The Financial Crisis and White Collar Crime

This book is dedicated to my wonderful, patient, loving and supporting wife, Ruth, who I love very much. It is also dedicated to my grandparents, Jack, Mary, Sam, Mercia and Sue. You will never be forgotten.

The Financial Crisis and White Collar Crime

The Perfect Storm?

Nicholas Ryder

Professor in Financial Crime, Department of Law, University of the West of England, UK

Edward Elgar

Cheltenham, UK • Northampton, MA, USA

Published by
Edward Elgar Publishing Limited
The Lypiatts
15 Lansdown Road
Cheltenham
Glos GL50 2JA
UK

Edward Elgar Publishing, Inc.
William Pratt House
9 Dewey Court
Northampton
Massachusetts 01060
USA

A catalogue record for this book
is available from the British Library

Library of Congress Control Number: 2013957767

This book is available electronically in the ElgarOnline.com Law Subject Collection, E-ISBN 978 1 78100 100 4

MIX
Paper from responsible sources
FSC® C013056

ISBN 978 1 78100 099 1

Typeset by Columns Design XML Ltd, Reading
Printed and bound in Great Britain by T.J. International Ltd, Padstow

Contents

Foreword

During the last five years, the world has witnessed economic crime committed by financial institutions and international corporations on a gargantuan scale. Senior bank executives have presided over the reckless, and on occasions, fraudulent acquisition and sale of mortgage-backed securities, publicly representing to financial market participants that these investments were safe whilst privately betting on their collapse. In some instances the executives recklessly turned a blind eye to the fact that these securities had been falsely valued; in others they were clueless about the nature of the securities which had been established and how they were traded. Meanwhile, at the same time as these securities were traded, the LIBOR interest rate was rigged by many of the lending banks, with the avowed intention of presenting a false picture to the financial markets as well as boosting their corporate profits – and profit bonuses. As if this malign activity were not enough, at least one leading bank added to its range of criminality by assisting customers to dishonestly evade huge amounts of tax which were desperately needed by government to support public services. And there is yet more. Instances of large-scale insider dealing and other forms of market manipulation have come to light involving a number of different and unconnected financial markets participants. Cases of fraud and corruption involving some of the largest companies in the world abound. Then, there are the money laundering and breach of sanctions cases involving the top clearing banks. The offending conduct has been international in its nature, taking place on financial markets stretching from New York through London and Frankfurt to Tokyo and Hong Kong. When coupled with the astonishing degree of incompetence and irresponsibility demonstrated by those in control of leading financial institutions and some of the largest listed companies, as well as their professional advisers on occasions, the combined effect has been to bring the global economy to its knees.

It is quite extraordinary that, against this background, there have been so few criminal prosecutions. In the United States the prosecutors have secured a small number of large scalps in insider dealing cases, but on both sides of the Atlantic the criminal process has left the senior bankers unscathed. Instead, a handful of rogue traders have been prosecuted. It is difficult to feel too much sympathy for the rogue traders, although that said, it is worth remembering that their conduct did not take place in a vacuum. Weak corporate governance procedures, associated with a warped conception of market place ethics, formed the backdrop to their activities. In addition, when compared with the United States, it is surprising that there has been little academic research activity in Britain on the topic of economic crime and its broader impact. In particular, the relationship between economic crime and the global financial crisis remains largely unexplored. There has been a paucity of academic work on how the international community should best respond to the challenges which financial crime presents.

Professor Nicholas Ryder, a noted legal academic with expertise in the areas of economic crime and banking regulation, has performed an invaluable service to both the academic and practitioner community by producing a monograph which addresses these core issues. His analysis of the factors which contributed to the global financial crisis and the role played by economic crime is most instructive, and it is followed by an insightful critique of the legislative, regulatory and enforcement responses in the United States and United Kingdom. Professor Ryder's conclusions are powerful, and those responsible for policing the financial markets should take careful note of the recommendations which he puts forward. I unhesitatingly commend this excellent work.

Jonathan Fisher QC
Devereux Chambers and London School of Economics

Preface

This monograph is an extension of the other research I have conducted on banking regulation, the financial crisis and white collar crime. Since the start of the most recent financial crisis, a great deal of literature has been written on the crisis and the factors that contributed to it. Many excellent texts and articles have identified such factors, including weak banking regulation, the deregulation of consumer credit laws, high risk banking, greed, the sub-prime mortgage crisis, securitisation, deregulation of banking laws, convenient credit, irresponsible or predatory lending and weak macroeconomic policies. This monograph seeks to offer an alternative interpretation, but one that contributes to the vast area of academic literature by arguing that there is one, previously under-researched factor: white collar crime. The hypothesis of this book is that white collar crime is an important factor that contributed towards the financial crisis. This is demonstrated in Chapters 2 and 3, which seek to illustrate how instances of white collar crime associated with, for example, sub-prime mortgages and LIBOR contributed towards the largest economic crisis since the Wall Street Crash and subsequent Great Depression.

The monograph concentrates on the impact of the global financial crisis in two specific jurisdictions – the United States of America and the United Kingdom. These countries were carefully selected and present a unique opportunity to compare and contrast the different approaches towards combating the problems associated with the global financial crisis. Interestingly, the United States and the United Kingdom have adopted similar financial regulatory policies towards the global financial crisis. This includes, for example, the publication of numerous reviews by the Department of Treasury, the Federal Reserve, the Bank of England, the Financial Services Authority, HM Treasury and official independent inquiries. Similarities are also seen in the plethora of legislative reform enacted in both countries, including the Emergency Economic Stabilization Act 2008, the Housing and Economic Recovery Act 2008, the American Recovery and Reinvestment Act 2009, and the Dodd–Frank Wall Street Reform Act 2012 in the United States. While legislators in the United Kingdom introduced the Banking (Special

Provisions) Act 2009, the Financial Services Act 2010, the Financial Services Act 2012 and the Banking Reform Act 2013.

Interestingly, the search for the culprits who caused the global financial crisis has demonstrated a number of differences in the approaches of the two countries. For example, one of the first measures introduced by President Barack Obama was the Fraud Enforcement and Recovery Act 2009 and the creation of the Financial Fraud Enforcement Task Force. These measures are of great significance for two reasons. First, the Fraud Enforcement and Recovery Act was introduced as a direct response to white collar crime that was associated with the global financial crisis. Secondly, this legislation also attempted to redress the imbalance created by President George Bush who tasked the Federal Bureau of Investigation with tackling the 'War on Terror' at the expense of white collar crime, by providing the Department of Justice with additional funding. This response can be contrasted with that adopted in the United Kingdom, where there has been no direct legislative response to the white collar crime that is associated with the global financial crisis. The Coalition government has only introduced new criminal offences under the remit of the Financial Services Act 2012 and proposals under the Banking Reform Act 2013.

Another important contrast between the policies adopted in the United States and United Kingdom relates to the prosecution strategies adopted by law enforcement agencies and regulatory bodies. For instance, in the United States the Federal Bureau of Investigation has handled any criminal prosecutions while the Securities and Exchange Commission has used its extensive civil enforcement powers. Importantly, there is a clear division between the roles of both agencies. However, it is important to note that the Department of Justice has failed to secure any high profile convictions of bankers allegedly involved in criminal activity. It has decided to pursue civil fraud actions as opposed to criminal prosecutions.

This monograph also highlights the increasing use of deferred prosecution agreements in the United States, especially in relation to the LIBOR scandal. In the United Kingdom, the enforcement actions have been pursued by the Financial Services Authority and the Serious Fraud Office. However, there has been some reluctance from either agency to actively pursue alleged wrongdoers. For example, both of these agencies were very averse to investigate the alleged manipulation of LIBOR and it will be argued that it was due to pressure from the government and commentators that record financial penalties were imposed on banks and that traders have been arrested and charged. Not one of the bankers purportedly involved in illegal activities during the global financial crisis has been convicted in either the US or UK. Furthermore, in the UK not one director has been disqualified under the Company Directors Disqualification Act 1986 for their conduct during the global financial crisis, despite strong rhetoric from the Department of Business, Innovation and Skills. This position can be contrasted with that adopted by the Securities and Exchange Commission. A key part of the discussion of the response in the United Kingdom will emanate from the sparse resources provided for the Serious Fraud Office by the Coalition government. Once again, this is an important contrast between the policies in the United States and the United Kingdom. Furthermore, the monograph will consider the potential impact that the National Crime Agency will have on those involved in white collar crime and it will note that the Coalition government has missed an ideal opportunity by not creating the Economic Crime Agency.

Acknowledgements

This monograph is the culmination of what seems several years of work! I would like to thank Georgina Bensted for her excellent work as my research assistant for this project. Her dedication and hard work were a real inspiration during this endeavour. I am very grateful to my Commercial Law students (especially the classes of 2012 and 2013) who have listened to me lecture (or rant) about this topic over the last two years. I would also like to thank Ben Booth and the staff of Edward Elgar for their continued patience and support (thanks for the extension or two!) during the duration of this project. There are two people in particular who have put up with me during the writing of this monograph – my wife, Ruth and son, Ethan. Without their support and love this monograph would not have been possible. It is to them that I dedicate this book.

Abbreviations

ABS	Asset backed securities
AIG	American International Group
APA	Asset Protection Agency
APS	Asset Protection Scheme
BBA	British Bankers' Association
CDO	Collateralised debt obligations
CFTC	Commodity Futures Trading Commission
CPMA	Consumer Protection Markets Authority
CRA	Credit rating agency
DBIS	Department of Business, Innovation and Skills
DoJ	Department of Justice
DPA	Deferred Prosecution Agreements
ECA	Economic Crime Agency
ESMA	European Securities and Markets Authority
EU	European Union
FBI	Federal Bureau of Investigation
FCA	Financial Conduct Authority
FCTC	Futures Commodities Trading Commission
FERA	Fraud Enforcement and Recovery Act
FFETF	Financial Fraud Enforcement Task Force
FIFU	Financial Institution Fraud Unit
FinCEN	Financial Crimes Enforcement Network
FPC	Financial Policy Committee
FSA	Financial Services Authority
FSCS	Financial Services Compensation Scheme
FSMA	Financial Services and Markets Act 2000
FSOC	Financial Stability Oversight Council
GFC	Global financial crisis
IMF	International Monetary Fund

IMM	International Money Management
IOSCO	International Organization of Securities Commissions
LIBOR	London inter-bank offered rate
MBA	Mortgage Bankers' Association
NCA	National Crime Agency
NFA	National Fraud Authority
NFIB	National Fraud Intelligence Bureau
NFMT	National Fraud Mortgage Team
NFRC	National Fraud Reporting Centre
NPA	Non-prosecution Agreements
OFT	Office of Fair Trading
PRA	Prudential Regulatory Authority
RBS	Royal Bank of Scotland
RMBS	Residential mortgage backed securities
SARs	Suspicious activity reports
SEC	Securities and Exchange Commission
SFO	Serious Fraud Office
SIB	Securities and Investment Board
TARP	Troubled Asset Relief Program
UK	United Kingdom
US	United States

1. Introduction

> The global financial crisis has revealed massive financial frauds and misconduct that have long been a part of our markets but have been submerged by the euphoria that has dominated these markets … white collar and corporate crimes have long been part of markets and are among the most difficult crimes for the legal system to deal with, let alone control. This is especially so where these crimes are of enormous proportions or involve some of the most powerful individuals or corporations in a society. Their seeming invulnerability to regulation is enhanced in boom times and this is further buttressed by powerful political forces supporting corporate risk taking. These political forces have served to muzzle or curtail the activities of enforcement agencies either directly, through the lack of adequate resources, or indirectly, by promoting ideologies which legitimise the minimal role of government in markets and a preference for industry self-regulation.[1]

While the vulnerabilities that created the potential for crisis were years in the making, it was the collapse of the housing bubble – fuelled by low interest rates, easy and available credit, scant regulation, and toxic mortgages – that was the spark that ignited a string of events, which led to a full-blown crisis in the fall of 2008. Trillions of dollars in risky mortgages had become embedded throughout the financial system, as mortgage-related securities were packaged, repackaged, and sold to investors around the world. When the bubble burst, hundreds of billions of dollars in losses in mortgages and mortgage-related securities shook markets as well as financial institutions that had significant exposures to those mortgages and had borrowed heavily against them. This happened not just in the United States but around the world. The losses were magnified by derivatives such as synthetic securities.[2]

---

[1] Tomasic, R. 'The financial crisis and the haphazard pursuit of financial crime' (2011) Journal of Financial Crime, 18(1), 7–31, at 7.

[2] Financial Crisis Inquiry Commission *Final report of the National Commission on the causes of the financial and economic crisis in the United States* (Financial Crisis Inquiry Commission: Washington DC, 2011) at xvi. For a useful summary of the Financial Crisis Inquiry Commission see Angelides, P. 'FICF and the crisis: preventing the next financial meltdown' (2012) UMKC Law Review, Summer, 80, 949–964.

1.1 THE FINANCIAL CRISIS: AN INTRODUCTION

The most recent financial crisis is believed to have originated within the United States (US) subprime mortgage market.[3] The lending practices of subprime lenders fuelled the flames of the worst economic crisis since the 1929 Wall Street Crash and subsequent Great Depression.[4] It is important to emphasise that the threat of a financial crisis was originally outlined in 1998 by the then head of the Commodity Futures Trading Commission (CFTC) Brooksley Born.[5] Furthermore, this was a view supported by the Federal Bureau of Investigation (FBI) when they asked President George Bush for additional agents and resources to tackle the forthcoming tsunami of mortgage fraud cases.[6] The origins of the subprime crisis are to be found in the mortgages provided by subprime lenders, which included 'prime loans', 'alt-A loans' and 'subprime loans'. A 'prime loan' is a financial instrument that is used by debtors with a good credit rating.[7] An 'alt-A' loan is used by debtors who generally have a good credit rating that contains some shortcomings.[8] Conversely, a 'subprime loan' is aimed at 'high-risk borrowers who

---

[3] Edmonds, T., Jarrett, T. and Woodhouse, J. *Credit crunch time line* (House of Commons Library: London, 2010) at 1.

[4] *Ibid.*

[5] Ramirez, M. 'Criminal affirmance: going beyond the deterrence paradigm to examine the social meaning of declining prosecution of elite crime' (2013) Connecticut Law Review, February, 45, 865–931, at 875.

[6] *Ibid.*

[7] According to Mitchell, 'lenders steered minorities into taking out subprime loans, though they may have qualified for prime loans that had much lower interest rates and more favourable terms for the borrower'. See Mitchell, T. 'Growing inequality and racial economic gaps' (2013) Howard Law Journal, Spring, 56, 849–890 at 884.

[8] Such shortcomings according to Messerschmitt could include an inability to 'verify their income or have high debt-to-income ratios'. See Messerschmitt, D. 'Overview of the subprime mortgage market' (2007) Review of Banking and Financial Law, Fall, 27, 3–11, at 3. Furthermore, US lenders also offered other high risk lending instruments, including 'No Income, No Jobs or Assets' loans, and exploding adjustable rate mortgages. See Jackson, K. 'The scandal beneath the financial crisis: getting a view from a moral–cultural mental model' (2010) Harvard Journal of Law and Public Policy, 33, 735–778, at 767 and Carrillo, J. 'Dangerous loans: consumer challenges to adjustable rate mortgages' (2008) Berkeley Business Law Journal, 5, 1–43. Also see Seitz, N., Gilsinan, J., Millar, J., Fisher, J., Harshman, E., Islam, M. and Yeager, F. 'Bank integrity: the case of subprime lending' (2009) Company Lawyer, 30(9), 271–276, at 272.

typically have poor credit histories'.[9] It is the latter of these loans that contributed towards the financial crisis. Subprime loans grew at an unprecedented level between 1994 and 2006, when the total amount of money via this financial instrument increased from $35bn to $600bn, accounting for a quarter of all US mortgages.[10] In 2006 an additional 3m subprime loans were instigated, extending the total value of unsettled debt to $3tn.[11] However, it is important to point out that the introduction of such legislation as the Fair Housing Act 1968 and the extended remit of the Civil Rights Act 1968 contributed towards the increased use of subprime loans.[12] Despite the obvious merits of both pieces of legislation, the then available 30 year mortgages were still prohibitive to many borrowers, thus forcing them to use subprime lenders. When the subprime mortgage market spectacularly collapsed in the summer of 2007, what followed has simply been described as 'the worldwide financial crisis'.[13] The impact of the subprime mortgage crisis was hastened by the 'repackaging' or 'rebranding' and 'selling' of mortgage portfolios, a

---

[9] *Ibid.*, at 3. For an excellent discussion of subprime loans see Bar-Gill, O. 'The law, economics and psychology of subprime mortgage contracts' (2009) Cornell Law Review, 93, Rev. 1073–1151. A subprime loan has been defined as 'mortgage loan to a borrower with sub-standard credit'. See *Henry v Lehman Commercial Paper, Inc.*, 471 F.3d 977, 984 (9th Cir. 2006) as cited in Johnston, K., Greer, J., Biermacher, J. and Hummel, J. 'The subprime morass: past, present and future' (2008) North Carolina Banking Institute, March, 12, 125–139, at 125. A subprime borrower has been defined as 'borrowers displaying a high credit risk of delinquency'. See Dose, D. 'Subprime: price of infringements' (2008) International Business Law Journal, 4, 558–568, at 559. For a more detailed discussion of the definition see Department of Treasury, Office of Comptroller, Federal Reserve System, Federal Deposit Insurance Corporation, Office of Thrift Supervision and National Credit Union Association 'Statement on subprime mortgage lending', 29 June 2007, available from http://www.occ.gov/news-issuances/news-releases/2007/nr-ia-2007-64a.pdf, accessed 5 March 2013.

[10] White, A. 'The case for banning subprime mortgages' (2008) University of Cincinnati Law Review, Winter, 77, 617–644, at 618. This is a view supported by Nguyen, T. and Pontell, H. 'Fraud and inequality in the subprime mortgage crisis' in Deflem, M. (ed.), *Economic crisis and crime* (Emerald: Bingley, 2011) at 12. For an interesting discussion of the problems associated with and the legality of subprime mortgages see Brescia, R. 'Tainted loans: the value of mass torts approach in subprime mortgage litigation' (2009) University of Cincinnati Law Review, 78, 1–79. Also see Financial Crisis Inquiry Commission above, n 2, at 70.

[11] Bar-Gill above, n 9, at 1073.

[12] Nguyen and Pontell above, n 10, at 5.

[13] Seitz *et al* above, n 8, at 271.

process referred to as 'securitisation'.[14] This process 'aims to provide finance [for banks] by selling assets, by transforming a loan as a financial relationship into a tradable bond and therefore into a transaction'.[15] Securitisation influenced the subprime mortgage crisis in two ways. First, the repackaging of mortgages made it extremely difficult, if not impossible, for investors to avoid 'ill-advised' or 'unsuitable' transactions.[16] Secondly, a large collection of US mortgages were in the possession of banks in many different countries around the world,[17] and it soon became apparent that many of these mortgages were toxic, thus contributing to the spread of the financial crisis.[18]

The first evidence of the financial crisis appeared in April 2007, when New Century Financial, one of the US's largest subprime lenders,[19] announced it had outstanding liabilities of $100bn and had filed for bankruptcy protection.[20] The early problems of the subprime market were acknowledged by then Federal Reserve Chairman, Ben Bernanke, who said that 'the credit losses associated with subprime [loans] have come to

---

[14] Securitisation is a financial practice that 'efficiently allows risk and capital [that] enables companies to access capital markets'. See Schwarcz, S. 'The future of securitisation' (2008) *Duke Public Law and Legal Theory Research Paper Series No. 223*¸ at 1 as cited in Gray, J. and Akseli, O. *Financial regulation in crisis? The role of law and the failure of Northern Rock* (Edward Elgar: Cheltenham, 2011) at 2.

[15] Bavoso, V. 'Financial innovation and structured finance: the case of securitisation' (2012) Company Lawyer, 34(1), 3–12, at 4.

[16] For a critical overview of securitisation see Macchiavello, E. 'Securitisation in microfinance and global financial crisis: innovation or Trojan horse?' (2013) Journal of International Banking Law and Regulation, 28(3), 109–122, at 113–114 and Nwogugu, M. 'Illegality of securitisation: bankruptcy issues and theories of securitisation' (2008) Journal of International Banking Law and Regulation, 23(7), 363–377.

[17] For an interesting discussion of the problems associated with subprime mortgages see White above, n 10.

[18] For an excellent discussion of the problems associated with toxic mortgages see Murdock, C. 'Why not tell the truth? Deceptive practices and the economic meltdown' (2010) Loyola University Chicago Law Journal, 41, 801–884.

[19] Linn, C. 'The way we live now: the case for mandating fraud reporting by persons involved in real estate closings and settlements' (2009) Journal of Financial Crime, 16(1), 7–27, at 10.

[20] See Cresswell, J. 'Mortgage lender New Century Financial files for bankruptcy', 2 April 2007, available from http://www.nytimes.com/2007/04/02/business/worldbusiness/02iht-loans.5.5118838.html, accessed 21 November 2012.

light and they are fairly significant … some estimates are in the order of between $50bn and $100bn'.[21] The subprime mortgage market affected Lehman Brothers, which filed for chapter 11 bankruptcy in 2008.[22] Lehman Brothers was once described as 'one of the largest financial services firms in the world … [it] operated in over forty countries and had more than 650 legal entities outside of the US'.[23] Essentially, Lehman Brothers did not raise sufficient capital to continue operating in response to rising interest rates and a rating reduction for its assets.[24] This institution was severely criticised because of its highly leveraged operations before the financial crisis which resulted in a 'debt-to-equity ratio' of 32 to 1.[25] Additionally, the US government was forced to intervene and rescue the Federal National Mortgage Association (Fannie Mae) and the Federal Home Loan Mortgage Corporation (Freddie Mac).[26] Both of these institutions were created in 1938 by President

---

[21] New York Times 'Bernanke: subprime hit could top $100bn', 19 July 2007, available from http://money.cnn.com/2007/07/19/news/economy/bernanke/, accessed 21 November 2012.

[22] See Wearden, G., Teather, D. and Treanor, J. 'Banking crisis: Lehman Brothers files for bankruptcy protection', 15 September 2008, available from http://www.guardian.co.uk/business/2008/sep/15/lehmanbrothers.creditcrunch, accessed 21 November 2012. For a more detailed account of this see Estrada, E. 'The immediate and lasting impacts of the 2008 economic collapse – Lehman Brothers, General Motors and the secured credit markets' (2011) University of Richmond Law Review, 45, 1111–1142.

[23] Altman, J. 'A test case in international bankruptcy protocols: the Lehman Brothers insolvency' (2011) San Diego International Law Journal, 12, 463–495, at 464.

[24] For a damning indictment of the activities of Lehman Brothers see Valukas, A.R., Examiner In re Lehman Brothers Holding Inc., Report, Chapter 11 Case No. 08-13555, United States Bankruptcy Court for the Southern District of New York, available from http://www.distressedvolatility.com/2010/03/full-examiner-report-of-lehman-brothers.html, accessed 25 March 2013.

[25] See Lehman Brothers Holdings Inc., *Quarterly report* (Form 10-Q), 89 (31 May 2008), available from http://www.rns-pdf.londonstockexchange.com/rns/8436Z_1-2008-7-24.pdf, accessed 25 March 2013 as cited in Rosato, J. 'Down the road to perdition: how the flaws of Basel II led to the collapse of Bear Stearns and Lehman Brothers' (2011) Connecticut Insurance Law Journal, 17, 475–500, at 490.

[26] For an interesting commentary on the role of both of these institutions see Reiss, D. 'The role of the Fannie Mae/Freddie Mac duopoly in the American housing market' (2009) Journal of Financial Regulation and Compliance, 17(3), 336–348. It is important to note that both Fannie Mae and Freddie Mac were the subject of intense criticism prior to the outbreak of the most recent financial crisis in 2007. See for example Krehely, K. 'Government sponsored enterprises:

Roosevelt as part of the New Deal legislation to 'serve as mortgage lenders for consumers and potential home buyers'.[27] They are both government sponsored enterprises, which according to Carnell are 'federally chartered, privately owned, privately managed financial institutions that have only specialized lending and guarantee powers and that bond market investors perceive as implicitly backed by the federal government'.[28] Lavargna took the view that the key role of government sponsored enterprises 'lies in the "securitization" of primary loans. The enterprises buy loans from primary lenders, pool the loans into portfolios, and then sell the portfolios to investors and others in the capital markets'.[29] However, it soon became apparent that Fannie Mae and Freddie Mac were heavily exposed by the subprime mortgage market. For example, both institutions accounted for 34 per cent of subprime loans and 59 per cent of 'alt-A' loans.[30] This is a view supported by Reiss, who stated that 'the two firms [Fannie Mae and Freddie Mac] had a much greater exposure to the disastrous "Alt-A" subsector than they

---

a discussion of the federal subsidy of Fannie Mae and Freddie Mac' (2002) North Carolina Banking Institute, 6, 519–544 and Strickland, J. 'The proposed regulatory changes to Fannie Mae and Freddie Mac: an analysis' (2004) Northern Carolina Banking Institute, 8, 267–287.

[27] Patel, A. 'The bailout of Fannie Mae and Freddie Mac' (2008) Review of Banking and Financial Law, 28, 21–30, at 22.

[28] Carnell, R. 'Handling the failure of a government-sponsored enterprise' (2005) Washington Law Review, 80, 565–642, at 570 as cited in Reiss above, n 26, at 337.

[29] Lavargna, C. 'Government-sponsored enterprises are "too big to fail" balancing public and private interests' (1993) Hastings Law Journal, 44, 991–1083, at 999.

[30] Marshall, J. *US Congressional debates on the financial crisis: key players, policy and future regulation – House of Commons Research Paper 09/58* (House of Commons Library: London, 2009) at 21. A former officer of Fannie Mae stated that this organisation 'guarantee[s] or hold[s] 10.5m nonprime loans worth $1.6tn – one in three of all subprime loans, and nearly two in three of all so-called Alt-A loans, often called "liar loans"'. The New York Times reported that Edward Pinto, a former chief credit officer at Fannie Mae, stated that Fannie Mae and Freddie Mac participated in 'an orgy of junk mortgage development' which resulted in them becoming 'vast repositories of subprime and similarly risky loans'. See Browning, L. 'Ex-officer faults mortgage giants for "orgy" of nonprime loans', 9 December 2008, available from http://www.nytimes.com/2008/12/10/business/10fannie.html, accessed 25 March 2013.

had previously let on'.[31] By the middle of 2007 Fannie Mae and Freddie Mac experienced combined losses of $190bn,[32] which resulted in a US government bailout of $1.4tn.[33] Reiss added that 'these two sectors were rife with predatory lending practices, Fannie and Freddie may be seen as complicit with these practices even though they did not engage in them directly'.[34] Other institutions which suffered during the early part of the financial crisis included American International Group (AIG), then the world's largest insurance company.[35] AIG was heavily involved in the trade of derivatives[36] and as a result faced significant liquidity problems due to heavy losses in credit default swaps.[37] In September 2008, AIG's shares slumped by 19 per cent on the New York Stock Exchange. This was followed by a further 61 per cent crash in share prices.[38] Therefore, the US government was forced to intervene and agreed to lend AIG $85bn in exchange for an 80 per cent stake of the company.[39] AIG's

---

31 Reiss, D. 'Fannie Mae and Freddie Mac and the future of federal housing finance policy: a study of regulatory privilege' (2011) Alabama Law Review, 62, 907–955, at 931.

32 Squire, R. 'Shareholder opportunism in a world of risky debt' (2010) Harvard Law Review, 123, 1151–1213, at 1191.

33 *Ibid.*

34 Reiss above, n 31 at 931.

35 For a more detailed discussion of the collapse of AIG see Selvarajah, P. 'The AIG bailout and AIG's prospects for repaying government loans' (2010) Review of Banking and Financial Law, 29, 363–371 and Silva, Y. 'The "too big to fail" doctrine and the credit crisis' (2008) Review of Banking and Financial Law, 28, 115–131.

36 A derivative can be defined as a 'legally binding agreement whose values are derived from the value of an underlying commodity, financial instrument or reference rate'. See Malkawi, B. 'Financial derivatives between Western legal tradition and Islamic finance: a comparative approach' (2011) Journal of International Banking Law and Regulation, 26(6), 276–284, at 276.

37 For an excellent and detailed discussion of credit default swaps see Smith, M. 'The legal nature of credit default swaps' (2010) Lloyd's Maritime and Commercial Law Quarterly, August, 3, 386–410.

38 See Smith, A. 'Stocks slump on AIG, housing', 17 September 2008, available from http://money.cnn.com/2008/09/17/markets/stockswatch/index.htm, accessed 25 March 2013.

39 Karnitschnig, M., Solomon, D., Pleven, L. and Hilsenrath, J. 'U.S. to take over AIG in $85 billion bailout; central banks inject cash as credit dries up', 16 September 2008, available from http://online.wsj.com/article/SB122156561931242905.html, accessed 25 March 2013. Also see Securities and Exchange Commission 'Credit agreement between American International Group and Federal Reserve Bank of New York', 22 September 2008, available from http://www.sec.gov/Archives/edgar/data/5272/000095012308011496/y71452exv99w1.htm,

exposure at the height of the financial crisis was $169bn,[40] and it was not until 2012 that the company managed to repay all of its outstanding liabilities to the US government.[41] Bear Stearns, then the fifth largest investment bank in the US,[42] also benefited from emergency funding and it was jointly purchased by the government and JP Morgan at a 93 per cent discount, a meagre $2 per share.[43] It is interesting to note that prior to its takeover by the government and JP Morgan, Bear Stearns shares were trading at $170.[44] Rosato took the view that 'JP Morgan acquired Bear Stearns in a federally orchestrated and assisted effort to save the financial markets from imminent peril'.[45] Therefore, the total losses arising from the subprime crisis exceeded $600bn.[46] The total losses of the financial crisis are explicitly illustrated in the following quote from Barak: '[the] Wall Street debacle accounted for more than $20tn in lost wealth … cost some 20m workers their jobs worldwide … domestically, cost taxpayers $700bn in TARP bailouts funds … and between 2007 and the end of 2012, cost 4m American households their homes [due] to

---

accessed 25 March 2013. For an interesting discussion of the takeover of AIG see Rosemeyer, M. 'Is the government's takeover of AIG constitutionally permissible?' (2009) Entrepreneurial Business Law Journal, 4, 243–266.

[40] Squire above, n 32, at 1187.

[41] Tracer, Z. 'AIG stock sale repays bailout as U.S. Government profits', 11 September 2012, available from http://www.bloomberg.com/news/2012-09-11/aig-stock-prices-at-32-50-share-as-treasury-cuts-stake.html, accessed 28 March 2012.

[42] Nikolić, B. 'Rise and fall of regulatory state in financial markets' (2013) Journal of International Banking Law and Regulation, 28(1), 1–8 at 1. For a more detailed discussion of the collapse of Bear Sterns see Ben-Ishai, S. and Lubben, S. 'A comparative study of bankruptcy as bailout' (2011) Brooklyn Journal of Corporate, Financial and Commercial Law, 6, 79–101.

[43] Sorkin, A. and Thomas Jnr, L. 'JP Morgan acts to buy ailing Bear Sterns at huge discount', 16 March 2008, available from http://www.nytimes.com/2008/03/16/business/16cnd-bear.html?_r=0, accessed 25 March 2013. For a more detailed commentary on the collapse of Bear Stearns see Broughman, A. 'The collapse of Bear Stearns, or: skinny dipping on the street' (2010) Ohio Northern University Law Review, 36, 191–213 and Reinhart, V. 'A year of living dangerously: the management of the financial crisis' (2011) Journal of Economic Perspectives, 25(1), 71–90, at 76–79.

[44] Sorkin, A. 'JP Morgan pays $2 a share for Bear Stearns', 17 March 2008, available from http://www.nytimes.com/2008/03/17/business/17bear.html?_r=0, accessed 7 October 2013.

[45] Rosato above, n 25, at 490.

[46] Patterson, L. and Koller, C. 'Diffusion of fraud through subprime lending' in Deflem, M. (ed.), *Economic crisis and crime* (Emerald: Bingley, 2011) at 26.

mortgage foreclosures'.[47] The International Monetary Fund (IMF) estimated that the cost of the financial crisis between 2008 and 2009 was $11.9tn, or 20 per cent of annual global output.[48]

The initial US response to the financial crisis was led by the Federal Reserve and the Department of Treasury. The reactions of both institutions were described as 'swift and substantial' and 'focused first on providing liquidity in the financial sector'.[49] Nevertheless, as the impact of the financial crisis deepened their responses broadened to protect levels of financial stability and to prevent the depreciation of the dollar.[50] The Federal Reserve 'played a major role in addressing liquidity problems by providing a number of avenues for financial institutions to receive short term loans using collateral that the market would not accept at such generous rates'.[51] It approached the financial crisis by utilising four mechanisms.[52] First, it reduced US interest rates.[53] Secondly, the Federal Reserve introduced a 'Term Auction Facility' to increase access to short-term liquidity.[54] Under this scheme the Federal Reserve auctioned funds for deposit taking institutions 'against the wide variety of collateral that can be used to secure loans'.[55] Thirdly, it announced the 'Terms Securities Lending Facility', a weekly loan service that 'promoted liquidity in Treasury and other collateral markets and thus fostered the

---

47 Barak, G. 'The flickering desires for white collar crime studies in the post-financial crisis: will they ever shine brightly?' (2013) Western Criminology Review, 13(3), 61–71, at 63.

48 Button, M. 'Editorial: fraud, corruption and the financial crisis' (2011) International Journal of Law, Crime and Justice, 29, 137–139 at 137.

49 Choi, J. and Papaioannou, M. 'Financial crisis and risk management: reassessing the Asian financial crisis in light of the American financial crisis' (2010) East Asia Law Review, Summer, 5, 442–466, at 455.

50 *Ibid.*

51 Marshall above, n 30, at 3.

52 *Ibid.*, at 13.

53 For a rationale for maintaining low interest rates since the dawn of the financial crisis see Federal Reserve 'Why are interest rates being kept at a low level?', n/d, available from http://www.federalreserve.gov/faqs/money_12849.htm, accessed 23 September 2013.

54 For a brief explanation see Federal Reserve 'Term Auction Facility', n/d, available from http://www.federalreserve.gov/newsevents/reform_taf.htm, accessed 23 September 2013.

55 Federal Reserve 'Press Release', 21 December 2007, available from http://www.federalreserve.gov/newsevents/press/monetary/20071212a.htm, accessed 8 August 2012.

functioning of financial markets more generally'.[56] Under this scheme $200bn of Department of Treasury's securities were auctioned to increase the bank liquidity levels. The fourth scheme introduced by the Federal Reserve was the enforced takeover of Bear Stearns.[57] The first legislative measure introduced to tackle the problems associated with the financial crisis was the Economic Stimulus Act 2008. President George Bush stated that the Act is:

> large enough to have an impact – amounting to more than $152bn this year [2008], or about 1 percent of GDP. The Bill provides temporary tax incentives for businesses to make investments in their companies so that we create new jobs … the Bill provides individual tax relief in the form of tax rebates.[58]

The principal objective of the Economic Stimulus Act 2008 was to stimulate the economy.[59] In order to achieve this objective, the Act contained three particular objectives. First, to provide tax rebates for low income families amounting to $266m.[60] Secondly, it aimed to encourage businesses to invest in qualifying property.[61] Thirdly, it was designed to increase the loan limits for Fannie Mae, Freddie Mac and the Federal Housing Administration.[62] The second legislative instrument introduced and signed by President George Bush was the Emergency Economic Stabilization Act 2008.[63] The preamble to the Act outlined its aims as 'to provide authority for the Federal Government to purchase and insure certain types of troubled assets for the purposes of providing stability to and preventing disruption in the economy and financial system and

---

[56] Federal Reserve 'Term Securities Lending Facility', n/d, available from http://www.federalreserve.gov/monetarypolicy/tslf.htm, accessed 8 August 2012.

[57] Federal Reserve 'Press Release', 14 March 2008, available from http://www.federalreserve.gov/newsevents/press/monetary/20080314a.htm, accessed 8 August 2012.

[58] The White House 'President Bush signs H.R. 5140, the Economic Stimulus Act of 2008', 13 February 2008, available from http://georgewbush-whitehouse.archives.gov/news/releases/2008/02/20080213-3.html, accessed 23 September 2013.

[59] Deeds, J. 'The flawed logic of congress in the Economic Stimulus Act of 2008' (2010) Journal of Law and Family Studies, 12, 299–313, at 302.

[60] Economic Stimulus Act 2008, §101. See Fairfax, L. 'The legal origins of theory in crisis' (2009) Brigham Young University Law Review, 1571–1617, at 1590.

[61] Economic Stimulus Act 2008, §102–03.

[62] Economic Stimulus Act 2008, §201–02.

[63] Emergency Economic Stabilization Act of 2008, Public Law 110–343.

protecting taxpayers'.[64] After signing the Act President George Bush stated that it seeks to 'address this problem [the financial crisis] head on by providing a variety of new tools to the government – such as allowing us to purchase some of the troubled assets, and creating a new government insurance program that will guarantee the value of others'.[65] The most significant and perhaps controversial aspect of this Act was the creation of the Troubled Asset Relief Program (TARP). The Emergency Economic Stabilization Act 2008 was described as the 'most significant economic intervention by the federal government in the financial system since the Great Depression'.[66] It provided the Secretary of the Department of Treasury with approximately $700bn to purchase mortgages and other assets which had prevented financial institutions,[67] families and small companies from accessing credit.[68] Essentially, the Act 'injected capital into troubled financial institutions by purchasing preferred stock'.[69] The next legislative measure was the American Recovery and Reinvestment Act 2009, or 'stimulus' or 'stimulus package' Act, which provided $787bn of federal funding.[70] The Act had five objectives: to preserve and create jobs and promote economic recovery;[71] to assist those most impacted by the recession;[72] to provide investments needed to increase economic efficiency by spurring technological advances in science and health;[73] to invest in transportation, environmental protection

---

[64] Public Law 110–343.

[65] The White House 'President Bush discusses Emergency Economic Stabilization Act of 2008', 3 October 2008, available from http://georgewbush-whitehouse.archives.gov/news/releases/2008/10/20081003-11.html, accessed 5 August 2013.

[66] Anderberg, K. and Epstein, J. 'Transatlantic developments' (2008) Compliance Officer Bulletin, October, 60, 1–40, at 38. However, it is important to note that the Act has been heavily criticised. See for example Ghosh, S. and Mohamed, S. 'The troubled asset relief program (TARP) and its limitations: an analysis' (2010) International Journal of Law and Management, 52(2), 124–143.

[67] This would include for example 'banks, savings associations, credit unions, security brokers or dealers, and insurance companies'. Ghosh and Mohamed, *ibid.*

[68] For a more detailed discussion of this Act see Ruby, J. 'Sound of fury, confused alarms, and oversight: congress, delegation, and effective responses to financial crises' (2010) Harvard Journal on Legislation, 47, 209–252.

[69] Paez, G. 'LTCM and other major hedge fund failures: part 2' (2009) Journal of International Banking Law and Regulation, 24(6), 304–312, at 309.

[70] Fairfax above, n 60, at 1596.

[71] American Recovery and Reinvestment Act 2009, s. 3(a)(1).

[72] American Recovery and Reinvestment Act 2009, s. 3(a)(2).

[73] American Recovery and Reinvestment Act 2009, s. 3(a)(3).

and other infrastructure that will provide long-term economic benefits;[74] and to stabilise State and local government budgets, in order to minimise and avoid deductions in essential services and counterproductive state and local tax increases.[75] President Barack Obama stated that the Act was the 'beginning of the first steps to set our economy on a firmer foundation, paving the way to long-term growth and prosperity' and described it as the 'most sweeping economic recovery package in our history'.[76] The American Recovery and Reinvestment Act 2009 was described by one commentator as 'one of the most massive and far-reaching pieces of legislation in American history'.[77] Additionally, the Dodd–Frank Wall Street Reform Act 2012, 'a broad-ranging financial market reform',[78] was signed by President Barack Obama in response to the problems caused by the subprime crisis.[79] It aimed to reduce the frequency of bailouts for financial firms.[80] Furthermore, the Dodd–Frank Wall Street Reform Act altered the responsibility of existing regulatory bodies such as the Financial Stability Oversight Council (FSOC) and the Securities and Exchange Commission (SEC).[81]

The impact of the financial crisis was also felt in Europe when IKB Industriebank posted losses of £475m due to its exposure to the US subprime market.[82] Further losses attributed to the subprime market were

---

[74] American Recovery and Reinvestment Act 2009, s. 3(a)(4).

[75] American Recovery and Reinvestment Act 2009, s. 3(a)(5).

[76] President Barack Obama 'Remarks upon signing the American Recovery & Reinvestment Act', 17 February 2009, available from http://www.presidentialrhetoric.com/speeches/02.17.09.html, accessed 27 March 2013.

[77] Rappis, J. 'Tax aspects of the American Recovery and Reinvestment Act of 2009: on the road to recovery?' (2009) Wisconsin Lawyer, 82, 10–14, at 10.

[78] Engert, A. 'Transnational hedge fund regulation' (2010) European Business Organization Law Review, 11(3), 329–378, at 353. For a brief analysis of the Act see Scott, H. 'A general evaluation of the Dodd–Frank US financial reform legislation' (2010) Journal of International Banking Law and Regulation, 25(10), 477–480.

[79] Yeager, F., Seitz, N., Islam, M., Harshman, E., Gilsinan, J., Fisher, J. and Millar, J. 'US legislation designed to improve corporate governance: an exploration' (2012) Company Lawyer, 33(1), 25–32, at 25.

[80] Scott, H. 'The competitive impact of financial regulatory reform' (2011) Journal of International Banking Law and Regulation, 26(11), 527–530, at 528.

[81] Barfield, R., Du Plessis, S. and Fell, P. 'Basel III – implications for risk management and supervision' (2011) Compliance Officer Bulletin September, 89, 1–26, at 23.

[82] BBC 'Sub-prime crisis to cost IKB $1bn', 3 September 2007, available from http://news.bbc.co.uk/1/hi/business/6976517.stm, accessed 21 November 2012. In July 2007 IKB received an €8.1bn bailout from KfW, a state owned

reported by UBS, which wrote off 4.2bn Swiss francs in October 2007.[83] By May 2008 the main credit losses linked to the subprime market had reached a then unprecedented scale. For example, Citigroup announced losses of $40.7bn, UBS $38bn, Merrill Lynch $31.7bn, HSBC $15.6bn, Bank of America $14.9bn, Morgan Stanley $12.6bn, Royal Bank of Scotland (RBS) $12bn, JP Morgan Chase $9.7bn, Washington Mutual $8.3bn, Deutsche Bank $7.5bn, Wachovia $7.3bn, Credit Agricole $6.6bn, Credit Suisse $6.3bn, Mizuho Financial $5.5bn, Bear Stearns $3.2bn and Barclays $3.2bn.[84] The effect of the subprime market was also felt by nation states.[85] For example, in December 2008 the European Union (EU) agreed a series of financial packages and measures aimed at bolstering growth to counteract the problems associated with the financial crisis. The problems were exacerbated in April 2009, when the EU ordered France, Spain, Greece and the Republic of Ireland to reduce their budgetary deficits.[86] Furthermore, there were still concerns about the

German bank. See Maximilian, J. 'The sub-prime crisis, the credit squeeze and Northern Rock: the lessons to be learned' (2008) Journal of Financial Regulation and Compliance, 16(1), 19–34, at 20. For a more detailed discussion of the impact of the subprime crisis on IKB see Kaal, W. and Painter, R. 'Initial reflections on evolving standards: constraints on risk taking by directors and officers in Germany and the United States' (2010) Seton Hall Law Review, 40, 1433–1485.

[83] Reuters, 'Timeline: UBS investment bank mishaps and upheavals', 15 September 2007, available from http://mobile.reuters.com/article/topNews/idUSTRE78E2FM20110915, accessed 21 November 2012. The losses increased to 10bn francs. See Reuters 'UBS writes off $10 billion in subprime losses', 12 October 2007, available from http://www.msnbc.msn.com/id/22180574/ns/business-real_estate/t/ubs-writes-billion-subprime-losses/; BBC News 'Timeline: sub-prime losses' 19 May 2008, available from http://news.bbc.co.uk/1/hi/business/7096845.stm, accessed 21 November 2012.

[84] BBC News, *ibid.*

[85] This has been referred to as the 'Euro zone debt crisis'. See Buchheit, L. and Mitu Gulati, G. 'The Eurozone debt crisis: the options now' (2013) Capital Markets Law Journal, 8(1), 54–61.

[86] BBC News 'Timeline: the unfolding eurozone crisis', 13 June 2012, available from http://www.bbc.co.uk/news/business-13856580, accessed 11 March 2013. It is important to note that there were still concerns about the levels of debt in Portugal, Spain and the Republic of Ireland. See BBC News 'Greece's debt reaches 300bn euros', 10 December 2009, available from http://news.bbc.co.uk/1/hi/business/8406665.stm, accessed 26 February 2013. The impact of the high levels of debt in Greece was also felt in other EU Member States including France. See for example Gonon, F. 'Greece and Armageddon' (2011) European Lawyer, 109, 5.

levels of debt in Portugal, Spain and the Republic of Ireland.[87] In May 2010, the EU and IMF announced that it had agreed a €110bn financial package to rescue Greece,[88] which was soon followed by an €85bn bailout for the Republic of Ireland.[89] In response to the continuing debt problems, the euro zone established a permanent bailout fund, the European Stability Mechanism, which is the 'euro zone's rescue fund [that] will be able to recapitalise struggling banks directly'.[90] Portugal was the next EU state to receive emergency liquidity from the EU, which totalled €78bn.[91] In June 2011 Greece received a second financial bailout from the euro zone totalling €96.3bn.[92] In the same month Italy introduced an austerity based budget of €50bn,[93] but this did little to dissuade Standard and Poor from reducing Italy's credit worthiness from A+ to A.[94] In October 2011, the Bank of England provided £75bn into the

---

87 BBC News 'Europe's PIGS: country by country', 11 February 2011, available from http://news.bbc.co.uk/1/hi/business/8510603.stm, accessed 26 February 2013. For an interesting discussion of the impact of the crisis in Greece see Quintin, Y. 'Alis…da in wonderland or Greek tragedy? The dynamics of credit default swaps and the "voluntary" Greek restructuring of 2011/2012' (2012) International Business Law Journal, 2, 277–291.

88 Prime Minister's Office 'Prime Minister's speech', 2 May 2010, available from http://www.primeminister.gov.gr/english/2010/05/02/meeting-of-cabinet-prime-ministers-speech/, accessed 26 February 2013.

89 BBC News 'Irish Republic 85bn euro bail-out agreed', 20 November 2010, available from http://www.bbc.co.uk/news/world-europe-11855990, accessed 26 February 2013.

90 Seyad, S. 'The impact of the proposed banking union on the unity and integrity of the European Union's single market' (2013) Journal of International Banking Law and Regulation, 28(3), 99–108, at 104.

91 BBC News 'Portugal's 78bn euro bail-out is formally approved', 17 May 2011, available from http://www.bbc.co.uk/news/business-13408497, accessed 26 February 2013.

92 Minder, R. 'Portugal agrees to a $116 billion bailout', 3 May 2011, available from http://www.nytimes.com/2011/05/04/business/global/04portugal.html?_r=0, accessed 26 February 2013.

93 CNN 'Italian Cabinet OKs 47 billion-euro austerity package', 30 June 2011, available from http://articles.cnn.com/2011-06-30/world/italy.austerity.measures_1_austerity-package-finance-minister-giulio-tremonti-pierluigi-bersani?_s=PM:WORLD, accessed 26 February 2013.

94 Hawles, A. 'Italy downgrade adds to eurozone contagion fears', 20 September 2011, available from http://www.guardian.co.uk/business/2011/sep/20/italy-downgrade-eurozone-contagion-fear, accessed 26 February 2013. For a more detailed discussion of CRAs see McVea, H. 'Credit rating agencies, the subprime mortgage debacle and global governance: the EU strikes back' (2010) International and Comparative Law Quarterly, 59(3), 701–730.

United Kingdom's (UK's) economy via quantitative easing.[95] However, this in addition to the austerity measures introduced by the Coalition government since 2010 had little impact and in February 2013 the UK lost its AAA rating by Moody's for the first time since 1978.[96] This decision was soon followed by a decision by the Fitch credit rating agency (CRA) to also downgrade the UK to AA+ in April 2013.[97] In March 2013, the IMF and EU announced that they wanted all bank customers in Cyprus to pay a levy in return for a €10bn bailout.[98]

In the UK the first victim of the financial crisis was Northern Rock, which was granted emergency funding by the Bank of England,[99] as the lender of last resort.[100] Interestingly, only two months prior to securing the emergency funding, Northern Rock declared it had 'continued to expand its business at a rapid rate … [and] its loans to customers underwent a net increase of £10.7bn'.[101] Furthermore, it announced an increase in its interim dividend of 30.3 per cent.[102] Nonetheless, the Financial Services Authority (FSA) expressed concerns about the bank's

---

[95] Allen, K. 'Quantitative easing boosted by £75bn by Bank of England', 6 October 2011, available from http://www.guardian.co.uk/business/2011/oct/06/quantitative-easing-75bn-bank-of-england, accessed 26 February 2013.

[96] BBC News 'UK loses top AAA credit rating for first time since 1978', 23 February 2013, available from http://www.bbc.co.uk/news/business-21554311, accessed 26 February 2013.

[97] BBC News 'Fitch downgrades UK credit rating to AA+', 19 April 2013, available from http://www.bbc.co.uk/news/business-22219382, accessed 7 October 2013.

[98] BBC News 'Europe markets follow Asia's down after Cyprus bailout deal', 18 March 2013, available from http://www.bbc.co.uk/news/business-21823432, accessed 18 March 2013. For a more detailed discussion of the impact of the bailout in the UK see BBC News 'Why Cyprus's rescue matters to us', 16 March 2013, available from http://www.bbc.co.uk/news/business-21812853, accessed 18 March 2013.

[99] BBC News 'Northern Rock gets bank bailout', 13 September 2007, available from http://news.bbc.co.uk/1/hi/business/6994099.stm, accessed 21 November 2012.

[100] For an excellent discussion of the role of central banks as lenders of last resort see Lastra, R. 'Lender of last resort, an international perspective' (1999) International and Comparative Law Quarterly, 48(2), 340–361.

[101] HM Treasury Select Committee *The run on the Rock* (HM Treasury Select Committee: London, 2008) at 14.

[102] *Ibid.*, at 25.

financial position following its stress testing in May 2007.[103] Subsequently, evidence presented to the HM Treasury Select Committee suggested that in August 2007 the Bank of England, HM Treasury and the FSA were fully aware of Northern Rock's financial predicament prior to its collapse.[104] Following the announcement of the emergency funding, thousands of Northern Rock customers famously queued to withdraw their savings from the failing institution,[105] which saw the bank's shares drop by 40 per cent.[106] In response, HM Treasury announced that it had increased the levels of the Financial Services Compensation Scheme (FSCS) to guarantee 100 per cent of the first £35,000 of customers' savings.[107] In February 2008, HM Treasury Select Committee published

---

[103] *Ibid.*, at 31. According to the FSA stress testing is 'an important element in firms' planning and risk management processes, helping them to identify, analyse and manage the risks within their businesses'. See Financial Services Authority 'Stress testing', n/d, available from http://www.fsa.gov.uk/about/what/international/stress_testing, accessed 4 February 2012. For a more detailed discussion of stress testing see Financial Services Authority *Stress and scenario testing – feedback on CP08/24 and final rules* (Financial Services Authority: London, 2009) and Dunbar, K. 'Forecasting and stress testing the risk-based capital requirements for revolving retail exposures' (2012) Journal of Banking Regulation, 13(3), 249–263.

[104] For a detailed discussion about the tripartite authorities and their role in financial regulation in the United Kingdom see Clayton, N. 'Many hands make light work: the tripartite arrangement as part of the legislative reforms to banking legislation in the UK – a spectrum of views from a spectrum of institutions' (2010) Law and Financial Markets Review, 4(4), 366–393. For an excellent discussion of how the regulatory agencies and government responded to the financial crisis in the United Kingdom see Singh, D. 'UK approach to financial crisis management' (2011) Transnational Law and Contemporary Problems, 19, 868–922 and Brown, E. 'A comparison of the handling of the financial crisis in the United States, the United Kingdom and Australia' (2010) Villanova Law Review, 55, 509–574.

[105] See for example Thelwell, E. 'Northern Rock customers queue for cash as crisis hits high street', 14 September 2007, available from http://www.telegraph.co.uk/finance/markets/2815686/Northern-Rock-customers-queue-for-cash-as-crisis-hits-high-street.html, accessed 8 December 2012.

[106] See generally Ryder, N. 'An unhappy coupling' (2008) New Law Journal, 158(7319), 609.

[107] HM Treasury 'Northern Rock plc deposits', 9 October 2007, available from http://webarchive.nationalarchives.gov.uk/20100407010852/http://www.hm-treasury.gov.uk/press_104_07.htm, accessed 28 February 2013. For a more detailed discussion see Singh, D. and LaBrosse, J. 'Northern Rock, depositors and deposit insurance coverage: some critical reflections' (2010) Journal of Business Law, 2, 55–84.

its damning report into the collapse and nationalisation of Northern Rock.[108] This was followed by the publication of the FSA's own review of its supervision of Northern Rock.[109] The government introduced the Banking (Special Provisions) Act 2008 that resulted in the nationalisation of Northern Rock.[110] This was followed by the Banking Act 2009 which introduced the Special Resolution Regime for failing banks; established the bank insolvency order and a new bank administration order.[111] It soon transpired that Northern Rock was not isolated as other UK financial institutions faced similar problems. For example, the retail business of Bradford & Bingley was purchased by Santander while its mortgage and loans were nationalised.[112] The Labour government announced that it had recapitalised Lloyds TSB, HBOS and RBS.[113] In order to protect these banks, the Asset Protection Scheme (APS) was created by HM Treasury

---

[108] HM Treasury Select Committee above, n 101.

[109] The report identified several weaknesses in its approach, including insufficient administrative engagement with Northern Rock, weak managerial oversight of its supervision, deficient resources supervising the bank and 'lack of intensity by FSA in ensuring that all available risk information was properly utilised to inform its supervisory actions'. See Richards-Carpenter, P., Sautter, E., Hayes, A., Kynoch, N., Stark, P., Baker, M., Dehra, S., Rosser, S., Plange, V. and Ali, M. 'Annual review for 2008' (2008/2009) Compliance Officer Bulletin December/January 62, 1–38, at 3. Also see Financial Services Authority *The supervision of Northern Rock: a lessons learned review* (Financial Services Authority: London, 2008).

[110] S.I. 2008/432.

[111] For a more detailed commentary on the Act see Singh, D. 'The UK Banking Act 2009, pre-insolvency and early intervention: policy and practice' (2011) Journal of Business Law, 1, 20–42.

[112] See HM Treasury 'Bradford & Bingley plc', 29 September 2007, available from http://webarchive.nationalarchives.gov.uk/+/http://www.hm-treasury.gov.uk/press_97_08.htm, accessed 8 December 2012 and HM Treasury 'Government guarantee arrangements: Bradford & Bingley plc', 29 September 2008, available from http://webarchive.nationalarchives.gov.uk/+/http://www.hm-treasury.gov.uk/press_98_08.htm, accessed 13 August 2012. For a more detailed discussion see Bates, C., Gibbons, K., Gray, R., Machin, J., Motani, H. and Plews, T. 'Bradford and Bingley plc: break-up under the Banking (Special Provisions) Act 2008' (2008) Financial Regulation International, November, 1–4.

[113] The Chancellor of the Exchequer (Mr. Alistair Darling), HC Deb, 13 October 2008, c539–42, available from http://www.publications.parliament.uk/pa/cm200708/cmhansrd/cm081013/debtext/81013-0003.htm#0810132000002, accessed 8 December 2012. It is important to note that each of these measures required approval from the EU under its competition law regime. See for example Ed. 'RBS measure and restructuring plan approved' (2010) EU Focus, 33–34.

to improve levels of confidence in the UK banking sector by limiting its losses and by supporting its economic revival.[114] In light of these problems the Financial Services Act received Royal Assent on 8 April 2010,[115] which provided the FSA with a new financial stability statutory objective,[116] new powers relating to the salary structure of the financial services sector,[117] rules relating to 'living wills',[118] the prohibition of short selling,[119] a widening of the circumstances in which it may utilise its investigative powers,[120] an extension of its enforcement powers,[121] a series of consumer protection improvements[122] and new powers to force the assembly of information by authorised firms.[123] These measures were amended by the Financial Services Act 2012, a Coalition government statutory measure that resulted in the 'rebranding' of the FSA to the Financial Conduct Authority (FCA),[124] and the creation of the Prudential

---

114 HM Treasury 'The Asset Protection Scheme', n/d, available from http://www.hm-treasury.gov.uk/apa_aps.htm, accessed 2 December 2012.

115 For a more detailed discussion of the provisions of the Financial Services Act 2010 see Willmott, N., McGowan, P., Ghusn, M., Brocklehurst, V., Aikens, R., Bailey, S., Scodie, M., Palmer, J., Whorton, R. and Gold, A. 'Equipping the modern regulator: assessing the new regulatory powers under the Financial Services Act 2010' Compliance Officer Bulletin, July/August, 78, 1–28.

116 Financial Services Act 2010, s. 1.

117 Financial Services Act 2010, ss. 4–6.

118 Financial Services Act 2010, s. 7. For a brief account see Raaijmakers, G., Silverentand, L., Rank, P. and Noome, M. 'Living wills for banks' (2011) Financial Regulation International, May, 16–19 and Financial Services Authority 'Speech by Thomas F. Huertas, Director, Banking Sector, FSA and Vice Chairman, CEBS, Wharton School of Management, University of Pennsylvania Philadelphia', 16 February 2010, available from http://www.fsa.gov.uk/pages/Library/Communication/Speeches/2010/0212_th.shtml, accessed 7 October 2013.

119 Financial Services Act 2010, s. 8. For a more detailed commentary see Moosa, I. 'The regulation of short selling: a pragmatic view' (2012) Journal of Banking Regulation, 13(3), 211–227 and Juurikkala, O. 'Credit default swaps and the EU Short Selling Regulation: a critical analysis' (2012) European Company and Financial Law Review, 9(3), 307–341.

120 Financial Services Act 2010, ss. 9–13.

121 Financial Services Act 2010, ss. 9–13.

122 Financial Services Act 2010, ss. 14–17.

123 Financial Services Act 2010, ss. 18–19.

124 The FCA has been referred to by some commentators as the 'son of the FSA'. See Anon. 'Reform of financial regulation gathers pace with son of FSA' (2011) Company Law Newsletter, 297, 103.

Regulation Authority (PRA)[125] and Financial Policy Committee (FPC)[126] that is housed within the Bank of England.[127]

1.2 RATIONALE

One of the most important questions that has been addressed by many commentators since the outbreak of the financial crisis is what variables contributed or caused the largest financial crisis since the Great Depression and Wall Street Crash?[128] The FSA stated that 'the origins of the greatest post-war financial crisis can be traced back to a combination of macroeconomic factors and financial market developments. The resulting exuberance in pricing credit and volatility risk developed into a self-reinforcing cycle, exacerbated by a failure to develop appropriate macro-prudential policy responses.'[129] In particular, the FSA identified six factors it felt contributed to the financial crisis, including the macroeconomic imbalances increasing complexity of the securitised credit model; rapid extension of credit and falling credit standards; property price booms; increasing leverage in the banking and shadow banking system; underestimation of bank and market liquidity risk, and a self-reinforcing cycle of irrational exuberance.[130] The Department of Treasury stated that there were five factors that contributed towards the financial crisis, including a breakdown in underwriting standards for subprime mortgages; a significant erosion of market discipline; flaws in CRAs; risk management weaknesses at some large US and European financial institutions; and ineffective regulatory policies.[131] Additionally, the Federal Reserve concluded that there were five factors that contributed towards the financial crisis. These were a generalised run on global

---

[125] For a brief discussion see Walker, G. 'Prudential Regulation Authority' (2011) Financial Regulation International, October, 7–11.

[126] See for example Hill, C. 'Fund management update' (2013) Compliance Officer Bulletin, March, 104, 1–36, at 28.

[127] For a more detailed discussion see Brown, A. and Rice, B. 'Financial Services Act 2012' (2013) Company Secretary's Review, 36(21), 166–167.

[128] For a further discussion of this point see Chapter 2.

[129] Financial Services Authority *Financial risk outlook 2009* (Financial Services Authority: London, 2009) at 5.

[130] *Ibid.*, at 7–12.

[131] Department of Treasury 'President's Working Group on Financial Markets, policy statement on financial markets developments', 13 March 2008, available from http://www.treasury.gov/resource-center/fin-mkts/Documents/pwgpolicystatemktturmoil_03122008.pdf, accessed 14 August 2012.

financial institutions; the dependence of many financial systems on short-term funding; a vicious cycle of mark-to-market losses driving fire sales of asset backed securities; the realisation that financial firms around the world were pursuing similar (flawed) business models and were subject to similar risks; and global swings in risk aversion supported by instantaneous worldwide communications and a shared business culture.[132] Other well documented factors include the subprime mortgage crisis,[133] weak banking regulation,[134] high levels of consumer debt,[135] toxic debts,[136] securitisation,[137] deregulation of banking legislation,[138] ineffective macroeconomic policies,[139] weak credit regulation,[140] deregulation of consumer credit legislation,[141] self-regulated

---

132 Kamin, S.B. and DeMarco, L.P. *How did a domestic housing slump turn into a global financial crisis?*, Board of Governors of the Federal Reserve System International Finance Discussion Papers No. 994, January 2010, p. 6.

133 See for example European Commission *Report of the High-Level Group on Financial Supervision in the EU* (European Commission: Brussels, 2009) and Singh and LaBrosse above, n 107.

134 Hutchins, A. 'Flip that prosecution strategy: an argument for using RICO to prosecute large-scale mortgage fraud' (2011) Buffalo Law Review, 59(1), 293 at 306.

135 See generally Dickerson, M. 'Over-indebtedness, the subprime mortgage crisis, and the effect on US cities' (2009) Fordham Urban Law Journal, 36, 395–425.

136 Arsalidou, D. 'The banking crisis: rethinking and refining the accountability of bank directors' (2010) Journal of Business Law, 4, 284–310, at 292.

137 For a critical discussion of securitisation see Nwogugu, M. 'Securitisation is illegal: racketeer influenced and corrupt organisations, usury, antitrust and tax issues' (2008) Journal of International Banking Law and Regulation, 23(6), 316–332.

138 The arguments on the relationship between the financial crisis and banking deregulation relate to the impact of several pieces of legislation, including the Graham–Leach–Bailey Act 1999, the Depository Institutions Deregulation and Monetary Control Act 1980 and the Garn St Germain Depository Institutions Act 1982. See Levitin, A. 'The crisis without a face: emerging narratives of the financial crisis' (2009) University of Miami Law Review, 63, 999–1010, at 1004.

139 Gevurtz, G. 'The role of corporate law in preventing a financial crisis: reflections on in re Citigroup Inc shareholder derivative litigation' (2010) Pacific McGeorge Global Business and Development Law Journal, 23, 113, at 3.

140 Choi and Papaioannou above, n 49, at 443.

141 See for example the impact of the decision in *Marquette National Bank of Minneapolis v First Omaha Service Corp* 439 U.S., at 299. For a more detailed discussion of the impact of this case on the deregulation of the consumer credit market in the US see Schaefer, E. 'The Credit Card Act of 2009 was not enough: a national usury rate would provide consumers with the protection they need' (2012) University of Baltimore Law Review, Summer, 41, 741–767.

CRAs[142] and the culture of banking practices.[143] It is not the purpose of this monograph to review in detail each of the factors that have contributed towards the financial crisis, but to add to the existing literature by recognising the importance of the previously under-researched factor: white collar crime.

It is acknowledged that many factors created the perfect economic environment that was partly fuelled by and then exploited by white collar criminals. This is a view supported by Huisman, who stated that 'misconduct in the financial industry is widely seen as having triggered the credit crunch that has pushed the world into an economic crisis'.[144] The National Public Survey on White Collar Crime reported that 70 per cent of people believe that white collar crime contributed towards the financial crisis.[145] It has also been reported that there have been increases in white collar crime since the start of the financial crisis in 2008. For example, this includes insurance fraud,[146] credit card fraud,[147] business

---

142 See European Commission above, n 133.

143 See Tomasic above, n 1.

144 Huisman, W. 'White-collar crime and the economic crisis' (2012/2013) Newsletter of the European Society of Criminology, 11, at 8. This is a view supported by Gee, who stated that 'there is considerable evidence that fraud was a major cause of the recession, with widespread sale of financial securities based on sub-prime mortgages, which were known to be worthless'. See Gee, J. 'Fraud 2009 bad, 2010 better?' (2010) Computer Fraud and Security, 2010, February, 2, 13–15, at 13. However, it is important to acknowledge that not all commentators agree with the contention that white collar crime was an important variable that contributed towards the financial crisis. See for example Gill, M. 'Fraud and recessions: views from fraudsters and fraud managers' (2011) International Journal of Law, Crime and Justice, 39, 204–214.

145 Nationwide White Collar Crime Centre *National public survey on white collar crime* (Nationwide White Collar Crime Centre: Fairmont, 2011) at 20.

146 Rayner, G. 'Families turning to insurance fraud to beat credit crunch', 25 December 2008, available from http://www.telegraph.co.uk/finance/financial crisis/3949048/Families-turning-to-insurance-fraud-to-beat-credit-crunch.html, accessed 28 March 2013.

147 BBC News 'Credit crunch fuels fraud cases', 30 April 2008, available from http://news.bbc.co.uk/1/hi/business/7375091.stm, accessed 28 March 2013. In this report the BBC cited figures from the UK fraud prevention service CIFAS. See for example CIFAS '2007 fraud trends', January 2008, available from http://www.cifas.org.uk/secure/contentPORT/uploads/documents/Press%20 Release/2008/A%20-%202007%20Fraud%20Trends.pdf, accessed 28 March 2013.

fraud[148] and reported fraud by CIFAS.[149] However, it is very important to note that it is very difficult to accurately determine levels of white collar crime, let alone increases that are associated with a financial crisis. Huisman argued that an increase in white collar crime emanating from the financial crisis is largely attributed towards accounting fraud.[150] Other commentators, such as Nguyen and Pontell, asserted that prevalent mortgage fraud is associated with the financial crisis.[151] The link between the financial crisis and white collar crime is clearly illustrated by an increase in the related enforcement actions of the SEC, the CFTC, the FBI, the Department of Justice, the FSA, the FCA and the Serious Fraud Office (SFO). For example, since the start of the financial crisis the SEC has charged 161 companies and individuals, including 66 senior corporate officials, with related offences and 37 individuals have either been barred from acting as company directors or suspended from doing so. In addition it has imposed penalty orders of $1.53bn, enforced disgorgement orders totalling $800m and obtained $400m compensation for affected investors. The total amount of penalties amounts to $2.73bn.[152] Abramowitz and Sack took the view that:

> Enforcement statistics from the SEC reveal a constant steady uptick in enforcement actions. Fiscal years 2011 and 2012 brought the highest numbers ever for the agency, with 735 and 734 total actions in those respective years. In the SEC's 2012 annual report, Chairwoman Mary Schapiro noted that in connection with the financial crisis, the SEC has filed actions against 117 entities and individuals

---

148 Masters, B. 'Corporate fraud rises to £1.2bn', 19 January 2009, available from http://www.ft.com/cms/s/0/344179e6-e5c9-11dd-afe4-0000779fd2ac.html#axzz2OpRGItRM, accessed 28 March 2013.

149 See generally CIFAS *Fraudscape – depicting the UK's fraud landscape* (CIFAS: London, 2013). The increase in fraud associated with the financial crisis was also supported by CIFAS 'Fraud trends and recession go hand in hand', n/d, available from www.cifas.org.uk/default.asp?edit_id=899-5, accessed 19 October 2013 and Fraud Advisory Panel *11th annual review 2008/2009* (Fraud Advisory Panel: London, 2009) and Price Waterhouse Cooper *Fraud in a downturn* (Price Waterhouse Cooper: London, 2008).

150 Huisman, Q.W. 'Corporate crime and crisis: causation scenarios' in Deflem, M. (ed.), *Economic crisis and crime* (Emerald: Bingley, 2011) at 111. For a more detailed discussion of accounting fraud see Velikonja, U. 'Leverage, sanctions, and deterrence of accounting fraud' (2011) UC Davis Law Review, 44, 1281–1345.

151 Nguyen, T. and Pontell, H. 'Mortgage origination fraud and the global economic crisis' (2010) Criminology and Public Policy, 9(3), 591–612, at 592.

152 Securities and Exchange Commission 'SEC enforcement actions addressing misconduct that led to or arose from the financial crisis', 1 September 2013, available from http://www.sec.gov/spotlight/enf-actions-fc.shtml, accessed 7 October 2013.

(in 80 actions) including more than 50 CEOs, CFOs and other senior corporate officers, and obtained over $2.2 billion in monetary relief.[153]

Specific instances of enforcement action pursued by the SEC include Goldman Sachs agreeing to pay $550m to reconcile SEC charges related to subprime mortgage collateralised debt obligation[154] and CR Intrinsic agreeing to pay $600m to settle insider trading charges.[155] The CFTC has been heavily involved in the manipulation of the London inter-bank offered rate (LIBOR) by banks in the UK and US and has fined Barclays $200m,[156] UBS $700m,[157] RBS $325m[158] and ICAP $65m.[159] Abramowitz and Sack took the view that:

---

153 Abramowitz, E. and Sack, J. 'Why so few prosecutions connected to the financial crisis?' (2013) New York Law Journal, 250(46), 1–3, at 2.

154 Securities and Exchange Commission 'Goldman Sachs to pay record $550 million to settle SEC charges related to subprime mortgage CDO', 15 July 2010, available from http://www.sec.gov/news/press/2010/2010-123.htm, accessed 6 March 2013. A collateralised debt obligation has been defined as a 'debt instrument that allows investors with differing risk appetites to invest in a broad range of debt instruments that would normally reside on bank balance sheets'. See Alexander, K. 'The nature of modern credit markets' in Alexander, K. and Dhumale, R. (eds) *Research handbook on international financial regulation* (Edward Elgar: Cheltenham, 2012) at 11.

155 Securities and Exchange Commission 'CR Intrinsic agrees to pay more than $600 million in largest-ever settlement for insider trading case', 15 March 2013, available from http://www.sec.gov/news/press/2013/2013-41.htm, accessed 18 March 2013.

156 Commodities Futures Trading Commission 'CFTC orders Barclays to pay $200 million penalty for attempted manipulation of and false reporting concerning LIBOR and Euribor benchmark interest rates', 27 June 2012, available from http://www.cftc.gov/PressRoom/PressReleases/pr6289-12, accessed 12 August 2013. Also see Gensler, G. 'Libor, naked and exposed', 6 August 2012, available from http://www.nytimes.com/2012/08/07/opinion/libor-naked-and-exposed.html?_r=3&ref=opinionpiecesaboutlibor&, accessed 12 August 2013.

157 Commodities Futures Trading Commission 'CFTC orders UBS to pay $700 million penalty to settle charges of manipulation, attempted manipulation and false reporting of LIBOR and other benchmark interest rates', 19 December 2012, available from http://www.cftc.gov/PressRoom/PressReleases/pr6472-12, accessed 12 August 2013.

158 Commodities Futures Trading Commission 'CFTC orders The Royal Bank of Scotland plc and RBS Securities Japan Limited to pay $325 million penalty to settle charges of manipulation, attempted manipulation, and false reporting of yen and Swiss franc LIBOR', 6 February 2013, available from http://www.cftc.gov/PressRoom/PressReleases/pr6510-13, accessed 12 August 2013.

159 Commodities Futures Trading Commission 'CFTC charges ICAP Europe Limited, a subsidiary of ICAP plc, with manipulation and attempted manipulation of

> A similar upward trend has been documented at the CFTC. Fiscal year 2011 brought record highs with 99 enforcement actions, the highest tally in the agency's history and a 74 percent increase over the prior year, and more than 450 new investigations opened. In fiscal year 2012, the agency filed 102 enforcement actions and opened 350 new investigations.[160]

Additionally, the Department of Justice announced that RBS Securities Japan Limited, a wholly owned subsidiary of RBS, pleaded guilty to wire fraud and its role in influencing the Japanese yen LIBOR.[161] As part of a deferred prosecution agreement it has agreed to pay a $50m fine. Additionally, RBS Securities Japan Limited agreed to pay a $100m penalty to the Department of Justice.[162] Similarly, the FBI has seen a significant increase in its enforcement and investigative activities towards white collar crime, especially mortgage fraud, since the start of the financial crisis.[163] For example, at the time of writing the FBI is investigating 1,954 allegations of mortgage fraud, approximately 70 per cent of which exceed $1m; it made 1,079 indictments and secured 1,026 convictions in 2012, approximately $13bn was lost and there are 141 open investigations.[164] The increase in mortgage fraud is illustrated by also examining the number of mortgage fraud related suspicious activity reports (SARs) filed by the Financial Crimes Enforcement Network (FinCEN) with the US Financial Intelligence Unit.[165] In 2010, FinCEN received 70,472 mortgage loan fraud SARs, a 4 per cent increase from

---

yen Libor', 25 September 2013, available from http://www.cftc.gov/PressRoom/PressReleases/pr6708-13, accessed 8 October 2013.

160 Abramowitz and Sack above n 153, at 2.

161 Department of Justice 'RBS Securities Japan Limited agrees to plead guilty in connection with long-running manipulation of Libor benchmark interest rates', 6 February 2013, available from http://www.justice.gov/opa/pr/2013/February/13-crm-161.html, accessed 8 February 2013.

162 *Ibid.*

163 Fisher, L. 'Target marketing of subprime loans: racialised consumer fraud and reverse redlining' (2009) Journal of Law and Policy, 18, 121–155, at 144.

164 Federal Bureau of Investigation 'Mortgage fraud', n/d, available from http://www.fbi.gov/about-us/investigate/white_collar/mortgage-fraud/mortgage_fraud, accessed 6 March 2013.

165 For a more detailed discussion on the role of the Financial Crimes Enforcement Network see Ryder, N. *Money laundering – an endless cycle? A comparative analysis of the anti-money laundering policies in the United States of America, the United Kingdom, Australia and Canada* (Routledge Cavendish: Abingdon, 2012) at 49–52.

2009.[166] In 2011, FinCEN reported that 92,028 mortgage loan fraud SARs had been reported, an increase of 31 per cent from 2010.[167] The link between the financial crisis, subprime lending and mortgage fraud was also acknowledged by Patterson and Koller, who stated:

> The subprime mortgage products and processes that were made available in the 1990s, however, increased the population of potential offenders, increased temptation and suitable targets, and increased the ease at which motivated individuals could take advantage of the opportunities to commit crime. As such, it was not necessarily the routine of the housing/mortgage industry that was problematic, it was the actual category of subprime products that created an environment rich with white collar crime and opportunity.[168]

We have also seen increased enforcement activities of regulatory agencies in the UK since the start of the financial crisis in 2007. The FSA adopted what it refers to as a 'credible deterrence' approach towards its then financial crime statutory objective.[169] In 2007, the FSA imposed a total of £5.3m of financial sanctions on firms and individuals.[170] A year later, it reported that the figure had increased to £22.7m.[171] In 2009 the total amount of financial sanctions imposed by the FSA had risen to £35m.[172] The figures for 2010 and 2011 illustrated an increase to £89.1m[173] but then a fall to £66.1m.[174] 2012 represented the largest amount of financial

---

[166] Financial Crimes Enforcement Network *Mortgage loan fraud update suspicious activity report filings from January 1–December 31 2010* (Financial Crimes Enforcement Network: Washington DC, 2011) at 2.

[167] *Ibid.*

[168] Patterson and Koller above, n 46, at 33. This is a view supported by Barnett, H. 'The securitization of mortgage fraud' in Deflem, M. (ed.), *Economic crisis and crime* (Emerald: Bingley, 2011) at 67–68.

[169] Financial Services Authority 'Delivering credible deterrence', speech by Margaret Cole, Director of Enforcement, FSA, Annual Financial Crime Conference, 27 April 2009, available from http://www.fsa.gov.uk/library/communication/speeches/2009/0427_mc.shtml, accessed 8 March 2013.

[170] Financial Services Authority 'FSA fines table 2007', n/d, available from http://www.fsa.gov.uk/about/press/facts/fines/2007, accessed 8 March 2013.

[171] Financial Services Authority 'FSA fines table 2008', n/d, available from http://www.fsa.gov.uk/about/press/facts/fines/2008, accessed 8 March 2013.

[172] Financial Services Authority 'FSA fines table 2009', n/d, available from http://www.fsa.gov.uk/about/press/facts/fines/2009, accessed 8 March 2013.

[173] Financial Services Authority 'FSA fines table 2010', n/d, available from http://www.fsa.gov.uk/about/press/facts/fines/2010, accessed 8 March 2013.

[174] Financial Services Authority 'FSA fines table 2011', n/d, available from http://www.fsa.gov.uk/about/press/facts/fines/2011, accessed 8 March 2013.

sanctions imposed by the FSA, totalling a staggering £311.5m.[175] Prior to its merger into the FCA, by April 2013 the FSA had imposed fines totalling £135.8m and it would have been on course to exceed its figure from 2012.[176] These figures since 2011 have been influenced by the imposition of a series of record fines due to the LIBOR scandal. This includes, for example, the £59.5m fine on Barclays,[177] the £160m fine on UBS[178] and the £87.5m fine on RBS.[179] It is important to note that the FCA has continued to use the 'credible deterrence' strategy by virtue of the Financial Services Act 2012. It has been suggested by one commentator that the:

> FCA intends to pursue the policy of credible deterrence as vigorously as (if not more so than) the FSA has done. This will mean even higher penalties against high-profile targets, both firms and individuals. There has been a continuing trend of imposing significant, exemplary sanctions against senior individuals in the market, particularly in the context of market conduct cases.[180]

An example of the FCA continuing the credible deterrence policy is the financial sanctions it has imposed since the LIBOR scandal. For instance, in September 2013 the FCA fined ICAP Europe Limited £14m over its role in the LIBOR scandal.[181] Since April 2013, the FCA has imposed

---

175 Financial Services Authority 'FSA fines table 2012', n/d, available from http://www.fsa.gov.uk/about/press/facts/fines/2012, accessed 8 March 2013.

176 Financial Services Authority 'FSA fines table 2013', n/d, available from http://www.fsa.gov.uk/about/press/facts/fines/2013, accessed 8 March 2013.

177 Financial Services Authority 'Barclays fined £59.5m for significant failings in relation to LIBOR and EURIBOR', 27 June 2012, available from http://www.fsa.gov.uk/library/communication/pr/2012/070.shtml, accessed 8 February 2013.

178 Financial Services Authority 'UBS fined £160m for significant failings in relation to LIBOR and EURIBOR' 19 December 2012, available from http://www.fsa.gov.uk/library/communication/pr/2012/116.shtml, accessed 8 February 2013.

179 Financial Services Authority 'RBS fined £87.5m for significant failings in relation to LIBOR', 6 February 2013, available from http://www.fsa.gov.uk/library/communication/pr/2013/011.shtml, accessed 8 February 2013.

180 Travers Smith Regulatory Investigations Group 'FSA enforcement action: themes and trends' (2012) Compliance Officer Bulletin, May, 96, 1–30, at 2.

181 Financial Conduct Authority 'ICAP Europe Limited fined £14 million for significant failings in relation to LIBOR', 25 September 2013, available from http://www.fca.org.uk/news/list?ttypes=&yyear=&ssearch=ICAP, accessed 7 October 2013.

financial penalties totalling approximately £202m,[182] and the largest financial sanction imposed by the FCA was £137.6m on JP Morgan.[183]

Additionally, there has been an increase in the enforcement activities of the SFO, which was created as a result of the influential recommendations of the Roskill Report and the implementation of the Criminal Justice Act 1987.[184] The SFO is an independent government department that investigates and prosecutes serious, complex fraud and corruption.[185] The SFO was heralded as the UK's answer to the FBI, due to its combined investigative and prosecutorial powers. However, the SFO has led a troubled life and is perceived by many commentators as a failing organisation. Its reputation has been tarnished by several high profile failures, including for example Guinness,[186] Blue Arrow,[187] Maxwell,[188] Levitt[189] and Azil Nadir.[190] More recently, the SFO has been in the headlines for its handling of the bribery allegations against BAE Systems and its abandonment of the investigation into arms sales in Saudi

---

182 Financial Conduct Authority 'Fines table 2013', 1 October 2013, available from http://www.fca.org.uk/firms/being-regulated/enforcement/fines, accessed 7 October 2013.

183 Financial Conduct Authority 'JPMorgan Chase Bank N.A. fined £137,610,000 for serious failings relating to its Chief Investment Office's "London Whale" trades', 19 September 2013, available from http://www.fca.org.uk/news/jpmorgan-chase-bank-na-fined, accessed 8 October 2013.

184 Criminal Justice Act 1987, s. 1(1).

185 Serious Fraud Office 'Who we are', n/d, available from http://www.sfo.gov.uk/about-us/who-we-are.aspx, accessed 11 March 2013.

186 For a more detailed discussion see Sarker, R. 'The trials and errors of the Guinness four' (1995) Journal of Financial Crime, 3(1), 86–88 and Page, F. 'Defining fraud: an argument in favour of a general offence of fraud' (1997) Journal of Financial Crime, 4(4), 287–308.

187 For a more detailed discussion of this case see Cohen, H. 'What place does the criminal law have in the regulation of securities markets after the Blue Arrow trials?' (1992) Journal of International Banking Law, 7(10), 420–422 and Kirk, D. 'Blue Arrow: the SFO on trial' (1992) International Company and Commercial Law Review, 3(10), 331–333.

188 For a more detailed discussion see Sarker, R. 'Maxwell: fraud trial of the century (case comment)' (1996) Company Lawyer, 17(4), 116–117 and Honess, T. 'Juror competence in processing complex information: implications from a simulation of the Maxwell trial' (1998) Criminal Law Review, November, 763–773.

189 For a more detailed discussion see Sarker, R. 'The Serious Fraud Office – quo vadis?' (1995) Company Lawyer, 16(2), 56–61.

190 For a more detailed discussion see Gallagher, J., Lauchlan, J. and Steven, M. 'Polly Peck: the breaking of an entrepreneur?' (1996) Journal of Small Business and Enterprise Development, 3(1), 3–12.

Arabia.[191] The weaknesses of the SFO have been highlighted by several reports, including the de Grazia Review[192] and the HM Crown Prosecution Service Inspectorate in 2008[193] and 2012.[194] More recently, the SFO has been severely criticised over its poor handling of the Tchenguiz brothers' investigation.[195] However, it is important to note that the SFO has increased the frequency of its investigations and prosecutions against its tainted track record. For example, in its 2006/2007 Annual Report the SFO noted that since 2001 it had achieved a conviction rate of 61 per

---

191 For a more detailed discussion see Williams, S. 'The BAE/Saudi Al-Yamamah contracts: implications in law and public procurement' (2008) International and Comparative Law Quarterly, 57(1), 200–209 and Rose, C. 'Legislative comment: the UK Bribery Act 2010 and accompanying guidance: belated implementation of the OECD Anti- Bribery Convention' (2012) International and Comparative Law Quarterly, 61(2), 484–499. The decision by the SFO to terminate its investigation into the sale of arms in Saudi Arabia was subject to a judicial review and the Queen's Bench Divisional Court determined that the decision was unlawful. See *The Queen on the application of (1) Corner House Research (2) Campaign Against Arms Trade v The Director of the Serious Fraud Office (Defendant) and BAE Systems Plc (Interested Party),* Claim No. CO/1567/2007, High Court of Justice, Queen's Bench Division, Administrative Court, 18 April 2007. However, this decision was overturned on appeal by the House of Lords. See *R (on the application of Corner House Research and others) v Director of the Serious Fraud Office* [2008] UKHL 60, 30 July 2008, para. 11. For a more detailed discussion of this case and the related legal issues see Yihdego, Z. 'Arms trade and public controls: the right to information perspective' (2008) Northern Ireland Legal Quarterly, 59(4), 379–394; Spencer, J. 'Fiat justicia, ruatque concordia cum Arabe?' (2008) Cambridge Law Journal, 67(3), 456–458 and Roberts, A. 'Prosecution: director of SFO – lawfulness of decision to discontinue prosecution' (2009) Criminal Law Review, 1, 46–49.

192 de Grazia, J. *Review of the Serious Fraud Office – final report* (Serious Fraud Office: London, 2008).

193 HM Crown Prosecution Service Inspectorate *Review of the Fraud Prosecution Service* (HM Crown Prosecution Inspectorate: London, 2008).

194 HM Crown Prosecution Service Inspectorate *Report of the Attorney General on the inspection of the Serious Fraud Office* (HM Crown Prosecution Service Inspectorate: London, 2012).

195 See for example Neate, R. 'Tchenguiz brothers seek millions from Serious Fraud Office', 3 December 2012, available from http://m.guardian.co.uk/business/2012/dec/03/tchenguiz-brothers-millions-damages-sfo, accessed 18 March 2013, Russel, J. 'Tchenguiz brothers launch damages case against SFO', 2 December 2012, available from http://www.telegraph.co.uk/finance/financial-crime/9717240/Tchenguiz-brothers-launch-damages-case-against-SFO.html, accessed 18 March 2013.

cent.[196] However, this figure had increased to 71 per cent by 2006/2007.[197] In its next Annual Report, the conviction rate had increased to 68 per cent.[198] In 2009, the SFO achieved an impressive conviction rate of 91 per cent.[199] However, this figure fell to 84 per cent in 2010 and 73 per cent in 2011.[200] The regulatory performance of the SFO has been assisted by the introduction of the Bribery Act 2010.[201] Under the Act the SFO, or 'chief prosecutors of offences under the Bribery Act',[202] have been provided with additional prosecutorial powers by the creation of several new offences.[203] These include for example offering, promising or providing a bribe,[204] requesting, agreeing to receive or accepting a bribe,[205] bribery of foreign public officials[206] and failure of commercial organisations to prevent bribery.[207]

It is interesting to note that the increased enforcement activity of both the FSA and SFO could be associated with an announcement by the Coalition government of the creation of the single Economic Crime

---

196 Serious Fraud Office *Annual Report 2006/2007* (Serious Fraud Office: London, 2007) at 4.

197 *Ibid.*, at 4.

198 Serious Fraud Office *Annual Report 2007/2008* (Serious Fraud Office: London, 2008) at 5.

199 Serious Fraud Office *Annual Report 2009/2010* (Serious Fraud Office: London, 2010) at 2.

200 Serious Fraud Office *Annual report and accounts 2011/2012* (Serious Fraud Office: London, 2012) at 6.

201 A full detailed commentary on the Bribery Act 2010 is beyond the scope of this monograph. For a more detailed analysis see Wells, C. 'Who's afraid of the Bribery Act 2010?' (2012) Journal of Business Law, 5, 420–431; Yeoh, P. 'The UK Bribery Act 2010: contents and implications' (2012) Journal of Financial Crime, 19(1), 37–53 and Rose, C. 'The UK Bribery Act 2010 and accompanying guidance: belated implementation of the OECD Anti-Bribery Convention' (2012) International and Comparative Law Quarterly, 61(2), 484–499.

202 Breslin, B., Ezickson, D. and Kocoras, J. 'The Bribery Act 2010: raising the bar above the US Foreign Corrupt Practices Act' (2010) Company Lawyer, 31(11), 362–369, at 362.

203 For an excellent discussion on the enforcement of the Bribery Act 2010 see Monteith, C. 'The Bribery Act 2010: part 3: enforcement' (2011) Criminal Law Review, 2, 111–121.

204 Bribery Act 2010, s. 1.

205 Bribery Act 2010, s. 2.

206 Bribery Act 2010, s. 6.

207 Bribery Act 2010, s. 7.

Agency (ECA) in its Coalition Agreement.[208] The government stated that 'we take white collar crime as seriously as other crime and we are determined to simplify the confusing and overlapping responsibilities in this area in order to improve detection and enforcement'.[209] The government acknowledged that the regulatory structure then in place was unworkable due to conflicting priorities, overlapping roles and ineffective outcomes. However, the formation of the ECA was obstructed by differences of opinion within the Coalition government over its remit and the reaction of both the SFO and FSA.[210] The most significant factor that prevented its creation was the uncertainty over its ownership. It is to the bemusement of the author that HM Treasury, which managed the FSA and administered the UK's anti-money laundering and counter-terrorist financing policies, was not considered for this role. The ECA was to be managed by the Home Office, which hoped to end the UK's 'piecemeal' attitude towards tackling financial crime.[211] However, the Home Office mistakenly expected that the 'initial elements' of the agency would be in place by the middle of 2011.[212] In a soap opera-like twist, the Home Office decided against creating the ECA, and turned its attention to establishing the broader National Crime Agency (NCA), the objective of which was to tackle organised crime, fraud, and cyber crime, maintain border protection, and protect children and young people. The NCA is divided into four Command areas: Organised Crime Command, Border Policing Command, Economic Crime Command, and the Child Exploitation and Online Protection Centre.[213] The Home Office envisages the

---

[208] See HM Government *The Coalition: our programme for government* (HM Government: London, 2010) at 9. The proposal to create the Economic Crime Agency was first mooted by an excellent report by Jonathan Fisher QC. See Fisher, J. *Fighting fraud and financial crime – a new architecture for the investigation and prosecution of serious fraud, corruption and financial market crimes* (Policy Exchange: London, 2010).

[209] HM Treasury 'George Osborne, Chancellor of the Exchequer. Speech at The Lord Mayor's Dinner for Bankers and Merchants of the City of London, at Mansion House 16 June 2010', available from www.hm-treasury.gov.uk/press_12_10.htm, accessed 26 June 2010.

[210] See for example Palmer, A. and Ryder, N. 'The Economic Crime Agency' (2011) Financial Regulation International, April, 1–3.

[211] Home Office, Press Release, 'Home Office to take lead on economic crime', 17 January 2011, available from http://www.homeoffice.gov.uk/media-centre/news/economic-crime, accessed 23 October 2011.

[212] *Ibid.*

[213] Home Office *The National Crime Agency – a plan for the creation of a national crime-fighting capability* (London: Home Office, 2011).

role of the Economic Crime Command to 'ensure a coherent approach to the use of resources focussed on economic crime across the full range of agencies deploying them'.[214] Furthermore, the Economic Crime Command will 'maintain an overview' of a wide range of economic crime agencies, including the City of London Police and SFO.[215]

1.3 DEFINITIONS

The most recent financial crisis has been referred to by many commentators, especially those in the media, as the 'Credit Crunch'. It would seem a very easy term to define, and it could be interpreted as 'a severe shortage of money or credit'[216] or where 'creditors become reluctant to lend money to businesses or individuals'.[217] However, the phrase 'Credit Crunch' has attracted numerous interpretations and a degree of uncertainty as to its origin. For example, it has been claimed that the term was first used in 1966 to describe the restrictive credit conditions when financial institutions were reluctant to offer credit to borrowers.[218] It has also been said that the term can be traced to the Roman Republic in 88BC.[219] The term 'Credit Crunch' has been defined as 'unexplained sluggishness in the economy and that it should be reserved for a situation of widespread non-price rationing of credit'.[220] It has also been referred to as a period of time where interbank lending stops and it becomes more

---

[214] *Ibid.*, at 20.

[215] Home Office above, n 211, at 20.

[216] BBC News 'Credit crunch enters the lexicon', 3 July 2008, available from http://news.bbc.co.uk/1/hi/business/7487608.stm, accessed 21 November 2012.

[217] Financial Times Lexicon, n/d, available from http://lexicon.ft.com/Term?term=credit-crunch, accessed 21 November 2012.

[218] Owens, R. and Schreft, S. 'Identifying credit crunches' (1995) Contemporary Economic Policy, 13(2), 63–76.

[219] Brown, M. 'First credit crunch traced back to Roman republic', 28 November 2008, available from http://www.guardian.co.uk/business/2008/nov/28/credit-crunch-roman-republic-lecture, accessed 1 February 2013. Also see University of Oxford 'World's first credit crunch?', 27 November 2008, available from http://www.ox.ac.uk/media/news_releases_for_journalists/081127.html, accessed 1 February 2013.

[220] Peek, J. and Rosengren, E. Crunching the recovery: bank capital and the role of bank credit. *Conference Series [Proceedings]* (1992). Federal Reserve Bank of Boston, 151–186.

difficult to obtain and offer credit facilities.[221] The term 'Credit Crunch' has been frequently used by economists,[222] who have also offered a variety of definitions, resulting in further uncertainty as to 'what constitutes a credit crunch'.[223] For example, Bernanke and Lown defined it as 'a significant leftward shift in the supply curve for bank loans, holding constant both the safe real interest rate and the quality of potential borrowers'.[224] According to Clair and Tucker 'the phrase "credit crunch" has been used in the past to explain curtailment of the credit supply in response to both … a decline in the value of bank capital and … conditions imposed by regulators, bank supervisors, or banks themselves that require banks to hold more capital than they previously would have held'.[225] The Council of Economic Advisers offered the following definition of 'Credit Crunch': 'when the supply of credit is restricted below the range usually identified with prevailing market interest rates and the profitability of investment projects'.[226] Writing in 1980, Wojnilower characterised a credit crunch as 'cyclically significant retardations or reductions in credit and aggregate demand occur only when there is an interruption in the supply of credit'.[227] Other terms that are synonymous with the 'Credit Crunch' are 'financial crises' and 'banking crises'. According to Reinhart and Rogoff a banking crisis depends on the occurrence of two events. First, there must be 'bank runs that lead to the closure, merging or takeover by the public sector of one or more

---

221 Elliot, L. 'Credit crisis – how it all began', 5 August 2008, available from http://www.guardian.co.uk/business/2008/aug/05/northernrock.banking, accessed 8 February 2013.

222 Wojnilower, A.M. 'The central role of credit crunches in recent financial history' (1980) Brookings Papers on Economic Activity, 2, 277–339, at 287.

223 Clair, R. and Tucker, P. 'Six causes of the credit crunch (or, why is it so hard to get a loan?)' (1993) Federal Reserve Bank of Dallas Economic Review, 1–19, at 1.

224 Bernanke, B.S. and Lown, C.S. 'The Credit Crunch,' (1991) Brookings Papers on Economic Activity, 2, 205–247. This definition has been criticised by some commentators. See for example Clair and Tucker *ibid.*, at 2.

225 Clair and Tucker, *ibid.*

226 Council of Economic Advisers *Economic report of the President* (Government Printing Office, 1992) at 46.

227 See Wojnilower above, n 222, at 278. Kliesen and Tatom took the view that 'the traditional notion of a credit crunch originally involved the process known as disintermediation, a decline in savings-type deposits at banks and savings and loans that result in a decline in bank lending'. See Kliesen, K. and Tatom, J. 'The recent credit crunch: the neglected dimensions' (1992) Federal Reserve Bank of St. Louis Review, 74(5), 18–36, at 1.

financial institutions'.[228] Secondly, there must be 'large scale government assistance of an important financial institution (or group of institutions) that mark the start of a string of similar outcomes for other financial institutions'.[229] Another term associated with a 'Credit Crunch' is a 'Credit Squeeze', which, according to Mizen, is a 'milder version of a full-blown credit crunch ... [which] we observed in 2007 and early 2008'.[230]

The term 'white collar crime' has become synonymous with Professor Edwin Sutherland, who has been described as the 'most influential American criminologist of his day'.[231] He used the term in his 1939 presidential lecture to the American Sociological Society.[232] He defined 'white collar crime' as 'a crime committed by a person of respectability and high social status in the course of his occupation'.[233] In his seminal paper, Sutherland stated that:

> The present-day white-collar criminals, who are more suave and deceptive than the 'robber barons', are represented ... [by] many other merchant princes and captains of finance and industry, and by a host of lesser followers. Their criminality has been demonstrated again and again in the investigations of

---

228 Reinhart, C. and Rogoff, K. *This time is different – eight centuries of financial folly* (Princeton University Press: Princeton, 2009) at 10.

229 *Ibid.*

230 Mizen, P. 'The credit crunch of 2007–2008: a discussion of the background, market reactions, and policy responses' (2008) Federal Reserve Bank of St. Louis Review, 90(5), 531–567, at 531.

231 Green, S. 'The concept of white collar crime in law and legal theory' (2004) Buffalo Criminal Law Review, 8, 1–34, at 3.

232 See Sutherland, E. (1940) 'The white collar criminal', American Sociological Review, 5(1), 1–12, at 1.

233 Sutherland, E. *White collar crime* (Dryden: New York, 1949) 9, as cited in Wilson, S. 'Collaring the crime and the criminal? Jury psychology and some criminological perspectives on fraud and the criminal law' (2006) Journal of Criminal Law, 70(1), 75–92, at 79. This is a view supported by Gottschalk, who stated that 'the most economically disadvantaged members of society are not the only ones committing crime. Members of the privileged socio-economic class are also engaged in criminal behaviour. The types of crime may differ from those of the less privileged classes, such as lawyers helping criminal clients launder their money, executives bribing public officials to achieve public contracts, or accountants manipulating balance sheet to avoid taxes'. Gottschalk, P. 'Executive positions involved in white- collar crime' (2011) Journal of Money Laundering Control, 14(4), 300–312, at 302. For a more detailed commentary on the definitions of white collar crime see Simpson, S. 'White collar crime: a review of recent developments and promising directions for future research' (2013) Annual Review of Sociology, 39, 309–331, at 310–313.

> land offices, railways, insurance, munitions, banking, public utilities, stock exchanges, the oil industry, real estate, reorganization committees, receiverships, bankruptcies, and politics.[234]

One of the most important parts of this definition is that white collar crime is committed by people of a high social standing, a view supported by Benson and Simpson, who stated that 'criminal behaviour by members of the privileged socioeconomic class is labelled white-collar crime'.[235] Kempa described white collar crime as a 'wide concept that speaks generally to illegal behaviour that takes advantage of positions of professional authority and power – or simply the opportunity structures available within business – for personal or corporate gain'.[236] Friedrichs stated that white collar crimes are 'the large scale illegalities … committed on behalf of major financially privileged statuses, including violations of banking Acts, bribery, fraud, tax evasion, money laundering, insider trading, predatory lending, and other deceptive practices'.[237] Sutherland's definition has been described as his 'most famous and controversial legacy'.[238] However, Green suggested that the interpretation of the term is 'deeply contested', and that the definition provided 'was famously vague and inconsistent'.[239] Furthermore, Bookman argued that Sutherland's definition of white collar crime was too narrow.[240] This was a view supported by Leong, who noted that:

---

234 Sutherland above, n 232 at 2.

235 Benson, M.L. and Simpson, S.S. *White-collar crime: an opportunity perspective*, Criminology and Justice Series (Routledge: New York, 2009), as cited in Gottschalk, P. 'Gender and white-collar crime: only four percent female criminals' (2012) Journal of Money Laundering Control, 15(3), 362–373, at 362. For an excellent commentary on whether white collar criminals are privileged see Buell, S. 'Is the white collar offender privileged?' (2014) Duke Law, 63(4), 823–889.

236 Kempa, M. 'Combating white-collar crime in Canada: serving victim needs and market integrity' (2010) Journal of Financial Crime, 17(2), 251–264, at 252.

237 Friedrichs, D. *Trusted criminals: white collar crime in contemporary society* (Wadsworth Cengage Learning: Bellmont, 2010) at 190.

238 Wilson, G. and Wilson, S. 'Can the general fraud offence "get the law right"? Some perspectives on the "problem" of financial crime' (2007) Journal of Criminal Law, 71(1), 36–53, at 40.

239 Green above, n 231 at 3. For a more detailed discussion of the problems associated with the definition of white collar crime see Gilligan, G. 'The problem of, and with, financial crime' (2012) Northern Ireland Legal Quarterly, 63(4), 495–508.

240 Bookman, Z. 'Convergences and omissions in reporting corporate and white collar crime' (2008) DePaul Business and Commercial Law Journal, 6, 347–392, at 355.

> the definition of white-collar crime is criticised for being too narrow as it does not include the differential associations between the 'upperworld' of corporations and the 'underworld' of criminal organisations. At the same time, it is criticised for being too broad as an all-encompassing category. In fact, the distinction between organised crime or 'business in crime' and the activities of white-collar offenders blurs, and organised crime often uses and abuses legitimate corporate enterprises.[241]

Further criticism over the definition afforded by Sutherland was offered by Podgor, who stated that 'the bottom line is that throughout the last 100 years no one could ever figure it [white collar crime] out'.[242] Friedrichs stated that by the 1970s there were two 'core types of white collar crime [that] have been widely recognised: corporate crime and occupational crime'.[243] Soothill went so far as to argue that 'there have been long-standing doubts and debates about whether these misbehaviours [white collar crime] can be considered to count as crime'.[244] Brody and Kiehl correctly asserted that the most significant limitation of Sutherland's definition is that it has not endured the progress and advancement of white collar crime to retain its status as the conventional definition. They concluded that 'many scholars continue to redefine and develop a more useful and working definition of the term'.[245] White collar crime has also been referred to as 'financial crime', 'economic crime' and 'illicit finance'.[246]

In the UK financial crime is defined as 'any offence involving fraud or dishonesty; misconduct in, or misuse of information relating to, a financial market; or handling the proceeds of crime'.[247] Graham stated

---

[241] Leong, A. 'Definitional analysis: the war on terror and organised crime' (2004) Journal of Money Laundering Control, 8(1), 19–36, at 22.

[242] Podgor, E. 'White collar crime: a letter from the future' (2007) Ohio State Journal of Criminal Law, 5, 247–255, at 247.

[243] Friedrichs, D. 'Wall Street: crime never sleeps' in Will, S., Handelman, S. and Brotherton, D. (eds), *How they got away with it – white collar criminals and the financial meltdown* (Columbia University Press: New York, 2013) at 9.

[244] Soothill, K. 'Blacklists and black sheep' (2010) Police Journal, 83(1), 5–10, at 10.

[245] Brody, R. and Kiehl, K. 'From white-collar crime to red-collar crime' (2010) Journal of Financial Crime, 17(3), 351–364, at 351.

[246] For a general discussion of these different types of white collar crime see Harrison, K. and Ryder, N. *The law relating to financial crime in the United Kingdom* (Ashgate: Farnham, 2013).

[247] Financial Services and Markets Act 2000, s. 6(3). Friedrichs defined 'financial crime' as 'large-scale illegality that occurs in the world of finance and financial institutions'. See Friedrichs above, n 237, at 9.

that there are two elements to this definition. First, 'there must be an offence, which is defined in clause 6(4) to include an act or omission which would be an offence if it had taken place in the UK. This definition therefore includes financial crimes committed abroad provided they would be offences were they to have taken place in the UK.'[248] Secondly, 'there are limitations to the "offence" definition, since not all offences constitute "financial crime" … "proceeds of crime" is not defined … this phrase is likely to be interpreted to include proceeds of crimes committed abroad'.[249] Fleming noted that 'financial crime as defined by FSMA relates to a broad and potentially indistinct range of offences'.[250] The FBI has provided a broad definition of 'financial crime', which includes corporate fraud, commodities and securities fraud, mortgage fraud, healthcare fraud, financial institution fraud, insurance fraud, mass marketing fraud and money laundering.[251] Definitions of the term 'financial crime' have also been presented by academics. For example, Gottschalk states that it is 'a crime against property, involving the unlawful conversion of property belonging to another to one's own personal use and benefit', stating that it is often 'profit driven … to gain access to and control over property that belonged to someone else'.[252]

Now that the main terms have been defined, it is necessary to outline and justify why the US and UK have been selected as case studies for this monograph.

1.4 WHY THE UNITED STATES OF AMERICA?

The US presents an interesting case study for this monograph. This is because, for example, the origins of the financial crisis can be traced to its subprime mortgage sector, which has been heavily linked to a

---

[248] Graham, T. 'Financial Services and Markets Bill: investigations and enforcement in the context of the financial crime objective' (2000) Journal of International Financial Markets, 2(3), 88–93, at 88.

[249] *Ibid.*

[250] Fleming, M. *FSA's Scale & Impact of Financial Crime project (phase one): Critical Analysis Occasional Paper Series 37* (Financial Services Authority: London, 2009) at 2.

[251] Federal Bureau of Investigation 'Financial crimes report to the public', available from http://www.fbi.gov/stats-services/publications/financial-crimes-report-2010-2011/financial-crimes-report-2010-2011#Financial, accessed 21 March 2012.

[252] Gottschalk, P. 'Categories of financial crime' (2010) Journal of Financial Crime 17(4), 441–458, at 441.

significant increase in mortgage fraud. The association between the subprime mortgage market and fraud was identified by Podgor, who stated that:

> The subprime market was out of control and because it was not sufficiently monitored there were instances of fraud. In some instances, the frauds that were eventually prosecuted had caused enormous losses. The high loss figures may have been due in part to the length of time that these frauds had gone undetected.[253]

Since the start of the financial crisis in 2007, there have been several high profile white collar crimes that have either emanated from it or been exposed by it. These include the Ponzi related frauds committed by Bernard Madoff and Allen Stanford and the rampant increase in mortgage fraud. One of the key questions that commentators have asked is how were both Madoff and Stanford able to avoid detection for so many years? Therefore, an excellent opportunity exists to review the performance of the SEC, FBI and other US regulatory agencies in light of these regulatory mishaps.[254] Furthermore, US regulatory agencies such as the SEC and FBI have instigated numerous investigations and prosecutions and imposed record financial penalties for the illegal activities of firms that have contributed towards the financial crisis. However, it is also important to stress that these agencies, along with the Department of Justice, have failed to secure any high profile Wall Street related criminal convictions for the alleged culprits.

Another reason why the US was selected for this research is that there has been a dramatic rethink of its white collar crime policy since the start of the financial crisis. This is partly due to the diversion by President George Bush of resources and staff from white collar crime agencies to the 'War on Terror' following the terrorist attacks in September 2001. As will be explained in this monograph, this decision was to have a detrimental and catastrophic impact on the initial regulatory and enforcement response to white collar crime during the financial crisis. This was dramatically reversed by President Obama, who signed the Fraud Enforcement Recovery Act 2009, which resulted in a significant increase in funding for the Department of Justice and other related agencies to

---

[253] Podgor, E. 'White-collar-crime and the recession: was the chicken or egg first?' (2010) University of Chicago Legal Forum, 205–222, at 209–210.

[254] For a general critique of the performance of the Securities and Exchange Commission during the Madoff case see Hardouin, P. 'The aftermath of the financial crisis' (2011) Journal of Financial Crime, 18(2), 148–161, at 149.

tackle white collar crime associated with the financial crisis.[255] Additionally, President Obama authorised the creation of the Financial Fraud Enforcement Task Force, which aimed to 'hold accountable those who helped bring about the last financial crisis, and to prevent another crisis from happening'.[256]

The final reason why the US was selected as a case study relates to its response to previous financial crises where white collar crime was a contributory factor. This includes, for example, the robust stance illustrated during the Savings and Loans Crisis and the response to the collapse of Enron and WorldCom. This assists in determining if the policies adopted since the 2007 financial crisis are similar and effective.

1.5 WHY THE UNITED KINGDOM?

As previously outlined in this chapter, the financial crisis has had a dramatic impact on the economic performance of the UK and adversely affected the performance of its banking sector. Evidence suggests that since the start of the financial crisis there has been a steady increase in the amount and instances of white collar crime. For example, the National Fraud Authority estimated that the extent of fraud in the UK increased from £38.4bn in 2011 to £73bn in 2012.[257] Additionally, KPMG reported that the extent of fraud in the UK had increased to a record high in 2011.[258] The UK provides a unique comparator to the US

---

255 For a more detailed discussion of the Fraud Enforcement and Recovery Act 2009 see Titolo, M. 'Retroactivity and the Fraud Enforcement and Recovery Act of 2009' (2011) Indiana Law Journal, Winter, 86, 257–302.

256 Financial Crimes Enforcement Network 'Financial Fraud Enforcement Task Force', n/d, available from http://www.fincen.gov/fraudenftaskforce.html, accessed 18 March 2013. For a more detailed discussion of the Financial Fraud Enforcement Network see Ramirez, M. 'Prioritizing justice: combating corporate crime from task force a top priority' (2010) Marquette Law Review, 93, 971–1019.

257 National Fraud Authority *Annual fraud indicator 2011* (National Fraud Authority: London, 2011) at 3. Interestingly, the figure in 2010 was £30bn. See National Fraud Authority *Annual fraud indicator 2010* (National Fraud Authority: London, 2010) at 3. Also see National Fraud Authority *Annual fraud indicator 2012* (National Fraud Authority: London, 2012) at 3.

258 KPMG is one of the world's leading accountancy firms. KPMG 'Boom time for fraudsters as austerity bites', 30 January 2012, available from http://www.kpmg.com/uk/en/issuesandinsights/articlespublications/newsreleases/pages/fraud-barometer-boom-time-for-fraudsters-as-austerity-bites.aspx, accessed 18 March 2013. Also see Allen, K. 'Recession pushes white-collar crime to new

due to the policy adopted by the Coalition government towards banking regulation and the prevention of white collar crime. The UK's white collar crime strategy has significantly altered since publication of the Coalition Agreement in 2010. Initially, it anticipated amalgamating the SFO, the Office of Fair Trading and the FSA into a single financial crime agency, the ECA. The ECA was to be managed by the Home Office in an attempt to end the fragmented approach towards tackling financial crime.[259] However, the Home Office decided against creating the ECA, and turned its attention to establishing the broader NCA. This reversal by the Home Office presents a new landscape towards the regulation and enforcement of white collar crime in the UK.

Another reason why the UK was chosen as a case study relates to the significant enforcement response to white collar crime associated with the financial crisis by the SFO and FSA. For example, the FSA has imposed a higher number of financial penalties since 2010, which have been largely based on the LIBOR scandal. Similarly, the SFO has also illustrated an increase in the number of prosecutions, especially in relation to mortgage fraud and the manipulation of LIBOR. An important factor that also needs to be taken into consideration is the impact of the Financial Services Act 2012 on banking regulation and white collar crime.[260] In addition to replacing the ineffective FSA the Act also aimed to redress the regulatory and legislative deficiencies regarding certain types of white collar crime. The Financial Services Act 2012 provides that the FCA has a number of operational objectives, including, for example, consumer protection,[261] integrity[262] and competition.[263] One issue that has not been included in the 2012 Act is the FSA's financial crime statutory objective.[264] However, the Financial Services Act does state that the FCA, when discharging its general functions, must have regard to 'the importance of taking action to minimize the extent to which it is possible for a business … to be used for a purpose of being

---

highs', 31 December 2009, available from http://www.guardian.co.uk/business/2009/dec/31/fraud-recession-kpmg-report, accessed 18 March 2013.

259 Home Office, Press Release, 'Home Office to take lead on economic crime', 17 January 2011, available from http://www.homeoffice.gov.uk/media-centre/news/economic-crime, accessed 23 October 2011.

260 For a more detailed discussion of the role of the FCA see Marshall, H., Leonard, C., Bibby, R.P., Paul, R. and Zahabi, E. 'Annual review 2012' (2013) Compliance Officer Bulletin, January, 102, 1–30.

261 Financial Services Act 2012, s.1(C).

262 Financial Services Act 2012, s.1(D).

263 Financial Services Act 2012, s.1(E).

264 Financial Services and Markets Act 2000, s. 6.

connected with financial crime'.[265] Furthermore, financial crime is also an important part of the FCA's integrity objective.[266] What is clear is that the FCA will continue to use the FSA's 'enforcement responsibilities' and 'it is clear that the FCA intends to pursue the policy of credible deterrence as vigorously as the FSA has done'.[267]

One of the most important reasons why the UK was selected as a case study is that the Coalition government has introduced and implemented a series of austerity cuts in the area of white collar crime enforcement, whereas the US government has increased funding. The budget of the SFO has been slashed by the Coalition government since the 2010 general election, which initially was seen to have prevented its investigation into the manipulation of LIBOR.[268] In 2007/2008 its annual budget was £43.3m, in 2008/2009 it was £53.2m, yet the figure has now been reduced to £32.1m in 2013/2014 and £30.8m in 2014/2015.[269] The problems associated with funding cuts were highlighted by Thomas LJ, who stated that more funding would allow the SFO to 'deal with investigations with clarity'.[270]

1.6 CONTENTS OVERVIEW

Chapters 2 and 3 of the monograph seek to add to the existing literature by identifying and commenting on the relationship between white collar crime and the 2007 financial crisis. It is not the intention of these chapters to reengage in a detailed commentary of the contributing variables, such as the subprime mortgage crisis, weak banking regulation, high levels of consumer debt, toxic debts, securitisation, ineffective

---

[265] Financial Services Act 2012, s. 1B(5).

[266] Financial Services Act 2012, s.1(D)(2)(b).

[267] Travers Smith Regulatory Investigations Group above, n 180, at 6.

[268] Brady, B. and Owen, J. 'Budget cuts killed off LIBOR inquiry', 1 July 2012, available from http://www.independent.co.uk/news/uk/politics/budget-cuts-killed-off-libor-inquiry-7901940.html, accessed 18 March 2013. Also see Russell, J. 'SFO given just £2m to enforce Bribery Act', 30 January 2011, available from http://www.telegraph.co.uk/finance/newsbysector/banksandfinance/8290808/SFO-given-just-2m-to-enforce-Bribery-Act.html, accessed 18 March 2013.

[269] Serious Fraud Office above, n 200, at 7.

[270] Rowley, E. 'Serious Fraud Office needs proper funding, warns Tchenguiz judge', 24 May 2012, available from http://www.telegraph.co.uk/finance/financial-crime/9288330/Serious-Fraud-Office-needs-proper-funding-warns-Tchenguiz-judge.htmlm, accessed 18 March 2013.

macroeconomic policies, weak credit regulation, deregulation of consumer credit legislation, self-regulation of CRAs and the culture of banking practices. Therefore, the main area of discussion, debate and analysis is the association between the financial crisis and white collar crime. Chapter 2 identifies several factors that support the contention that this relationship is a significant a factor as those previously documented. These variables include, *inter alia*, subprime mortgages, CRAs, predatory lending, mortgage fraud, Ponzi schemes and the 'Financial War on Terror'. The third chapter provides a detailed commentary on specific examples of white collar crime and how they contributed towards the financial crisis. In particular, the chapter concentrates on mortgage fraud, Ponzi schemes, market manipulation, misleading statements and the manipulation of LIBOR.

Chapters 4 and 5 seek to critically reflect on the responses in the US and UK towards white collar crime associated with the financial crisis. Chapter 4 begins by outlining and identifying the policies adopted in the US towards white collar crime since the start of the financial crisis. The first part of the chapter briefly outlines the initial measures introduced by President George Bush. The next part then offers a detailed analytical review of the legislative measures introduced to counteract the problems associated with the financial crisis. Some of the legislative measures include, for example, the Emergency Economic Stabilization Act 2008, the Housing and Economic Recovery Act 2008, the American Recovery and Reinvestment Act 2009, the Fraud Enforcement and Recovery Act 2009 and the Dodd–Frank Wall Street Reform Act 2012. The chapter then moves on to assess the regulatory response towards white collar crime emanating from the financial crisis. This involves an analysis of the functions of several federal regulatory agencies. The final part of Chapter 4 examines the law enforcement response to white collar crime and the financial crisis. This section is divided into two parts: criminal and civil sanctions. Particular reference is made to the use of deferred prosecution agreements, the increased use of financial sanctions by the SEC and CFTC, the instigation of civil fraud suits against CRAs and the lack of criminal proceedings.

The aim of the Chapter 5 of this monograph is to critically consider the response in the UK towards the relationship between white collar crime and the financial crisis. The chapter begins by seeking to identify the UK's policy towards white collar crime since the start of the financial crisis. This is achieved by undertaking a detailed analytical review of the overabundance of policy review documents that have been commissioned by the former Labour and current Coalition governments. This section of the chapter highlights and critiques the meaningful policy disparities between each of the two governments. This is clearly determined in three instances. The second part of the chapter outlines and critically considers the impact of the legislative responses towards the association between white collar crime and the financial crisis. Reference is made to the relevant statutory provisions of the Financial Services Act 2012, the Courts and Crime Act 2013 and the Financial Services (Banking Reform) Act 2013. The penultimate part of the chapter outlines and judiciously critiques the regulatory response to the association between white collar crime and the financial crisis. Particular attention is given to the role of the FSA, the SFO, the NCA and the FCA. The final part of the chapter critiques the enforcement of white collar crime during the financial crisis, and particular attention is drawn to the use of financial penalties, at the expense of instigating criminal proceedings.

Chapter 6 of the monograph draws together the findings and conclusions of the research and offers a commentary on the response to white collar crime originating from the financial crisis.

2. The financial crisis: An alternative interpretation – Part I

The first decade of the twenty-first century exemplifies the macroeconomic boom–bust–boom cycle. By 2007 and 2008, the economy dropped to historic lows last seen during the Great Depression. In the drama that unfolded as the 'Great Recession,' banks, Wall Street executives, government officials, investors, and home buyers were all eventually cast as both villain and victim. In the ensuing mess of finger-pointing, bailouts, and cries for reform, the arch-villain emerged: Bernie Madoff. He bilked thousands of investors out of billions of dollars. Madoff certainly was not the only Ponzi architect, though he was perhaps the biggest. Since Madoff's scheme collapsed, authorities have uncovered Ponzi schemes of all shapes and sizes. Unfortunately, for those who fell under the Ponzi spell, their ability to seek restitution is both incomplete and inconsistent[1]

2.1 INTRODUCTION

The aim of this chapter is to add to the existing literature by identifying the relationship between white collar crime and the 2007 financial crisis. The main area of discussion, debate and commentary in this chapter is the link between the financial crisis and white collar crime. The chapter identifies several examples that support the contention that this relationship is as significant a variable as any that contributed towards the financial crisis. The examples include, *inter alia*, subprime mortgages and mortgage fraud, CRAs, predatory lending, Ponzi schemes and the 'Financial War on Terror'.

[1] Gabel, J. 'Midnight in the garden of good faith: using clawback actions to harvest the equitable roots of bankrupt Ponzi schemes' (2011) Case Western Reserve Law Review, 62, 19–78, at 21.

2.2 THE FINANCIAL CRISIS AND WHITE COLLAR CRIME

> Every great crisis reveals the excessive speculations of many houses which no one before suspected.[2]

It is the contention of this monograph that white collar crime is one of key variables that contributed towards the 2007 financial crisis. As outlined in the previous chapter, an increasing number of commentators have concluded that white collar crime either triggered the financial crisis[3] or was a significant contributory factor.[4] The association between the financial crisis and white collar crime is illustrated by the significant increase in related enforcement activities in both the United States and United Kingdom.[5] It is also important to note that the relationship or bond between white collar crime and the financial crisis can be demonstrated by undertaking a brief historical review of previous financial crises. For example, it has been argued that white collar crime was a key factor that contributed towards the Wall Street Crash and subsequent Great Depression. For example, Lynn Turner, a former chief accountant for the SEC, noted 'the amount of gimmickry and outright fraud dwarfs any period since the early 1970's, when major accounting scams like Equity Funding surfaced, and the 1920's, when rampant fraud helped cause the crash of 1929'.[6] Kuttner noted that between 1932 and 1934 'the Senate Banking Committee, led by its Chief Counsel Ferdinand Pecora, ferreted out the deeper fraud and corruption that led to the Crash of 1929 and the Great Depression'.[7] This is a view supported by Romano, who

---

[2] Bagehot, W. *Lombard Street – a description of the money market* (John Murray: London, 1922) at 150, as cited in Galbraith, J. *The great crash 1929* (Houghton: Boston, 1988) at 135.

[3] Huisman, W. 'White-collar crime and the economic crisis' (2012/2013) Newsletter of the European Society of Criminology, 11, at 8.

[4] Nationwide White Collar Crime Centre *National public survey on white collar crime* (Nationwide White Collar Crime Centre: Fairmont, 2011) at 20.

[5] For a more detailed discussion of the responses to white collar crime that originated during the financial crisis see Chapters 4 and 5.

[6] Berenson, A. 'Watching the firms that watch the books', 5 December 2001, available from http://www.nytimes.com/2001/12/05/business/05INVE.html?pagewanted=1, accessed 4 June 2013.

[7] Kuttner, R. 'A real Pecora Commission', 31 May 2009, available from http://www.huffingtonpost.com/robert-kuttner/a-real-pecora-commission_b_209572.html, accessed 4 June 2013.

also stated that according to the Pecora Commission the Great Depression was caused by 'market manipulation, fraud, and abuse by financial firms'.[8] The Pecora Commission also 'exposed widespread fraud and other distasteful practices',[9] and unearthed 'widespread fraud and abuse on Wall Street, including self-dealing and market manipulation among investment banks and their securities affiliates'.[10] It is also very interesting to note that one Charles Ponzi introduced his first 'pyramid' fraud scheme in Florida in 1925, just before the onset of the Wall Street Crash.[11] Furthermore, the Congressional Research Service took the view that 'in the Great Depression after 1929, Congress examined the mixing of the "commercial" and "investment" banking industries that occurred in the 1920s. Hearings revealed conflicts of interest and fraud in some banking institutions' securities activities.'[12]

It is also possible to draw parallels between the 2007 financial crisis and the Savings and Loans Crisis in the late 1980s and early 1990s.[13] Harrell took the view that:

> No discussion of the … Great Credit Contraction that has followed would be complete without a discussion of mortgage fraud. Again there is a sense of deja vu in this; those of us who followed this area of law during the previous credit and housing boom and collapse, characterized by the deposit insurance crises of the late 1980s and early 1990s, may recall the public focus throughout that period on fraud and abuse by savings and loans kingpins and other financial insiders.[14]

---

[8] Romano, R. 'The Sarbanes–Oxley Act and the making of quack corporate governance' (2005) Yale Law Journal, May, 114, 1521–1603, at 202.

[9] Ruby, J. 'Sound and fury, confused alarms and oversight: congress, delegation, and effective responses to financial crises' (2010) Harvard Journal on Legislation, 47, 209–252, at 245. See Committee on Banking and Currency *Stock exchange practices* (United States Government: Washington DC, 1934) at 301–318.

[10] Schapiro, M. 'SEC Chair Mary L. Schapiro, testimony concerning the state of the financial crisis before the Financial Crisis Inquiry Commission' 14 January 2013, available from http://www.sec.gov/news/testimony/2010/ts011410mls.htm, accessed 4 June 2013.

[11] Galbraith above, n 2, at 4–5.

[12] Jackson, W. *Glass–Steagall Act: commercial vs. investment banking* (Congressional Research Services: Washington DC, 1987) at 2.

[13] For a more detailed discussion of the factors that contributed towards the 'Savings and Loan Crisis' see Laughlin, R. 'Causes of the Savings and Loan Crisis' (1991) Fordham Law Review, 59, 6(11), 301–322.

[14] Harrell, A. 'The great credit contraction: who, what, when, where and why?' (2010) Georgia State University Law Review, Summer, 26, 1209–1258, at

It is important to note that many institutions, including the US government, initially did not believe that white collar crime played a significant part in the Savings and Loans Crisis.[15] This financial crisis had a disastrous impact on the related providers, and their numbers diminished from 4,500 to 2,400, at a cost to the US taxpayer of $150bn.[16] However, due to a significant increase in the number of bank collapses it soon became apparent that 'corrupt insiders were responsible for bringing down financial institutions'.[17] Evidence that white collar crime was a key factor in the Savings and Loans Crisis was offered by Pontell and Calavita, who stated that 'crime and fraud were central factors in the savings and loan crisis'.[18] Further evidence of the link between the Savings and Loans Crisis and fraud was offered by one commentator who argued that it was caused by 'bribery and outright embezzlement'.[19] This is a view supported by McDonald, who stated that 'fraud and insider abuse caused the savings and loans crisis'.[20] Pizzo *et al* famously stated that the 'Savings and Loans Crisis' was caused by 'a financial mafia of swindlers, mobsters, greedy savings and loans executives, and con men … [and an] orgy of avarice and fraud'.[21] Gray described the Savings and

1231. This is a view supported by Jordan, who stated that fraud 'permeated the entire savings and loan industry and had ramifications beyond the immediate impact on individual institutions insured by the Federal Savings and Loan Insurance Corporation'. See Jordan, S. 'Victimisation on main street: Occupy Wall Street and the mortgage fraud crisis' (2011) Fordham Urban Law Journal, December, 39, 485–510, at 502.

[15] Green, M. 'After the fall: the criminal law enforcement response to the S&L crisis' (1991) Fordham Law Review, May, 59, 155–192, at 163. For an interesting discussion of legislative response towards fraud and the Savings and Loan Crisis see United States General Accounting Office *Savings and loan crisis – federal response to fraud in financial institutions* (United States General Accounting Office: Washington DC, 1990).

[16] Smith, S. 'Reforming the law of adhesion contracts: a judicial response to the subprime mortgage crisis' (2010) Lewis and Clark Law, Fall, 1035–1121, at 1060.

[17] Green above, n 15, at 163.

[18] Pontell, H. and Calavita, K. 'The savings and loans industry' (1993) Crime and Justice, 18, 203–242, at 203.

[19] Felsenfeld, C. 'The savings and loan crisis' (1991) Fordham Law Review, May, 59, 7–56, at 35.

[20] McDonald, J. 'Similarities between the savings & loans crisis and today's current financial crisis: what the past can tell us about the future' (2009) Defence Counsel Journal, October, 76, 470–480, at 473.

[21] Pizzo, S., Fricker, M. and Muolo, P. *Inside job: the looting of America's savings and loans* (McGraw-Hill: New York, 1989) at 298, as cited in Zimring, F.

Loans Crisis as a 'story of unbridled power and influence corrupting the political process, crooked management perpetrating massive fraud and insider abuse'.[22] In its 1989 report, the Senate Committee, citing the Department of Justice, stated that:

> the most prevalent forms of fraud and insider abuse [in the Savings and Loans Crisis] include nominee loans, double pledging of collateral, reciprocal loan arrangements, land flips, embezzlement, and check kiting. In addition, witnesses have told the Committee of extravagant parties, exorbitant spending on frivolous corporate aircraft, lavish office suites, and numerous other squanderings of federally-insured deposit monies.[23]

Other examples of financial scandals that are associated with white collar crime are the Enron and WorldCom collapses. This resulted in the creation of the Corporate Fraud Task Force and the enactment of the Sarbanes–Oxley Act 2002.

2.3 THE FINANCIAL CRISIS, SUBPRIME MORTGAGES AND WHITE COLLAR CRIME

> Last year [2008], the Treasury Department received 62,000 reports of mortgage fraud – more than 5,000 each month. The number of criminal mortgage fraud investigations opened by the FBI has more than doubled over the past three years.[24]

The origins of the financial crisis can be traced to the US subprime mortgage sector.[25] The subprime mortgage sector is supported by lenders

---

and Hawkins, G. 'Crime, justice, and the savings and loans crisis' (1993) Crime and Justice, 18, 247–288, at 264.

[22] Gray, E. 'Warnings ignored: the politics of the crisis' (1990) Stanford Law and Policy Review, Spring, 2, 138–145, at 138.

[23] Bailey, S. 'Chopping at the roots: a proposal to change the focus of criminal laws dealing with savings and loan fraud' (1997) American Journal of Criminal Law, Spring, 24, 401–439, at 411.

[24] The White House 'Remarks by the President at the signing of the Helping Families Save Their Homes Act and the Fraud Enforcement and Recovery Act', 20 May 2009, available from http://www.whitehouse.gov/the_press_office/Remarks-by-the-President-at-Signing-of-the-Helping-Families-Save-Their-Homes-Act-and-the-Fraud-Enforcement-and-Recovery-Act/, accessed 17 June 2013.

[25] For an interesting discussion of the subprime model see Seitz, N., Gilsinan, J., Fisher, J., Harshman, E., Islam, M., Yeager, F. and Millar, J. 'The U.S. subprime mortgage crisis: what have we learned?' (2010) Company Lawyer, 31(11), 355–361. This is a view supported by several commentators including

providing subprime loans which can be defined as 'mortgages that … have a higher risk of default associated with them' and that 'this type of financial transaction is offered to debtors with lower credit scores and higher mortgage-loan-to-value'.[26] Subprime loans have also been referred to as:

> non-traditional, higher risk loans that frequently carry above market interest rates and, in the case of loans secured by real estate, may also contain so-called 'negative amortisation' features. In the mortgage market, these loans were made by US lenders with low 'teaser' rates to borrowers who may not have the financial strength to qualify for traditional mortgages. In some cases, the loans were made with less documentation and credit verification than traditional mortgages.[27]

Therefore, a very simplistic definition of a subprime loan could be loans offered to unsafe and riskier borrowers.[28]

Singh and LaBrosse took the view that the financial crisis was 'caused by the creeping levels of mortgage defaults in the subprime market in the US'.[29] This is a view supported by Seitz *et al*, who noted that the 'crisis was fuelled by subprime lending'.[30] The losses incurred as a result of the

---

McDonald, O. 'The American mortgage market' (2012) Company Lawyer, 33(6), 183–184; Yeoh, P. 'Hedge funds: from privileged child to locust and now bogeyman?' (2012) Company Lawyer, 33(2), 42–49, at 42.

[26] Fox, M. and David, H. 'Lessons from the US subprime mortgage crisis' (2008) Journal of International Banking Law and Regulation, 23(9), 449–457, at 449. Subprime mortgages have also been referred to as 'underlying risky assets' by Morgan, G. 'Reforming OTC markets: the politics and economics of technical fixes' (2012) European Business Organization Law Review, 13(3), 391–412, at 404.

[27] Slevin, P. 'Bad vibrations: subprime-sparked legal action' (2007) European Lawyer, 72, 18–19, at 18.

[28] Bar-Gill, O. 'Seduction by plastic' (2004) Northwestern University Law Review, 98, 1373–1434, at 1382.

[29] Singh, D. and LaBrosse, J. 'Northern Rock, depositors and deposit insurance coverage: some critical reflections' (2010) Journal of Business Law, 2, 55–84, at 56. Also see Anderson, T., David, L. and Fox, M. 'The US financial sector status update: road to recovery or highway to hell?' (2009) Journal of International Banking Law and Regulation, 24(10), 491–500, at 492.

[30] Seitz, N., Gilsinan, J., Fisher, J., Harshman, E., Islam, M., Yeager, F. and Millar, J. 'Bank integrity: the case of subprime lending' (2009) Company Lawyer, 30(9), 271–276, at 271. For a similar view see Succurro, M. 'Bankruptcy systems and economic performance across countries: some empirical evidence' (2012) European Journal of Law and Economics, 33(1), 101–126, at 102. The global impact of the problems caused by subprime mortgages was also

collapse of the subprime mortgage sector were staggering. For example, according to the IMF the total losses associated with subprime lending in 2008 initially totalled $945m.[31] The Wall Street Journal reported that the total losses from the financial crisis were $15tn.[32] The bursting of the subprime mortgage sector resulted in numerous corporate insolvencies and significant losses for both investors and banks.[33] In 2010, it was estimated that losses attributed to banks from the financial crisis amounted to $2.28bn.[34]

It has been suggested that the blame for the subprime crisis is associated with the actions of the Federal Reserve. For example, Doise noted that 'it [the Federal Reserve] indeed allowed an excessive growth of monetary liquidity which generated low interest rates, thereby giving an incentive not only to resort to an *aggressive* [author's emphasis] sale

---

noted by Arora, who stated that 'the effect of a banking crisis does not contain itself within national boundaries and, as we have seen recently, a subprime mortgage that started in the United States rapidly developed into a destructive force that shook the global banking sector and economies to the core'. See Arora, A. 'The corporate governance failings in financial institutions and directors' legal liability' (2011) Company Lawyer, 32(1), 3–18, at 7.

[31] International Monetary Fund *Global financial stability report: containing systemic risks and restoring financial soundness* (International Monetary Fund: Washington DC, 2008) at 10, as cited in Morgan, H. 'Credit rating agencies and regulatory reform: the case of Moody's Investors Services' (2012) Journal of International Banking Law and Regulation, 26(8), 389–397, at 389.

[32] Yoon, A. 'Total global losses from financial crisis: $15 trillion', 1 October 2012, available from http://blogs.wsj.com/economics/2012/10/01/total-global-losses-from-financial-crisis-15-trillion/, accessed 21 October 2013. For an excellent discussion of the financial impact of the financial crisis see Atkinson, T., Luttrell, D. and Rosenblum, H. 'How bad was it? The costs and consequences of the 2007–09 financial crisis' (2013) Dallas Fed, Staff Papers, 1–22.

[33] Wen, S. 'The magnitude of shareholder value as the overriding objective in the UK: the post-crisis perspective' (2011) Journal of International Banking Law and Regulation, 26(7), 325–337, at 331. Kenagy *et al* took the view that 'banks were increasingly enamoured with highly leveraged, complex investments based on the rising housing market and the proliferating securitisation of loans made in the prime and subprime mortgage market'. See Kenagy, R., Anderson, T. and Fox, M. 'Regulation and the impact of political lobbying on the investment banking industry' (2013) Journal of International Banking Law and Regulation, 28(5), 171–180, at 175. This is a view supported by Yeoh, P. 'Self-regulation, regulation, co-regulation: the credit rating industry case' (2013) Journal of Business Law, 2, 186–211, at 198.

[34] Crutsinger, M. 'IMF trims loss estimate from financial crisis', 20 April 2010, available from http://www.nbcnews.com/id/36662585/, accessed 21 October 2013.

of loans, but also, for investors and financial institutions, an accurate search for high yields'.[35] Therefore, it is possible to argue that the Federal Reserve, by reducing interest rates to encourage consumer borrowing and expenditure, indirectly promoted predatory lending. This will be further explored towards the end of this chapter.

Conversely, Fox and David argued that some of the blame for subprime lending is associated with the activities of borrowers.[36] Akseli linked the roots of the subprime crisis with 'a number of interrelated financial, sociological and legal trends'. This included, for example, 'the growth of wealth and its utilisation in investments, whether or not in an effective way; the financial sector and individuals' ability to take risk; and deficiencies in corporate governance and financial supervision'.[37]

The subprime mortgage sector burst when property prices began to decrease and the number of foreclosures began to increase.[38] Singh and LaBrosse noted that 'the credit crunch caused creeping levels of mortgage defaults in the subprime market in the United States'.[39] Nesvetailova stated that the 'problems of the US subprime industry became apparent … in 2006, when the first wave of mortgage defaults hit lending institutions'.[40] This was preceded by a period of economic growth when the average property price doubled, at a rate higher than the wages of many householders.[41] This housing bubble was expedited by the Federal Reserve, which decided to maintain low interest rates between 1999 and 2004, making it much easier for people to gain access to subprime

---

[35] Doise, D. 'Subprime: price of infringements' (2008) International Business Law Journal, 4, 558–568, at 558.

[36] Fox and David above, n 26 at 449.

[37] Akseli, O. 'Securitisation, the financial crisis and the need for effective risk retention' (2013) European Business Organization Law Review, 14(1), 1–27, at 5.

[38] Marshall, J. *US Congressional debates on the financial crisis: key players, policy and future regulation – House of Commons Research Paper 09/58* (House of Commons Library: London, 2009) at 2. According to statistical data from Reuters, the number of delinquencies increased and several subprime lenders became insolvent. See Reuters 'Timeline: the credit crunch of 2007/2008', 5 August 2008, available from http://www.reuters.com/article/gc06/idUSL155564520080805, accessed 10 August 2012.

[39] Singh and LaBrosse above, n 29, at 55.

[40] Nesvetailova, A. 'The crisis of invented money: liquidity illusion and the global credit meltdown' (2010) Theoretical Inquiries in Law, January, 11, 125–147, at 128.

[41] Marshall, J. *The financial crisis in the US: key events, causes and responses – House of Commons Research Paper 09/034* (House of Commons Library: London, 2009) at 10.

mortgages. As outlined above, a subprime mortgage or loan is unlike a prime loan because of the risks attached.[42] These types of mortgages, due to their very nature, place the debtor under severe pressure to repay the loan, due to irresponsible lending or even predatory lending practices.[43] These lending practices contributed to record levels of defaults, repossessions and an increase in consumer debt. Dickerson stated that 'too many people in the United States are overwhelmed by debt. While we were once a country of thrift, consumer indebtedness has become an ubiquitous phenomenon that affects people in both urban and rural areas and from all socio-economic groups.'[44] The total amount of US household debt in 1977 was $946.7bn; this had increased to $13.825tn by 2006.[45] Research suggests that the levels of household debt from mortgages in the US increased every year from 1982 to 2007.[46] However, the level of debt increased at an increasingly fast rate between 2000 and 2007, resulting in personal debt levels in excess of $13.9tn in 2008.[47] Therefore, as a direct result of providing subprime mortgages, there was a significant increase in the number of mortgage defaults, housing repossessions and reduction in house prices.[48] Nguyen and Pontell stated that 'as the crisis unfolds, a significant number of families have lost their homes or are financially trapped in their current mortgages and simply waiting for their homes to be taken from them'.[49] The increase in the number of repossessions and mortgage defaults has resulted in an increase in mortgage fraud.

---

[42] Westercamp, K. 'A crack in the façade and the whole building came tumbling down: a critical examination of the central banks' response to the sub-prime mortgage loan crisis and global financial economic turmoil' (2009) Transnational Law and Contemporary Problems, Winter, 11, 197–244, at 213.

[43] *Ibid.*

[44] Dickerson, M. 'Over-indebtedness, the subprime mortgage crisis, and the effect on US cities' (2009) Fordham Urban Law Journal, 36, 395–425, at 396.

[45] *Ibid.*, at 410.

[46] Ruben, M. 'Forgive us our trespasses? The rise of consumer debt in modern America', February 2009, available from http://www.csa.com/discoveryguides/debt/review.pdf, accessed 14 August 2012, at 1.

[47] Federal Reserve Board *Flow of funds accounts of the United States: flows and outstandings third quarter 2008* (Board of Governors of the Federal Reserve System: Washington DC, 2008).

[48] Dickerson above, n 44, at 396.

[49] Nguyen, T. and Pontell, N. 'Fraud and inequality in the subprime mortgage crisis' in Deflem, M. (ed.) *Economic crisis and crime* (Emerald: Bingley, 2011) at 5.

Mortgage fraud is the most prominent white collar crime associated with subprime lending and the financial crisis.[50] It has been described as 'one of the fastest growing white collar crimes in the US'[51] and 'one of the most pervasive problems in lending today'.[52] Koller took the view that:

> the subprime mortgage products and processes that were made available in the 1990s ... increased the population of potential [white collar] offenders, increased temptation and suitable targets, and increased ease at which motivated individuals could take advantage of the opportunities to commit crime. As such, it was not necessarily the routines of the housing/mortgage industry that were problematic, it was the actual category of subprime 'products' that created an environment rich with white collar crime motivation and opportunity.[53]

This is a view supported by Nguyen and Pontell, who confirmed the link between white collar crime and subprime loans by stating that 'investigations have found that the growth of nonprime lending attracted a great deal of fraud'.[54] Furthermore, Harrell took the view that 'no discussion of the housing boom of 1993–2006 and the great credit contraction that has followed would be complete without a discussion of mortgage fraud'.[55] Dilley and Weller noted that 'the origins of the credit crunch lie with the sub-prime lending and the ensuing house price bubble in the US. Mortgage fraud – by borrowers, brokers and appraisers – was a key contributor.'[56] Similarly, the FBI stated that during the subprime mortgage crisis 'mortgage fraud perpetrators ... [took] advantage of industry

---

50 The mortgage sector in the USA constitutes approximately 20 per cent of the country's gross domestic product. See Heroy, J. 'Other people's money: how a time-gap in credit reporting may lead to fraud' (2008) North Carolina Banking Institute, 12, 321–351, at 322.

51 Federal Bureau of Investigation 'Looking ahead resolve not to be scammed', 29 December 2006, available from http://www.fbi.gov/news/stories/2006/december/scams_122906, accessed 23 May 2013.

52 Jacobus, C. 'Mortgage fraud: recognition and prevention' (2008) Texas Bar Journal, March, 71, 188–192, at 188.

53 Koller, C. *Diffusion of innovation and fraud in the subprime mortgage market.* OhioLink ETD, 2010, available from http://etd.ohiolink.edu/send-pdf.cgi/Koller%20Cynthia.pdf?ucin1282050951, accessed 23 May 2013, as cited in Nguyen and Pontell above, n 49, at 33.

54 *Ibid.*

55 Harrell above, n 14, at 1231.

56 Dilley, B. and Weller, F. 'Mortgage fraud and the credit crunch' (2008) Fighting Fraud, Summer, 35, 1–31, at 11.

personnel attempting to generate loans to maintain current standards of living'.[57] Therefore, the FBI concluded that 'subprime mortgage issues remain a key factor in influencing mortgage fraud directly and indirectly'.[58] This is a view supported by McCann, who noted that 'mortgage fraud perpetrated by these unregulated private mortgage brokers may have contributed to the instability and loss in the residential lending market that contributed to the mortgage crisis'.[59] It is very interesting to note that the threat posed by mortgage fraud *was* recognised by the FBI in 2004, when it stated 'if fraudulent practices become systemic within the mortgage industry and mortgage fraud is allowed to become unrestrained, it will ultimately place financial institutions at risk and have adverse effects on the stock market'.[60] Furthermore, the FBI warned that 'it [mortgage fraud] has the potential to be an epidemic'.[61] Black stated that despite this blunt warning from the FBI, 'no one in the industry, including regulators, ranks of investors or creditors, or law enforcement personnel took effective action against the epidemic'.[62]

Mortgage fraud has been defined by the FBI as 'the intentional misstatement, misrepresentation, or omission by an applicant or other interested parties, relied on by a lender or underwriter to provide funding

---

[57] Federal Bureau of Investigation 'Swecker, C. former FBI Assistant Director, Criminal Investigative Division, introductory statement: House Financial Services Subcommittee on Housing and Community Opportunity' 7 October 2004, available from http://www.fbi.gov/news/testimony/fbis-efforts-in-combating-mortgage-fraud, accessed 22 October 2013.

[58] *Ibid.*

[59] McCann, N. 'Federal law enforcement in the home mortgage lending market enhanced by the Fraud Enforcement Act and Recovery Act of 2009' (2010) Loyola Consumer Law Review, 22, 352–390, at 354. Also see Schuck, C. 'A new use of the responsible corporate officer doctrine: prosecuting industry insiders for mortgage fraud' (2010) Lewis and Clark Law Review, 14, 371–395, at 371.

[60] Federal Bureau of Investigation 'John S. Pistole, Deputy Director Federal Bureau of Investigation, statement before the House Committee on the Judiciary', 1 April 2009, available from http://www.fbi.gov/news/testimony/fbi-efforts-to-combat-mortgage-fraud-and-other-financial-frauds, accessed 17 June 2013.

[61] Frieden, T. 'FBI warns of mortgage fraud "epidemic"', 17 September 2004, available from http://www.cnn.com/2004/LAW/09/17/mortgage.fraud/, accessed 23 May 2013.

[62] Black, K. 'Neo-classical economic theories, methodology, and praxis optimize criminogenic environments and produce recurrent intensifying crisis' (2011) Creighton Law Review, 44, 597–644, at 622.

for, to purchase, or to insure a mortgage loan'.[63] It also includes providing misleading information when making a mortgage application.[64] There are traditionally two types of mortgage fraud – fraud for property and fraud for profit,[65] which can be divided into different subcategories.[66] For example, this includes misrepresentation, occupancy fraud, appraisal fraud, identity theft, straw purchasing and flipping.[67] Common mortgage fraud schemes include property flipping, straw buyers and equity skimming.[68] Other mortgage fraud systems include builder bailout, buy and bail, chunking, double selling, fictitious loan, phantom sale, reverse mortgage fraud and short sale fraud.[69] The FBI noted that other types of mortgage fraud scams 'involve material misstatement, misrepresentation, or omission relating to a real estate transaction which is relied on by one or more parties to the transaction'.[70] They added that these schemes include 'foreclosure rescue schemes, loan modification schemes, illegal property flipping, builder bailout/condo conversions, equity skimming, silent second, home equity conversion mortgage, commercial real estate loans and air loans'.[71]

The extent of mortgage fraud is difficult, if not impossible, to determine. For example, the FBI estimated that the extent of mortgage fraud in 2006 was $4.2bn.[72] In 2007 it described mortgage fraud as 'an

---

63 Federal Bureau Investigation, above n 57.

64 Vacco, P. 'RESPA and avoiding mortgage fraud: what goes on the HUD settlement statement?' (2008) Illinois Bar Journal, May, 96, 248–249, at 249.

65 O'Donnell, M. and Planer, K. 'If it sounds too good to be true: identifying and avoiding common mortgage fraud scams' (2008) New Jersey Lawyer, October, 254, 54–57, at 54.

66 Gans, K. 'Anatomy of a mortgage meltdown: the story of the subprime crisis, the role of fraud, and the efficacy of the Idaho Safe Act' (2011) Idaho Law Review, 48, 123–174, at 146.

67 *Ibid.*

68 Jacobsen, B. and Barnhill, M. 'Drawing the short straw – mortgage fraud and straw buyers' (2008) Utah Bar Journal, July/August, 21, 9–13, at 11–12.

69 Anon. 'Banking and financial services policy report' (2010) The Monitor, 29(4), 19–23, at 21.

70 Federal Bureau of Investigation 'Financial crimes report to the public – fiscal years 2010–2011', n/d, available from http://www.fbi.gov/stats-services/publications/financial-crimes-report-2010-2011/financial-crimes-report-2010-2011#Mortgage, accessed 19 June 2013.

71 *Ibid.*

72 Federal Bureau of Investigation 'Mortgage fraud report 2006', May 2007, available from http://www.fbi.gov/stats-services/publications/mortgage-fraud-2006/2006-mortgage-fraud-report, accessed 23 May 2013.

escalating problem',[73] yet the total amount of mortgage fraud related losses dropped to $813m.[74] Nonetheless, in 2008 the reported losses from mortgage fraud increased by 83.4 per cent to $1.4bn.[75] In its 2009 Mortgage Fraud Report, the FBI cited figures from CoreLogic, which estimated that the total amount of losses related to mortgage fraud had increased to $14bn.[76] CoreLogic estimated that the extent of mortgage fraud in 2011 was $12bn.[77] In its 2012 mortgage fraud report CoreLogic projected that the level of mortgage fraud had increased to $13bn.[78] These statistical data are supported by research conducted by the Mortgage Asset Research Institute, which advised that 'mortgage fraud is more prevalent now than in the heyday of the origination boom and … it will continue to rise'.[79]

The link between mortgage fraud and the financial crisis is clearly illustrated by the significant increase in the number of related SARs submitted to FinCEN. For example, between 1996 and 2006 FinCEN received 82,851 mortgage fraud related SARs.[80] During this period the number of suspected instances of mortgage fraud reported to FinCEN increased by approximately 1,400 per cent.[81] Furthermore, in 2008 FinCEN stated that between 2006 and 2007 it received 37,313 mortgage

---

[73] Federal Bureau of Investigation 'Mortgage fraud report 2007', April 2008, available from http://www.fbi.gov/stats-services/publications/mortgage-fraud-2007, accessed 18 October 2013.

[74] *Ibid.*

[75] Federal Bureau of Investigation 'Mortgage fraud report 2008', 2009, available from http://www.fbi.gov/stats-services/publications/mortgage-fraud-2008/2008-mortgage-fraud-report, accessed 17 June 2013.

[76] Federal Bureau of Investigation '2009 mortgage fraud report year in review', n/d, available from http://www.fbi.gov/stats-services/publications/mortgage-fraud-2009, accessed 17 June 2013.

[77] CoreLogic *2011 Mortgage fraud trends report* (CoreLogic: Irvine, 2011) at 1.

[78] *Ibid.*

[79] Creseney, A., Eng, G.E. and Nuttal, S. 'Regulatory investigations and the credit crisis: the search for villains' (2009) American Criminal Law Review, Spring, 46, 225–273, at 226. Hereafter Creseney *et al.*

[80] Financial Crimes Enforcement Network *Mortgage loan fraud: an industry assessment based upon suspicious activity report analysis* (Financial Crimes Enforcement Network: Washington DC, 2006) at 4.

[81] Mahallati, N. 'Chapter 174: California's dedicated mortgage fraud statute' (2010) McGeorge Law Review, 41, 712–724, at 717. Also see Simpson, S. 'Making sense of white-collar crime: theory and research' (2011) Ohio State Journal of Criminal Law, Spring, 8, 481–502, at 495.

fraud SARs.[82] This figure represented 45 per cent of the total mortgage fraud related reports it received between 1996 and 2006. In 2010 the number of mortgage fraud related SARs received by FinCEN numbered 70,472.[83] The number of SARs increased significantly to 92,028 in 2011.[84] Lexis Nexis reported that in 2011 FinCEN received 93,508 mortgage fraud related SARs from 2010, an increase of approximately 33 per cent.[85] This position was succinctly summarised by Smith, who concluded: 'the past decade has witnessed an explosion of mortgage fraud, with reports to the federal government of suspected criminal behaviour rising by a magnitude of over eighteen times from 2000 to 2008'.[86] However, it has been argued that the figures from FinCEN represent only a small percentage of the true extent of mortgage fraud. For example, Black took the view that 'the total SARs figure is only a faint indication of the true incidence of mortgage fraud'.[87] It is also interesting to note that 'mortgage fraud, far from abating, has only expanded since the foreclosure crisis began'.[88] Schuck took the view that:

> Many believe that mortgage fraud played a starring role in the dramatic rise and fall of the housing market. In the time period leading up to the mortgage meltdown, lending institutions relaxed standards and rewarded mortgage professionals with commissions based upon the quantity not quality of loans closed. The combination of the lowered lending standards, skyrocketing home prices, and the securitization of loans masked the exponential rise in mortgage fraud.[89]

---

[82] Financial Crimes Enforcement Network *Mortgage loan fraud: an update on trends based on analysis of suspicious activity reports April 2008* (Financial Crimes Enforcement Network: Washington DC, 2008) at 4.

[83] Financial Crimes Enforcement Network *Mortgage loan fraud update – suspicious activity report filings from January–December 31 2010* (Financial Crime Enforcement Network: Washington DC, 2011) at 2.

[84] Financial Crimes Enforcement Network *Mortgage loan fraud* (Financial Crime Enforcement Network: Washington DC, 2012) at 2.

[85] Lexis Nexis *The Lexis Nexis 14th annual mortgage fraud report* (Lexis Nexis: London, 2012) at 3.

[86] Smith, J. 'The structural causes of mortgage fraud' (2010) Syracuse Law Review, 60, 473–500, at 473.

[87] Black above, n 62, at 623.

[88] Fisher, L. 'Target marketing of subprime loans: racialised consumer fraud and reverse redlining' (2009) Journal of Law and Policy, 18, 121–155, at 144.

[89] Schuck above, n 59, at 372.

Further evidence of the link between mortgage fraud and the financial crisis is also illustrated by an increase in the investigative and enforcement activities of the FBI. For example, since the start of the financial crisis we have witnessed a 400 per cent increase in the number of mortgage fraud investigations undertaken by the FBI.[90] Furthermore, in response to the increase in mortgage fraud the FBI has established 84 mortgage fraud task forces; there have been approximately 2,000 investigations, over 1,000 indictments and over 1,100 convictions.[91] Moye summarised the overall impact of mortgage fraud from a law enforcement perspective:

> From 2007 through 2010, the number of federal mortgage fraud cases increased from 1,200 to over 3,000. Almost 70 per cent of those fraud cases involved losses exceeding $1m. In June 2010, the Department of Justice announced the results of Operation Stolen Dreams, the largest mortgage fraud sweep in history. The sweep lasted three and a half months, involved 1,517 defendants, 863 indictments, 525 arrests, and involved over $3.05bn in losses. Finally, the sweep resulted in over 191 civil enforcement actions and $196m in recoveries.[92]

Mortgage fraud poses a significant threat in the UK. According to the Association of Chief Police Officers (ACPO), the annual level of mortgage fraud in the UK is approximately £700m.[93] However, it must be noted that the Council of Mortgage Lenders took the view that 'we do not believe that the report [by ACPO] presented evidence of "confirmed mortgage fraud" of around £700m'.[94] Sandra Quinn, the Programme Director of the NFA stated that 'mortgage fraud is only a small fraction

---

90 Heroy, above n 2, at 323.

91 Federal Bureau of Investigation 'Mortgage fraud', n/d, available from http://www.fbi.gov/about-us/investigate/white_collar/mortgage-fraud/mortgage_fraud, accessed 23 May 2013. Also see Dooley, D. and Radke, M. 'Does severe punishment deter financial crimes?' (2010) Charleston Law Review, 4, 619–659, at 624–626.

92 Moye, J. 'Let's put the fear in the FERA! Suggestions to make the Fraud Enforcement and Recovery Act of 2009 a strong fraud deterrent' (2011) Southern Illinois University Law Journal, Spring, 35, 421–432, at 421–422.

93 Association of Chief Police Officers 'Police committed to tackling mortgage fraud', Press Release, 5 March 2008, available from www.acpo.police.uk, accessed 15 May 2013.

94 Council of Mortgage Lenders '£700 million fraud claim not substantiated' (2008) Council of Mortgage Lenders News and Views, 5(18), 5.

of the UK's mortgage market. But it is a serious criminal threat.'[95] Conversely, it has been argued that the figure of £700m is cautious and that the amount could be as high as £7bn.[96] More recently, the NFA estimated that the extent of mortgage fraud was £1bn.[97] The NFA took the view that mortgage fraud can also lead to the collapse of companies and subsidise other illegal activities.[98] It added that in the UK 'falling house prices and tightening credit conditions have shed significant new light on the extent to which criminals have exploited the mortgage process to defraud lenders'.[99]

2.4 CREDIT RATING AGENCIES AND WHITE COLLAR CRIME

> The story of the credit rating agencies is a story of a colossal failure ... the result is that our entire financial system is now at risk.[100]

One of the most important factors that contributed towards the financial crisis is the role of CRAs.[101] A CRA can be defined as 'a company that assigns credit ratings to companies issuing a variety of debt obligations, and also to the specific debt instruments themselves, including preferred

---

95 Attorney General's Office and Sandra Quinn 'The national fraud strategy', speech to Council of Mortgage Lenders, 13 February 2008, available from www.attorneygeneral.gov.uk, accessed 15 May 2013.

96 Costello, M. and Spence, A. 'Lenders face huge hit on mortgages fraudulently obtained by crime gangs', 30 August 2008, available from http://www.thetimes.co.uk/tto/business/industries/banking/article2158313.ece, accessed 23 May 2013.

97 National Fraud Authority *Annual fraud indicator 2013* (National Fraud Authority: London, 2013) at 42. Also see National Fraud Authority *Working together to stop mortgage fraud: progress report* (National Fraud Authority: London, 2011) at 4; Financial Services Authority *Mortgage fraud against lenders – a thematic review of lenders' systems and controls to detect and prevent mortgage fraud* (Financial Services Authority: London, 2011) at 3; and National Fraud Authority *Annual fraud indicator 2012* (National Fraud Authority: London, 2012) at 17.

98 *Ibid.*

99 National Fraud Authority, *Annual fraud indicator*, above n 97, at 8.

100 Evans, C. 'What makes you so special? Ending the credit rating agencies' special status and access to confidential information' (2012) Valparaiso University Law Review, Summer, 46, 1091–1137, at 1091.

101 Coors, C. 'Credit rating agencies – too big to fail?' (2012) Journal of International Banking Law and Regulation, 27(1), 27–32, at 27.

stock'.[102] A Wall Street securities analyst, John Moody, is perceived by many commentators as the instigator of the credit rating system. Evans noted that in 1909 Moody 'synthesised all available information about an issuer and its securities into a single letter rating for the security'.[103] CRAs play an important role in the global economy[104] and they seek to 'provide investors with an indication of the likelihood that a given debt obligation will be repaid as well as the expected loss in the event of a default'.[105] Therefore, according to McVea, CRAs 'provide standardized assessments of the future probability that a debtor will default on the liabilities owed to creditors … [they] assess the credit risk associated with holding specific debt or debt-like securities'.[106] Thus it can be argued that CRAs have three distinctive functions. First, they provide information to the investor and issuer. Secondly, they act as a certification body. Thirdly, they seek to provide ratings for standardisation.[107] The most prominent CRAs – Standard and Poor's, Moody's, and Fitch – issue similar but not duplicate ratings systems.[108] There are over 150 CRAs, which will analyse and scrutinise approximately 750,000 securities valued at approximately $30tn every year.[109]

---

[102] Hurst, T. 'The role of credit rating agencies in the current worldwide financial crisis' (2009) Company Lawyer, 30(2), 61–64, at 61.

[103] Evans above, n 100, at 1099.

[104] Ellis, N., Fairchild, L. and D'Souza, F. 'Is imposing liability of credit rating agencies a good idea? Credit rating agency reform in the aftermath of the global financial crisis' (2012) Stanford Journal of Law, Business and Finance, Spring, 17, 175–222, at 176. Hereinafter Ellis *et al.*

[105] Brownlow, B. 'Rating agency reform: preserving the registered market for asset backed securities' (2011) North Carolina Banking Institute, March, 15, 111–138, at 114.

[106] McVea, H. 'Credit rating agencies, the subprime mortgage debacle and global governance: the EU strikes back' (2010) International and Comparative Law Quarterly, 59(3), 701–730, at 704.

[107] Johannson, T. 'Regulating credit rating agencies: the issue of conflicts of interest in the rating of structured finance products' (2010) Journal of Banking Regulation 12, 1–23, at 3.

[108] McVea stated that 'a designation of AAA represents the highest rating, followed by AA, then A, then BBB and so on. Sometimes ratings are accompanied by a + or an x or some other modifying designation. Ratings ranging from AAA to BBB – represent "investment grade", a designation which has significant consequences for a security's marketability, particularly with regard to institutional investors'. See McVea above n 106, at 704.

[109] Harper, S. 'Credit rating agencies deserve credit for the 2007–2008 financial crisis: an analysis of CRA liability following the enactment of the Dodd–Frank Act' (2011) Washington and Lee Law Review, 68, 1925–1972, at 1940.

The conduct and operation of CRAs during the financial crisis have been questioned and criticised.[110] Indeed, several commentators have argued that the conduct of CRAs contributed towards the financial crisis. For example, Hurst argued that 'there is widespread agreement that credit rating agencies deserve a significant portion of the blame [for the financial crisis]'.[111] Similarly, White suggested that 'when the histories are written of the US subprime residential mortgage debacle … the world financial crisis that followed, the three large US-based credit-rating agencies – Moody's, Standard & Poor's and Fitch – will surely be seen as central parties to the debacle; and rightly so'.[112] This is a view supported by Coors, who stated that 'credit rating agencies are widely perceived as being complicit in the global financial crisis … especially the big three US rating agencies, – Moody's, Standard & Poor's and Fitch have lost credibility in the eyes of many nations and investors'.[113] Therefore, two important questions must be answered. First, why have CRAs attracted such a high level of criticism? Secondly, what is the link with white collar crime?

The first question has been answered by many commentators who have convincingly argued that the 'flawed ratings of mortgage-backed securities and collateralised debt obligations by the top three US based credit rating agencies – Moody's, Standard & Poor's, and Fitch – are among the main causes of the debacle'.[114] One of the main criticisms of CRAs is also that they inexplicably allocated advantages ratings to mortgage backed securities (MBSs) and collateralised debt obligations (CDOs), which resulted in these multifaceted and complicated securities that attracted numerous investors, but which also contributed towards the flawed demand for domestic US properties.[115] This is a view supported by Harper, who noted that 'CRAs played an important role in the financial crisis … CRAs have been criticised for misconstruing the risks

---

[110] Johannson above, n 107, at 1. Also see Partnoy, F. 'Rethinking regulation of credit-rating agencies: an institutional investor perspective' (2010) Journal of International Banking Law and Regulation, 25(4), 188–199, at 188.

[111] Hurst above, n 102, at 61. This is a view supported by Abdurakhmanova, S. 'Using unsolicited credit ratings to regulate the credit rating agencies' (2013) Fordham Journal of Corporate and Financial Law, 18, 451–488, at 452.

[112] White, L. 'Credit-rating agencies and the financial crisis: less regulation of CRAs is a better response' (2010) Journal of International Banking Law and Regulation, 25(4), 170–179, at 171.

[113] Coors above, n 101, at 27.

[114] Morgan above, 31, at 389.

[115] *Ibid.*

associated with complex financial instruments that fuelled the United States' housing bubble, such as MBSs and CDOs'.[116]

It can be argued that CRAs contributed towards the financial crisis in two ways.[117] First, the CRAs unsuccessfully calculated the credit risks of CDOs. Secondly, they failed to supervise and prevent the conflicts of interest between themselves and issuers.[118] The miscalculation could be explained by an overly optimistic attitude towards their ratings.[119] The buoyant outlook adopted by CRAs towards mortgage backed securities 'fuelled the residential real estate bubble in the United States'.[120] As a result, it has been argued, CRAs 'underestimated the probability of default in the underlying CDOs and … they failed to review their ratings promptly'.[121] Therefore, one of the major criticisms of CRAs can be directed at their regulation, or lack of regulation, which is predominantly based only on their reputation.[122]

CRAs are loosely regulated by the International Organization of Securities Commissions (IOSCO), which 'develops, implements, and promotes adherence to internationally recognized standards for securities regulation'.[123] IOSCO issued its first 'Code' for CRAs in 2003,[124] a

---

116 Harper above, n 109, at 1926.

117 Grinshteyn, A. 'Horseshoes and hand grenades: the Dodd–Frank Act's (almost) attack on credit rating agencies' (2011) Hofstra Law Review, Summer, 937–978, at 925.

118 *Ibid.*

119 Piekarski, M. 'Ratings agency accountability' (2008) Review of Banking and Financial Law, Spring, 27, 272–284, at 273.

120 Ellis *et al* above, n 104.

121 Johannson above, n 107, at 6.

122 *Ibid.*, at 7. For a useful discussion of the self-regulation system for CRAs in the United States see Lupica, L. 'Credit rating agencies, structured securities, and the way out of the abyss' (2009) Review of Banking and Financial Law, Spring, 28, 639–673, at 663–667 and Bai, L. 'The performance disclosures of credit rating agencies: are they effective reputational sanctions?' (2010) NYU Journal of Law and Business, 7, 47–104, at 54–59.

123 The International Organization of Securities Commission 'General information', n/d, available from http://www.iosco.org/about/, accessed 24 April 2013. For a more detailed commentary on IOSCO see McVea, H. 'Hedge fund asset valuations and the work of the International Organization of Securities Commissions (IOSCO)' (2008) International and Comparative Law Quarterly, 57(1), 1–24.

124 The International Organization of Securities Commission *Report on the activities of credit rating agencies* (International Organization of Securities Commission: Madrid, 2003).

revised version in 2004[125] and an updated version in 2008.[126] It is important to stress that the 'Code' is *not* legally binding and can therefore be described as *guidance* or a *best practice* for regulation.[127] Therefore, the effectiveness of the 'Code' must be questioned given its voluntary nature, a point graphically illustrated by the fact that approximately two thirds of CRAs have not implemented its provisions.[128] Another criticism that can be made is that IOSCO has no powers to enforce the 'Code'.[129] It is interesting to note that prior to the financial crisis, there was no legislative regulation of CRAs from the EU.[130] However, since the start of the financial crisis they have 'been among the institutions most targeted for heightened regulatory oversight'.[131] The EU responded to the criticism and published a number of Regulations and Directives aimed at regulating CRAs.[132] The proposals sought to introduce 'rigorous rules' to ensure that CRAs do not have any conflict of interests, that they act in a

---

[125] The International Organization of Securities Commission *Report on the activities of credit rating agencies* (International Organization of Securities Commission: Madrid, 2008).

[126] *Ibid.*

[127] For an interesting discussion on the levels of compliance with the 'Code' see Committee of European Securities Regulators *CESR's report to the European Commission on the compliance of credit rating agencies with the IOSCO Code* (Committee of European Securities Regulators: Paris, 2006).

[128] International Organization of Securities Commission 'IOSCO update on credit rating agencies oversight' 3 March 2009, available from http://www.iosco.org/news/pdf/IOSCONEWS138.pdf, accessed 24 April 2013, as cited in Coors above, n 101, at 29. For an interesting discussion of the effectiveness of such measures see Ferran, E. and Alexander, K. 'Can soft law bodies be effective? The special case of the European Systemic Risk Board' (2010) European Law Review, 35(6), 751–776.

[129] Charles, K. 'Regulatory imperialism: the worldwide export of European regulatory principles on credit rating agencies' (2010) Minnesota Journal of International Law, Summer, 19, 399–451, at 409.

[130] Johannson above, n 107, at 8.

[131] Bonewitz, P. 'Implications of reputation economics on regulatory reform of the credit rating industry' (2010) William and Mary Business Law Review, April, 1, 391–430, at 394.

[132] See for example Regulation (EC) No. 1060/2009 of the European Parliament and of the Council of 16 September 2009 on credit rating agencies; Directive 2009/65/EC of the European Parliament and of the Council of 13 July 2009 on the coordination of laws, regulations and administrative provisions relating to undertakings for collective investment in transferable securities; and Directive 2009/111/EC of the European Parliament and of the Council of 16 September 2009. For an excellent discussion of the effectiveness of Regulation 1060/2009 see Ligere, E. 'Legislative comment EU Regulation 3642/09 on credit

plain and clear manner, and that they maintain the rigour and quality in rating methodology.[133] In 2011, the EU published a new Regulation that governed the operations of CRAs.[134] Additionally, the European Securities and Markets Authority (ESMA) has been given extensive supervision and regulatory powers to regulate CRAs that are registered in the EU.[135]

Before the introduction of the Credit Rating Agency Reform Act in 2006, CRAs 'operated with scant government oversight for much of their ... history'.[136] This is a view supported by Ellis *et al*, who noted that 'historically ... CRAs have faced minimal external regulation which helped shape the largely self-regulatory environment'.[137] President George Bush signed the Credit Rating Agency Reform Act 2006, which was the first real attempt to regulate CRAs following the collapse of Enron and WorldCom.[138] The aim of the Act was to 'improve ratings

---

rating agencies' (2010) Journal of International Banking Law and Regulation, 25(1), 1–4.

133 Ed. 'Credit rating agencies to be regulated' EU Focus, 2008, 244, 2–4, at 2. It has also been argued that CRAs could fall under the Basel II framework: Coskun, D. 'Credit-rating agencies in the Basel II framework: why the standardised approach is inadequate for regulatory capital purposes' (2010) Journal of International Banking Law and Regulation, 25(4), 157–169.

134 Regulation (EU) No. 513/2011 of the European Parliament and of the Council of 11 May 2011 amending Regulation (EC) No. 1060/2009 on credit rating agencies.

135 ESMA was created by Regulation (EU) No. 1095/2010 of the European Parliament and of the Council of 24 November 2010 establishing a European Supervisory Authority (European Securities and Markets Authority), amending Decision No. 716/2009/EC and repealing Commission Decision 2009/77/EC Official Journal L 331, 15/12/2010, p. 84. For a more detailed discussion of this regulatory agency see Moloney, N. 'Reform or revolution? The financial crisis, EU financial markets law, and the European Securities and Markets Authority' (2011) International and Comparative Legal Quarterly, 60(2), 521–533 and Schammo, P. 'The European Securities and Markets Authority: lifting the veil on the allocation of powers' (2011) Common Market Law Review, 48(6), 1879–1913.

136 Evans above n 100, at 1111. For an alternative and interesting account of the regulation of credit rating agencies see White above, n 112.

137 Ellis *et al* above, n 104, at 180.

138 Grinshteyn above, n 117, at 953. For a more detailed discussion of the collapse of Enron and its relationship with CRAs see Coskun, D. 'Credit rating agencies in a post-Enron world: Congress revisits the NRSRO concept' (2008) Journal of Banking Regulation, 9(4), 264–283, and for a critical discussion of the role of the Securities and Exchange Commission see Mulligan, C. 'From AAA to F: the credit rating agencies failed America and what can be done to protect

quality for the protection of investors and in the public interest by fostering accountability, transparency, and competition in the credit rating industry'.[139] Jones noted that the limited accountability of CRAs is one of the major reasons why 'the mortgage bubble was able to form'.[140] The 2006 Act introduced a series of amendments to the Securities and Exchange Act 1934, which required the registration of nationally recognised statistical rating organizations (NRSROs).[141] In 1975, the SEC categorised some CRAs as NRSROs, which provided reassurances for investors that they were a reliable source.[142] Nonetheless, the Credit Rating Agency Reform Act has attracted criticism for its narrow scope and failure to deal with the conflict of interests of CRAs.[143] These

---

investors' (2009) Boston College Law Review, September, 50, 1275–1305, at 1284–1285.

[139] S. Rep. No. 109-326, at 1 (2006). The Act was supported by rules published by the SEC, see Oversight of Credit Rating Agencies Registered as Nationally Recognized Statistical Rating Organizations, Exchange Act Release No. 34-55857, 72 Fed. Reg. 33,563 (12 June 2007). As cited in Bai above, n 122, at 48. For a balanced commentary on the rules introduced by the Securities and Exchange Commission see Neuman, N. 'A Sarbanes–Oxley for credit rating agencies? A comparison of the roles of auditors' and credit rating agencies' conflicts of interest played in recent financial crises' (2010) University of Pennsylvania Journal of Business Law, Spring, 12, 921–946. For further support for a Sarbanes–Oxley approach towards the regulation of CRAs see Hatchett, D. 'Sox it to 'em: using Sarbanes–Oxley as a model for regulating conflicts of interest in the credit rating industry' (2012) Alabama Law Review, 63, 407–428.

[140] Jones, R. 'The need for a negligence standard of care for credit rating agencies' (2010) William and Mary Business Law Review, 1, 201–231, at 223.

[141] Credit Rating Agency Reform Act §4(a), 120 Stat. at 1329. For a useful commentary on the rules introduced by the Securities and Exchange Commission following the introduction of the Credit Rating Agency Reform Act see Curzon, E., Kaswell, S. and Rosenblat, A. 'SEC proposed for registration of credit rating agencies' (2007) Banking Law Journal, May, 124, 438.

[142] Murphy, B. 'Credit rating immunity? How the hands-off approach towards credit rating agencies led to the subprime credit crisis and the need for greater accountability' (2010) Oklahoma Law Review, Summer, 62, 735–792, at 744. However, the weaknesses of the NRSROs were illustrated by a 2008 SEC report. Securities and Exchange Commission *Summary report of issues identified in the Commission staff's examinations of select credit rating agencies* (Securities and Exchange Commission: Washington DC, 2008).

[143] Evans above n 100, at 1116. For a more in-depth commentary on the effectiveness of the 2006 Act see Bonewitz above, n 131, at 420–424 and Krebs, J. 'The rating agencies: where we have been and where do we go from here?' (2009) Journal of Business, Entrepreneurship and the Law, Fall, 3, 133–164, at 157–158.

concerns resulted in Lynch concluding that 'credit rating agencies [still] enjoy a relative lack of regulatory oversight'.[144] The most important function of a CRA is the setting of its credit ratings, yet the Credit Rating Agency Reform Act prevented the SEC from 'regulating the substance of credit ratings or the policies and procedures by which credit rating agencies determined credit ratings'.[145] It should have been the intention and purpose of the Credit Rating Agency Reform Act to regulate this type of activity. This anomaly has not been rectified – the Dodd–Frank Wall Street Reform and Consumer Protection Act 2010 does *not* grant the SEC the power to regulate this activity.[146] Evans noted that the Dodd–Frank Act 'like its predecessor … also permits certain industry abuses to continue and is not without its unintended consequences and short-falls'.[147] However, the 2010 Act does require CRAs to register with the SEC, which has imposed strict internal controls on CRAs that seek to diminish any potential conflicts of interest and improve levels of public disclosure.[148] Furthermore, the Act also provides the SEC with an extensive array of enforcement powers that could be used against CRAs which abuse the registration requirements.[149] The Act also provides litigants with a number of civil options to pursue actions against CRAs.[150]

It has also been asserted that CRAs are 'slow to react to market events or acting pro-cyclically … examples include the collapse of established corporations, such as Enron, AIG, or Lehman Brothers'.[151] The response

---

144 Lynch, T. 'Deeply and persistently conflicted: credit rating agencies in the current regulatory environment' (2009) Case Western Reserve Law Review, Winter, 59, 227–304, at 227–228.

145 Credit Rating Agency Reform Act of 2006, 15 U.S.C. § 78o-7(c)(2).

146 For an interesting critique of the Dodd–Frank Wall Street Reform and Consumer Protection Act see Hill, C. 'Limits on Dodd–Frank's rating agency reform' (2011) Chapman Law Review, Spring, 15,133–148.

147 Evans above n 100, at 1116.

148 Boylan, S. 'Will credit rating agency reforms be effective?' (2012) Journal of Financial Regulation and Compliance, 20(4), 356–366, at 359.

149 Boylan noted that the Securities and Exchange Commission is able to impose financial penalties, impose corrective training, and censure and prevent CRAs from issuing ratings. *Ibid.*

150 Dodd–Frank Wall Street Reform and Consumer Protection Act 2010, ss. 931–939H. For a brief discussion of the civil liability of CRAs see Fitzpatrick, T. and Sagers, C. 'Faith-based financial regulation: a primer on oversight of credit rating organizations' (2009) Administrative Law Review, Summer, 61, 557–610, at 599–603.

151 Coors above, n 101, at 27.

of CRAs has also been criticised in relation to the downgrading of Penn Central Railroad, the US recession in 2001, and WorldCom and Enron.[152] One only has to undertake a brief review of the collapse of Enron to illustrate how CRAs contributed to its fall. Enron was established in 1985 by Kenneth Lay as a result of the merger of Houston Natural Gas and InterNorth. Kenneth Lay appointed Jeff Skilling who, in conjunction with his team of executives, was able to offset Enron's losses by exposing several accountancy ambiguities. In December 2001, a month after a proposed merger of Enron had failed, the company filed for chapter 11 bankruptcy protection. Subsequently, Jeff Skilling was convicted of wire and securities fraud. He was acquitted on several other charges, including insider trading, and received a 24 year custodial sentence.[153] Kenneth Lay was convicted of wire and securities fraud, but died prior to the sentencing hearing in 2006.[154] Until its collapse in 2001, Enron had continued to receive respectable credit ratings from Standard and Poor's, Fitch, and Moody's.[155] Coskun argued that 'credit ratings were important for Enron, because … [they] provided Enron the stability to operate and expand its trading business … [they] also gave Enron the opportunity to access the capital markets to meet its liquidity needs'.[156] In October 2001, two months prior to its collapse, the Wall Street Journal reported that Enron had notified the CRAs of a $2.2bn write-down due to accounting modifications.[157] As a result of this, the SEC commenced an

---

152 Hurst above, 102, at 63.

153 However, it is important to note that the 24 year sentence was reduced in June 2013 by ten years. See Hays, K. and Driver, A. 'Former Enron CEO Skilling's sentence cut to 14 years', 22 June 2013, available from http://uk.reuters.com/article/2013/06/21/us-enron-skilling-idUSBRE95K12520130621, accessed 18 October 2013 and Wilson, S. 'Former Enron boss Jeffrey Skilling has jail sentence cut to 14 years', 21 June 2013, available from http://www.telegraph.co.uk/news/worldnews/northamerica/usa/10136104/Former-Enron-boss-Jeffrey-Skilling-has-jail-sentence-cut-to-14-years.html, accessed 18 October 2013.

154 See Peters, J. and Romeo, S. 'Enron founder dies before sentencing', 5 July 2006, available from http://www.nytimes.com/2006/07/05/business/05cnd-lay.html?_r=0, accessed 18 October 2013.

155 Coskun, D. 'Supervision of credit rating agencies: the role of credit rating agencies in finance decisions' (2009) Journal of International Banking Law and Regulation, 24(5), 252–261, at 255.

156 *Ibid.*

157 Smith, R. and Emshwiller, J. 'Enron faces collapse as Dynegy bolts and stock price, credit standing dive', 29 November 2001, available from http://online.wsj.com/article/SB1006963515929275680.html, accessed 13 October 2013.

investigation into the operations and transactions of Enron.[158] Nonetheless, the CRAs did not respond and reduce their rating of Enron, despite allegations of fraud. The *traditional* investigation into the collapse of Enron condemned the inactivity of CRAs:

> the rating agencies failed to detect Enron's problems – or take sufficiently seriously the problems they were aware of – until it was too late because they did not exercise the proper diligence. They did not ask sufficiently probing questions and, despite their mission to make long-term credit assessments, did not sufficiently consider factors affecting the long-term health of the company, particularly accounting irregularities and overly complex financing structures.[159]

The link between the actions of CRAs and white collar crime has gathered significant momentum. For example, the actions of the CRAs and evidence presented to the US Senate Permanent Subcommittee on Investigations resulted in the following damning indictment:

> Evidence gathered by the Subcommittee shows that the credit rating agencies were aware of problems in the mortgage market, including an unsustainable rise in housing prices, the high risk nature of the loans being issued, lax lending standards, and rampant mortgage fraud. Instead of using this information to temper their ratings, the firms continued to issue a high volume of investment grade ratings for mortgage backed securities.[160]

Of particular relevance to this section of the chapter is the introduction of a wide range of civil sanctions for fraud. The US Financial Institutions Reform, Recovery and Enforcement Act 2008 provides regulatory agencies with the ability to pursue and impose civil penalties on perpetrators

---

[158] Berenson, A. 'S.E.C. opens investigation into Enron', 1 November 2001, available from http://www.nytimes.com/2001/11/01/business/sec-opens-investigation-into-enron.html, accessed 18 October 2013.

[159] Committee on Governmental Affairs United States Senate *Financial oversight of Enron: the SEC and private-sector watchdogs* (Committee on Governmental Affairs United States Senate: Washington DC, 2002) at 6. Also see Securities and Exchange Commission *Report on the role and function of credit rating agencies in the operation of the securities markets* (Securities and Exchange Commission: Washington DC, 2002).

[160] United States Senate Permanent Subcommittee on Investigations – Committee on Homeland Security and Governmental Affairs *Wall Street and the financial collapse* (United States Senate Permanent Subcommittee on Investigations – Committee on Homeland Security and Governmental Affairs: Washington DC, 2011) at 7.

involved in banking fraud.[161] Furthermore, the Act permits the removal of relevant persons and the prevention of their future involvement in the institution concerned.[162] This enforcement action was brought by the Department of Justice via the Financial Institutions Reform, Recovery and Enforcement Act of 1989.[163] In particular, the Department of Justice is attempting to recover money for mail fraud, wire fraud and financial institution fraud. Furthermore the Act also permits the Department of Justice to pursue civil penalties that are equivalent to the losses suffered by federally insured financial institutions.[164] In February 2013, the Department of Justice charged Standard and Poor's with fraud,[165] and is seeking $5bn in losses suffered by federally insured institutions.[166] The Department of Justice has accused Standard and Poor's of 'intentionally making "limited, adjusted and delayed updates" to its rating criteria and analytical models during a key period stretching from 2004 to 2007'.[167]

---

[161] 12 U.S.C. § 1818(i) 2006. For a brief discussion see Rowlett, J. 'The chilling effect of the Financial Institutions Reform, Recovery and Enforcement Act of 1989 and the Bank Fraud Prosecution Act of 1990: has Congress gone too far?' (1993) American Journal of Criminal Law, Winter, 20, 239–262, at 244–246.

[162] 12 U.S.C. § 181(e) (2006).

[163] 12 U.S.C. § 1833a.

[164] Department of Justice 'Attorney General Eric Holder speaks at the press conference announcing lawsuit against S&P', 5 February 2013, available from http://www.justice.gov/iso/opa/ag/speeches/2013/ag-speech-130205.html, accessed 28 May 2013.

[165] Although it is interesting to note that several US media outlets reported that regulatory agencies were considering civil actions for fraud against Standard and Poor's as early as 2011. See for example Touryalai, H. 'Fraud charges against ratings agencies won't help investors', 17 June 2011, available from http://www.forbes.com/sites/halahtouryalai/2011/06/17/fraud-charges-against-ratings-agencies-wont-help-investors/, accessed 29 May 2013 and Blackden, R. 'SEC investigates role of ratings agencies Moody's and Standard & Poor's ahead of the financial crisis', 18 June 2011, available from http://www.telegraph.co.uk/finance/financial crisis/8583387/SEC-investigates-role-of-ratings-agencies-Moodys-and-Standard-and-Poors-ahead-of-the-financial-crisis.html, accessed 29 May 2013.

[166] Viswanatha, A. and LaCapra, L. 'U.S. government slams S&P with $5 billion fraud lawsuit', 5 February 2013, available from http://mobile.reuters.com/article/idUSBRE9130U120130205?irpc=932, accessed 29 May 2013.

[167] The Economist 'America's Justice Department charges Standard & Poor's with fraud', 13 February 2013, available from http://www.economist.com/news/finance-and-economics/21571448-americas-justice-department-charges-standard-poors-fraud-victim-support, accessed 28 May 2013. The case is *U.S. v McGraw-Hill*, 13-00779, U.S. District Court, Central District of California (Santa Ana).

The Department of Justice is seeking civil penalties under the Financial Institutions Reform, Recovery and Enforcement Act of 1989 for three purported frauds by Standard and Poor's: mail fraud,[168] wire fraud[169] and financial institution fraud.[170] In particular, the Department of Justice alleges that Standard and Poor's:

> engaged in a scheme to defraud investors in structured financial products known as Residential Mortgage-Backed Securities and Collateralized Debt Obligations. The lawsuit alleges that investors, many of them federally insured financial institutions, lost billions of dollars on CDOs for which S&P issued inflated ratings that misrepresented the securities' true credit risks. The complaint also alleges that S&P falsely represented that its ratings were objective, independent, and uninfluenced by S&P's relationships with investment banks when, in actuality, S&P's desire for increased revenue and market share led it to favor the interests of these banks over investors.[171]

Furthermore, the Department of Justice alleged that Standard and Poor's:

> engaged in a scheme to defraud investors in financial products known as Residential Mortgage-Backed Securities, or RMBS, and Collateralized Debt Obligations, or CDOs. We allege that, by knowingly issuing inflated credit ratings for CDOs – which misrepresented their creditworthiness and understated their risks – S&P misled investors, including many federally insured financial institutions, causing them to lose billions of dollars. In addition, we allege that S&P falsely claimed that its ratings were independent, objective, and not influenced by the company's relationship with the issuers who hired S&P to rate the securities in question – when, in reality, the ratings were affected by significant conflicts of interest, and S&P was driven by its desire to increase its profits and market share to favor the interests of issuers over investors.[172]

The Attorney General described the alleged behaviour as 'egregious' and added that it 'goes to the very heart of the recent financial crisis'.[173] He concluded that the 'action is an important step forward in our ongoing efforts to investigate – and punish – the conduct that is believed to have

[168] 18 U.S.C. § 1341.
[169] 18 U.S.C. § 1343.
[170] 18 U.S.C. § 1344.
[171] Department of Justice 'Department of Justice sues Standard & Poor's for fraud in rating mortgage-backed securities in the years leading up to the financial crisis', 5 February 2013, available from http://www.justice.gov/opa/pr/2013/February/13-ag-156.html, accessed 28 May 2013.
[172] Department of Justice above, n 164.
[173] Department of Justice above, n 171.

contributed to the worst economic crisis in recent history'.[174] In response to the announcement from the Department of Justice, the Huffington Post reported that the 'civil charges against the credit rating agency were the administration's most aggressive action to date against those deemed responsible for contributing to the worst financial crisis since the Great Depression'.[175] Standard and Poor's responded by issuing the following statement:

> We will vigorously defend S&P against these unwarranted claims. S&P has always been committed to serving the interests of investors and all market participants by providing independent opinions on creditworthiness based on available information. At all times, our ratings reflected our current best judgments about RMBS and the CDOs in question. Unfortunately, S&P, like everyone else, did not predict the speed and severity of the coming crisis and how credit quality would ultimately be affected. Although we deeply regret that these 2007 CDO ratings did not perform as expected, 20/20 hindsight is no basis to take legal action against the good-faith opinions of professionals. The fact is that S&P's ratings were based on the same subprime mortgage data available to the rest of the market – including U.S. Government officials who in 2007 publicly stated that problems in the subprime market appeared to be contained. Every CDO cited by the DOJ also independently received the same rating from another rating agency.[176]

Standard and Poor's issued a motion to dismiss the civil fraud action of the Department of Justice, arguing that the claim is 'too vague'.[177] The

---

174 *Ibid.*

175 Wagner, D. and Rexrode, C. 'S&P lawsuit: U.S. accuses ratings agency of fraud in lead up to financial crisis', 5 February 2013, available from http://www.huffingtonpost.com/2013/02/05/sp-lawsuit_n_2621561.html, accessed 28 May 2013.

176 Standard&Poors Rating Service 'Standard & Poor's says DOJ civil lawsuit is unjustified and without legal merit', 5 February 2013, available from http://img.en25.com/Web/StandardPoorsRatings/DOJLawsuit.pdf, accessed 29 May 2013. Ellis *et al* stated that 'if ratings are not accurate assessments of the credit risk, as we saw during the Global Financial Crisis, this inaccuracy can place the solvency of such financial institutions at risk'. See Ellis *et al* above n 104, at 182–183.

177 Lopez, L. and Viswanatha, A. 'S&P asks federal judge to dismiss U.S. civil fraud lawsuit', 22 April 2013, available from http://www.reuters.com/article/2013/04/22/sandp-fraud-lawsuit-idUSN9E8KE00P20130422, accessed 29 May 2013. For a more detailed discussion of this see Standard&Poors Rating Service 'S&P brief in support of motion to dismiss', 22 April 2013, available from http://www.standardandpoors.com/spf/upload/Ratings_US/USvMcGraw-HillMemorandumin SupportofDefendantsnMotion.pdf, accessed 29 May 2013.

Department of Justice has responded by filing a request to dismiss Standard and Poor's motion to dismiss.

It is interesting to note that, despite its staunch rhetoric towards this civil fraud claim from the Department of Justice, Standard and Poor's continues to settle claims that it exaggerated credit ratings before the financial crisis.[178] In order for a litigant to be able to successfully sue a CRA, they would have to prove that CRAs did not trust or accept their own ratings at the time they were provided. In the case of *Fait v Regions Financial Corporation*,[179] the court held that investors must be able to illustrate that CRAs did not believe their own ratings, thus making any future litigation against them almost bullet proof. The Dodd–Frank Wall Street Reform and Consumer Protection Act 2010 created a new cause of action against CRAs. By virtue of section 933, a private cause of action can be pursued against 'credit rating agencies by placing statements made by the credit rating agencies on the same level as statements made by a registered public accounting firm or a securities analyst under the securities laws'.[180] This section of 'the Act applies the enforcement and penalty provisions of the Exchange Act onto rating agencies, allowing for civil suits against CRAs'.[181] Additionally, section 939G of the Act removed a controversial exemption from liability for CRAs under Rule 436(g).[182] However, it is important to note that the US judiciary has been very reluctant to allow such actions against CRAs.[183]

2.5 PREDATORY LENDING AND WHITE COLLAR CRIME

> Home ownership is a fundamental aspect of American life – a dream to which many aspire. On the other hand, purchasing a home is one of the most complex and expensive transactions that a typical person will be involved in.

---

[178] Foley, S. 'McGraw-Hill reveals $77m S&P settlement', 30 April 2013, available from http://www.ft.com/cms/s/0/97d716bc-b187-11e2-9315-00144feabdc0.html#axzz2UgVAYfge, accessed 29 May 2013.

[179] 665 F.ed 105 (2d Cir. 2011).

[180] Dodd–Frank Wall Street Reform and Consumer Protection Act sec. 933(a), §15E(m)(1), 124 Stat. at 1883.

[181] Cane, M., Shamir, A. and Jodar, T. 'Below investment grade and above the law: a past, present and future look at the accountability of credit rating agencies' (2012) Fordham Journal of Corporate and Financial Law, 17, 1063–1126, at 117.

[182] This rule was introduced as a result of the Securities Act 1933.

[183] Grinshteyn above, n 117, at 941.

> Practically all homes are purchased with the aid of outside financing, and such financing typically comes in the form of a mortgage.[184]

It has been suggested that predatory lending practices are one of the important factors that contributed towards the financial crisis.[185] The most comprehensive definition of predatory lending was afforded by the Department of Treasury's Task Force on Predatory Lending:

> Predatory lending – whether undertaken by creditors, brokers, or even home improvement contractors – involves engaging in *deception* or *fraud, manipulating* the borrower through aggressive sales tactics, or taking *unfair* advantage of a borrower's lack of understanding about loan terms … that, alone or in combination, are *abusive* or make the borrower more vulnerable to abusive practices.[186]

It has been argued that *any* loan could be categorised as predatory lending where the debtor does not have adequate funds to meet the monthly repayments.[187] Furthermore, it has been suggested that even 'aggressive lending practices can amount to predatory lending'.[188] Predatory lending has been described as 'real, pervasive, and destructive',[189] 'harsh lending practices',[190] 'a catalogue of onerous lending practices'[191] and a 'syndrome of loan abuses that benefit mortgage brokers, lenders,

---

184 Putney, A. 'Rules, standards, and suitability: finding the correct approach to predatory lending' (2003) Fordham Law Review, April, 71, 2101–2139, at 2103–2104.

185 Shelley, M. and Jackson, M. 'Sub-prime lending, its deficiencies and the government responses' (2008) Journal of International Banking Law and Regulation, 23(10), 523–537, at 527.

186 Department of Treasury Task Force on Predatory Lending *Curbing predatory home mortgage lending* 1 (Treasury Task Force on Predatory Lending: Washington DC, 2000) at 1.

187 Nwogugu, M. 'Corporate governance and high-risk finance: alternative methods for financing domestic/foreign emerging growth companies with inadequate collateral' (2005) Journal of International Banking Law and Regulation, 20(10), 541–558, at 544.

188 Putney above, n 184, at 2105.

189 Peterson, C. 'Predatory structured finance' (2007) Cardozo Law Review, April, 28, 2185–2282, at 2189.

190 *Ibid.*

191 Engel, K. and McCoy, P. 'A tale of three markets: the law and economics of predatory lending' (2002) Texas Law Review, 80(6), 1255–1281, at 1260.

and securitizes to the serious detriment of borrowers'.[192] In some instances, lenders have been accused of 'intentionally target[ing] individuals and demographic groups whom they identify as most vulnerable'.[193] Engel and McCoy noted that:

> predatory lending is a syndrome of abusive loan terms or practices that involve one or more of the following five problems: loans structured to result in seriously disproportionate net harm to borrowers, harmful rent seeking, loans involving fraud or deceptive practices, other forms of lack of transparency in loans that are not actionable as fraud, and loans that require borrowers to waive meaningful legal redress.[194]

Predatory lending can be divided into two categories. First, the lending activity includes *illegal* lending practices such as *fraud*.[195] Secondly, predatory lending behaviour that is not necessarily illegal but actions that are 'misused by unprincipled lenders'.[196] Examples of conduct that amounts to predatory lending include 'credit insurance, balloon payments, padded fees, rapid refinancing, broker kickbacks disguised as yield spread premiums, high pressure marketing, and of course, high rates'.[197] Davenport argued that predatory lending 'provide[s] an overview of the types of predatory tactics prevalent in the subprime industry. These categories include loan "flipping", charging of excessive fees and "packing", lending without regard to the borrower's ability to repay or "equity stripping", and outright fraud'.[198] The Federal Trade Commission stated that:

> Predatory lending in the subprime mortgage market covers a wide range of practices. While the practices are quite varied, there are common traits. They generally aim either to extract excessive fees and costs from the borrower or

---

192 Guentes, N. 'Defrauding the American dream: predatory lending in Latin communities and reform of California's lending law' (2009) California Law Review, August, 97, 1279–1335, at 1285.

193 Davenport, T. 'An American nightmare: predatory lending in the subprime home mortgage industry' (2003) Suffolk University Law Review, 36, 531–557, at 541.

194 Engel and McCoy above, n 191, at 1260.

195 McNonagle, D. 'In pursuit of safety and soundness: an analysis of the OCC's anti-predatory lending standard' (2004) Fordham Urban Law Journal, November, 31, 1533–1554, at 1538.

196 Ibid.

197 Peterson, C. 'Federalism and predatory lending: unmasking the deregulatory agenda' (2005) Temple Law Review, Spring, 1–98, at 13.

198 Davenport above, n 193, at 541.

to obtain outright the equity in the borrower's home. This is often accomplished through a combination of aggressive marketing practices, high-pressure sales tactics, and loan terms, such as prepayment penalties, that inhibit a borrower's ability to go elsewhere for credit.[199]

Forrester offered a damning indictment of predatory lending, and stated:

The effects of predatory lending are devastating for the individuals who are victims and for their neighbourhoods. At best, the victims of predatory lenders end up paying too much in fees and interest for their loans. The worst case scenario is that they lose their homes to foreclosure. A dramatic increase in foreclosures in inner-city neighbourhoods has followed the increase in subprime lending in recent years. For individuals and families, the loss of a home to foreclosure is devastating, both financially and psychologically. Foreclosures caused by predatory lending have a negative impact on neighbourhoods as well since the impact of foreclosures may be concentrated in low-income areas. Vacant homes caused by foreclosures can cause a decrease in property values and an increase in crime, thereby destabilizing at-risk neighbourhoods. Therefore, predatory lending has an impact beyond the homeowners who obtain predatory loans.[200]

Shelley and Jackson noted that predatory lending encourages 'situations where borrowers are unable to meet loan repayments because of the loan conditions, not because of unforeseen changes to their financial position. It goes beyond a borrower not understanding terms and conditions to a deliberate intent on the part of the lender to take advantage of the borrower.'[201] Davenport added that the 'goals of all predatory lenders are easy to identify: to increase profit by charging the borrower excessive rates and fees and/or to take the equity in the borrower's home'.[202] It has been argued that the foundations of predatory lending were put in place by legislation that was originally designed to prevent such practices, end redlining (refusing people access to credit based on where they live) and increase consumers' access to credit. For example, the Fair Housing Act 1968, the Community Reinvestment Act 1977 and the Financial Services Modernization Act 1999 contributed to 'the seeds of predatory lending

---

199 Federal Trade Commission 'Predatory lending practices in the subprime industry', 24 May 2000, available from http://www.ftc.gov/os/2000/05/predatory testimony.htm, accessed 21 October 2013.

200 Forrester, J. 'Still mortgaging the American dream: predatory lending, pre-emption, and federally supported lenders' (2006) University of Cincinnati Law Review, Summer, 74, 1303–1371, at 1350.

201 Shelley and Jackson above, n 185, at 534.

202 Davenport above, n 193, at 541.

and pursuit of unacceptable risk … blossom[ing] into the carnivorous plants of financial meltdown'.[203] Other legislation that has attempted to limit the impact of predatory lending includes the Truth in Lending Act 1968, the Home Ownership Equity Protection Act 1994, the Equal Credit Opportunity Act 1949 and the Federal Trade Commission Act 1914.[204]

The link between predatory lending, fraud and the financial crisis has been acknowledged by several commentators. For example, Ament took the view that 'one of the more egregious forms of predatory lending involves fraud [and] two basic forms of fraud exist in the predatory lending market'.[205] The first type of fraud relates to not disclosing certain types of legally required information and the second is connected to illegal activity that seeks to defraud providers of credit.[206] It has also been argued that predatory lending involves 'deception or fraud, manipulating the borrower through aggressive sales tactics, or taking unfair advantage of a borrower's lack of understanding about loan terms'.[207] The link between predatory lending and fraud has also been recognised by the judiciary. For example, in *American Financial Services Association v Toledo* the court stated that predatory lending involves 'the use of fraud or deception, manipulation of the borrower through aggressive sales tactics, or taking unfair advantage of a borrower's lack of understanding of loan terms'.[208] It has been argued by Engel and McCoy that:

> the most blatant forms of predatory lending involve the age-old problem of fraud … all of the deceptive practices in this category are violations of existing laws, such as state fraud statutes, state consumer-protection laws, state fiduciary duties, and federal disclosure statutes such as the Truth in Lending Act or the Real Estate Settlement Procedures Act.[209]

By its very nature, predatory lending amounts to unfair, misleading, deceitful and even fraudulent conduct on the part of the lender. It is impossible to determine how many of the subprime loans issued before the start of the financial crisis fell within the definition of predatory

---

[203] Seitz *et al* above, n 30, at 274.

[204] Davenport above, n 193, at 541.

[205] Ament, H. 'Predatory lending: what will stop it?' (2009) Journal of Business and Technology Law, 4, 371–394, at 387–388.

[206] *Ibid.*, at 379.

[207] Department of Treasury Task Force on Predatory Lending above, n 186.

[208] 830 N.E.2d 1233 (Ohio Ct. App. 2005), rev'd, 859 N.E.2d 923 (Ohio 2006) at 1238.

[209] Engel and McCoy above, n 191, at 1267.

lending.[210] It is important to note that by 2006 '$600bn of subprime loans were originated, most of which were securitized. That year, subprime lending accounted for 23.5 per cent of all mortgage originations.'[211] Therefore, it can be argued that some of the subprime loans that contributed towards the financial crisis were conducted in a fraudulent manner.

There have been several attempts to regulate predatory lending. The Truth in Lending Act 1968 'attempts to create a uniform terminology for all consumer credit contracts that facilitates comparison shopping and informed decision making. TILA requires lenders to give consumers a disclosure statement that expresses some of the most important provisions of a credit contract in federally defined terminology'.[212] Davenport added that the purpose of the Truth in Lending Act was to 'assure a meaningful disclosure of credit terms so that the consumer will be able to compare more readily the various credit terms available to him and avoid the uninformed use of credit'.[213] Furthermore, the Real Estate Settlement Procedures Act 1974 tried to regulate unreasonable systems and high costs in closing mortgages.[214] More recently, the Home Ownership and Equity Protection Act 1994 amended the 'Truth in Lending Act to more directly respond to the problem of predatory home mortgage lending'.[215] This Act bans 'several terms common in predatory loans, including balloon payments for loans which mature in less than five years, payment arrangements that cause negative arrangements, increases in the interest rate after default, and most prepayment penalties'.[216] Putney noted that the Act's main 'method of operation is to set a system of triggers that activate additional scrutiny and restrictions on loans that go beyond certain criteria. The two triggers for high cost are APR of the loans or its associated fee.'[217] However, the Home Ownership and Equity Protection Act has been criticised for not going far enough.[218] This is a view

---

[210] See Bruce, H., Gruenstein, D., Herbert, C. and Scheessele, R. 'Subprime foreclosures: the smoking gun of predatory lending?', n/d, available from http://www.huduser.org/publications/polleg/hpcproceedings.html, accessed 21 October 2013.

[211] Financial Crisis Inquiry Commission *Financial Crisis Inquiry Commission report* (Financial Crisis Inquiry Commission: Washington DC, 2011) at 99.

[212] Peterson above, n 189, at 2227.

[213] Davenport above, n 193, at 546.

[214] Peterson above, n 189 at 2226.

[215] *Ibid.*, at 2227.

[216] Davenport above, n 193, at 548–549.

[217] Putney above, n 184, at 2115.

[218] *Ibid.*, at 2116.

supported by Forrester, who noted that 'very few subprime loans exceeded the interest rate threshold ... the free trigger excludes reasonable fees paid to third parties ... it does not apply to high-cost mortgages, reverse mortgages, or home equity lines of credit'.[219] The Fair Debt Collection Practices Act 1977 seeks to promote and maintain standards of civility in the collection of debts. For example, Peterson stated that the Act 'forbids harassment, false or misleading representations, and a variety of other unfair collection tactics, including threatening foreclosure when not legally entitled to do so'.[220] Other measures include the Mortgage Reform and Anti-Predatory Lending Act 2007. This Act created a 'Nationwide Mortgage Licensing System and Registry' which 'require[d] individual mortgage brokers and bank employees to obtain a national licence, through registration on a national database after meeting minimum education in certification standards'.[221] A legislative measure that was introduced to tackle the problems associated with such lending practices was the Credit Card Accountability, Responsibility and Disclosure Act 2009. Nonetheless, the effectiveness of these measures has been questioned. For example, Ament concluded that 'Predatory lending has devastated the mortgage market and as foreclosures rise, politicians and scholars are in the unenviable position of finding a solution. The ineffectiveness of regulations ... only compounds matters.'[222]

Writing in 2003 Putney argued that 'a spate of prosecutions and settlements suggests that law enforcement agencies are beginning to take the issue seriously'.[223] However, Putney warned that 'the difficulty in moving against predatory lenders is twofold. First, identifying predatory loans can be tricky ... the second problem is that legitimate subprime lenders are apt to be harmed by any attempt to regulate predatory lenders'.[224] Several large financial sanctions have been imposed on US financial institutions over their predatory lending practices. The Federal Trade Commission Act 1914 prohibits unjust and misleading practices.[225] The Act provides the Federal Trade Commission with the ability and flexibility to determine what amounts to unjust and misleading practices. Furthermore, the Federal Trade Commission is charged with enforcing

[219] Forrester above, n 200, at 1317.
[220] Peterson above, n 189, at 2228.
[221] Shelley and Jackson above, n 185, at 533.
[222] Ament above, n 205, at 393.
[223] Putney above, n 184, at 2103–2106.
[224] *Ibid.*, at 2108.
[225] 15 U.S.C. 45(a)(1) 2006.

the Federal Trade Commission Act and is provided with an array of enforcement powers. Forrester took the view that:

> the Federal Trade Commission has filed enforcement actions against lenders engaged in predatory lending activities ... between 1998 and 2003, the Federal Trade Commission filed nineteen complaints and reached settlements in most of these cases. Most of the settlements required compensation to consumers and an agreement by the lender to stop certain practices.[226]

For example, Household International paid a $484m settlement to the Federal Trade Commission,[227] Ameriquest paid $325m for conducting predatory lending practices,[228] Bank of America agreed a $335m settlement with the Department of Justice over discriminatory lending practices[229] and Wells Fargo also reached a settlement with the Department of Justice for $175m to resolve fair lending claims.[230] Furthermore, in September 2008 the Federal Trade Commission reached an agreement with Bear Stearns and EMC Mortgage for $28m; they admitted engaging in 'unlawful practices in servicing consumers' home mortgage loans'.[231] There has been some debate about whether or not predatory lending is a criminal offence. For example, Hunt argued that 'criminal fraud statutes could be enthusiastically brought to bear on the most egregious cases of racialized predatory lending through any number of mail or wire fraud

---

[226] Forrester above, n 200, at 1318.

[227] Santanu, R. and Chakrabarti, B. 'Operational risk and the banking sector' (2005) Journal of International Banking Law and Regulation, 20(10), 535–540, at 536.

[228] Connecticut Department of Banking 'Ameriquest to pay $325 million for predatory lending practices that bilked consumers', 23 January 2006, available from http://www.ct.gov/dob/cwp/view.asp?a=2245&q=309018, accessed 21 October 2013.

[229] Isidore, C. 'BofA settles unfair lending claims for $335 million', 21 December 2011, available from http://money.cnn.com/2011/12/21/news/companies/bank_america_settlement/, accessed 21 October 2013.

[230] Department of Justice 'Justice Department reaches settlement with Wells Fargo resulting in more than $175 million in relief for homeowners to resolve fair lending claims', 12 July 2012, available from http://www.justice.gov/opa/pr/2012/July/12-dag-869.html, accessed 21 October 2013.

[231] Federal Trade Commission 'Bear Stearns and EMC Mortgage to pay $28 million to settle FTC charges of unlawful mortgage servicing and debt collection practices', 9 September 2008, available from http://www.ftc.gov/opa/2008/09/emc.shtm, accessed 21 October 2013.

provisions'.[232] However, Engel and McCoy stated that 'criminal fraud actions afford little or no relief to victims of predatory lending'.[233] At the time of writing no criminal convictions have been achieved in this area.

2.6 CONCLUSION

The number of factors that have contributed towards the financial crisis are numerous and extremely complex. A majority of research and commentary on the causes of the financial crisis has identified a set of common factors, including the subprime mortgage collapse, unethical banking practices, weak banking regulation, the development and evolution of complicated financial instruments, macroeconomic policy and access to convenient credit. This chapter has adopted a somewhat alternative interpretation of the causes of the financial crisis and has presented evidence that supports the contention of this monograph that white collar crime is an equally important factor.

The first type of white collar crime that contributed towards the financial crisis, mortgage fraud, is directly linked to its primary cause: the collapse of the subprime mortgage market. The subprime mortgage sector grew at a spectacular rate before the onset of the financial crisis in 2007. For example, by 2006 the number of subprime mortgages had peaked and accounted for over 25 per cent of all US mortgages. Financial institutions, which were eager to profit from subprime mortgages, contributed to their rapid growth. However, when the subprime market collapsed in 2007 a number of financial institutions suffered significant losses, with many applying for bankruptcy protection. Additionally, homeowners suffered as a result of the failure and there was a dramatic increase in the number of repossessions, which resulted in the discovery of widespread instances of mortgage fraud. The chapter has provided evidence from the FBI, which in 2004 warned of the threat posed by mortgage fraud and asked President George Bush for additional funding to counteract this perceived threat. Evidence has also been presented to illustrate that the annual levels of mortgage fraud have increased since the onset of the financial crisis in 2007. Further evidence that supports the contention that mortgage fraud contributed to the financial crisis is illustrated by two related examples – the increase in related enforcement

[232] Hunt, C. 'In the racial crosshairs: reconsidering racially targeted predatory lending under a new theory of economic hate crime' (2003) University of Toledo Law Review, Winter, 3, 211–315, at 217.

[233] Engel and McCoy above, n 191, at 1302.

activities by the FBI and the number of mortgage fraud related SARs filed with FinCEN. The FBI, largely due to additional funding granted by legislation introduced by President Barack Obama, has investigated numerous allegations of mortgage fraud, created several mortgage fraud related task forces and prosecuted over 1,000 instances of mortgage fraud. The number of mortgage fraud related SARs filed by financial institutions to FinCEN has increased to record levels. Therefore, it is my contention that mortgage fraud was an important factor that contributed towards the most recent financial crisis.

A great deal of criticism has been directed at the role of CRAs prior to and during the financial crisis. The chapter provided evidence that has questioned the effectiveness of the current regulation of CRAs. The ineffectiveness of the role and performance of CRAs was graphically illustrated prior to the collapse of Enron in 2001, when little action was taken regarding the company's financial performance following the publication of evidence in the Wall Street Journal. The sluggish or unhurried response was heavily criticised by commentators and resulted in the introduction of the Credit Rating Agency Reform Act 2006, following the collapse of Enron and WorldCom. As argued earlier in this chapter, the aim of this Act was to increase the levels of protection afforded to investors, and improve the methods of accountability for CRAs and transparency. Some commentators have suggested that the ambition to improve the accountability and transparency of CRAs has categorically failed; for example Jones contended that the ineffective accountability of CRAs was an important reason why the 'mortgage bubble was able to form'.[234] The primary function of a CRA is to determine credit ratings, a system that is not without contention or criticism, as illustrated prior to the collapse of Enron. However, the Credit Rating Agency Reform Act 2006 *stopped* the SEC from formally regulating this activity. This loophole has not been remedied by the Dodd–Frank Wall Street Reform and Consumer Protection Act 2010. The only enforcement action that has been instigated against a CRA is by the Department of Justice, which has charged Standard and Poor's with fraud and is seeking $5bn. However, this action is aimed at seeking civil penalties under the Financial Institutions Reform, Recovery, and Enforcement Act 1989 and there is little indication that the Department of Justice will be seeking criminal charges against Standard and Poor's.

A related factor to mortgage fraud is predatory lending. The term, which is extremely difficult to define, has become associated with

---

234 Jones above, 140 at 223.

financial crisis largely due to the unethical, immoral and sometimes fraudulent lending activities of lenders. Predatory lending practices have resulted in many borrowers entering into financial instruments that they were never able to repay. This raises a very important question: did the lenders knowingly engage in practices that encouraged, deceived or misrepresented the borrower to enter into a financial arrangement? If the lender did knowingly engage in such practices the only sanction that can be imposed is the customary financial sanction by the Federal Trade Commission or the Department of Justice. There is no federal legislation that specifically criminalises predatory lending, only legislation that attempts to regulate the terms and conditions of credit agreements. This is unsatisfactory, and it is strongly recommended that legislation is enacted to formally criminalise fraudulent predatory lending. This view has been supported by judicial precedent where the courts have recognised that fraud is a key part of the definition for predatory lending. Another possible solution would be to create a Mortgage Fraud Statute that could be used to target instances of predatory lending. However, it could be argued that the existing provisions under the Wire Fraud Statute and Mail Fraud Statute could easily be used by federal prosecutors.

3. The financial crisis: An alternative interpretation – Part II

3.1 INTRODUCTION

The purpose of this third chapter is to continue to illustrate the connection between the financial crisis and white collar crime. The chapter begins by highlighting the link between the financial crisis and Ponzi fraud schemes, with particular attention given to the fraud schemes implemented by Bernard Madoff and Allen Stanford. This part also provides a commentary on how the financial crisis contributed towards an increase in the number of Ponzi related schemes. The chapter then moves on to consider the relationship between the al-Qaeda terrorist attacks in September 2001 and the financial crisis. This segment of the chapter concentrates on how the instigation of the 'War on Terror' and 'Financial War on Terrorism' by President George Bush indirectly contributed towards an increase in white collar crime before and during the most recent financial crisis. This argument is illustrated by the adverse influence this decision was to have on the ability of law enforcement agencies, in particular the FBI, to be able to tackle mortgage fraud. It is important to note that mortgage fraud has already been identified in Chapter 2 as one of the variables that contributed towards the financial crisis. The chapter then moves on to critically consider the significant increase in occurrences of market misconduct. This part of the chapter is heavily influenced by the significant increase in the enforcement actions pursued by the SEC against a wide range of financial institutions that contributed towards the financial crisis. The last part of the chapter carefully examines the link between the financial crisis and the manipulation or rigging of LIBOR.

3.2 THE FINANCIAL CRISIS AND PONZI SCHEMES

From the very start, the credit crunch has been described as the crisis of Ponzi finance. The increasingly popular use of the term, as well as the collapses of

> the financial pyramids of Bernie Madoff and Allen Stanford, has put Minsky's scholarship at the centre of crisis commentary.[1]

This section discusses the association between Ponzi fraud schemes and the financial crisis. A Ponzi scheme can be defined as a 'fraudulent investment operation that pays investors with money received from new investors rather than from bona fide profits from the investment'.[2] It has also been referred to as a 'form of fraud in which belief in the success of a fictive enterprise is fostered by a payment of quick returns to investors from money invested by others'.[3] It has been defined by the SEC as:

> An investment fraud that involves the payment of purported returns to existing investors from funds contributed by new investors. Ponzi scheme organizers often solicit new investors by promising to invest funds in opportunities claimed to generate high returns with little or no risk. With little or no legitimate earnings, Ponzi schemes require a constant flow of money from new investors to continue. Ponzi schemes inevitably collapse, most often when it becomes difficult to recruit new investors or when a large number of investors ask for their funds to be returned.[4]

The FBI offered the following definition of a Ponzi fraud scheme:

> A Ponzi scheme is an investment fraud that involves the payment of purported returns to existing investors from funds contributed by new investors. Ponzi schemes often share common characteristics, such as offering overly consistent returns, unregistered investments, high returns with little or no risk, or

---

[1] Nesvetailova, A. 'The crisis of invented money: liquidity illusion and the global credit meltdown' (2010) Theoretical Inquiries in Law, January, 11, 125–147, at 142.

[2] Bale, R. and Volpe, T. 'Ponzi schemes and financial fraud regulation' (2011) Brief, Summer, 40, 8. Ponzi fraud schemes have also been referred to as 'pyramid schemes'. Also see Perri, F. and Brody, R. 'The optics of fraud: affiliations that enhance offender credibility' (2012) Journal of Financial Crime, 19(4), 355–370, at 357.

[3] Anderson, T., Lane, H. and Fox, M. 'Consequences and responses to the Madoff fraud' (2009) Journal of International Banking Law and Regulation, 24(11), 548–555, at 548.

[4] Securities and Exchange Commission 'SEC enforcement actions against Ponzi schemes', n/d, available from http://www.sec.gov/spotlight/enf-actions-ponzi.shtml, accessed 28 October 2013.

> secretive or complex strategies. This arrangement gives investors the impression there is a legitimate, money-making enterprise behind the subject's story, but in reality, unwitting investors are the only source of funding.[5]

The term 'Ponzi scheme' or 'Ponzi fraud' has become 'synonymous with fraud … [these] transactions are simple in the execution: the fraudsters retain the investor's capital in exchange for empty promises of high returns'.[6] The term has become synonymous with white collar criminals, including for example William '520 per cent' Miller[7] and Lou Pearlman.[8] However, the term 'Ponzi fraud' is most famously associated with the actions of Charles Ponzi in the United States of America prior to the Wall Street Crash and Great Depression.[9] The origins of Charles Ponzi's scheme can be traced to 1918, when he created his own company that continued to promote his simplistic pyramid fraud scheme which promised investors high returns on their investments. In many instances, the victims of his fraud reinvested not only their 'returns' in Ponzi's pyramid scheme, but also their life savings. Charles Ponzi's scheme was becoming very unstable and it eventually collapsed, resulting in the insolvency of six banks and investors losing approximately $20m. Ponzi was initially charged with 86 counts of mail fraud, yet at trial he admitted to one charge and was sentenced to five years' imprisonment.

There is evidence to suggest that the most recent financial crisis has resulted in a significant increase in the exposure and instances of Ponzi related frauds. For example, according to one study approximately 150 Ponzi schemes with losses exceeding $16.5bn have been exposed since the start of the financial crisis (between 2007 and 2009).[10] Furthermore, the relationship between the financial crisis and Ponzi related fraud

---

[5] Federal Bureau of Investigation 'Financial crimes report to the public – fiscal years 2010–2011 (1 October 2009–30 September 2011)', n/d, available from http://www.fbi.gov/stats-services/publications/financial-crimes-report-2010-2011, accessed 4 June 2013.

[6] Gabel, J. 'Midnight in the garden of good faith: using clawback actions to harvest the equitable roots of bankrupt Ponzi schemes' (2011) Case Western Reserve Law Review, 62, 19–78, at 21.

[7] *Ibid.*, at 27–28.

[8] *Ibid.*, at 30.

[9] For a more detailed discussion of Charles Ponzi see Gradwohl, D. and Corbett, K. 'Equity receiverships for Ponzi schemes' (2010) Seton Hall Legislative Journal, 34, 181–225, at 183–189.

[10] Anderson, C. 'Ponzi schemes' collapses nearly quadrupled in '09', 29 December 2009, available from http://www.law.com/jsp/article.jsp?id=1202437299784, accessed 20 October 2013.

schemes is clearly illustrated by referring to the number of enforcement actions pursued by the SEC against the perpetrators of this white collar crime.[11] According to Johnston *et al* there has been a 21 per cent increase in the number of Ponzi fraud related enforcement actions conducted by the SEC.[12] For example, the SEC stated that:

> Since fiscal year 2010, the SEC has brought more than 100 enforcement actions against nearly 200 individuals and 250 entities for carrying out Ponzi schemes. In these actions, more than 65 individuals have been barred from working in the securities industry. The SEC also has worked closely with the U.S. Department of Justice and other criminal authorities on parallel criminal and civil proceedings against Ponzi scheme operations.[13]

Furthermore, the FBI has instigated over 1,500 Ponzi fraud related investigations since 2008, an increase of 150 per cent.[14] In its Financial Crimes Report for 2010/2011, the FBI reported that it had noticed a 52 per cent increase in securities, commodities and investment fraud and that a majority of these cases were Ponzi schemes.[15] The relationship between the financial crisis and fraudulent Ponzi schemes was further acknowledged by the FBI, which stated: 'the current financial crisis resulted in the exposure of several large Ponzi schemes perpetrated not on an individual community level, but on a corporate national level by executives of what were once considered legitimate companies'.[16] The FBI added: 'the recent financial crisis led to the identification of numerous investment fraud schemes, many of which were Ponzi schemes we have increased the number of agents investigating such schemes by 61 per cent'.[17] However, it is very important to note that 'the recession serves as the impetus to provide a transparency that brings to light Ponzi schemes and existing frauds'.[18] This is a view supported by Drew and Drew, who acknowledged that 'one of the ironies of the global financial

---

11 For a detailed list of Ponzi fraud related enforcement actions undertaken by the SEC see Chapter 4.

12 Johnston, K., Johnson, K. and Hummel, J. 'Ponzi schemes litigation risks: what every financial services company should know' (2010) North Carolina Banking Institute, 14, 29–57, at 29.

13 Securities and Exchange Commission above, n 4.

14 *Ibid.*

15 Federal Bureau of Investigation above, n 5.

16 *Ibid.*

17 *Ibid.*

18 Pontell, H. and Calavita, K. 'The savings and loans industry' (1993) Crime and Justice, 18, 203–242, at 218.

crisis is that it has been the single greatest catalyst for fraud identification in financial services for many decades'.[19]

The most infamous Ponzi fraud scheme associated with the financial crisis is that of Bernard Madoff.[20] In 2008, Madoff was arrested and accused of orchestrating one of the largest US Ponzi frauds. The impact of the fraud is extensive: 'it is estimated that thousands of investors lost somewhere between twenty and sixty-five billion dollars. Madoff purported to invest the savings of some four thousand clients, and these investors spanned across forty-eight of the fifty states, as well as throughout Europe, Latin America, and Asia.'[21] Indeed, it was noted that 'the fallout after the fraud was exposed was wide-reaching, coinciding as it did with a credit crunch that hit both the US and the UK'.[22] Drew and Drew took the view that:

> History shows that numerous individuals have followed in the path of Charles Ponzi. Madoff is arguably the most successful Ponzi scheme operator, being able to manage and grow his scheme for almost two decades. The liquidity crunch saw the eventual demise of Madoff's Ponzi scheme, as a result of the global financial crisis. The global financial crisis sparked a general run on investment withdrawals sparked by falls on the stock market and worsening economic climate. Like investors worldwide, Madoff's investors sought to consolidate and move out of the market. Madoff and his networks were unable to attract sufficient new investments to cover investor withdrawals.[23]

In 2009, Madoff pleaded guilty and was sentenced to 150 years' imprisonment. Judge Chin, who sentenced Madoff, described his crimes as 'extraordinarily evil' and justified the maximum sentence because it would act as a deterrent and also because of the harm he had caused to

---

19 Drew, J. and Drew, M. 'Ponzimonium: Madoff and the red flags of fraud' (2012) Griffith Business School Discussion Papers Finance, 2010-07, at 3.

20 For an excellent discussion of the Bernard Madoff case see Hurt, C. 'Evil has a new name (and a new narrative): Bernard Madoff' (2009) Michigan State Law Review, Winter, 947–987.

21 Nunziato, M. 'Aiding and abetting, a Madoff family affair: why secondary actors should be held accountable for securities fraud through the restoration of the private right of action for aiding and abetting liability under the federal security laws' (2010) Albany Law Review, 73, 603–643, at 603–604.

22 Anon. 'Bernard Madoff: the Ponzi scam', 16 June 2009, available from http://www.telegraph.co.uk/finance/financetopics/bernard-madoff/5547213/Bernard-Madoff-the-Ponzi-scam.html, accessed 3 June 2013.

23 Drew, J. and Drew, M. 'The identification of Ponzi schemes – can a picture tell a thousand frauds?' (2010) Griffith Law Review, 19, 51–70, at 53.

his victims.[24] Judge Chin stated: 'the message must be sent that Mr Madoff's crimes were extraordinarily evil, and that this kind of irresponsible manipulation of the system is not merely a bloodless financial crime that takes place just on paper, but that instead, as we have heard, one that takes a staggering human toll'.[25]

Another high profile Ponzi scheme that was exposed by the financial crisis was that of Allen Stanford, who was convicted[26] and sentenced to 110 years for devising a 20 year investment fraud worth $7bn. The trial judge described Stanford's actions as 'one of the most egregious frauds ever presented to a trial jury in federal court'.[27]

The association between the financial crisis and Ponzi schemes is well documented. For instance, Drew and Drew noted: 'the global financial crisis has seen investors withdraw funds from investment schemes around the world seeking the safe harbour of cash and bonds. As new investment dried up and investor redemptions were lodged in record numbers, a raft of Ponzi and pyramid-like schemes have been uncovered.'[28] Furthermore, Bale and Volpe stated that:

> The downfalls of Madoff and Stanford were a harbinger of things to come. According to a study by the Associated Press, about 150 Ponzi schemes were exposed in 2009 with estimated losses of more than $16.5bn. This was a

---

[24] Smith, A. 'Madoff sentenced to 150 years, CNN', 30 June 2009, available from http://money.cnn.com/2009/06/29/news/economy/madoff_prison_sentence/index.htm, accessed 17 August 2012.

[25] Smith, F. 'Madoff Ponzi scheme exposes "the myth of the sophisticated investor"' (2010) University of Baltimore Law Review, 40, 215–283, at 226.

[26] Allen Stanford was convicted of 'one count of conspiracy to commit wire and mail fraud, four counts of wire fraud, five counts of mail fraud, one count of conspiracy to obstruct an SEC investigation, one count of obstruction of an SEC investigation, and one count of conspiracy to commit money laundering'. See Federal Bureau of Investigation 'Allen Stanford convicted in Houston for orchestrating $7 billion investment fraud scheme', 6 March 2012, available from http://www.fbi.gov/houston/press-releases/2012/allen-stanford-convicted-in-houston-for-orchestrating-7-billion-investment-fraud-scheme, accessed 4 June 2012.

[27] Federal Bureau of Investigation 'Allen Stanford gets 110 years for orchestrating $7 billion investment fraud scheme', 14 June 2012, available from http://www.fbi.gov/houston/press-releases/2012/allen-stanford-gets-110-years-for-orchestrating-7-billion-investment-fraud-scheme, accessed 4 June 2013. For a more detailed discussion of the Ponzi scheme used by Allen Stanford see Taylor III, P., Pinguelo, D. and Cedrone, T. 'The reverse-morals clause: the unique way to save talent's reputation and money in a new era of corporate crimes and scandals' (2010) Cardozo Arts and Entertainment Law Journal, 28, 65–113, at 86–87.

[28] Drew and Drew above, n 19, at 1.

> substantial increase over 2008 when the AP study indicated that 40 Ponzi schemes had been uncovered. From 2008 to 2009, Securities and Exchange Commission restraining orders against Ponzi scheme operators increased 82 per cent and Commodity Futures Trading Commission civil filings against Ponzi schemes doubled.[29]

They added that the frequency of Ponzi schemes has increased during the financial crisis.[30] Furthermore, the New York Times reported that, as a result of the exposure and the Madoff Ponzi scheme and his conviction, there has been a significant increase in the enforcement activities of the CFTC. The report suggested that there was a 45 per cent increase in the CFTC's Ponzi fraud related enforcement activities between 2010 and 2011.[31] This is a point illustrated by the so called 'infamous Madoff runners up': Allen Stanford (Stanford Group entities, $7.2bn), Thomas J. 'Tom' Petters (Petters Worldwide Group, $3.65bn),[32] Paul Greenwood (Westridge Capital Management, $1.3bn),[33] Joel Steinger (Mutual Benefits Corp., $1.25bn),[34] Scott W. Rothstein (Rothstein Rosenfeldt Adler, $1.2bn)[35] and Nevin

---

29 Bale and Volpe above, n 2, at 8.

30 *Ibid.*

31 Protess, B. 'Post-Madoff, a greater awareness of Ponzi schemes', 14 November 2011, available from http://dealbook.nytimes.com/2011/11/14/post-madoff-a-greater-awareness-of-ponzi-schemes/, accessed 3 June 2013.

32 Thomas Petters was convicted of fraud and sentenced to 50 years in prison after devising a $3.65bn fraud. See Burton, T. 'Petters gets 50-year term for running Ponzi scheme', 9 April 2010, available from http://online.wsj.com/article/SB10001424052702304198004575171881879666308.html, accessed 3 June 2013.

33 In July 2010, Paul Greenwood pleaded guilty to conspiracy and securities fraud worth approximately $1.3bn. See Hurtado, P. 'Paul Greenwood, WG Trading hedge fund manager, pleads guilty to fraud', 28 July 2010, available from http://www.bloomberg.com/news/2010-07-28/paul-greenwood-wg-trading-hedge-fund-manager-to-plead-guilty-to-fraud.html, accessed 28 October 2013.

34 Joel Steinger has been accused of conspiracy to commit mail fraud, mail fraud and money laundering and is awaiting trial in two associated cases. See *United States v Joel Steinger, et al*, Case No. 08-21158-CR-Scola and *United States v Joel Steinger et al.*, Case No. 12-20123-CR-Rosenbaum. For more information see United States Department of Justice 'Ft. Lauderdale man convicted of money laundering and obstruction of justice in connection with MBC fraud', 8 February 2013, available from http://www.justice.gov/usao/fls/PressReleases/130228-01.html, accessed 3 June 2013.

35 Scott W. Rothstein pleaded guilty for his role in masterminding an elaborate Ponzi fraud scheme worth $1.2bn and was sentenced to 50 years in

Shapiro (Capitol Investments, $880m).[36] Thus it can be argued that the financial crisis has not only resulted in an increase in the detection of Ponzi fraud schemes, but has also influenced a significant increase in this particular type of white collar crime.

3.3 THE FINANCIAL CRISIS AND THE 'WAR ON TERROR'

An unforeseen factor that contributed towards the financial crisis was the instigation of the 'War on Terror' by President George Bush in September 2001. As a direct result of the al-Qaeda terrorist attacks in September 2001, the maintenance of Homeland Security became *the* top priority for President Bush and his administration. An integral part of this policy that would have an adverse impact on the wider white collar crime policy was the 'Financial War on Terrorism'. This would result in the implementation of a counter-terrorist financing strategy that resulted in this white collar crime being plucked from political obscurity and being driven, wrongly, to the top of the US white collar crime strategy, at the expense of mortgage fraud. Until this decision, US white collar crime strategies concentrated on money laundering. Following the terrorist attacks President George Bush signed Presidential Executive Order 13,224 and the Uniting and Strengthening America by Providing Appropriate Tools Required to Intercept and Obstruct Terrorism Act 2001. Presidential Executive Order 13,224 attempted to 'block [and freeze] all assets and interests in property of certain terrorists and individuals and entities materially supporting them'. Since its implementation the US government has attempted to deny terrorists admittance to the international financial system and limit their ability to raise funds. The Patriot Act 2001 contains a comprehensive package of provisions which aimed to bolster the anti-terrorist financing regulatory regimes. Title III of the Act increases reporting obligations and permits the Secretary of the Treasury to impose additional money laundering requirements on financial and

prison. For more information pertaining to this case see United States Department of Justice 'First year report – Financial Fraud Enforcement Task Force' (2011) United States Attorney Bulletin, 59(2), 4.3.4.

[36] Nevin Shapiro pleaded guilty to a Ponzi fraud worth approximately $880m and was sentenced to a 20 year imprisonment in 2011. See Voreacos, D. 'Wholesale grocery owner gets 20-year sentence in $930 million Ponzi scam', available from http://www.bloomberg.com/news/2011-06-07/nevin-shapiro-gets-20-years-in-880-million-ponzi-scheme.html, accessed 4 June 2013.

credit institutions.[37] The Act introduced a series of regulations which are aimed at detecting terrorist financing prior to its introduction to the US financial system.[38] Under the Act, financial institutions are required to file a suspicious activity report to the Financial Crimes Enforcement Network if they suspect money or finances are being used for the purposes of terrorism. The reporting requirements imposed significant administrative burdens on financial institutions that already had to comply with reporting requirements under the Banking Secrecy Act 1970.[39]

The terrorist attacks in September 2001 resulted in a significant alteration in policy and the instigation of the ill-conceived and controversial 'Financial War on Terror'. However, it is important to note that 'Financial War on Terror' was not an original notion by President George Bush because it was initially used by President Bill Clinton in 1998.[40] Nonetheless, the correlation between the financial crisis and the financing of terrorism is based on the 'War on Terror' and the subsequent adverse implications for wider white collar crime strategies. For example, it is strongly asserted that President George Bush mistakenly prioritised tackling terrorism at the expense of white collar crime. This argument is clearly illustrated by the following evidence and discussion that highlights how President Bush, despite numerous warnings from the FBI and other commentators of the threat posed by mortgage fraud and the subprime mortgage crisis, continued to give precedence to the 'War on Terror'. For example, in 2004 the New York Times stated:

> Since 2004, FBI officials have warned that mortgage fraud posed a looming threat, and the bureau has repeatedly asked the Bush administration for more money to replenish the ranks of agents handling non-terrorism investigations, according to records and interviews. But each year, the requests have been

---

[37] Title III is also known as the International Money Laundering Abatement and Anti-terrorist Financing Act 2001.

[38] USA Patriot Act 2001, ss 311 to 330.

[39] For a more detailed discussion see Ryder, N. *Money laundering – an endless cycle? A comparative analysis of the anti-money laundering policies in the United States of America, the United Kingdom, Australia and Canada* (Routledge Cavendish: Abingdon, 2012) at 59–64.

[40] Ryder, N. 'A false sense of security? An analysis of legislative approaches towards the prevention of terrorist finance in the United States and the United Kingdom' (2007) Journal of Business Law, November, 821–850, at 822.

denied, with no new agents approved for financial crimes, as policy makers focused on counterterrorism.[41]

The ‘War on Terror’ resulted in the Department of Justice altering its priorities from white collar crime towards tackling terrorism. Baker argued that as a result ‘the Justice Department, led by organized-crime prosecutors, [became] … an extension of the Defence Department in the “War on Terrorism”, as the USA Patriot Act provides a new role for law enforcement in fighting terrorism. The boundaries between war and law enforcement are now very blurry.’[42] The impact of the ‘War on Terror’ on the Department of Justice was recognised by the then Attorney General, who noted that the

> War on terrorism became the overriding focus of the Department of Justice and my mission as Attorney General became clear: to transform a peacetime Justice Department ill-prepared for the challenges of 9/11, into a wartime Justice Department focused on the defence of life and liberty by ushering in a new culture of prevention.[43]

As a result of this alteration in priorities, the FBI and a larger number of United States Attorneys’ officers became responsible for ‘fighting the domestic portion of the War on Terror’.[44] Therefore, an indirect result of the War on Terror on the financial crisis was the diversion of resources in the FBI away from white collar crime teams towards countering terrorism. Brooks stated that, as a result, the FBI:

> Assigned some 4,000 of its 11,500 special agents to counterterrorist activities [and] this expansion of US police powers also brought about a refocusing of police powers and a realignment of federal, state, and local police agencies, as all levels of police now more than ever focus[ed] on terrorism. This surge in

---

[41] Lichtblau, E., Johnston, D. and Nixon, R. ‘F.B.I. struggles to handle financial fraud cases’, 18 October 2008, available from http://www.nytimes.com/2008/10/19/washington/19fbi.html?_r=2&scp=1&sq=white%20collar%20crime&st=cse&oref=slogin&, accessed 3 May 2013. Hereafter Lichtblau *et al.*

[42] Baker, J. ‘Reforming corporations through threats of federal prosecution’ (2004) Cornell Law Review, January, 89, 310–353, at 347.

[43] Ashcroft, J. ‘Reflections on events and changes at the Department of Justice’ (2009) Harvard Journal of Law and Public Policy, Summer, 32, 813–830, at 813.

[44] Richman, D. and Stuntz, W. ‘Al Capone’s revenge: an essay on the political economy of pretextual prosecution’ (2005) Columbia Law Review, March, 105, 583–639, at 587.

counterterrorism was not effective. These FBI agents were pulled from other areas and they did not have the training and skills of a counterterrorism specialist.[45]

The diversion of resources resulted in the New York Times concluding that 'the FBI is struggling to find enough agents and resources to investigate criminal wrongdoing tied to the country's economic crisis'.[46] In 2004, an assistant director of the FBI described the threat posed by mortgage fraud as having 'the potential to be an *epidemic* [author's emphasis]' and that 'we think we can prevent a problem that could have as much impact as the Savings and Loans crisis'.[47] This was supported by a report on Reuters which stated that 'the FBI, after years spent focusing on national security, is struggling to find agents and resources to investigate wrongdoing tied to the country's economic crisis'.[48] Furthermore, the Los Angeles Times reported that 'a massive shift of FBI agents to anti-terrorism and counterintelligence duties has undermined the work of fraud investigators, who are taking on fewer scam artists and corporate miscreants and taking longer to complete cases'.[49] The reduction in white collar crime FBI agents was recognised by the Financial Crisis Enquiry Commission Report that stated that the number of assigned agents dropped from 2,342 to fewer than 2,000.[50] It added that in 2007 only 150 agents were available to investigate over 54,000 mortgage fraud related SARs filed with FinCEN.[51] Lathrop noted that despite numerous pleas by law enforcement agencies and the Mortgage Bankers' Association for

---

[45] Brooks, B. 'Law enforcement's role in US counterterrorism strategy' (2010) Police Journal, 83(2), 113–125, at 114.

[46] Lichtblau *et al.* above, n 41.

[47] Frieden, T. 'FBI warns of mortgage fraud "epidemic"', 17 September 2004, available from http://www.cnn.com/2004/LAW/09/17/mortgage.fraud/, accessed 23 May 2013.

[48] Michaud, C. 'FBI resources limited for economic probes: report', 18 October 2008, available from http://www.reuters.com/article/2008/10/18/us-fbi-resources-idUSTRE49H23S20081018?feedType=RSS&feedName=domestic News, accessed 3 May 2013.

[49] Eckard, E. 'FBI shift crimps white-collar crime probes – with more agents moved to anti-terrorism duty, corporate fraud cases are routinely put on hold, prosecutors say', 30 August 2004, available from http://articles.latimes.com/2004/aug/30/business/fi-fbi30, accessed 3 May 2013.

[50] The Financial Crisis Enquiry Commission *The financial crisis inquiry report – final report of the National Commission on the causes of the financial and economic crisis in the United States* (The Financial Crisis Enquiry Commission: Washington DC, 2011) at 190.

[51] *Ibid.*, at 190–191.

more federal funding to tackle mortgage fraud, it was consistently rejected by President George Bush and his administration.[52] This was acknowledged by Robert Mueller, Director of the FBI, who informed the Financial Crisis Enquiry Commission Report that he had asked for more resources to tackle fraud but 'didn't get what we had requested'.[53] However, the former Attorney General Alberto Gonzales argued that: 'I don't think anyone can credibly argue that [mortgage fraud] is more important than the war on terror. Mortgage fraud doesn't involve taking loss of life so it doesn't rank above the priority of protecting neighbourhoods from dangerous gangs or predators attacking our children.'[54]

Nonetheless, the stance by President George Bush towards mortgage fraud has been criticised by several commentators. For example, Gabilondo argued that 'it was devotees of deregulation – George W. Bush in the White House and Alan Greenspan at the Federal Reserve – who let subprime debt mushroom thanks to easy money and, it would come to light later, systematic mortgage fraud'.[55] Additionally, it has been argued that the Bush administration disregarded the threat posed by mortgage fraud. Therefore, Creseney *et al* concluded that:

> The obstacles inherent in investigating mortgage fraud have been exacerbated by federal law enforcement resource and manpower shortages. Following the September 11th attacks, the FBI shifted more than 1,800 agents, nearly one third of all agents in criminal programs, including many of those trained in financial investigations, to counterterrorism and intelligence duties. In the years prior to the credit crisis, the FBI mounted several investigations into mortgage fraud, but its repeated warnings of the threat mortgage fraud posed and its requests for additional resources for non-terrorism investigations were left unaddressed by policymakers. By 2007, the number of FBI agents nationwide pursuing mortgage fraud had shrunk to about 100, in sharp contrast to the roughly 1,000 agents that were deployed on banking fraud during the S&L crisis of the 1980s and 1990s. In addition, because mortgage fraud cases are often one-off incidents involving relatively small losses, law enforcement officials have faced a difficult trade-off between going after low-impact, widespread cases or focusing on the smaller number of more

---

[52] Lathrop, D. 'FBI lacks resources to fight boom in mortgage fraud: 2,500 agents reassigned to terrorism weren't replaced', 5 July 2007 available from http://www.highbeam.com/doc/1G1-125637095.html, accessed 3 May 2013.

[53] Financial Crisis Enquiry Commission above, n 50 at 163.

[54] *Ibid.*

[55] Gabilondo, J. 'Dodd–Frank, liability structure, and financial instability cycles: neither a (Ponzi) borrower nor a lender be' (2011) Wake Forest Law Review, Fall, 46, 469–489, at 481.

complicated mortgage scams that have higher impact, but that require more resources to pursue.[56]

However, the policy towards mortgage fraud has gained significant momentum since President Barack Obama came into office in January 2009. One of the first legislative measures introduced to tackle white collar crime associated with the financial crisis was the Fraud Enforcement and Recovery Act 2009. The origins of this legislation are to be found in an initial legislative attempt to combat mortgage fraud that was tabled in April 2007 by Senators Barack Obama and Dick Durbin.[57] The Bill was entitled 'Stopping Mortgage Transactions which Operate to Promote Fraud, Risk, Abuse, and Underdevelopment Act'.[58] The Bill stated that it was illegal 'to defraud any natural person, financial institution,[59] or other borrower in connection with the extension of credit that is secured by either real property or personal property that is to be used as a primary dwelling'. Furthermore, it provided that it was illegal to 'obtain, by means of false or fraudulent pretences, representations, or promises, any money or property, … from a natural person in connection with an extension of consumer credit'.[60] The Bill sought to impose tough criminal sanctions upon people convicted of mortgage fraud – a custodial sentence of 35 years and fines of up to $5m. The proposals also aimed to enlarge the breadth of reports and evidence received by FinCEN. However, the Bill was not signed into law by President George Bush as it ran out of Congressional time. Therefore the Fraud Enforcement and Recovery Bill was introduced by the Chairman of the Committee on the Judiciary, Patrick Leahy, Senators Grassley and Kaufman and co-sponsored by Senators Klobuchar and Schumer in February 2009. After signing the Bill on 20 May 2009, President Barack Obama stated: 'the Fraud Enforcement and Recovery Act will protect the American people from giving the federal government new tools and resources to prevent fraud'.[61] The aim of this Act was twofold. First, to improve the

---

[56] Creseney, A., Eng, G.E. and Nuttal, S. 'Regulatory investigations and the credit crisis: the search for villains' (2009) American Criminal Law Review, Spring, 46, 225–273, at 238–239.

[57] However, it is important to note that this was not the first version of the Bill to be introduced by Senators Barack Obama and Dick Durbin, which was originally tabled in February 2006.

[58] It is more commonly referred to as the Stop Fraud Act.

[59] S. 1222, Sec 2 § 1351(a)(1).

[60] S. 1222, Sec 2 § 1351(a)(2).

[61] The White House 'Reforms for American homeowners and consumers – President Obama signs the Helping Families Save their Homes Act and the Fraud

levels of responsibility and accountability for frauds that had arisen during the financial crisis. Secondly, the Act provided a substantial increase in funding for the Justice Department and other law enforcement agencies to tackle mortgage fraud. In particular the Act empowered the government to distribute approximately $500bn for 2010 and 2011 for 'additional government enforcement activity'.[62] Furthermore, the Department of Justice was given $330m to investigate any suspected instances of mortgage fraud and to pursue any potential prosecutions that arose from those investigations. However, Creseney *et al* warned that:

> Even with the increased resources that federal law enforcement agencies are beginning to devote to mortgage fraud, it is unlikely that they will be successful in systematically prosecuting the frauds that may have triggered the credit crisis. The potential amount of fraud in the mortgage industry, coupled with the complexity of fraud investigations and federal resource constraints, makes systematic prosecution difficult.[63]

The link between the terrorist attacks in September 2001, the financial crisis and white collar crime has been directly influenced by the decision by President George Bush to prioritise terrorism and national security over white collar crime. The diversion of resources away from mortgage fraud, despite several warnings and pleas from the FBI, left it unprepared and ill-equipped to deal with the incoming tsunami of mortgage fraud cases.

3.4 THE FINANCIAL CRISIS AND MARKET MISCONDUCT

Further evidence of the link between the financial crisis and white collar crime is illustrated by increased enforcement activities for market misconduct used by the SEC. These have been concisely divided into three subcategories. First, conduct by financial institutions that has concealed from investors risks, terms and improper pricing in CDOs and other complex structured products. Secondly, behaviour that has resulted in

---

Enforcement and Recovery Act', 20 May 2009, available from http://www.whitehouse.gov/the_press_office/Reforms-for-American-Homeowners-and-Consumers-President-Obama-Signs-the-Helping-Families-Save-their-Homes-Act-and-the-Fraud-Enforcement-and-Recovery-Act, accessed 28 October 2013.

[62] Kirkland Alert, 'The Fraud Enforcement and Recovery Act 2009', Kirkland and Ellis LLP.

[63] Creseney *et al.*, above n 56, at 243.

misleading disclosures to investors about mortgage related risks and exposure. Thirdly, where financial institutions have hidden the extent of risky mortgage related and other investments in mutual funds and other financial products.[64]

3.4.1 Concealed from Investors Risks, Terms and Improper Pricing in CDOs and Other Complex Structured Products

One of the highest profile actions instigated by the SEC was against Goldman Sachs, which was described by one commentator as 'high-dollar, high-profile and unprecedented'.[65] Here, the SEC accused Goldman Sachs of defrauding investors by misleading them as the housing market stumbled by excluding important pieces of information about how certain financial commodities were linked to subprime mortgages.[66] In particular, the SEC alleged that Goldman Sachs 'structured and marketed a synthetic collateralized debt obligation that hinged on the performance of subprime residential mortgage-backed securities' and that 'Goldman Sachs failed to disclose to investors vital information about the collateralized debt obligation'.[67] According to Buell, 'the theory of the case was that Goldman had sold a German bank a derivative product tied to the fate of a basket of mortgage-backed securities, while simultaneously obscuring the weaknesses of the securities in that basket'.[68] In response to the allegations, Goldman Sachs stated that it was 'disappointed that the SEC would bring this action related to a single transaction in the face of an extensive record which establishes that the accusations are unfounded

---

[64] Securities and Exchange Commission 'SEC enforcement addressing misconduct that led or arose from the financial crisis', n/d, available from http://www.sec.gov/spotlight/enf-actions-fc.shtml#keyStatistics, accessed 1 June 2013.

[65] Deckant, N. 'Criticisms of collateralised debt obligations in the wake of the Goldman Sachs scandal' (2010) Review of Banking and Financial Law, Fall, 30, 407–442, at 407.

[66] Securities and Exchange Commission 'SEC charges Goldman Sachs with fraud in structuring and marketing of CDO tied to subprime mortgages', 16 April 2010, available from http://www.sec.gov/news/press/2010/2010-59.htm, accessed 17 June 2013. The complaint was filed in the United States District Court for the Southern District of New York.

[67] *Ibid.* Goldman Sachs was charged with breaching the Securities Act 1933 (s. 17(a)) and the Securities and Exchange Act 1934 (s. 10(b)).

[68] Buell, S. 'What is securities fraud?' (2011) Duke Law Journal, December, 61, 511–581, at 513.

in law and fact'.[69] Davidoff *et al* noted that 'the complaint alleged that Goldman Sachs violated the anti-fraud provisions of the federal securities laws in connection with a 2007 synthetic collateralized debt obligation transaction, ABACUS'.[70] In July 2010, Goldman Sachs admitted that its marketing materials 'contained incomplete information' and that it 'regretted that the marketing materials did not contain that disclosure'.[71] Therefore, it agreed to pay a record financial penalty of $550m and also agreed to alter its business practices. The SEC stated that this was its 'largest penalty ever assessed against a financial services firm … [and that] this settlement is a stark lesson to Wall Street firms'.[72] However, it is very important to put the amount of the fine into context. For example, in the first quarter of 2010, it was reported that Goldman Sachs announced profits of $3.46bn, and it has been argued that the '*largest* [author's emphasis] well received penalty' represented 'two weeks of profits'.[73] The settlement between the SEC and Goldman Sachs has also been questioned by MacDonald, who took the view that:

> Since most consent judgments are announced the same day as a complaint is filed, settling with the Commission at least mitigates the negative publicity and may even be a financial windfall. Goldman Sachs, after announcing its

---

69 Barr, C. 'SEC charges Goldman Sachs with fraud', 16 April 2010, available from http://money.cnn.com/2010/04/16/news/companies/sec.goldman.fortune/, accessed 18 June 2013.

70 Davidoff, S., Morrison, A. and Wilhelm Jr, W. 'The SEC v Goldman Sachs: reputation, trust, and fiduciary duties in investment banking' (2012) Journal of Corporation Law, 37, 529–553, at 530. For a more detailed commentary on the transactions see Tuch, A. 'Conflicted gatekeepers: the Volcker Rule and Goldman Sachs' (2012) Virginia Law and Business Review, Fall, 7, 365–420, at 393–396 and Davidoff, S. and Hill, C. 'Limits of disclosure' (2013) Seattle University Law Review, 36, 599–637, at 609–617.

71 Securities and Exchange Commission 'Goldman Sachs to pay record $550 million to settle SEC charges related to subprime mortgage CDO', 15 July 2010, available from http://www.sec.gov/news/press/2010/2010-123.htm, accessed 17 June 2013.

72 *Ibid*. For a more detailed discussion see Deckant above, n 65.

73 Wang, M. 'Goldman's SEC settlement by the numbers: we do the math', 15 July 2010, available from www.propublica.org/blog/item/what-the-goldman-sachs-settlement-means-in-context, as cited in Cava, B. 'Quid pro quo corruption is "so yesterday": restoring honest services fraud after Skilling and Black' (2011) University of California, Fall, 12, 1–29.

consent to one of the largest financial penalties in Commission history, had its stock price rise by more than 10%.[74]

However, the enforcement activities of the SEC against Goldman Sachs have attracted a high level of criticism and have been described as 'unconstitutional'.[75] Similarly, Buell argued that 'because Goldman admitted nothing – the great case of "U.S. Charges Goldman Sachs with Fraud" simply evaporated, leaving hardly a trace beyond the $550 million fine that swelled the SEC's coffers'.[76] Furthermore, the enforcement action was described as 'inefficient because it wasted scarce Commission resources on an enforcement action with dubious merit and resulted in needless damage to Goldman Sachs' reputation, corporate image and market capitalization'.[77]

Another example of conduct of concealment from investors related to JP Morgan Securities. The SEC charged the company with misleading investors in a multifaceted mortgage securities contract when the US housing sector began to fall.[78] The SEC alleged that 'J.P. Morgan marketed highly-complex CDO investments to investors with promises that the mortgage assets underlying the CDO would be selected by an independent manager looking out for investor interests', but failed to inform investors that a 'prominent hedge fund that would financially profit from the failure of CDO portfolio assets heavily influenced the CDO portfolio selection'.[79] JP Morgan Securities consented to the final judgment, but without admitting or denying the charges, and agreed to pay $153.6m. Bell noted that 'JP Morgan paid $18.6 million in disgorgement of profits, $2 million in prejudgment interest, and a $133 million penalty'.[80]

---

[74] MacDonald, R. 'Setting examples, not settling: towards a new SEC enforcement paradigm' (2012) Texas Law Review, 91, 419–447, at 433.

[75] Sekhon, V. 'Enforcement of material non-disclosure under federal securities laws' (2011) Stanford Journal of Law, Business and Finance, Spring, 16, 273–287, at 286.

[76] Buell above, n 68, at 514.

[77] Sekhon above, n 75.

[78] Securities and Exchange Commission 'J.P. Morgan to pay $153.6 million to settle SEC charges of misleading investors in CDO tied to U.S. housing market', 21 June 2011, available from http://www.sec.gov/news/press/2011/2011-131.htm, accessed 17 June 2013.

[79] *Ibid.*

[80] Bell, S. 'Clarity and predictability at the SEC: Abacus, Citigroup, and the political economy of securities fraud settlements' (2012) Columbia Business Law Review, 865–912, at 885.

The SEC also targeted certain transactions entered into by Citigroup's primary broker-dealer subsidiary, which was accused of misleading investors of a $1bn CDO that was associated with the housing market. In particular, the SEC alleged that the 'CDO defaulted within months, leaving investors with losses while Citigroup made $160 million in fees and trading profits'.[81] The SEC stated that 'securities laws demand that investors receive more care and candor than Citigroup provided to these CDO investors ... investors were not informed that Citgroup had decided to bet against them and had helped choose the assets that would determine who won or lost'.[82] However, it is important to note that the settlement was rejected by Judge Jed Rakoff, who said that it was extremely complicated 'to discern from the limited information before the court what the SEC is getting from this settlement other than a quick headline'.[83] He did however state that 'Citi's alleged conduct arguably [was] more egregious than that in Goldman Sachs'.[84]

In another case, the SEC accused ICP Asset Management and its President with 'fraudulently managing investment products tied to the mortgage markets as they came under pressure'. In particular, the SEC alleged that:

> At the direction of its owner and president Thomas Priore, ICP Asset Management LLC defrauded four multi-billion-dollar collateralized debt obligations (CDOs) by engaging in fraudulent practices and misrepresentations that caused the CDOs to lose tens of millions of dollars. Priore and his companies also improperly obtained tens of millions of dollars in advisory fees and undisclosed profits at the expense of their clients and investors.[85]

In December 2012, ICP and its President Thomas Priore agreed to pay penalties of $23m and settle the SEC allegations.[86] The SEC stated that

---

[81] Securities and Exchange Commission 'Citigroup to pay $285 million to settle SEC charges for misleading investors about CDO tied to housing market', 19 October 2011, available from http://www.sec.gov/news/press/2011/2011-214.htm, accessed 17 June 2013.

[82] *Ibid.*

[83] *SEC v Citigroup Global Markets Inc.*, 827 F. Supp. 2d 328, 334 (S.D.N.Y. 2011), as cited in Bell above, n 80.

[84] *Ibid.*, at 889.

[85] The Securities and Exchange Commission alleged that the defendants had breached the Securities Act 1933, s. 17(a), Securities Exchange Act 1934, s. 10(b) and 15(c)(1)(a) and the Investment Advisers Act 1940, s. 204, 206(1), 206(2), 206(3) and 206(4).

[86] Securities and Exchange Commission 'N.Y.-based investment advisory firm and founder settle SEC charges for fraudulent management of CDOs', 7

'the settlement with Priore and ICP sends a clear message that investment advisers must always act in the best interests of their advisory clients, even if those clients are sophisticated investors ... when advisers put their own interests ahead of their clients' interests, the SEC will seek to hold them accountable'.[87]

The SEC also charged the subsidiary Mizuho Financial Group and three of its former employees with misleading investors in a CDO by utilising 'dummy assets' to escalate a transactions credit rating. In particular, the SEC alleged that:

> Mizuho structured and marketed Delphinus CDO 2007-1, a CDO that was backed by subprime bonds at a time when the housing market was showing signs of severe distress. The deal was contingent upon Mizuho obtaining credit ratings it used to market the notes to investors. When its employees realized that Delphinus could not meet one rating agency's newly announced criteria intended to protect CDO investors from the uncertainty of ratings downgrades, they submitted to the rating firm a portfolio containing millions of dollars in dummy assets that inaccurately reflected the collateral held by Delphinus. Once the firm rated the inaccurate portfolio, Mizuho closed the transaction and sold the notes to investors using the misleading ratings.[88]

Mizuho Financial Group agreed to settle the SEC charges and paid $127.5m. Additionally, the firm's three former employees also agreed to charges.[89]

3.4.2 Misleading Disclosures to Investors about Mortgage Related Risks and Exposure

The SEC has also utilised its enforcement powers where financial institutions have provided misleading disclosures to investors. For example, Citigroup was accused by the SEC of deliberately misleading investors over its exposure to subprime mortgage assets.[90] The SEC alleged that:

September 2012, available from http://www.sec.gov/news/press/2012/2012-184.htm, accessed 17 June 2013.

[87] *Ibid.*

[88] Securities and Exchange Commission 'SEC charges Mizuho Securities USA with misleading investors by obtaining false credit ratings for CDO', 18 July 2012, available from http://www.sec.gov/news/press/2012/2012-139.htm, accessed 18 June 2013.

[89] *Ibid.*

[90] Securities and Exchange Commission 'SEC charges Citigroup and two executives for misleading investors about exposure to subprime mortgage assets',

> In response to intense investor interest on the topic, Citigroup repeatedly made misleading statements in earnings calls and public filings about the extent of its holdings of assets backed by subprime mortgages. Between July and mid-October 2007, Citigroup represented that subprime exposure in its investment banking unit was $13bn or less, when in fact it was more than $50bn.

Citigroup agreed to settle the allegations and paid a $75m penalty, while its former Chief Financial Officer paid $100,000 and its former Head of Investor Relations agreed to pay $80,000.[91]

Another example relates to the enforcement activities pursued by the SEC against employees of American Home Mortgage. Here, the SEC charged the employees with accountancy fraud and deliberately misleading investors about their worsening financial predicament due to its exposure to the subprime crisis. As a result, the former employees of the firm agreed to pay a settlement worth $2.45m.[92] The SEC stated that 'these senior executives did not just occupy a front row seat to the mortgage meltdown – they were part of the show … as the housing market imploded, these executives kept secret that the company's holdings were collapsing like a house of cards'.[93]

One of the largest settlements reached by the SEC was against Credit Suisse and JP Morgan, which were charged with 'misleading investors in offerings of residential mortgage-backed securities'.[94] In particular, the SEC alleged that:

> J.P. Morgan misstated information about the delinquency status of mortgage loans that provided collateral for an RMBS offering in which it was the underwriter. J.P. Morgan received fees of more than $2.7m, and investors sustained losses of at least $37m on undisclosed delinquent loans. J.P. Morgan also is charged for Bear Stearns' failure to disclose its practice of obtaining and keeping cash settlements from mortgage loan originators on problem

---

29 July 2010, available from http://www.sec.gov/news/press/2010/2010-136.htm, accessed 17 June 2013.

91 *Ibid.*

92 Securities and Exchange Commission 'SEC charges former American Home Mortgage executives for misleading investors about company's financial condition', 28 April 2009, available from http://www.sec.gov/news/press/2009/2009-92.htm, accessed 17 June 2013.

93 *Ibid.*

94 Securities and Exchange Commission 'SEC charges J.P. Morgan and Credit Suisse with misleading investors in RMBS offerings', 16 November 2012, available from http://www.sec.gov/news/press/2012/2012-233.htm, accessed 17 June 2013.

> loans that Bear Stearns had sold into RMBS trusts. The proceeds from this bulk settlement practice were at least $137.8m.[95]

Both JP Morgan ($296.9m) and Credit Suisse ($120m) agreed to settle the SEC accusations. Robert Khuzami, the Director of the SEC's Division of Enforcement, said:

> Today, we are announcing actions against two major investment firms that will pay a combined total of almost $420 million for engaging in misconduct in connection with hundreds of residential mortgage backed securities – transactions that involve the pooling together of residential mortgages that are then securitized and sold to investors by Wall Street.[96]

The Wall Street Journal described this as the 'first tangible victory in a wide-ranging investigation into Wall Street's sale of mortgage-backed securities before the onset of the financial crisis and the collapse of the U.S. housing market'.[97]

The SEC has also taken action against New Century for misrepresenting investors as its lenders' subprime mortgage was collapsing. The position was exacerbated as New Century was then the US's largest subprime lender. The SEC alleged that New Century 'failed to disclose important negative information, including dramatic increases in early loan defaults, loan repurchases, and pending loan repurchase requests. Defendants knew this negative information from numerous internal reports they regularly received.'[98] The SEC indicted three of the company's former officers (Brad Morrice, Patti Dodge and David Kenneally) with securities fraud.[99] In July 2010, the SEC accepted a settlement from the three former employees, who each agreed to pay over $1.5m and to a five year ban from acting as a director or officer.[100]

---

95 *Ibid.*

96 Securities and Exchange Commission 'Remarks during news conference call about enforcement actions against J.P. Morgan and Credit Suisse', 16 November 2012, available from http://www.sec.gov/news/speech/2012/spch111612rk.htm, accessed 18 June 2013.

97 Berthelsen, C., Eaglesham, J. and Jones, K. 'SEC, two banks settle over loans', 16 November 2012, available from http://online.wsj.com/article/SB10001424127887324735104578123242727307524.html, accessed 18 June 2013.

98 Securities and Exchange Commission 'SEC charges former officers of subprime lender New Century with fraud', 7 December 2009, available from http://www.sec.gov/news/press/2009/2009-258.htm, accessed 18 June 2013.

99 *Ibid.*

100 *Ibid.*

3.4.3 Concealed the Extent of Risky Mortgage Related and Other Investments in Mutual Funds and Other Financial Products

One of the biggest firms to collapse at the start of the financial crisis was Bear Stearns. In June 2008, the SEC decided to indict two former managers of the ailing financial institution for fraudulently misleading investors about the monetary state of two of its biggest hedge funds and their risk of exposure during the global financial crisis. In particular, the SEC alleged that:

> when the hedge funds took increasing hits to the value of their portfolios during the first five months of 2007 and faced escalating redemptions and margin calls, then-BSAM senior managing directors Ralph R. Cioffi and Matthew M. Tannin deceived their own investors and certain institutional counterparties about the funds' growing troubles until they collapsed and caused investor losses of approximately $1.8bn.[101]

In June 2012, a court approved the SEC settlement with the two former employees of Bear Stearns, Ralph Cioffi and Matthew Tannin, who were each ordered to pay $1.05m.[102]

Another example of a firm providing misleading statements to investors was Charles Schwab, which settled charges in 2011 and agreed to a financial sanction of $118m.[103]

3.5 LIBOR

> LIBOR and EURIBOR also have a wider impact on other markets. Barclays' misconduct could have caused serious harm to participants in any of these markets. Harm could have been caused by Barclays' misconduct if the final reference rates were affected by Barclays' actions on any given day. Barclays' misconduct also created the risk that the integrity of LIBOR and EURIBOR

---

[101] Securities and Exchange Commission 'SEC charges two former Bear Stearns hedge fund managers with fraud', 19 June 2008, available from http://www.sec.gov/news/press/2008/2008-115.htm, accessed 18 June 2013.

[102] Securities and Exchange Commission 'Court approves SEC settlements with two former Bear Stearns hedge fund portfolio managers; SEC bars managers from regulated industries', 25 June 2012, available from http://www.sec.gov/litigation/litreleases/2012/lr22398.htm, accessed 18 June 2013.

[103] Securities and Exchange Commission 'SEC charges Schwab entities and two executives with making misleading statements', 11 January 2011, available from http://www.sec.gov/news/press/2011/2011-7.htm, accessed 28 October 2013.

> would be called into question and that confidence in or the stability of the UK financial system would be threatened.[104]

One of the most recent types of white collar crime associated with the financial crisis is the manipulation of LIBOR. LIBOR has been defined as 'the rate at which an individual contributor panel bank could borrow funds, were it to do so by asking for and then accepting interbank offers in reasonable market size, just prior to 11.00am London time'.[105] Another definition was offered by the BBC: 'the rate at which banks in London lend money to each other for the short-term in a particular currency. A new Libor rate is calculated every morning by financial data firm Thomson Reuters based on interest rates provided by members of the British Bankers' Association'.[106] Another term that needs to be defined is EURIBOR, 'the rate at which euro interbank term deposits are being offered within the EMU7 zone by one prime bank to another at 11:00 am Brussels time'.[107] The LIBOR and EURIBOR have been described by the United Kingdom's FSA as 'benchmark reference rates fundamental to the operation of both UK and international financial markets, including markets in interest rate derivatives contracts'.[108] Both the LIBOR and EURIBOR 'are used across the world for a range of financial products by a wide variety of financial market participants, for both hedging and speculative purposes'.[109] The importance of the LIBOR and EURIBOR rates and their integrity is illustrated by the fact that they play a central role in the global financial markets.[110] For example, it has been reported that the value of the contracts attached to LIBOR is between $300tn and $800tn.[111]

---

104 Financial Services Authority *Final notice to Barclays Bank Plc* (Financial Services Authority: London, 2012) at 1.

105 British Bankers' Association 'LIBOR definitions', n/d, available from http://www.bbalibor.com/bbalibor-explained/definitions, accessed 1 October 2012.

106 BBC News 'Timeline: Libor-fixing scandal', 26 September 2012, available from http://www.bbc.co.uk/news/business-18671255, accessed 1 October 2012.

107 EURIBOR 'About EURIBOR', n/d, available from http://www.euribor-ebf.eu/euribor-org/about-euribor.html, accessed 1 October 2012.

108 Financial Services Authority above, n 104, at 1.

109 HM Treasury *The Wheatley review of LIBOR: initial discussion paper* (HM Treasury: London, 2012) at 10.

110 Financial Services Authority above, n 104.

111 HM Treasury above, n 109, at 10.

LIBOR has been described as 'a benchmark that gauges the interest rate, credit premium and liquidity premium that a leading bank would expect to be offered by another similar institution'.[112] According to Lim, 'LIBOR is a reference index sponsored by the British Bankers' Association [that is] used to calculate interest rates on a range of global financial instruments in excess of $350tn.'[113] LIBOR is managed and regulated by the British Bankers' Association (BBA), which is the UK trade body of the banking and financial services sector.[114] The administration of LIBOR is the duty of BBA LIBOR Ltd, which is a subsidiary of the BBA, and managed by the LIBOR Manager.[115] To complicate matters even more, Thomson Reuters is accountable for the collection of submissions from participating banks and presenting them for inspection and assessment.[116] Additionally, the contributing banks are also expected to ensure and maintain the quality of the submissions they make to LIBOR.[117] HM Treasury stated that:

> It [LIBOR] was established in the 1980s in order to provide a fair and standardised interest rate benchmark for loans, thereby facilitating the growth of the syndicated loans market. Standardised inter-bank rates were attractive as a benchmark for investors and borrowers as they allowed the lending banks to pass on changes in the funding costs of an average bank over the course of the duration of the loan. The development of LIBOR was also driven, from an early stage, by the growth in new financial instruments such as forward rate agreements, which also required a standardised interest rate benchmark.[118]

The first evidence of wrongdoing regarding the LIBOR was witnessed in 2005. Here, the FSA alleged that Barclays Bank attempted to manipulate the dollar LIBOR and the EURIBOR rates of interest after being asked by derivative traders and other banking institutions. The misconduct took place in both London and New York. Further breaches took place between February 2006 and October 2007 when Barclays sought to further manipulate the EURIBOR and the US LIBOR. This period is particularly significant as it includes the start of the financial crisis and

---

112 *Ibid.*, at 9.

113 Lim, C. 'Libor, strategy, and the international cartel investigations' (2013) Journal of European Competition Law and Practice, first published online 8 January 2013, doi:10.1093/jeclap/lps077, at 1.

114 British Bankers' Association 'About us', n/d, available from http://www.bba.org.uk/about-us, accessed 1 October 2012.

115 HM Treasury above, n 109, at 16.

116 *Ibid.*, at 16.

117 *Ibid.*

118 *Ibid.*, at 9.

the near collapse of Northern Rock. During this period, the FSA determined that Barclays continued to control LIBOR submissions to provide a misleading depiction of its credit quality so that it could continue to raise funds. This resulted in several media outlets questioning the reliability of these submissions.[119] Further concerns about the submissions were voiced by the New York Federal Reserve, which stated that it had communications which implied that the LIBOR submissions were 'being set unrealistically low' by the banks.[120] In 2008, the Wall Street Journal also queried the reliability of LIBOR and stated that 'the concern: some banks don't want to report the high rates they're paying for short-term loans because they don't want to tip off the market that they're desperate for cash. The Libor system depends on banks to tell the truth about their borrowing rates.'[121] Lim argued that it was 'during the … financial crisis between 2006 to 2008, [that] competition authorities allege … the Contributor Panel Banks shared information to undervalue daily submissions and hide weaknesses in balance sheets caused by the collapse of Lehman Brothers and Northern Rock'.[122] The reliability of the submissions also came to the attention of the CFTC after a compliance officer at Barclays raised concerns about problematic actions by other banks to the BBA and FSA. The CFTC stated that the compliance officer informed the FSA that:

> Barclays believed that LIBOR submissions by the panel banks were distorted due to market illiquidity; that Barclays had been consistently the highest or one of the two highest submitters but was concerned to go higher given the negative media reporting about Barclays; that Barclays had concerns about the trillions of dollars of derivatives fixed off LIBOR; and that there were 'problematic actions' by some banks.[123]

---

[119] See for example the excellent report by Gilbert, M. 'Barclays takes a money-market beating', 3 September 2012, available from http://www.bloomberg.com/apps/news?pid=newsarchive&sid=a8uEKKBYY7As, accessed 1 October 2012.

[120] New York Federal Reserve 'USD Libor', 28 August 2008, available from http://www.newyorkfed.org/newsevents/news/markets/2012/libor/August_28_2007_mass_distribution_emails.pdf, accessed 1 October 2012.

[121] Mollenkamp, C. 'Bankers cast doubt on key rate amid crisis', 16 April 2008, available from http://online.wsj.com/article/SB120831164167818299.html, accessed 1 October 2012.

[122] Lim above, n 113, at 1. Also see Edwards, C., Hardiman, P., Madden, M. and McClelland, J. 'Implications for commercial organisations of the global investigations into LIBOR' (2012) Banking Law Journal, October, 129, 831.

[123] Commodity Futures Trading Commission *Order instituting proceedings pursuant to sections 6(c) and 6(d) of the Commodity Exchange Act, as amended,*

Further concerns about the LIBOR were raised by the Bank of International Settlements, which stated that banks had several reasons for providing a misleading quote during a shortage of funding:

> However, transparency raises questions about the information signalled by contributing banks through their quotes. There may be circumstances in which contributing banks deliberately choose to disclose biased quotes. If there is uncertainty about the liquidity position of a contributing bank, the bank will be wary of revealing any information that might add to this uncertainty for fear of increasing its borrowing costs.[124]

Here, the FSA concluded:

> Where Barclays made submissions which took into account the requests of its own Derivatives Traders, or sought to influence the submissions of other banks, there was a risk that the published LIBOR and EURIBOR rates would be manipulated. Barclays could have benefitted from this misconduct to the detriment of other market participants. Where Barclays acted in concert with other banks, the risk of manipulation increased materially.[125]

Furthermore, the FSA also concluded that Barclays acted inappropriately between September 2007 and May 2009 by 'making LIBOR submissions which took into account concerns over the negative media perception of Barclays' LIBOR submissions'.[126] This is of particular relevance to the link between the financial crisis and the illegal activities of Barclays. This was a point raised by the FSA, which reported:

> Liquidity issues were a particular focus for Barclays and other banks during the financial crisis and banks' LIBOR submissions were seen by some commentators as a measure of their ability to raise funds. Barclays was identified in the media as having higher LIBOR submissions than other contributing banks at the outset of the financial crisis. Barclays believed that other banks were making LIBOR submissions that were too low and did not

---

making findings and imposing remedial sanctions (Commodity Futures Trading Commission: Washington DC, 2012) at 22.

[124] Detrixhe, J. 'Libor reported as rigged in '08 proving 2012's revelation', 19 July 2012, available from http://www.bloomberg.com/news/2012-07-18/libor-reported-as-rigged-in-08-crisis-proving-revelation-in-12.html, accessed 3 October 2012.

[125] Financial Services Authority above, n 104, at 3.

[126] *Ibid.*

> reflect market conditions. The media questioned whether Barclays' submissions indicated that it had a liquidity problem. Senior management at high levels within Barclays expressed concerns over this negative publicity.[127]

The FSA added that the concerns raised by members of senior management of Barclays resulted in 'instructions being given by less senior managers at Barclays to reduce LIBOR submissions in order to avoid negative media comment'.[128] The FSA concluded that this conduct breached 11 of its Principles of Business and imposed a then record financial sanction of £59.5m for breaches of its Handbook. The FSA noted that:

> Barclays' misconduct was serious, widespread and extended over a number of years. The integrity of benchmark reference rates such as LIBOR and EURIBOR is of fundamental importance to both UK and international financial markets. Firms making submissions must not use those submissions as tools to promote their own interests. Making submissions to try to benefit trading positions is wholly unacceptable. This was possible because Barclays failed to ensure it had proper controls in place. Barclays' behaviour threatened the integrity of the rates with the risk of serious harm to other market participants. The FSA continues to pursue a number of other significant cross-border investigations in this area and the action we have taken against Barclays should leave firms in no doubt about the serious consequences of this type of failure.[129]

The HM Treasury Select Committee concluded that these findings have 'been a reputational disaster for Barclays. They have led directly to the loss of its Chief Executive and its Chief Operating Officer.'[130] Furthermore, the conduct of Barclays resulted in condemnation from the Select Committee:

> The attempted manipulation of Barclays' LIBOR submissions with the intention of personal gain continued for four years. It is shocking that it flourished for so long. Any system may fail for a short period, but compliance at Barclays was persistently ineffective. Even when Barclays' compliance had indications that something was awry, it failed to take the opportunity to

---

[127] *Ibid.*, at 3.

[128] *Ibid.*

[129] Financial Services Authority 'Barclays fined £59.5 million for significant failings in relation to LIBOR and EURIBOR', 27 June 2012, available from http://www.fsa.gov.uk/library/communication/pr/2012/070.shtml, accessed 1 October 2012.

[130] HM Treasury Select Committee *Fixing LIBOR: some preliminary findings* (HM Treasury: London, 2012) at 10.

> strengthen the bank's controls. Nor was there any pressure from senior executives within Barclays to ensure that effective LIBOR controls were in place, as it was considered low-risk, in particular where LIBOR setters sat, with no presence of the compliance function. These are serious failures of governance within Barclays, for which the board is responsible.[131]

It is very important to note that Barclays received a significant discount on the financial penalty imposed. In his evidence to the HM Treasury Select Committee, Bob Diamond, Barclays' former Chief Executive stated that:

> Clearly there was behaviour that was reprehensible; but as soon as this was recognised Barclays put all forces – if there's a mistake, if there's a problem, how do we handle it? What do we do about it? At Barclays it has been three years with three of the most important regulatory agencies in the world looking at millions of files; and all three regulatory agencies applauding Barclays for its co-operation, analysis and proactivity. We hired two external firms to work with two members of senior management, reporting to the chairman of the board and the chairman of the audit committee. The attitude of Barclays three years ago when this was recognised was, 'Let's get to the bottom of it. Let's identify the problem; take the actions necessary; learn our lessons and, if any of our customers and clients got hurt, let's make them good.' That attitude is recognised by the three regulatory agencies in what they wrote, but it is not coming out in the court of public opinion over the past week.[132]

The investigation by the FSA highlighted several instances of manipulation of the LIBOR rate by Barclays' employees. For example, the FSA referred to an e-mail from a US derivative trader to Manager A revealing that Barclays' Submitter 'submits our settings each day, we influence our settings based on the fixings we all have'.[133] Furthermore, in February 2008 another US dollar derivative trader said to a manager at Barclays that the bank's Submitter was tendering 'the highest LIBOR of anybody … He's like, I think this is where it should be. I'm like, dude, you're killing us.' The manager then instructed the trader to 'just tell him to keep it, to put it low'. Trader B said that he had 'begged' the Submitter to put in a low LIBOR submission and the Submitter had said he would 'see what I can do'.[134] Other examples of manipulation by Barclays included a series of e-mail exchanges between two US dollar derivative traders

131 *Ibid.*, at 21.
132 *Ibid.*, at 8.
133 Financial Services Authority above, n 104, at 11.
134 *Ibid.*

who asked for a 'low three month US dollar LIBOR submission for the coming Monday'. In one of the e-mails, the trader stated: 'We have an unbelievably large set on Monday (the IMM). We need a really low 3m fix, it could potentially cost a fortune. Would really appreciate any help.' The other trader stated that 'I really need a very low 3m fixing on Monday – preferably we get kicked out. We have about 80 yards [billion] fixing for the desk and each 0.1 [one basis point] lower in the fix is a huge help for us. So 4.90 or lower would be fantastic.'[135]

In addition to the record financial sanction imposed by the FSA, the CFTC ordered Barclays to pay a $290m fine for attempted manipulation and false reporting concerning LIBOR and EURIBOR benchmark interest rates.[136] The CFTC's Director of Enforcement stated:

> The American public and our markets rely upon the integrity of benchmark interest rates like LIBOR and Euribor because they form the basis for hundreds of trillions of dollars of transactions and affect nearly every corner of the global economy … banks that contribute information to those benchmarks must do so honestly. When a bank acts in its own self-interest by attempting to manipulate these rates for profit, or by submitting false reports that result from senior management orders to lower submissions to guard the bank's reputation, the integrity of benchmark interest rates is undermined. The CFTC launched this investigation to protect the markets and the public from such illegal conduct, and today's action demonstrates that we will bring the full force of our authority to bear as we carry out that mission.[137]

Additionally, Barclays entered into an agreement with the Department of Justice to pay a $160m penalty.[138] Assistant Attorney General Breuer stated that:

> LIBOR and EURIBOR are critically important benchmark interest rates … because mortgages, student loans, financial derivatives, and other financial products rely on LIBOR and EURIBOR as reference rates, the manipulation

---

135 *Ibid.*, at 12.

136 Commodity Futures Trading Commission 'CFTC orders Barclays to pay $200 million penalty for attempted manipulation of and false reporting concerning LIBOR and Euribor benchmark interest rates', 27 June 2012, available from http://www.cftc.gov/PressRoom/PressReleases/pr6289-12, accessed 1 October 2012.

137 *Ibid.*

138 Department of Justice 'Barclays Bank PLC admits misconduct related to submissions for the London Interbank Offered Rate and the Euro Interbank Offered Rate and agrees to pay $160 million penalty', 27 June 2012, available from http://www.justice.gov/opa/pr/2012/June/12-crm-815.html, accessed 1 October 2012.

> of submissions used to calculate those rates can have significant negative effects on consumers and financial markets worldwide. For years, traders at Barclays encouraged the manipulation of LIBOR and EURIBOR submissions in order to benefit their financial positions; and, in the midst of the financial crisis, Barclays management directed that U.S. Dollar LIBOR submissions be artificially lowered. For this illegal conduct, Barclays is paying a significant price. To the bank's credit, Barclays also took a significant step toward accepting responsibility for its conduct by being the first institution to provide extensive and meaningful cooperation to the government. Its efforts have substantially assisted the Criminal Division in our ongoing investigation of individuals and other financial institutions in this matter.[139]

Several other banks have been sanctioned by US and UK regulatory authorities for manipulating LIBOR. For example the FSA imposed a financial sanction of £87.5m on the Royal Bank of Scotland for conduct between January 2006 and November 2010.[140] The overall sanction would have been £125m had it not been for a 30 per cent discount granted by the FSA. The conduct of the bank's employees was not limited to the UK – it occurred in Japan, Singapore and the US. According to the FSA, the illegal conduct was extensive and '219 requests for inappropriate submissions were documented – an unquantifiable number of oral requests, which by their nature would not be documented, were also made. At least 21 individuals including derivatives and money market traders and at least one manager were involved in the inappropriate conduct.'[141] Tracey McDermott, the FSA's Director of Enforcement and Financial Crime, stated:

> The integrity of benchmark reference rates such as LIBOR is of fundamental importance to both UK and international financial markets. The findings set out in our notice today demonstrate a failure by RBS to take that wider context into account. The failures at RBS were all the more serious because of the attempts not only to influence the submissions of RBS but also of other panel banks and the use of interdealer brokers to do this. During the course of the FSA's work on LIBOR, RBS provided the FSA with an attestation that its LIBOR related systems and controls were adequate. This was not correct. Primary responsibility for the conduct of the individuals within firms and the efficacy of the controls that are in place, rests with those firms. The FSA takes it very seriously when firms tell us that they have appropriate systems but do not. The extent and nature of the misconduct relating to LIBOR has cast a

---

139 *Ibid.*

140 Financial Services Authority 'RBS fined £87.5m for significant failings in relation to LIBOR', 6 February 2013, available from http://www.fsa.gov.uk/library/communication/pr/2013/011.shtml, accessed 8 February 2013.

141 *Ibid.*

> shadow on the reputation of this industry and we expect firms to take steps to ensure that this can never happen again. This is the third penalty we have imposed in relation to LIBOR related misconduct. The size and scale of our continuing investigations remains significant.[142]

In addition to the fine imposed by the FSA, regulatory agencies in the US also imposed a raft of financial penalties on RBS. For instance, the Department of Justice announced that RBS Securities Japan Limited, a wholly owned subsidiary of RBS, pleaded guilty to wire fraud and its role in influencing the Japanese yen LIBOR.[143] As part of a deferred prosecution agreement it has agreed to pay a $50m fine. Additionally, it has agreed to pay a $100m penalty to the Department of Justice. Assistant Attorney General Breuer stated that:

> As we have done with Barclays and UBS, we are today holding RBS accountable for a stunning abuse of trust … The bank has admitted to manipulating one of the cornerstone benchmark interest rates in our global financial system, and its Japanese subsidiary has agreed to plead guilty to felony wire fraud. The department's ongoing investigation has now yielded two guilty pleas by significant financial institutions. These are extraordinary results, and our investigation is far from finished. Our message is clear: no financial institution is above the law.[144]

The CFTC imposed the largest financial penalty on RBS and RBS Securities Japan Limited, of $325m. The fine was imposed for manipulation, attempted manipulation and the false reporting of the yen and Swiss franc LIBOR.[145] The CFTC's Director of Enforcement stated that:

> the integrity of LIBOR depends on truthful information provided by a select group of some of the world's most important banks. The public is deprived of an honest benchmark interest rate when a group of traders sits around a desk

---

142 *Ibid.*

143 Department of Justice 'RBS Securities Japan Limited agrees to plead guilty in connection with long-running manipulation of Libor benchmark interest rates', 6 February 2013, available from http://www.justice.gov/opa/pr/2013/February/13-crm-161.html, accessed 8 February 2013.

144 *Ibid.*

145 Commodity Futures Trading Commission 'CFTC orders The Royal Bank of Scotland plc and RBS Securities Japan Limited to pay $325 million penalty to settle charges of manipulation, attempted manipulation, and false reporting of yen and Swiss franc LIBOR' 6 February 2013, available from http://www.cftc.gov/PressRoom/PressReleases/pr6510-13, accessed 8 February 2013.

> for years falsely spinning their bank's LIBOR submissions, trying to manufacture winning trades. That's what happened at RBS.[146]

These financial sanctions have been imposed for the misconduct of traders during the financial crisis. These will not be the last set of sanctions imposed by law enforcement and regulatory agencies, as many other financial institutions are still under investigation. In the UK, the SFO has charged three former traders with conspiracy to defraud, and its counterpart in the US, the Department of Justice, announced similar charges in 2013.

3.6 CONCLUSION

The aim of this chapter has been to add to the existing literature on the variables that contributed towards the financial crisis. It seeks, like the previous chapter, to illustrate the increasingly important role that white collar crime played in the biggest financial crisis since the Great Depression.

The first type of white collar crime discussed in this chapter that contributed to, and possibly thrived in, the financial crisis was Ponzi related frauds. The financial crisis has resulted in the discovery of many instances of these frauds. The highest profile Ponzi schemes exposed by the financial crisis were those instigated by the faces of the financial crisis, Bernard Madoff and Allen Stanford. However, the chapter has determined that there is more evidence that associates Ponzi frauds with the financial crisis than previously believed. For example, despite the notoriety and media frenzy that followed the arrests and convictions of Madoff and Stanford, research has noted that there was a 400 per cent increase in the number of Ponzi related frauds in 2009. The link between Ponzi fraud schemes and the financial crisis has also been clearly illustrated by the dramatic increase in related investigative and enforcement activities of the FBI, SEC and CFTC. For example, the CFTC instigated 32 enforcement actions against alleged Ponzi fraud schemes in 2011. This represented a 45 per cent increase from 2010. Furthermore, the FBI reported that it had seen a 150 per cent increase in Ponzi related fraud since 2008. Examples cited by the FBI during the financial crisis include Lee Farkas, the former Chairman of Taylor, Bean and Whitaker, who was sentenced to 30 years' imprisonment in 2011; Nevin Shapiro, who pleaded guilty to a Ponzi fraud scheme in September 2010 and was

---

[146] *Ibid.*

sentenced to 20 years' imprisonment; Paul Greenwood, a managing partner at WG Trading and Westridge Capital Management, who pleaded guilty to conspiracy and securities fraud; and Scott Rothstein, who was sentenced to 50 years in prison for coordinating a Ponzi scheme worth $1.6bn. Similarly, the SEC has also witnessed a significant increase in Ponzi related frauds and reported that it has originated over 100 enforcement actions against approximately 200 people and nearly 250 entities for undertaking Ponzi related frauds. The SEC also noted that it has seen an increase in Ponzi fraud schemes, leading to a 21 per cent increase in Ponzi fraud investigations.

The most contentious example of white collar crime contributing towards the financial crisis is the instigation of the War on Terror by President George Bush following the al-Qaeda terrorist attacks in September 2001. The decision to promote Homeland Security was to have a substantial adverse impact on the ability of the FBI to tackle mortgage fraud. The War on Terror resulted in both the redistribution of resources that would have originally been used to tackle white collar crime towards promoting national security, and the changing of its priorities away from white collar crime towards combating terrorism. Therefore, the FBI was unable to sufficiently tackle the threat posed by white collar crime and in particular mortgage fraud. As a result the number of white collar crime prosecutions and investigations dropped. The FBI highlighted the threat posed by mortgage fraud on several occasions in 2004 and stated that this type of white collar crime posed the largest threat to the US economy since the Savings and Loans Crisis in the 1980s. However, several requests for additional funding from the FBI were dismissed by President George Bush. It is thus the conclusion of this chapter that the FBI was ill-prepared to tackle the uncontrolled spread of mortgage fraud prior to and during the financial crisis. This position has now been redressed by the introduction of legislation by President Barack Obama that has resulted in increased funding for the FBI and Department of Justice. Nonetheless, the ability of the FBI to tackle white collar crime has been severely weakened by the decision of President George Bush to instigate the War on Terror in 2001.

As will be outlined in Chapter 4, the SEC has instigated numerous enforcement proceedings against a wide range of financial institutions for market misconduct. This includes deliberately misleading investors, concealing information from investors and providing misleading information. The highest profile example of white collar crime that is associated with the financial crisis is the manipulation of LIBOR. This particular example can be contrasted with the other types of white collar crime described in this monograph because of its global reach and impact.

Regulatory and law enforcement agencies in the US, UK, Japan and Switzerland have imposed record financial sanctions on banks and arrested low level traders and charged them with related offences. For example, as will be discussed in Chapters 4 and 5, law enforcement agencies in both the US and UK have indicted or charged traders with fraud related offences. Furthermore, several banks have also been convicted of white collar crime related offences associated with the manipulation of LIBOR and have had record financial sanctions imposed on them. It is extremely likely that there will be more sanctions imposed on those other financial institutions which were allegedly involved in the manipulation of LIBOR.

4. United States of America – Policy, legislative, regulatory and enforcement responses

> When the economy turns sour, revelations of criminal conduct and excessive practices that appear to have contributed to the downturn often lead the public to demand a swift and forceful response. The government responds by passing laws criminalizing the behavior at issue, increasing punishments for established offenses, and increasing the number of prosecutors and regulators. Unfortunately, this government response is often driven as much by the politics of the day as by any rational consideration of how to design a system that will prevent criminal conduct and excessive practices from becoming widespread during the next bull market.[1]

> The beginning of the twenty-first century has seen the drawing of a new era of criminality. This new era has been planned and perpetuated not by such traditional criminal players as organised crime or drug cartels, but instead by the large multinational corporations that are essential actors in both the economy and society at large.[2]

4.1 INTRODUCTION

The purpose of this chapter is to critically reflect on the response in the United States of America to white collar crime originating from the financial crisis. The first part of the chapter outlines the policy and legislative responses to the financial crisis introduced by President George Bush and President Barack Obama. This includes a brief evaluation of the Emergency Economic Stabilization Act 2008, the Housing and Economic Recovery Act 2008, the American Recovery and Reinvestment Act 2009, the Fraud Enforcement and Recovery Act 2009, and the

[1] Valukas, A. 'White-collar crime and economic recession' (2010) University of Chicago Legal Forum, 1–21, at 8.

[2] Markoff, G. 'Arthur Andersen and the myth of the corporate death penalty: corporate criminal convictions in the twenty-first century' (2013) University of Pennsylvania Journal of Business Law, 15, 797–836, at 799.

Dodd–Frank Wall Street Reform Act 2012. The chapter then moves on to appraise the regulatory responses to white collar crime deriving from the financial crisis. This involves a detailed analysis of the responses of the SEC, the FBI, the Futures Commodities Trading Commission (FCTC) and the Department of Justice. The final part of the chapter diagnostically inspects the law enforcement response to white collar crime since the commencement of the financial crisis. This section will be divided into two parts – criminal and civil sanctions.

4.2 POLICY AND LEGISLATIVE RESPONSE

The initial policy response to the financial crisis was jointly led by the Federal Reserve and the Department of Treasury. Both of these institutions were initially concerned with providing economic assistance to maintain the financial stability of the US economy and supporting several of the largest failing financial institutions. These actions were supported by several legislative instruments.

4.2.1 Economic Stimulus Act 2008

The first legislative measure introduced to tackle the financial crisis was the Economic Stimulus Act 2008.[3] The objective of this legislation was to stimulate the US economy using three mechanisms.[4] First, the Act provided tax rebates for low income families totalling $266m.[5] Secondly, the Economic Stimulus Act 2008 aimed to encourage businesses to invest in qualifying property.[6] Thirdly, it was designed to increase the loan

[3] President George Bush stated that the Act is 'large enough to have an impact, amounting to more than $152bn … the Act provides temporary tax incentives for businesses to make investments in their companies … [it also] provides individual tax relief in the form of tax rebates'. See The White House 'President Bush signs H.R. 5140, the Economic Stimulus Act of 2008', 13 February 2008, available from http://georgewbush-whitehouse.archives.gov/news/releases/2008/02/20080213-3.html, accessed 23 September 2013.

[4] Deeds, J. 'The flawed logic of Congress in the Economic Stimulus Act of 2008' (2010) Journal of Law and Family Studies, 12, 299–313, at 302.

[5] Economic Stimulus Act 2008, §101. See Fairfax, L. 'The legal origins of theory in crisis' (2009) Brigham Young University Law Review, 1571–1617, at 1590.

[6] Economic Stimulus Act 2008, §102–3.

limits for Fannie Mae, Freddie Mac and the Federal Housing Administration.[7] Harrell took the view that the 'Economic Stimulus Act increased the government sponsored enterprise lending limits while extending federal guaranties to cover their liabilities, and provided $350bn for Federal Housing Association lending programs'.[8] Additionally, the 2008 Act permitted the Department of Treasury to manage TARP, to recapitalise banks, and to support AIG and the car manufacturing industry. However, the impact of the Economic Stimulus Act has been questioned. For example Deeds stated that, despite its unprecedented cross-party support, the 'legislation has not satisfied its purposes. American families, while maybe a little richer … are not in a safer financial condition. The government had good motives, but ended up spending $152bn on a plan that has not succeeded.'[9]

4.2.2 Emergency Economic Stabilization Act 2008

The second legislative instrument introduced by President George Bush was the Emergency Economic Stabilization Act 2008.[10] The preamble to the legislation outlined its aims as 'to provide authority for the Federal Government to purchase and insure certain types of troubled assets for the purposes of providing stability to and preventing disruption in the economy and financial system and protecting taxpayers'.[11] President George Bush stated that the Act 'addresses this problem [the financial crisis] head on by providing a variety of new tools to the government – such as allowing us to purchase some of the troubled assets, and creating a new government insurance program that will guarantee the value of others'.[12] The most significant and perhaps controversial aspect of this Act was the creation of TARP. TARP is a Department of Treasury fund which aimed to inject $700bn into the financial services sector by purchasing troubled assets and equity from financial institutions. It has been suggested that these funds were used to 'forestall the failure of

---

7 Economic Stimulus Act 2008, § 201–2.

8 Harrell, A. 'The great credit contraction: who, what, when, where and why' (2010) Georgia State University Law Review, 26, 1209–1258, at 1249.

9 Deeds above, n 4, at 313.

10 Emergency Economic Stabilization Act of 2008, Public Law 110–343. The Act was signed into law on 3 October 2008.

11 *Ibid.*

12 The White House 'President Bush discusses Emergency Economic Stabilization Act of 2008', 3 October 2008, available from http://georgewbush-whitehouse.archives.gov/news/releases/2008/10/20081003-11.html, accessed 5 August 2013.

major banks'.[13] The initial proposal was published in September 2008,[14] and supported by draft legislation that would allow the Department of Treasury to borrow money to purchase mortgage related assets.[15] This proposal has been referred to as the 'Paulson Plan',[16] which consisted of a mere three pages of text that totalled 849 words, requesting $700bn of government funding.[17] The then Secretary of the Department of Treasury, Henry Paulson, 'called congressional leaders together and told them that it was imperative that they provide him with a $700bn bailout fund to purchase the toxic assets of the nation's banks, or else there would be an economic meltdown'.[18] This part of the proposal was described as 'the most significant economic intervention by the federal government in the financial system since the Great Depression'.[19] The proposal was extremely controversial because it would mean that the '[Department of Treasury] secretary's purchasing decisions would be final, and not subject to judicial review … Paulson apparently believed that by purchasing mortgage-related assets, the government would help reduce uncertainty about banks' balance sheets, allowing them to borrow if they turned out

[13] Scott, H. 'A general evaluation of the Dodd–Frank US financial reform legislation' (2010) Journal of International Banking Law and Regulation, 25(10), 477–480, at 477.

[14] A full text of the proposal can be accessed from the New York Times 'Text of draft proposal for bailout plan', 20 September 2008, available from http://www.nytimes.com/2008/09/21/business/21draftcnd.html, accessed 7 August 2013.

[15] Posner, E. and Vermeule, A. 'Crisis governance in the administrative state: 9/11 and the financial meltdown of 2008' (2009) University of Chicago Law Review, Fall, 76, 1613–1681, at 1624.

[16] For an excellent discussion of the Paulson Plan see Veronesi, P. and Zingales, L. 'Paulson's gift', 2008, unpublished working paper, University of Chicago Booth School of Business, available from http://faculty.chicagobooth.edu/brian.barry/igm/P_gift.pdf, accessed 6 August 2013.

[17] Davidoff, S. and Zaring, D. 'Regulation by deal: the government's response to the financial crisis' (2009) Administrative Law Review, Summer, 61, 463–541, at 513.

[18] Murdock, C. 'Why not tell the truth? Deceptive practices and the economic meltdown' (2010) Loyola University Chicago Law Journal, Summer, 41, 801–884, at 852.

[19] Anderberg, K. and Epstein, J. 'Transatlantic developments' (2008) Compliance Officer Bulletin, October, 60, 1–40, at 38.

to be solvent'.[20] The Paulson Plan was described by the New York Times as 'the most incredible powers ever bestowed on one person over the economic and financial life of the nation. It is the financial equivalent of the Patriot Act [2001].'[21] Henry Paulson stated before the US Senate Banking Committee:

> We have proposed a program to remove troubled assets from the system. This troubled asset relief program has to be properly designed for immediate implementation and be sufficiently large to have maximum impact and restore market confidence. It must also protect the taxpayer to the maximum extent possible, and include provisions that ensure transparency and oversight while also ensuring the program can be implemented quickly and run effectively.[22]

The proposal was presented before the US Senate Banking Committee, which completely rebuffed the ideas and described them as undesirable.[23] The Chairman of the Senate Banking Committee, Christopher Dodd, described the proposal as 'not acceptable … stunning and unprecedented in its scope and lack of detail … after reading this proposal, I can only conclude that it is not only our economy that is at risk … but our Constitution'.[24]

TARP is administered by the Office of Financial Stability, a sub-division of the Department of Treasury,[25] which is supported by the

---

[20] Posner and Vermeule above, n 15, at 1624–1625. The lack of judicial oversight of the proposal was regarded as extremely 'controversial'. See Davidoff and Zaring above, n 17, at 515.

[21] Sorkin, A. 'Bailout above the law', 22 September 2009, available from http://www.nytimes.com/2008/09/23/business/23sorkin.html?_r=0, accessed 7 August 2013. As cited in Shah, A. 'Emergency Economic Stabilization Act of 2008' (2009) Harvard Journal on Legislation, Summer, 46, 569–584, at 575.

[22] Department of Treasury 'Testimony by Secretary Henry M. Paulson, Jr. before the Senate Banking Committee on turmoil in US credit markets: recent actions regarding government sponsored entities, investment banks and other financial institutions', 23 September 2008, available from http://www.treasury.gov/press-center/press-releases/Pages/hp1153.aspx, accessed 7 August 2013.

[23] See Isidore, C. 'Bailout plan under fire', 23 September 2008, available from http://money.cnn.com/2008/09/23/news/economy/bailout_hearing/, accessed 7 August 2013.

[24] Lander, M. and Myers, S. 'Buyout plan for Wall Street is a hard sell on Capitol Hill', 23 September 2008, available from http://www.nytimes.com/2008/09/24/business/economy/24fannie.html?_r=1&, accessed 7 August 2013.

[25] For a brief discussion of the Office of Financial Stability see Kelly, J. 'Transparency and bank supervision' (2010) Albany Law Review, 73, 421–446, at 427–429 and Verret, J. 'The bailout through a public choice lens: government

Federal Reserve.[26] TARP was divided into six different programme areas: the US car industry,[27] credit market programmes,[28] investment into AIG,[29] bank investment,[30] the housing market[31] and executive compensation.[32] The scheme allowed the Department of Treasury to purchase bad mortgage related securities which had inhibited the movement and availability of credit.[33] Brewer and Klingenhagen stated that 'the initial

---

controlled corporations as a mechanism for rent transfer' (2010) Seton Hall Law Review, 40, 1521–1579, at 1561.

[26] Duran, C. 'The economic crisis and the role of law in monetary policy: a study of the political and social accountability of the Brazilian Central Bank (Bacen), the European Central Bank (ECB) and the Federal Reserve (Fed)' (2012) Journal of International Banking Law and Regulation, 27(8), 306–317, at 310.

[27] It is interesting to note that the auto industry in the US had received TARP loans prior to the Obama administration via the Chrysler Corporation Loan Guarantee Act 1979. For a brief discussion of the use of TARP with the auto industry under President Barack Obama see Block, C. 'A continuum approach to systemic risk and too-big-to-fail' (2012) Brooklyn Journal of Corporate, Financial and Commercial Law, Spring, 6, 289.

[28] For a more detailed discussion see Department of Treasury 'Credit market programs', n/d, available from http://www.treasury.gov/initiatives/financial-stability/TARP-Programs/credit-market-programs/Pages/default.aspx, accessed 5 August 2013 and Diamant, S. 'Neil Barofsjy's sig tarp: "difficult, rigorous, and independent" oversight of the TARP' (2011) North Carolina Banking Institute, 15, 313–332, at 324.

[29] For a more detailed discussion see Department of Treasury 'Investment in American International Group (AIG)', n/d, available from http://www.treasury.gov/initiatives/financial-stability/TARP-Programs/aig/Pages/default.aspx, accessed 5 August 2013.

[30] For a more detailed discussion see Department of Treasury 'Bank investment programs', n/d, available from http://www.treasury.gov/initiatives/financial-stability/TARP-Programs/bank-investment-programs/Pages/default.aspx, accessed 5 August 2013.

[31] For a more detailed discussion see Department of Treasury 'Executive compensation', n/d available from http://www.treasury.gov/initiatives/financial-stability/TARP-Programs/executive-comp/Pages/default.aspx, accessed 5 August 2013.

[32] Department of Treasury 'TARP programs', n/d, available from http://www.treasury.gov/initiatives/financial-stability/TARP-Programs/Pages/default.aspx, accessed 5 August 2013.

[33] Johnson, A. 'Bush signs $700 billion financial bailout bill', 3 October 2013, available from http://www.nbcnews.com/id/26987291/ns/business-stocks_and_economy/t/bush-signs-billion-financial-bailout-bill/, accessed 5 August 2013. Ghosh and Mohamed took the view that 'TARP was originally intended to be a lending programme and one that would increase liquidity by encouraging

participation in the TARP was essentially mandated by the Treasury Department to the largest banks in the US, in the hope of restoring confidence in the banking system and the markets'.[34] This was a view supported by Goddard *et al*, who stated that 'TARP was quickly adapted into a vehicle for public-funded bank recapitalizations, including the Bank of America and Citigroup.'[35] The Department of Treasury was granted a great deal of flexibility in determining how the TARP funds were to be allocated.[36] Therefore, it was unsurprising that a detailed and rigorous administrative regime was introduced to ensure its effective management. The administrative regime included the creation of the Office of Special Inspector General, the Financial Stability Oversight Board, Comptroller General and the Congressional Oversight Panel.[37] Additionally, those financial institutions that benefited from TARP were also required to adhere to a strict set of compliance regulations.[38] TARP has been described as being 'instrumental in stabilizing the financial system and setting the foundation for economic recovery'.[39] Nonetheless, it is unsurprising, given the amount of funding provided and the flexibility granted to the Department of Treasury, that its effectiveness has been questioned.[40] For example, one of the most controversial and damning indictments of TARP was its *favourable* treatment of financial executives in rescued banks.[41] The TARP Standards for Compensation

---

the flow of credit between the banks and from banks to customers'. See Ghosh, S. and Mohamed, S. 'The troubled asset relief program (TARP) and its limitations: an analysis' (2010) International Journal of Law and Management, 52(2), 124–143, at 125.

[34] Brewer, E. and Klingenhagen, A. 'Be careful what you wish for: the stock market reactions to bailing out large financial institutions: evidence from the USA' (2010) Journal of Financial Regulation and Compliance, 16(1), 56–69, at 57.

[35] Goddard, J., Molyneux, P. and Wilson, J. 'The financial crisis in Europe: evolution, policy responses and lessons for the future' (2009) Journal of Financial Regulation and Compliance, 17(4), 362–380, at 371.

[36] Lin, D. 'Bank recapitalizations: a comparative perspective' (2013) Harvard Journal on Legislation, Summer, 50, 513–544, at 513.

[37] Ghosh and Mohamed above, n 33, at 128–130.

[38] For a more detailed discussion see Hausemann, Y. and Bechtold-Orth, E. 'Changing remuneration systems in Europe and the United States: a legal analysis of recent developments in the wake of the financial crisis' (2010) European Business Organization Law Review, 11(2), 195–229, at 209–210.

[39] Lin above, n 36, at 513.

[40] Ghosh and Mohamed above, n 33, at 131–135.

[41] For an excellent discussion of this issue see Chason, E. 'The uneasy case for deferring banker pay' (2013) Louisiana Law Review, Summer, 73, 923–977

and Corporate Governance seek to impose limits on the amount of compensation and to stop inducements for senior executive officers (SEOs) to take ill-advised or unnecessary risks that endanger the TARP recipient.[42] For example, this includes a provision that permits the recovery of any 'bonus, retention award, or incentive compensation paid to a SEO or the next twenty most highly compensated employees based on materially inaccurate statements of earnings, revenues, gains, or other criteria'.[43] Additionally, there is a ban on making 'golden parachute payments to a SEO or any of the next five most highly compensated employees'.[44]

It is important to note that the original version of TARP used by President George Bush has been amended since the election of President Barack Obama. The 'Financial Stability Plan' permitted Timothy Geithner, the then Secretary of the Department of Treasury, to determine how to spend $350bn of TARP funding.[45] At the launch of the Financial Stability Plan, Timothy Geithner stated that 'we are establishing three new programs to clean up and strengthen the nation's banks, bring in private capital to restart lending, and to go around the banking system

---

and Krawiec, K. 'Financial reform during the Great Recession: Dodd–Frank, executive compensation, and the Card Act – don't screw Joe the plumber: the sausage-making of financial reform' (2013) Arizona Law Review, Spring, 55, 53–103. Also see Emergency Economic Stabilization Act 2008, s. 111 and Hausemann and Bechtold-Orth above, n 38, at 210.

42 Department of Treasury '31 CFR Part 30 RIN 1505–AC09 TARP standards for compensation and corporate governance' 28394 Federal Register, Vol. 74, No. 113, 15 June 2009/Rules and Regulations, available from http://www.gpo.gov/fdsys/pkg/FR-2009-06-15/pdf/E9-13868.pdf, accessed 6 August 2013. For a more detailed discussion of this issue see Kennedy, K. 'Excessive executive compensation: prior federal attempts to curb perceived abuses' (2010) Houston Business and Tax Law Journal, 10, 196–261.

43 Department of Treasury, *ibid.*

44 *Ibid.* According to Lee the Emergency Economic and Emergency Stabilization Act 'banned "golden parachutes" and disallowed tax reductions for executives whose annual compensation exceeds $500,000 and whose companies received financial aid through the Troubled Asset Relief Programme'. See Lee, J. 'Regulatory regimes and norms for directors' remuneration: EU, UK and Belgian law compared' (2012) European Business Organization Law Review, 13(4), 599–637, at 617–618.

45 This has been referred to as 'the revised plan under the Obama administration to alleviate continuing distress in the US financial sector'. See Stutts, W. and Watts, W. 'Of herring and sausage: nordic responses to banking crises as examples for the United States' (2009) Texas International Law Journal, Summer, 44, 577–627, at 618.

directly to the markets that consumers and businesses depend on'.[46] The Financial Stability Plan had four objectives. First, to provide funding for banks via the Financial Stability Fund. Secondly, an 'aggregator bank' would accept damaged assets from failing banks. Thirdly, the Term Asset-Backed Securities Loan Facility would be broadened. Fourthly, a new system would be created to alter foreclosure procedures.[47] However, its main objective was to infuse $250bn of capital via taxpayers' money into the foremost US banks.[48] This was to be established in three steps. First, the government required banks to undertake a stress test that would result in the balance sheets of banks being sturdier.[49] The second part would see the creation of a Public–Private Investment Fund that would offer both funding and capital that could be utilised to influence 'private capital to help get private markets working again'.[50] Thirdly, the government agreed to provide $1tn to support the Consumer and Business Lending Initiative that was aimed at supporting the secondary lending markets.[51] In essence, the Geithner plan intended to foster private investors and private capital to purchase toxic assets.[52]

4.2.3 Housing and Economic Recovery Act 2008

Another legislative measure introduced by President George Bush was the Housing and Economic Recovery Act 2008.[53] This Act had two very important objectives: to improve the levels of regulation for Fannie Mae and Freddie Mac and to provide additional funding to prevent the

---

[46] Department of Treasury 'Secretary Geithner introduces financial stability plan', 2 October 2009, available from http://www.treasury.gov/press-center/press-releases/Pages/tg18.aspx, accessed 7 August 2013.

[47] See Stutts and Watts above, n 45, at 618–619.

[48] Brewer and Klingenhagen above, n 34, at 57.

[49] Department of Treasury above, n 46. For a brief discussion of stress testing in the US see Abramovich, A. 'Comparative analysis of stress testing in the United States and Europe' (2011) North Carolina Banking Institute, March, 15, 333–353.

[50] *Ibid.*

[51] Department of Treasury above, n 46. This measure could be divided into two parts: the legal loan programme and the legacy securities programme. See Murdock above, n 18, at 874.

[52] Ghosh and Mohamed above, n 33, at 136.

[53] Pub. L. No. 110–289, 122 Stat. 2654 (2008). For an excellent and detailed commentary on the Act see Novogradac, M. and Graff, G. 'Impact of the Housing and Economic Recovery Act of 2008 on current and future low-income housing tax credit properties' (2008) Journal of Affordable Housing, 18(1), 47–70.

foreclosure of properties.[54] The first objective was to be achieved by replacing the Office of Federal Housing Enterprise Oversight with the Federal Housing Finance Agency.[55] Reiss stated that the Federal Housing Finance Agency 'has general regulatory authority over Fannie and Freddie as well as the Federal Home Loan Banks … it has been granted significantly more power'.[56] Additionally, the Housing and Economic Recovery Act 2008 provided the Department of Treasury with the ability to assist Fannie Mae and Freddie Mac if they faced insolvency.[57] The Housing and Economic Recovery Act 2008 provided $300bn for 'foreclosure prevention'.[58] However, the appropriateness of granting yet more additional funding has been questioned by several commentators.[59]

4.2.4 American Recovery and Reinvestment Act 2009

The foundations of the legislative responses from President Barack Obama are to be found in the publication of a White Paper that contained proposals to reform the US system of financial regulation.[60] The White Paper 'laid out a framework which later became the basis for the Dodd–Frank financial reform legislation, and which included a proposal

---

[54] Reiss, D. 'The role of the Fannie Mae/Freddie Mac duopoly in the American housing market' (2009) Journal of Financial Regulation and Compliance, 17(3), 336–348, at 340.

[55] *Ibid.* The objective of the Office of Federal Housing Enterprise Oversight was to 'ensure the capital adequacy and financial safety and soundness of two government sponsored enterprises, Fannie Mae and Freddie Mac'. See Nikolić, B. 'Rise and fall of regulatory state in financial markets' (2013) Journal of International Banking Law and Regulation, 28(1), 1–8, at 4.

[56] Reiss, D. 'Fannie Mae and Freddie Mac and the future of federal housing finance policy: a study of regulatory privilege' (2010) Alabama Law Review, 61, 907–955, at 919. Also see Hurley, C. 'Paying the price for too big to fail' (2010) Entrepreneurial Business Law Journal, 4, 349–387, at 359–360.

[57] Ibid.

[58] Mason, H. 'No one saw it coming – again systemic risk and state foreclosure proceedings: why a national uniform foreclosure law is necessary' (2012) University of Miami Law Review, Fall, 67, 41–93, at 58. Also see Fairfax above, n 5, at 1591.

[59] See for example Emerson, C. 'A troubled house of cards: examining how the Housing and Economic Recovery Act of 2008 fails to resolve the foreclosure crisis' (2008) Oklahoma Law Review, 61, 561–584.

[60] Department of Treasury *Financial regulatory reform – a new foundation: rebuilding financial supervision and regulation* (Department of Treasury: London, 2009).

for a new consumer financial protection agency'.[61] Bunting stated that the White Paper made 'significant and comprehensive regulatory reform [proposals] in response to what it identified as the most severe financial crisis since the Great Depression'.[62] President Barack Obama stated that:

> It is an indisputable fact that one of the most significant contributors to our economic downturn was an unraveling of major financial institutions and the lack of adequate regulatory structures to prevent abuse and excess. A culture of irresponsibility took root from Wall Street to Washington to Main Street. And a regulatory regime basically crafted in the wake of a 20th century economic crisis, the Great Depression, was overwhelmed by the speed, scope, and sophistication of a 21st century global economy … meanwhile, executive compensation, unmoored from long-term performance or even reality, rewarded recklessness rather than responsibility. And this wasn't just the failure of individuals; this was a failure of the entire system. The actions of many firms escaped scrutiny. In some cases, the dealings of these institutions were so complex and opaque that few inside or outside these companies understood what was happening. Where there were gaps in the rules, regulators lacked the authority to take action. Where there were overlaps, regulators lacked accountability for their inaction … with the reforms we're proposing today, we seek to put in place rules that will allow our markets to promote innovation while discouraging abuse.[63]

The White Paper contained five objectives: to promote an effective and robust supervision system for financial firms;[64] to create a comprehensive

---

[61] Zywicki, T. 'The Consumer Financial Protection Bureau: savior or menace?' (2013) George Washington Law Review, April, 81, 856–928, at 860.

[62] Bunting, W. 'The trouble with investment banks: cluelessness, not greed' (2011) San Diego Law Review, Summer, 48, 993–1073, at 995.

[63] The White House 'President Obama announces financial regulation reform', 18 June 2009, available from http://www.whitehouse.gov/video/President-Obama-Announces-Financial-Regulation-Reform/#transcript, accessed 6 August 2013. The White Paper correctly asserted that 'while this crisis had many causes, it is clear now that the government could have done more to prevent many of these problems from growing out of control and threatening the stability of our financial system. Gaps and weaknesses in the supervision and regulation of financial firms presented challenges to our government's ability to monitor, prevent, or address risks as they built up in the system. No regulator saw its job as protecting the economy and financial system as a whole.' See Department of Treasury above, n 60, at 2.

[64] In order to achieve the first objective, the Department of Treasury proposed to establish a Financial Services Oversight Council that would be tasked with attempting to recognise developing systemic risks and to improve cooperation between regulatory bodies. FSOC was created by Title I of the

supervision system of the financial markets;[65] to safeguard and protect consumers from financial abuse;[66] to provide the government with the tools it needs to manage financial crises;[67] and to improve international regulatory standards and to thus harmonise levels of international cooperation.[68]

The publication of the White Paper was soon followed by the introduction of the American Recovery and Reinvestment Act 2009.[69] The Act had three objectives, to 'create new jobs and save existing ones, to spur economic activity and invest in long-term growth and foster unprecedented levels of accountability and transparency in government spending'.[70] The Act is an integral part of President Barack Obama's 'economic stimulus plan'[71] and became the cornerstone of the President's

---

Dodd–Frank Wall Street Reform and Consumer Protection Act 2010. Its main objective is to 'identify risks and respond to emerging threats to financial stability'. See Department of Treasury 'Financial Stability Oversight Council – about FSOC', n/d, available from http://www.treasury.gov/initiatives/fsoc/about/Pages/default.aspx, accessed 23 September 2013.

65 In order to establish comprehensive supervision of financial markets the Department of Treasury proposed improved regulation of the securitisation markets, complete regulation of over-the-counter derivatives, and an extension of the regulatory remit of the Federal Reserve to administer payment, clearing and settlement systems. See Department of Treasury above, n 60, at 3.

66 To ensure the Department of Treasury could protect consumers and investors from financial abuse it proposed a series of measures that included the creation of a new Consumer Financial Protection Agency, a set of robust and durable regulations that will increase not only the levels of transparency but also fairness.

67 The fourth objective would be achieved by creating and implementing a new system to resolve non-bank financial institutions whose collapse might have serious universal effects.

68 The final goal would be achieved by 'international reforms to support our efforts at home, including strengthening the capital framework; improving oversight of global financial markets; coordinating supervision of internationally active firms; and enhancing crisis management tools'. See Department of Treasury above, n 60, at 3–4. For a more detailed discussion of these objectives see Walker, G. 'US regulatory reform' (2009) Journal of Banking Regulation, 11(1), 1–5.

69 Moye, J. 'Are we bulletproof? A defensive business strategy to protect health care companies from False Claims Act litigation and corporate integrity agreements' (2010) University of Baltimore Law Forum, Fall, 41, 24–42, at 29.

70 Recovery.gov 'The Recovery Act', n/d, available from http://www.recovery.gov/about/pages/the_act.aspx, accessed 8 August 2012.

71 Prior, I. and Skehill, L. 'Beware the federal government bearing gifts: how the American Recovery and Reinvestment Act of 2009 could become a

'stimulus package designed to jumpstart the economy'.[72] On signing the Act, President Barack Obama stated that the legislation was 'an investment package designed to provide a necessary boost to our economy in these difficult times and to create jobs, restore economic growth'.[73]

4.2.5 Fraud Enforcement and Recovery Act 2009

The clearest indicator of the link between white collar crime and the financial crisis was the introduction of the Fraud Enforcement and Recovery Act 2009.[74] This legislation was a *direct* response to white collar crime that 'contributed to the … economic collapse'.[75] Reidy went so far as to suggest that the Fraud Enforcement and Recovery Act 2009 was a reaction to what he described as 'economic calamity … ostensibly combating the type of chronic misconduct which may have helped foster economic instability rather than merely combating the acute symptoms of such instability'.[76] The Act was also viewed as a 'broad-based anti-fraud measure, designed to create more tools to prosecute fraud at all levels' and to 'help protect Americans from future frauds that exploit the economic assistance programs intended to restore and rebuild [the] economy'.[77] The Act was signed into law by President Barack Obama on 20 May 2009, and prior to signing the Act, he stated:

---

whistleblowing trojan horse' (2010) Suffolk University Law Review, 43, 565–586, at 566.

[72] Lewis, K. 'Rebuilding a house of cards: envisioning sustainable housing policy housing' (2009) Washington University Journal of Law and Policy, 35, 473–517, at 500.

[73] The White House 'Memorandum for the heads of executive departments and agencies', 20 March 2009, available from http://www.whitehouse.gov/the_press_office/Memorandum-for-the-Heads-of-Executive-Departments-and-Agencies-3-20-09/, accessed 7 August 2013. For a detailed discussion of the benefits of this legislation see The White House *Annual report to the President on progress implementing the American Recovery and Reinvestment Act of 2009* (The White House: Washington DC, 2010).

[74] Pub. L. No. 111–21, 123 Stat. 1617 (2009).

[75] Lover, C. 'The Fraud Enforcement and Recovery Act of 2009 and the expansion of the liability under the False Claims Act' (2012) Utah Law Review, 1129–1154, at 1129. Also see Dooley, D. and Radke, M. 'Does severe punishment deter financial crimes?' (2010) Charleston Law Review, Spring, 4, 619–659, at 639. This was a view supported by Moye above, n 69, at 29.

[76] Reidy, J. 'The problem of proceeds in the era of FERA' (2010) American Journal of Criminal Law, Summer, 5, 295–323, at 318.

[77] Lover above, n 75, at 1129. Also see Riley, C. and Johnston, J. 'Fraud Enforcement and Recovery Act of 2009: expanding fraud and False Claims Act

> Last year, the Treasury Department received 62,000 reports of mortgage fraud … the number of criminal mortgage fraud investigations opened by the FBI has more than doubled over the past three years. And yet, the federal government's ability to investigate and prosecute these frauds is severely hindered by outdated laws and a lack of resources. And that's why this bill nearly doubles the FBI's mortgage and financial fraud program, allowing it to better target fraud … That's why it provides the resources necessary for other law enforcement and federal agencies, from the Department of Justice to the SEC to the Secret Service, to pursue these criminals, bring them to justice … it's also why it expands Department of Justice's authority to prosecute fraud that takes place in many of the private institutions not covered under current federal bank fraud criminal statutes – institutions where more than half of all subprime mortgages came from as recently as four years ago.[78]

The Act contained five important provisions. First, it provided a significant increase in the funding for the Department of Justice and FBI to combat fraud.[79] Baer noted that 'over a two-year period, [the Act] authorized the injection of an additional $500m [to agencies] with jurisdiction over crimes ostensibly related to the financial crisis'.[80] The additional funding resulted in an increase in the number of appointed fraud related prosecutors and investigators.[81] The Department of Justice welcomed the additional funding and stated that the Act granted them essential 'further resources to increase the scope of our collective enforcement response'.[82] Secondly, the Fraud Enforcement and Recovery Act made some important amendments to fraud and money laundering

---

liability and increasing enforcement in the wake of the economic crisis' (2009) Banking and Financial Services Policy Report, July, 28(7), 1–7.

[78] President Barack Obama 'Protecting homeowners, protecting the economy', 24 August 2009, available from http://www.whitehouse.gov/blog/Protecting-Homeowners-Protecting-the-Economy, accessed 20 June 2013.

[79] It is of interest to note that this decision by President Barack Obama can be contrasted with the stance of President George Bush, who ignored requests from the FBI for additional funding to tackle fraud in 2004. For a more detailed discussion see Chapter 2. It has been estimated that the Act provided law enforcement agencies with an additional $500m to tackle fraud associated with the financial crisis. See Titolo, M. 'Retroactivity and the Fraud Enforcement and Recovery Act of 2009' (2011) Indiana Law Journal, Winter, 257–302, at 259.

[80] Baer, M. 'Choosing punishment' (2012) Boston University Law Review, March, 92, 577–640, at 607.

[81] Valukas above, n 1, at 13.

[82] United States Department of Justice 'Statement of Assistant Attorney General for the Criminal Division Lanny A. Breuer before the Senate Committee on the Judiciary', 26 January 2011, available from http://www.justice.gov/criminal/pr/testimony/2011/crm-testimony-110126.html, accessed June 2013.

legislation.[83] Thirdly, the Act increased the penalties for those convicted of mortgage fraud.[84] The significance of enhancing the penalties for mortgage fraud was supported by the chief sponsor of the Fraud Enforcement and Recovery Act, Senator Patrick Leahy, who stated: 'I want to not only get the people who did it, but I want to deter others from doing it in the future.'[85] He added that the mortgage industry acted dishonestly and 'are creating economic havoc and I want to make sure that we're able to go after them. I want to see people prosecuted … Frankly, I want to see them go to jail.'[86] Fourthly, the Act extended the definition of financial institutions to include private mortgage lending businesses and mortgage brokers.[87] Fifthly, the Fraud Enforcement and Recovery Act 2009 increased the supervision of TARP.[88] Additionally, the Act contained measures to tackle healthcare fraud,[89] it established the Financial Crisis Inquiry Commission,[90] extended the protection afforded

---

[83] This was specifically targeted at financial fraud and mortgage fraud. See McCann, N. 'Federal law enforcement in the home mortgage lending market enhanced by the Fraud Enforcement and Recovery Act of 2009' (2010) Loyola Consumer Law Review, 22, 354–390, at 355. For example, the Act imposes liability upon 'any person who … knowingly makes, uses, or causes to be made or used, a false record or statement material to a false or fraudulent claim'. See Tschoepe, J. 'A fraud against one is apparently a fraud against all: the Fraud Enforcement and Recovery Act's unprecedented expansion of liability under the False Claims Act' (2010) Houston Law Review, Fall, 47, 741–778, at 759.

[84] McCann noted that 'the penalties are enhanced by FERA's amendments to existing statutory law … the penalties for crimes affecting a "financial institution" as defined by section 20 carries an increased penalty under the mail, wire, and bank fraud statutes. Under the mail, wire, and bank fraud statutes, the penalty increases to a maximum of $1,000,000, and a maximum prison sentence of thirty years'. *Ibid.*, at 375. Also see 18 U.S.C. §§ 1341 and 18 U.S.C. §§ 1343, 1344.

[85] 155 Cong. Rec. S4531-01 (daily ed. 22 April 2009) (statement of Sen. Leahy), as cited in McCann above, n 83, at 378.

[86] 155 Cong. Rec. S2316 (daily ed. 13 February 2009) (statement of Patrick Leahy).

[87] Financial institutions were originally defined by 18 U.S.C. § 20(1) (2006).

[88] Lover above, n 75, at 1129.

[89] Moye, J. 'Let's put the fear in the FERA! Suggestions to make the Fraud Enforcement and Recovery Act of 2009 a strong fraud deterrent' (2011) Southern Illinois University Law Journal, Spring, 35, 421–432.

[90] See Titolo above, n 79, at 259.

to fraud related whistleblowers[91] and amended the False Claims Act 1986.[92] The False Claims Act now permits the government and private parties the ability to recuperate money that has been lost to fraud. This measure has become one of the most significant anti-fraud devices utilised by the government in civil fraud cases.[93]

The Fraud Enforcement and Recovery Act 2009 was welcomed by the Department of Justice, which stated that it 'would provide federal investigators and prosecutors with significant new tools and resources, both civil and criminal, with which to combat mortgage fraud, securities and commodities fraud and related offenses'.[94] McCann concluded that:

> the overall effect of the statutory enhancements and resources that FERA provides to federal law enforcement will be to more effectively police the home mortgage market. As a result of the federal government's commitment to preventing fraud, mortgage lending, investment in the lending market, and the ability of consumers to obtain housing, will be more secure.[95]

Despite the obvious merits of the Act, it has been criticised. For example, it has been asserted that the provisions amount to a rash and hasty response to the financial crisis.[96] Lowell argued that politicians have bowed to pressure from consumer groups and turned towards criminal law provisions.[97] The scope of the Act has been questioned by Valukas, who stated that merely providing additional funding and increasing the

---

[91] Donnini, G. 'White collar fraud investigations leading lawyers on analyzing recent trends, building a defense strategy, and developing compliance programs analyzing recent fraud trends' (2009) Aspatore, November, 1–12, at 4.

[92] For a detailed discussion of this see Handwerker, J., Solomon, M., Davar, M. and Harne, K. 'Congress declares checkmate: how the Fraud Enforcement and Recovery Act of 2009 strengthens the Civil False Claims Act and counters the courts' (2010) Journal of Business and Technology Law, 5, 295–323.

[93] See Titolo above, n 79, at 259.

[94] United States Department of Justice 'Letter to The Honorable Patrick J. Leahy Chairman, Committee on the Judiciary', 1 April 2009, available from http://www.justice.gov/ola/views-letters/111-1/040109-s386-fraud-enforcement-recovery-act.pdf, accessed 20 June 2013. Also see United States Department of Justice 'Statement of Lanny A. Breuer, Assistant Attorney General before the United States Senate Committee on the Judiciary', 22 September 2010, available from http://www.justice.gov/ola/testimony/111-2/09-22-10-breuer-financial-fraud.pdf, accessed 20 June 2013.

[95] McCann above, n 83, at 378–379.

[96] *Ibid.*, at 377.

[97] See for example Lowell, A. and Arnold, K. 'Corporate crime after 2000: a new law enforcement challenge or déjà vu?' (2003) American Criminal Law Review, Spring, 40, 219–240 and Moohr, G. 'The balance among corporate

number of fraud related prosecutions do not go far enough.[98] Moye stated that the Act 'does not go far enough to eradicate fraudulent claims submitted to the government and its programs. Clearly, the law attempts to tie up loose ends from the financial crisis, but it could go further to send a message to those violating the law.'[99] Nonetheless, the Fraud Enforcement and Recovery Act 2009 represents an attempt by President Barack Obama to redress some of the imbalances created by President George Bush, who wrongly prioritised the 'War on Terror' at the expense of mortgage fraud. The Act has allowed the Department of Justice and FBI, as will be outlined later in this chapter, to pursue white collar criminals who have contributed towards the financial crisis. This is demonstrated by the significant increase in mortgage fraud convictions and ongoing investigations by the FBI.

4.2.6 Dodd–Frank Wall Street Reform Act 2012

> In the fall of 2008, a financial crisis of a scale and severity not seen in generations left millions of Americans unemployed and resulted in trillions in lost wealth. Our broken financial regulatory system was a principal cause of that crisis. It was fragmented, antiquated, and allowed large parts of the financial system to operate with little or no oversight. And it allowed some irresponsible lenders to use hidden fees and fine print to take advantage of consumers.[100]

It is against this economic background that the most significant of legislative reforms was introduced by President Barack Obama: the Dodd–Frank Wall Street Reform and Consumer Protection Act 2010. The Act has been described by one commentator as 'the most sweeping

---

criminal liability, private civil suits, and regulatory enforcement' (2009) American Criminal Law Review, Fall, 46, 1459–1479.

[98] Valukas above, n 1, at 13. It is important to note that similar pieces of legislation were introduced to tackle white collar crime following the Savings and Loans Crisis. For a more detailed discussion of both of these issues see Zimring, F. and Hawkins, G. 'Crime, justice and the savings and loans crisis' (1993) Crime and Justice, 18, 247–288; Bailey, S. 'Chopping at the roots: a proposal to change the focus of criminal laws dealing with savings and loans fraud' (1997) American Journal of Criminal Law, Spring, 24, 401–439; and Green, M. 'After the fall: the criminal law enforcement response to the S&L crisis' (1991) Fordham Law Review, May, 59, 155–192.

[99] Moye above, n 89, at 429.

[100] The White House 'Wall Street reform: the Dodd–Frank Act', n/d, available from http://www.whitehouse.gov/economy/middle-class/dodd-frank-wall-street-reform, accessed 3 August 2013.

financial regulation passed in recent history [that] reflects the most substantial change to financial regulation since the 1930s'.[101] The Act, signed by President Obama in July 2010, is the 'centrepiece of the post-crisis financial regulation reform in the United States'.[102] President Barack Obama stated that:

> Over the past two years, we have faced the worst recession since the Great Depression. Eight million people lost their jobs. Tens of millions saw the value of their homes and retirement savings plummet. Countless businesses have been unable to get the loans they need and many have been forced to shut their doors. And although the economy is growing again, too many people are still feeling the pain of the downturn … while a number of factors led to such a severe recession, the primary cause was a breakdown in our financial system. It was a crisis born of a failure of responsibility from certain corners of Wall Street to the halls of power in Washington. For years, our financial sector was governed by antiquated and poorly enforced rules that allowed some to game the system and take risks that endangered the entire economy … unscrupulous lenders locked consumers into complex loans with hidden costs. Firms like AIG placed massive, risky bets with borrowed money. And while the rules left abuse and excess unchecked, they also left taxpayers on the hook if a big bank or financial institution ever failed. With this law, we'll crack down on abusive practices in the mortgage industry.[103]

The purpose of the legislation was to 'promote the financial stability of the United States by improving accountability and transparency in the financial system, to end "too big to fail", to protect the American taxpayer by ending bailouts, to protect consumers from abusive financial services practices, and for other purposes'.[104] The Dodd–Frank Wall Street Reform Act, at 848 pages in length, is one of the most detailed banking legislative reforms ever drafted. For example, the Act amended numerous areas of law and contained between 200 and 300 rule marking

---

[101] Grinshteyn, A. 'Horseshoes and hand grenades: the Dodd–Frank Act's (almost) attack on credit rating agencies' (2011) Hofstra Law Review, Summer, 39, 937–978, at 938.

[102] Omarova, S. 'The Dodd–Frank Act: a new deal for a new age?' (2011) North Carolina Banking Institute, March, 15, 83–98, at 83.

[103] The White House 'Remarks by the President at signing of Dodd–Frank Wall Street Reform and Consumer Protection Act', 21 July 2010, available from http://www.whitehouse.gov/the-press-office/remarks-president-signing-dodd-frank-wall-street-reform-and-consumer-protection-act, accessed 3 August 2012.

[104] Pub. L. No. 111–203, 124 Stat. 1376.

provisions.[105] The sheer size, length and scope of the Act 'put this piece of legislation in a class of its own'.[106] The Dodd–Frank Wall Street Reform Act 2010 introduced measures to, *inter alia*, 'alter the regulation of banks by the SEC, create a council of regulators to observe economic hazards, establish a new supervisory body to regulate consumer financial products, measures aimed at protecting whistle-blower protections and improve levels of shareholder protection'.[107] In relation to the regulation of banks, the Act established a plethora of new agencies, including the Council of Federal Regulators, the Financial Stability Oversight Council and the Consumer Financial Protection Bureau. The Act also abolished the Office of Thrift Supervision, which was merged into the Office of the Comptroller of the Currency.[108]

The reforms contained in the Dodd–Frank Wall Street Reform Act have been heavily criticised.[109] For example, they have been described as 'being invited to dinner and [only] served pictures of food',[110] and that 'it [the Dodd–Frank Act] may prove as ineffective as the Maginot Line'.[111] Furthermore, it has been suggested that the Act is not a 'Rooseveltian legislative milestone ... amid the hype and back-slapping ... the sad reality is that Dodd–Frank fails to address the fundamental problems that resulted in the sub-prime fiasco'.[112] The Dodd–Frank Wall Street Act has

---

105 See K&L Gates 'Financial services reform alert: Dodd Frank next steps', 16 August 2010, available from http://www.klgates.com/dodd-frank-next-steps-08-16-2010/, accessed 3 August 2013, as cited in Grinshteyn above, n 101, at 938.

106 Omarova above, n 102, at 85.

107 Luhrs, J. 'Encouraging litigation: why Dodd–Frank goes too far in eliminating the procedural difficulties in Sarbanes–Oxley' (2012) Hastings Business Law Journal, Winter, 8, 175–189, at 175–176.

108 Krawiec above, n 41, at 54.

109 Cooper, H. 'Obama signs overhaul of financial system', 21 July 2010, available from http://www.nytimes.com/2010/07/22/business/22regulate.html?_r=0, accesssed 3 August 2013.

110 Henry, J. and Kotlikoff, L. 'Financial reform, R.I.P.', 15 July 2010, available from http://www.forbes.com/2010/07/15/dodd-frank-failure-regulation-opinions-contributors-james-henry-laurence-kotlikoff-wall-street.html, accessed 3 August 2013.

111 Ramirez, S. 'Dodd–Frank as maginot line' (2011) Chapman Law Review, Spring, 15, 109–132, at 109. For a detailed and excellent critique of the Dodd–Frank Act see Wilmarth Jr, A. 'The Dodd–Frank Act: a flawed and inadequate response to the too-big-to-fail problem' (2011) Oregon Law Review, 89, 951–1057.

112 Halligan, L. 'Obama signs a bill that lets banks have US over a barrel once more', 26 July 2010, available from http://www.telegraph.co.uk/finance/

also been referred to as a short-term measure and while it may be able to 'prevent another subprime crisis, it will prove *unable* [author's emphasis] to prevent a future, more serious debt crisis'.[113] This was a view supported by McDonnel, who stated that the legislation 'will not end financial crises forever. But if the regulations are largely well done, they may postpone the next big crisis and make it both shorter and less severe when it does occur.'[114] The Act was condemned by one commentator as a 'plausible collection of cowardly interventions'.[115] Furthermore, the Act has also attracted complaints from commentators because of its weak approach towards the regulation of derivatives and because it does not give shareholders sufficient protection.[116]

4.3 REGULATORY AND LAW ENFORCEMENT RESPONSE

The regulatory response in the US has been heavily influenced by the introduction of legislation that specifically acknowledged the link between the financial crisis and white collar crime. This led to the creation of *another* task force, the Financial Fraud Enforcement Task Force, to tackle white collar crime emanating from the financial crisis. The responses of the SEC, FBI, Department of Justice and the CFTC are now judiciously appraised.

---

comment/liamhalligan/7908516/Obama-signs-a-bill-that-lets-banks-have-US-over-a-barrel-once-more.html, accessed 3 August 2013.

113 Ramirez above, n 111, at 110.

114 McDonnel, B. 'Don't panic! Defending cowardly interventions during and after the financial crisis' (2011) Penn State Law Review, Summer, 116, 1–75, at 5. Also see Murdock, C. 'The Dodd–Frank Wall Street Reform and Consumer Protection Act: what caused the financial crisis and will Dodd–Frank prevent future crises?' (2011) SMU Law Review, Fall, 64, 1243–1327.

115 *Ibid.*, at 3.

116 Nemeroff, M. 'Dodd–Frank: frankly an inefficient form of corporate governance' (2012) University of Florida Journal of Law and Public Policy, December, 23, 431–445, at 439–440.

4.3.1 Securities and Exchange Commission

> For years, traders in the financial markets stood more risk of getting struck by lightning on the golf course than they did of being arrested for swapping a few share tips on the same fairways.[117]

The SEC was established as a result of the Wall Street Crash and Great Depression and was initially designed to act as an 'economic watchdog'.[118] Its mission is to 'protect investors, maintain fair, orderly, and efficient markets, and facilitate capital formation'.[119] The SEC is 'responsible for the enforcement and regulation of the US and securities market … it is charged with regulating all companies that hold and trade public stock'.[120] The most pertinent part of the SEC for this chapter is its Division of Enforcement, which was established in August 1972. It is important to note that during this decade the SEC became more involved and committed to enforcing the provisions of the Securities Act 1933 and the Securities Exchange Act 1934.[121] The Division of Enforcement undertakes investigations for alleged breaches of securities legislation and prosecutes the SEC's civil suits.[122] Common remedies pursued include injunctions, financial penalties and the suspension or prohibition of people acting in certain positions.[123] The SEC is also permitted to provide compensation for the victims of fraud[124] and generate administrative proceedings before an SEC Administrative Law Judge. There are

---

[117] Lynn, M. 'UK crackdown on insider trading masks bigger problems', 4 April 2010, at 3, as cited in Montagano, C. 'The global crackdown on insider trading: a silver lining to the great recession' (2012) Indiana Journal of Global Legal Studies, 19, 575–598, at 576.

[118] Huynh, D. 'Preemption v. punishment: a comparative study of white collar crime prosecution in the United States and the United Kingdom' (2010) Journal of International Business and Law, Spring, 9, 105–135, at 108.

[119] Securities and Exchange Commission 'The investor's advocate: how the SEC protects investors, maintains market integrity, and facilitates capital formation', n/d, available from http://www.sec.gov/about/whatwedo.shtml, accessed 9 August 2013.

[120] See Huynh above, n 118, at 108.

[121] *Ibid.*, at 109.

[122] *Ibid.*, at 109.

[123] Securities and Exchange Commission 'About the Division of Enforcement', n/d, available from http://www.sec.gov/divisions/enforce/about.htm, accessed 8 August 2013.

[124] Sarbanes–Oxley Act 2002, s. 308. For a more general discussion of compensating the victims of fraud see Evans, A. 'The investor compensation fund' (2007) Journal of Corporation Law, Fall, 33, 233–290.

several different categories of proceedings that the SEC could pursue against wrongdoers, including a cease and desist order, a disgorgement order, the revocation of a licence or registration, or even suspension. The Division of Enforcement seeks to support and advise the SEC in 'executing its law enforcement function by recommending the commencement of investigations of securities law violations, by recommending that the Commission bring civil actions in federal court or as administrative proceedings before an administrative law judge, and by prosecuting these cases on behalf of the Commission'.[125] The SEC investigates a wide range of white collar crime activities, including allegations of misrepresentation, market manipulation, insider trading and selling unregistered securities.[126] From an enforcement perspective, it is very important to note that the SEC has an extensive array of civil enforcement powers, but it has *no* authority to instigate criminal proceedings. As outlined in Chapter 1, the SEC has imposed a record number of financial sanctions since the onset of the financial crisis. However, the effectiveness of these has been questioned. For example, Maher noted that:

> The SEC successfully obtained record settlements from those entities responsible; however, the individuals who are responsible are rarely affected by the settlements. One of the largest penalties paid by an executive to date was the former executive of Countrywide, who personally was ordered to pay $22.5m. Although the settlement is record-breaking for an individual executive, it is minimal to Angelo Mozilo, considering he has earned hundreds of millions of dollars even after Countrywide collapsed. According to reports, he received a total of $521.5m in total compensation from 2000 to 2008, prior to leaving Countrywide.[127]

Huynh took the view that:

> if the SEC staff determines a criminal prosecution is a viable option, they will recommend that the Justice Department pursue criminal proceedings. It is in the Department of Justice's discretion to pursue such criminals and if they do,

---

[125] Securities and Exchange Commission above, n 119.

[126] It is important to note that it was not until the 1980s that the SEC began to tackle insider trading due to the introduction of the Insider Trading Sanctions Act 1984. For a more detailed discussion see Bainbridge, S. 'A critique of the Insider Trading Sanctions Act 1984' (1985) Virginia Law Review, April, 71, 455–498.

[127] Maher, C. 'Crisis not averted: lack of criminal prosecutions leaves limited consequences for those responsible for the financial crisis' (2013) New England Journal on Criminal and Civil Confinement, 39, 459–476, at 463.

> the SEC works closely with them to prosecute those individuals and corporations who violate criminal laws.[128]

Huynh, citing Black, stated that only 10 per cent of cases originally investigated by the SEC are referred to the Department of Justice for further examination.[129] Maher stated that 'there is no indication that the Department of Justice plans to indict any of these executives for their actions'.[130] It is important to note that this position *must* be contrasted with that of the United Kingdom's Financial Services Authority and its replacement agency, the Financial Conduct Authority, which have the ability to commence criminal proceedings.[131]

Despite having an arsenal of enforcement powers the regulatory performance of the SEC during the financial crisis has been overshadowed, and perhaps permanently tarnished, as a result of the actions of Bernard Madoff. This is a point supported by Pontell *et al*, who stated: 'another way to meaningfully gauge the regulatory response or lack thereof in the current crisis is to consider the SEC's indifference to Bernard Madoff'.[132] They added:

> He [Bernard Madoff] was turned into the SEC by a competitor, Harry Markopolos … the fact that there was no follow up investigation of Madoff, who literally was delivered to the authorities, speaks volumes regarding the impotency of regulatory enforcement at the time. The 4,000-lb elephant was in the room and no one can – or wanted to – see it.[133]

Indeed, despite the SEC 'being created to protect investors from financial predators, the [SEC] has somehow *evolved* [author's emphasis] into a mechanism for protecting financial predators with political clout'.[134]

A brief review of the Bernard Madoff Ponzi scheme illustrates how the SEC failed to protect investors on numerous occasions. In 2008, Bernard

---

128 See Huynh above, n 118, at 109.

129 *Ibid.*, at 110. Also see Black, B. 'Should the SEC be a collection agency for defrauded investors?' (2008) Business Lawyer, February, 63, 317–346.

130 Maher above, n 127, at 463.

131 For a more detailed discussion of this see Chapter 5.

132 Pontell, H., Black, W. and Geis, G. 'Too big to fail, too powerful to prosecute? On the absence of criminal prosecutions after the 2009 financial meltdown' (2013) Crime, Law and Society, August, 10.1007/s10611-013-9476-4 at 3. Hereafter Pontell *et al.*

133 *Ibid.*

134 Lewis, M. and Einhorn, D. 'The end of the financial world as we know it', 3 January 2009, available from http://www.nytimes.com/2009/01/04/opinion/04lewiseinhorn.html?pagewanted=all&_r=0, accessed 2 October 2013.

Madoff was arrested by federal agents after being accused of orchestrating one of the largest Ponzi frauds ever encountered in the US. The impact of the fraud was extensive; as noted by Nunziato 'it is estimated that thousands of investors lost somewhere between $20bn and $65bn … Madoff purported to invest the savings of some four thousand clients … who spanned across forty-eight of the fifty states, as well as throughout Europe, Latin America, and Asia'.[135] Bernard Madoff established his firm, Bernard L. Madoff Securities, in 1960.[136] Additionally, Madoff also operated a secret investment company, which was not registered with the SEC until 2006.[137] In 2009, Bernard Madoff pleaded guilty to wire fraud, securities fraud, money laundering, mail fraud and perjury, and was sentenced to 150 years' imprisonment. Judge Chin rejected the defence's recommendation for a 12 year custodial sentence and described Madoff's crime as 'extraordinarily evil' that justified the maximum sentence as it would act as a deterrent and also because of the harm he had caused to his victims.[138]

One of the most significant questions that must be considered is how was Bernard Madoff able to avoid detection for so many years? The first reason lies with the ineffective regulatory stance of the SEC, which was described by Klock as an 'alarming level of incompetent examinations … [the SEC] is not capable of providing adequate protection for the integrity of our financial markets'.[139] Furthermore, it has been argued that the SEC *could* have prevented the Ponzi scheme on several occasions.[140] For example, the SEC received numerous warnings from many informants that Madoff's 'returns *defied* market realities'.[141] Valukas criticised the SEC, which 'had no interest in investigating successful funds whose investors were delighted with their returns. It therefore

---

135 Nunziato, M. 'Aiding and abetting, a Madoff family affair: why secondary actors should be held accountable for securities fraud through the restoration of the private right of action for aiding and abetting liability under the federal security laws' (2010) Albany Law Review, 73, 603–643, at 603–604.

136 Hurt, C. 'Evil has a new name (and a new narrative): Bernard Madoff' (2009) Michigan State Law Review, Winter, 947–987, at 952.

137 *Ibid.*

138 Smith, A. 'Madoff sentenced to 150 years, CNN', 30 June 2009, available from http://money.cnn.com/2009/06/29/news/economy/madoff_prison_sentence/index.htm, accessed 17 August 2012.

139 Klock, M. 'Lessons learned from Bernard Madoff: why we should partially privatise the Barney Fifes at the SEC' (2010) Arizona State Law Journal, 42, 783–835, at 784.

140 *Ibid.*, at 789–804.

141 Valukas above, n 1, at 4.

made only cursory investigations of Madoff's funds. Opportunities to expose his blatantly illegal practices were overlooked because of his very success.'[142] Bernard Madoff's Ponzi scheme was identified by Harry Markopolos, who had reported it to the SEC on several occasions.[143] The full extent of the fraud was outlined in his infamous memo sent to the SEC in 2005 entitled 'The World's Largest Hedge Fund is a Fraud'.[144] Importantly, Bernard Madoff was able to avoid detection for several decades due to his 'ability to cultivate notable relationships with key market regulators'.[145] For example, he was a member of the Financial Industry Regulatory Association's Board of Governors, a member of the SEC's Advisory Committee on Market Information; he was Chairman of the NASDAQ in the 1990s, a member of the board of the Securities Industry and Financial Markets Association, and a member of the Securities Traders' Association of New York.[146] Another reason why Madoff was allowed to deceive investors and regulators was due to his reputation as a 'trusted titan of Wall Street'.[147] Indeed, Nichols argued that 'Madoff was held in high esteem in the securities industry by regulators and other market participants'.[148] This led Hiznay to assert that

---

142 *Ibid.*

143 For a more detailed discussion on the regulatory performance of the SEC see Poser, N. 'Why the SEC failed: regulators against regulation' (2009) Brooklyn Journal of Corporate, Financial and Commercial Law, Spring, 3, 289.

144 Securities and Exchange Commission 'The world's largest hedge fund is a fraud', 7 November 2005, available from http://www.sec.gov/news/studies/2009/oig-509/exhibit-0293.pdf, accessed 13 October 2013. For a more detailed account see Markopolos, H. *No one would listen* (Wiley: New Jersey, 2010).

145 Colesanti, J. 'Another Madoff masquerade? Questioning "securities fraud" in the crime and its cleanup' (2012) Saint Louis University Law Journal, 56, 521–565, at 528.

146 Nichols, C. 'Addressing inept SEC enforcement efforts: lessons from Madoff, the hedge fund industry, and title IV of the Dodd–Frank Act for the US and global financial systems' (2011) Northwestern Journal of International Law and Business, 31, 637–698, at 645–646. The Securities and Exchange Commission admitted in 2009 that Madoff was a 'very-well connected, powerful, person'. See Securities and Exchange Commission *Office of Investigation's investigation of failure of the SEC to uncover Bernard Madoff's Ponzi scheme* (Securities and Exchange Commission: Washington DC, 2009) at 33.

147 Colesanti above, n 145, at 527.

148 Nichols above, n 146, at 644–645.

'critics have at least implicitly blamed Madoff's investors for permitting the fraud's proliferation'.[149]

The regulatory failings of the SEC were highlighted by a damning report by the SEC Office of Inspector General.[150] The Office of Inspector General 'revealed a surreal tale of anonymous tips, unheeded red flags and corroboration never sought, all commencing with a 1992 complaint about Madoff's unregistered activities'.[151] This is a view supported by Nichols, who stated that the SEC could have discovered the Madoff fraud on no less than ten separate occasions.[152] Harris noted that 'more than ample information was received by the SEC over the years to warrant an investigation into Bernard Madoff's activities ... but none of the five examinations and investigations initiated by the SEC was thoroughly or competently performed'.[153] Hiznay stated a popular view that 'critics are primarily targeting the SEC, flinging disapproval towards what many view as the agency's generally inadequate regulatory system'.[154] Furthermore, Nichols noted that 'the SEC failed to use its more than adequate enforcement powers ... it ignored red flags and failed to take basic steps within its legal authority to determine whether Madoff was operating a Ponzi scheme'.[155] Nichols concluded that:

> The SEC could have discovered his [Madoff's] fraud had its enforcement efforts not been so inept. The SEC had numerous opportunities to discover

---

[149] Hiznay, H. 'How the Bernard Madoff scandal exposed weaknesses in asset management regulation' (2009) Review of Banking and Financial Law, Spring, 28, 413–425, at 421.

[150] See generally Securities and Exchange Commission *Office of Investigation's Investigation of Failure of the SEC to uncover Bernard Madoff's Ponzi scheme* (Securities and Exchange Commission: Washington DC, 2009). Also see Financial Industry Regulatory Authority *Report of the 2009 special review committee on FINRA's examination program in light of the Stanford and Madoff schemes* (Financial Industry Regulatory Authority: Washington DC, 2010).

[151] Colesanti above, n 145, at 532. *Ibid.*, at 78–82, 95–96, 143, 149–150, 158, 234, 411–412. Dorn argued that the Securities and Exchange Commission 'had been asleep on watch'. See Dorn, N. 'Regulatory sloth and activism in the effervescence of financial crisis' (2011) University of Denver Law and Policy, 33(3), 428–448, at 431.

[152] Nichols above, n 146, at 661–666.

[153] Harris, J. 'Getting over Madoff: how the SEC must restore its credibility' (2010) Company Lawyer, 31(2), 33–34, at 33.

[154] Hiznay above, n 149, at 417.

[155] Nichols above, n 146, at 641.

> Madoff's fraud over a period of sixteen years. However, the SEC's enforcement efforts were abysmally inadequate because it failed to follow its own standard procedures when it investigated Madoff.[156]

The failings of the SEC illustrate a breakdown of communications and failings of the regulatory agency that was established to protect investors from white collar criminals like Bernard Madoff. It could be argued that the SEC failed to detect the extensive Ponzi fraud due to lack of resources or because it was understaffed. However, such arguments are unfounded as the SEC's ability to detect fraud has been criticised and some commentators have suggested that 'they [the SEC] couldn't find ice cream in a Dairy Queen'.[157]

4.3.2 Federal Bureau of Investigation

The FBI has been the most active law enforcement agency towards white collar crime associated with the financial crisis. For example, investigations by the FBI in 2011 resulted in 1,223 indictments and 1,082 convictions for mortgage fraud.[158] Furthermore, due to its investigations the FBI has secured $1.38bn in restitution, acquired fines totalling £116.3m, approximately $16m has been seized and $7.3m has been forfeited.[159] These actions have been influenced by the enactment of the Fraud Enforcement and Recovery Act 2009, which resulted in the FBI being granted additional funding which was used to employ more field agents, prosecutors and investigators to tackle mortgage fraud. However, the benefits and impact of this funding have been questioned. For example, Black takes the view that due to the large volume of referrals the FBI receives it 'can investigate only a tiny percentage of criminal referrals for mortgage fraud'.[160] Furthermore, according to statistical data

---

156 *Ibid.*, at 698.

157 Markopolos, H. 'Testimony before the US Senate Banking, Housing and Urban Affairs Committee', 4 February 2009, available from http://www.banking.senate.gov/public/index.cfm?FuseAction=Files.View&FileStore_id=a157968b-2c5f-4477-a9d6-7042fec46593, accessed 14 October 2013.

158 Federal Bureau of Investigation 'Financial crimes report to the public – fiscal years 2010–2011', n/d, available from http://www.fbi.gov/stats-services/publications/financial-crimes-report-2010-2011/financial-crimes-report-2010-2011#Mortgage, accessed 8 August 2013.

159 *Ibid.*

160 Black, W. 'The Department of Justice "chases mice while lions roam the campsite": why the department has failed to prosecute elite frauds that drove the financial crisis' (2012) UMKC Law Review, Summer, 80, 987–1019, at 998.

published in September 2013 there has been a significant fall in the number of white collar crime prosecutions brought by the FBI.[161] The report also illustrates that the total number of annual white collar crime prosecutions has fallen from approximately 5,500 in 1993 to approximately 2,500 in 2013.[162]

Nonetheless, the ability of the FBI to investigate and tackle mortgage fraud prior to the financial crisis was adversely affected by the decision of President George Bush to tackle the 'War on Terror' at the expense of white collar crime. This decision has been correctly criticised by many commentators and the FBI itself. It is very interesting to note that the FBI forewarned the Bush administration of the threat posed by mortgage fraud in 2004, before the onset of the financial crisis.[163] For example, Chris Swecker, the former Assistant Director of the FBI, stated that the 'potential impact of mortgage fraud on financial institutions and the stock market is clear. If fraudulent practices become systemic within the mortgage industry and mortgage fraud is allowed to become unrestrained, it will ultimately place financial institutions at risk and have adverse effects on the stock market.'[164] This warning was followed by a request for 'more investigators to address fraud in the mortgage industry'.[165] Mistakenly, these arguments were ignored by President George Bush.

It has been possible to review the performance of the FBI since the start of the financial crisis via statistical data from its annual mortgage fraud reports. These reports provide a useful and fascinating overview of the extent of mortgage fraud, as they outline emerging mortgage fraud schemes and summarise the actions of the FBI. In its 2006 mortgage fraud report the FBI outlined how it was liaising with the mortgage

---

[161] TRAC Reports 'Slump in FBI white collar crime prosecutions', 24 September 2013, available from http://trac.syr.edu/whatsnew/email.130924.html, accessed 17 October 2013.

[162] *Ibid.*

[163] See for example Lichtblau, E., Johnston, D. and Nixon, E. 'F.B.I. struggles to handle financial fraud cases', 19 October 2008, available from http://www.nytimes.com/2008/10/19/washington/19fbi.html?pagewanted=all&_r=0, accessed 8 August 2013.

[164] Federal Bureau of Investigation 'Chris Swecker, Assistant Director, Criminal Investigative Division, Federal Bureau of Investigation, before the House Financial Services Subcommittee on Housing and Community Opportunity', 7 October 2004, available from http://www.fbi.gov/news/testimony/fbis-efforts-in-combating-mortgage-fraud, accessed 8 August 2013.

[165] Ramirez, M. 'Criminal affirmance: going beyond the deterrence paradigm to examine the social meaning of declining prosecution of elite crime' (2013) Connecticut Law Review, February, 45, 865–931, at 876.

industry to respond to the increasing levels of mortgage fraud.[166] For example, the FBI signed a memorandum of agreement with the Mortgage Bankers' Association (MBA) in 2007.[167] John Robbins, the then Chairman of the MBA, stated:

> Fraud against lenders is a growing problem that hurts everyone throughout the mortgage process, from the lenders themselves, through the brokers and appraisers to the consumers and the communities we invest in … fraud is costing lenders billions of dollars each year and I want to thank the officials at the FBI for joining us in this partnership to give us another tool in the fight to stop fraud against mortgage lenders.[168]

Furthermore, the FBI established the National Fraud Mortgage Team (NFMT) in December 2008.[169] The main objectives of the NFMT were to improve existing affiliations with mortgage providers and originate new mechanisms to detect mortgage fraud. The FBI stated that the NFMT would 'assist field offices in addressing the financial crisis, from the mortgage fraud problem and loan origination scams to the secondary markets and securitization … [it would also] provide tools to identify the most egregious mortgage fraud perpetrators, [prioritize] investigative efforts, and [provide] information to evaluate resource needs'.[170] Additionally, the FBI is a key member of several mortgage fraud task forces and working groups.[171] For example, it is also a member of the Department of Justice National Mortgage Fraud and National Bank Fraud Working Groups and the Financial Fraud Enforcement Task Force.[172]

---

[166] Federal Bureau of Investigation 'Mortgage fraud report 2006', May 2007, available from http://www.fbi.gov/stats-services/publications/mortgage-fraud-2006/2006-mortgage-fraud-report#mf06_key, accessed 8 August 2013.

[167] *Ibid.*

[168] Mortgage Bankers' Association 'MBA signs memorandum of agreement with FBI to promote use of FBI's Mortgage Fraud Warning Notice', 8 March 2007, available from http://www.mortgagebankers.org/NewsandMedia/PressCenter/50728.htm, accessed 8 August 2013.

[169] Black, W. 'Neo-classical economic theories, methodology, and praxis optimize criminogenic environments and produce recurrent, intensifying crises' (2011) Creighton Law Review, 44, 597–645, at 640.

[170] Federal Bureau of Investigation '2008 Mortgage fraud report', n/d, available from http://www.fbi.gov/stats-services/publications/mortgage-fraud-2008/2008-mortgage-fraud-report, accessed 8 August 2013.

[171] *Ibid.*

[172] Federal Bureau of Investigation '2009 Mortgage fraud report', n/d, available from http://www.fbi.gov/stats-services/publications/mortgage-fraud-2009, accessed 8 August 2013.

Finally, the FBI established the Financial Institution Fraud Unit (FIFU) to 'oversee the investigation of financial industry fraud schemes perpetrated by individuals, as well as criminal organizations, which target our nation's financial institutions'.[173] FIFU seeks to:

> protect the public's interest by educating individuals and businesses about pervasive financial industry fraud schemes; working closely with federal, state, and local law enforcement agencies; and maintaining liaison contacts with our regulatory and industry partners. In addition, the FIFU obtains relevant intelligence data to prepare proactive strategies to neutralize current and emerging financial threats. The FIFU has oversight responsibilities of the mortgage fraud, financial institution fraud, credit card fraud, and bankruptcy fraud subprograms.[174]

The most important role that the FBI undertakes in relation to mortgage fraud is conducting investigations that result in the instigation of criminal proceedings. The success of this role will be discussed towards the end of this chapter.

4.3.3 Department of Justice

> The Department of Justice has brought few, if any, high profile criminal cases since 2008 charging important figures in the mortgage and financial industries, or otherwise addressing in criminal charges the financial transactions that contributed to the crisis. We have seen charges against ponzi schemers exposed by the sharp decline in securities prices in 2008 and 2009, and a slew of charges involving relatively low-level mortgage frauds, but the criminal cases brought by the department are widely seen as missing the heart of what causes the financial crisis.[175]

The Department of Justice has played an important role in tackling white collar crime associated with the financial crisis. The Attorney General Eric Holder Jr. testified before the Financial Crisis Inquiry Commission and stated:

> The Department has a long history of prosecuting financial fraud – and we will continue to do so. Working in concert with our Federal, state, local, tribal and territorial partners, the Justice Department is using every tool at our disposal – including new resources, advanced technologies and communications capabilities, and the very best talent we have – to prevent, prosecute and

173 Federal Bureau of Investigation above, n 166.

174 *Ibid.*

175 Abramowitz, E. and Sack, J. 'Why so few prosecutions connected to the financial crisis?', (2013) New York Law Journal, 250(46), 1–3, at 1.

> punish these crimes. And by taking dramatic action, our goal is not just to hold accountable those whose conduct may have contributed to the last meltdown, but to deter such future conduct as well.[176]

The Department of Justice claims to have 'investigated and held accountable those responsible for financial fraud' during the financial crisis.[177] For example, it has 'prosecuted some of the most significant financial crimes … bringing to justice … numerous individuals across the country who perpetrated investment, securities and other fraud schemes'.[178] This view is supported by Henning, but he noted that 'the cases are local in nature and do not involve large financial institutions'.[179]

One of the first measures introduced by the Department of Justice was the FFETF, which is one of several similar task forces established by the Department to tackle white collar crime. Other examples include the Corporate Fraud Task Force,[180] the Enron Task Force[181] and the National Procurement Fraud Task Force.[182] The FFETF replaced the Corporate Fraud Task Force,[183] which was created in 2002 following the collapse of

[176] Department of Justice 'Attorney General Eric Holder testifies before the Financial Crisis Inquiry Commission', 14 January 2010, available from http://www.justice.gov/ag/testimony/2010/ag-testimony-100114.html, accessed 2 October 2013.

[177] Department of Justice 'Accomplishments under the leadership of Attorney General Eric Holder', n/d, available from http://www.justice.gov/accomplishments/accomplishments.pdf, accessed 2 October 2013.

[178] *Ibid.*

[179] Henning, J. 'Making sure the buck stops here: barring executives for corporate violations' (2012) University of Chicago Legal Forum, 91–128, at 95.

[180] The Corporate Fraud Task Force was established by Executive Order 13271 of 9 July 2002. For a more detailed discussion see Ramirez, K. 'Prioritizing justice: combating corporate crime from task force to top priority' (2011) Marquette Law Review, Spring, 93, 971–1019.

[181] For a brief commentary see Brickey, K. 'Enron's legacy' (2004) Buffalo Criminal Law Review, 8, 221–276, at 230–231. It is important to note that this task force was disbanded in 2006. See Hurt, C. 'Of breaches of the peace, home invasions, and securities fraud' (2007) American Criminal Law Review, 44, 1365–1380, at 1367 fn 11.

[182] For a brief discussion of this task force see Kathuria, S. 'Best practices for compliance with new government contractor compliance and ethics rules under the federal acquisition regulation' (2009) Public Contract Law Journal, Summer, 38, 803–856, at 821.

[183] Podgor, E. 'Introduction: examining white collar crime with trifocals' (2011) Fordham Urban Law Journal, December, 39, 299–308, at 301.

Enron and WorldCom.[184] The aim of the Corporate Fraud Task Force was to 'provide direction for the investigation and prosecution of cases of securities fraud, accounting fraud, mail and wire fraud, money laundering … and other related financial crimes committed by commercial entities'.[185] Arogeti argued that the Corporate Fraud Task Force was created to 'restore market confidence and cut down on corporate fraud'.[186] The Corporate Fraud Task Force secured over 1,200 fraud related prosecutions which included numerous company chief executive officers, chief executives and chief financial officers.[187] President Barack Obama stated that the Financial Fraud Enforcement Task Force would assist the Department of Justice to 'investigate and prosecute significant financial crimes and other violations relating to the current financial crisis and economic recovery efforts'.[188] Dooley and Radke stated that the new task force was 'in response to the near melt-down of the US financial markets, implosion of the subprime mortgage loan sector … and growing evidence that … mortgage loan fraud and abuses in the secondary market … contributed to these two disasters'.[189] In essence, this Task Force specifically focused on white collar crime emanating from the financial crisis including mortgage and securities fraud.[190] Rasnak stated that the

184 For an interesting discussion of the Corporate Fraud Task Force see Bookman, Z. 'Convergences and omissions in reporting corporate and white collar crime' (2008) DePaul Business and Commercial Law Journal, Spring, 6, 347–362.

185 Exec. Order No. 13,271, 67 Fed. Reg. 46,091 (9 July 2002).

186 Arogeti, J. 'How much cooperation between government agencies is too much? Reconciling United States v Scrushy, the corporate fraud task force, and the nature of parallel proceedings' (2006) Georgia State University Law Review, Winter, 23, 427–453, at 430.

187 See Johnson, C. 'U.S. promotes its record on corporate crime', 18 July, 2007, available from http://www.washingtonpost.com/wp-dyn/content/article/2007/07/17/AR2007071701767.html, accessed 31 July 2013. Also see Department of Justice *First year report to the President – the Corporate Fraud Task Force* (Department of Justice: Washington DC, 2003) at 2.2; Department of Justice *Second year report to the President – the Corporate Fraud Task Force* (Department of Justice: Washington DC, 2004) at 3.2; and Department of Justice *The Corporate Fraud Task Force report* (Department of Justice: Washington DC, 2008) at 1.3–1.20.

188 Exec. Order No. 13519, 74 FR 60123, 2009 WL 3848641 (Pres.), as cited in Dooley and Radke above, n 75, at fn 18.

189 *Ibid.*, at 624.

190 Arnold, T. '"It's déjà vu all over again": using bounty hunters to leverage gatekeepers duties' (2010) Tulsa Law Review, 45, 419–469, at 450. Also see Montagano above, n 117.

aim of this Task Force was to 'bring together civil and criminal resources at all levels of government to hold perpetrators of financial fraud accountable'.[191] However, this claim must be questioned because the FFETF has tended to concentrate on civil cases and has not instigated any criminal proceedings.[192]

The Task Force contains representatives of a wide range of federal government departments, regulatory agencies and law enforcement agencies. For example, this includes *inter alia*, the Department of Treasury, the Department of Commerce, the SEC, the Department of Homeland Security, the Futures Trading Commission, the Federal Trade Commission, the Federal Deposit Insurance Corporation, the Board of Governors of the Federal Reserve System, the FBI, the US Secret Services and FinCEN.[193] Presidential Executive Order 13,519 provides that the objective of the FFETF is to:

> provide advice … for the investigation and prosecution of [significant] cases of bank, mortgage, loan, and lending fraud; securities and commodities fraud; retirement plan fraud; mail and wire fraud; tax crimes; money laundering; False Claims Act violations; unfair competition; discrimination; and other financial crimes and violations.[194]

Furthermore, this Task Force has five other objectives. First, it investigates and where possible prosecutes white collar crime and other illegal activities that have caused or arisen from the financial crisis. Secondly, it seeks to recover the proceeds from such crimes and violations. Thirdly, it attempts to address discrimination in the lending and financial markets. Fourthly, it aims to improve the levels of coordination and cooperation between local, state and federal investigative and prosecutorial agencies. Finally, the Task Force seeks to improve the level of interaction with a wide range of partners including financial institutions and consumers in order to improve the prevention and detection of fraud.[195] In order to achieve these objectives, the Task Force has purposely targeted and

---

191 Rasnak, S. 'USTP's civil enforcement activity targets mortgage fraud and mortgage rescue schemes' (2010) American Bankruptcy Institute Journal, March, 29, 18, at 72.

192 Abramowitz and Sack above, n 175, at 2.

193 Ramirez above, n 180, at 1005.

194 Exec. Order No. 13,519, 74 FR 60123, 2009 WL 3848641 (Pres.) as cited *ibid.*, at fn 71.

195 Financial Fraud Enforcement Task Force *First year report – Financial Fraud Enforcement Task Force* (Financial Fraud Enforcement Task Force: Washington DC, 2010) at 2.3.

prioritised fraud that is directly associated with the financial crisis. For example, this includes mortgage fraud, securities and commodities fraud, and the distribution of government funds via the American Recovery and Reinvestment Act and TARP.[196] It has been asserted that the Task Force will result in 'increased coordination and cooperation among the different federal and state authorities involved in the regulation of the financial markets'.[197] However, the structure of the FFETF is very similar to that adopted by the Corporate Fraud Task Force. The latter consisted of the Department of Justice, the SEC, the CFTC and the Federal Energy Regulatory Commission.[198] Nonetheless, the Corporate Fraud Task Force did result in the Department of Justice and SEC forming a closer working relationship towards tackling white collar crime. The Department of Justice would use its criminal enforcement powers while the SEC would complement these by using its wide reaching civil powers.[199] The FFETF is an attempt by President Barack Obama to improve the response towards white collar crime by adopting a coordinated response.[200]

One of the highest profile actions of the Task Force has been its 'Distressed Homeowner Initiative', which was launched in 2011.[201] The aim of this measure is to concentrate on fraud that targets homeowners who have fallen into arrears on their mortgage repayments. In such cases, the fraudster will approach the homeowner and promise them that they will be able to prevent the repossession or foreclosure of their property for a large fee. The fraudster promises that investors will purchase the homeowner's mortgage or in some cases will ask them to transfer the home ownership to the fraudulent investors.[202] In 2012, the Department of Justice reported that the scheme resulted in '530 criminal defendants

---

196 *Ibid.*, at 2.4.

197 Brotman, E. and Dougherty, E. 'Blue collar tactics in white collar crime' (2011) Champion, September, 35, 16–20, at 19.

198 Arogeti above, n 186, at 427.

199 *Ibid.*, at 428–429.

200 Sheppard, M. and Dougherty, E. 'Tapping into Wall Street – the government employs tougher tactics against money crimes' Criminal Justice, Winter, 26, 20–29, at 20.

201 Federal Bureau of Investigation 'Inside the FBI – podcast', 11 October 2012, available from http://www.fbi.gov/news/podcasts/inside/distressed-homeowner-mortgage-fraud.mp3/view, accessed 14 October 2013.

202 United States Department of Justice 'Financial Fraud Enforcement Task Force members reveal results of Distressed Homeowner Initiative', 9 October 2012, available from http://www.justice.gov/opa/pr/2012/October/12-ag-1216.html, accessed 1 August 2013. For more examples of these scams see House Lawyer 'Con artists fleece desperate homeowners', 14 December 2012, available

charged, including 172 executives, in 285 federal criminal indictments or informations filed … these cases involved more than 73,000 homeowner victims and total losses by those victims estimated by law enforcement at more than $1bn'.[203] The Attorney General, Eric Holder Jr., stated that these 'comprehensive efforts represent an historic, government-wide commitment to eradicating mortgage fraud and related offenses … the success of the Distressed Homeowner Initiative underscores our determination to pursue these and other financial fraud criminals around the country'.[204] He added that:

> Put simply, these comprehensive efforts represent an historic, government-wide commitment to eradicating mortgage fraud and related offenses across the country. And the results obtained by the many dedicated attorneys, experts, agents, and investigators who stand on the front lines of this work prove that our approach is working; that progress is possible; and that – as long as we continue to partner with a range of committed allies and engage the help of an informed public – there is good reason for confidence in where our anti-fraud efforts will take us from here.[205]

At first instance, the actions and results of the Distressed Homeowner Initiative appear to be very impressive. However, the figures were questioned by a Bloomberg report that suggested that the statistics incorporated investigations and actions two years prior to Barack Obama being elected President.[206] As a result of the investigation by Bloomberg,

---

from http://articles.washingtonpost.com/2012-12-14/news/35846475_1_lender-distressed-homeowner-initiative-loan-data, accessed 1 August 2013 and Financial Crimes Enforcement Network 'Remarks of Jennifer Shashly Calvery, Director of FinCEN Enforcement Network, Mortgage Bankers' Association, Fraud Issues Conference', 15 April 2013, available from http://www.fincen.gov/news_room/speech/pdf/20130415.pdf, accessed 1 August 2013.

[203] Department of Justice above, n 177. Also see Scannel, K. 'US cracks down on mortgage fraud', 9 October 2012, available from http://www.ft.com/cms/s/0/bcf3465c-122a-11e2-868d-00144feabdc0.html#axzz2aheJherM, accessed 1 August 2013.

[204] Department of Justice*, ibid.*

[205] Department of Justice 'Attorney General Eric Holder speaks at the Distressed Homeowner Initiative press conference', 9 October 2012, available from http://www.justice.gov/iso/opa/ag/speeches/2012/ag-speech-1210091.html, accessed 1 August 2013.

[206] Mattingly, P. and Schoenberg, T. 'U.S. mortgage fraud initiative included Bush-era case', 11 October 2012, available from http://www.bloomberg.com/news/2012-10-10/u-s-mortgage-fraud-initiative-data-included-older-cases.html, accessed 1 August 2013.

the statistics were corrected and restated by the FBI.[207] The report also suggested that the publication of the results was politically motivated as they were published a month before the 2012 presidential elections.[208]

Another important measure that was utilised by the Task Force was 'Operation Broken Dreams', which was launched in October 2010. The purpose of this initiative was to 'target mortgage fraudsters throughout the country'; it was 'the largest collective enforcement effort ever brought to bear in confronting mortgage fraud'.[209] It has been described as the 'government's largest mortgage fraud takedown to date'.[210] By June 2010, Operation Stolen Dream had identified 1,215 defendants, 486 arrests had been made, there were 673 indictments, there had been 135 complaints and 336 convictions, estimated losses of $2.3bn and over $10m had been seized.[211] Additionally, civil cases had been instigated against 400 defendants and the total number of civil enforcement actions was 191. After announcing these results, the Attorney General stated that 'mortgage fraud ruins lives, destroys families and devastates whole communities, so attacking the problem from every possible direction is vital … we will use every tool available to investigate, prosecute and prevent mortgage fraud, and we will not rest until anyone preying on vulnerable American homeowners is brought to justice'.[212]

It has been claimed that the creation of the FFETF clearly illustrates that the 'investigation and prosecution of financial and investment fraud

---

207 Mattingly, P. and Schoenberg, T. 'U.S. mortgage group forced to correct initiative stats', 9 August 2013, available from http://www.bloomberg.com/news/2013-08-09/u-s-mortgage-group-forced-to-correct-initiative-stats.html, accessed 14 October 2013. Also see Berger, J. 'DOJ, FBI admit they inflated claims about mortgage fraud crackdown last year', 14 August 2013, available from http://www.foxnews.com/politics/2013/08/14/doj-fbi-admit-inflated-claims-about-mortgage-fraud-crackdown-last-year/, accessed 14 October 2013.

208 Mattingly and Schoenberg, above n 206.

209 Department of Justice 'Coinciding with one-year anniversary of 'Operation Stolen Dreams,' three loan officers and a title agent charged in $2.5 million reverse mortgage and loan modification scheme', 6 July 2011, available from http://www.justice.gov/opa/pr/2011/July/11-civ-884.html, accessed 1 August 2013.

210 Federal Bureau of Investigation 'Operation Stolen Dreams: hundreds arrested in mortgage fraud sweep', 17 June 2010, available from http://www.fbi.gov/news/stories/2010/june/mortgage-fraud-sweep, accessed 1 August 2013.

211 *Ibid.*

212 Department of Justice 'Financial Fraud Enforcement Task Force announces results of broadest mortgage fraud sweep in history', 17 June 2010, available from http://www.justice.gov/opa/pr/2010/June/10-opa-708.html, accessed 1 August 2013.

is a primary concern [for the Obama administration]'.[213] However, the creation of *another* fraud related task force has been questioned. For example, Ramirez suggested that:

> Rather than combating the relentless waves of corporate criminality with a collection of ad hoc task forces that seek to coordinate policy among a vast array of offices and agencies, the DOJ should create a Corporate Crimes Division as a permanent base in the department from which to pursue national policy and to more efficiently investigate and prosecute such crimes.[214]

4.4 ENFORCEMENT RESPONSE

> Banks had made huge bets and bonuses with other people's money … it was wrong. It was irresponsible. And it plunged our economy into a crisis that put millions out of work.[215]

The enforcement response in the US has been led by the SEC, the CFTC, the Department of Justice and the FBI. The SEC and the CFTC have used their extensive array of civil enforcement sanctions against violaters of securities and fraud legislation, while the Department of Justice and FBI have attempted to commence criminal prosecutions against white collar criminals. The civil enforcement response has generated a superabundance of high profile, record breaking, headline grabbing and media friendly financial sanctions. Likewise, the criminal enforcement response has resulted in numerous low level prosecutions, especially those relating to mortgage fraud. The response to the most recent financial crisis can be contrasted to that adopted towards the Savings and Loans Crisis. For example, Black noted that:

> unlike the savings and loan debacle and the Enron-era accounting control frauds, where even the elite CEO frauds that drove those crises were prosecuted, the elite frauds that drove the current crisis have not even been subjected to a serious investigation. Indeed, Attorney General Michael B. Mukasey made the astounding admission that the FBI agents assigned to investigate mortgage fraud have investigated solely what he described as the

---

213 Saladrigas, C. 'Corporate criminal liability: lessons from the Rothstein debacle' (2012) University of Miami Law Review, Winter, 66, 435–469, at 464.

214 Ramirez above, n 180, at 973.

215 The White House 'Barack Obama, President of the United States, state of the union', 24 January 2012, available from www.whitehouse.gov/the-press-office/2012/01/24/remarks-president-state-union-address, accessed 21 October 2013.

> equivalent of 'white collar street crime'. We have the first major crisis of the modern era driven by an epidemic of accounting control fraud in which the elite, fraudulent CEOs have grown wealthy by engaging in fraud and done so with legal impunity.[216]

The next part of the chapter reviews the use of criminal sanctions against those white collar criminals during the financial crisis.

4.4.1 Criminal Sanctions

> Central to the American criminal justice system is an expectation that a known breach of the criminal law will yield punishment. In the aftermath of federal bailouts, expectations that CEOs would be held criminally accountable as had occurred after the fall of Enron abounded, and they still do. Yet, despite congressional investigations revealing known fraud and numerous fraud settlements worth billions, the Department of Justice has not criminally charged any of the key officers and managers of the financial institutions deemed 'too big to fail' or even those 'too big' that were allowed to fail anyway.[217]

US law enforcement agencies have a considerable collection of legislative provisions at their disposal to tackle white collar crime associated with the financial crisis. The prevention of fraud is an essential part of many criminal statutes.[218] For example, the Mail Fraud Statute criminalises mistreating the Post Office in continuance with any fraudulent activity.[219] Prosecutors must prove that the defendant intended to create a scheme to defraud the Post Office and it is not obligatory for the false representation to be communicated by mail, only that the mail system was to be used to conduct the fraudulent activity.[220] The Mail Fraud Statute has become one of the most popular fraud statutes with prosecutors. The law has been described as the 'prosecutor's secret weapon'[221] and has become the most important and powerful of fraud prosecutorial tools. The Act was amended and extended by the Anti-Drug Abuse Act

---

216 Black above, n 160, at 988.

217 Ramirez above, n 165, at 868.

218 Podgor, E. 'Criminal fraud' (1999) American University Law Review, 48, 729–768, at 730.

219 Act of 8 June 1872, ch. 335, § 301, 17 Stat. 283, 323, 18 U.S.C. § 1341.

220 Weintraub, L. 'Crime of the century: use of the mail fraud statute against authors' (1987) Boston University Law Review, 67, 507–549, at 524.

221 Greenwood, L. 'Mail and wire fraud' (2008) American Criminal Law Review, 45, 717–740, at 717.

1988[222] and the Violent Crime Control and Law Enforcement Act 1994.[223] Thus the Mail Fraud Statute now 'covers a full range of consumer frauds, stock frauds, land frauds, bank frauds, insurance frauds, and commodity frauds, but [also] areas such as blackmail, counterfeiting, election fraud, and bribery'.[224] The Mail Fraud Statute is often used in conjunction with the Wire Fraud Statute.[225] In order for a person to be convicted prosecutors must prove that there was a 'scheme to defraud that includes a material deception; with the intent to defraud; while using the mail, private commercial carriers, and/or wires in furtherance of that scheme; that did result or would have resulted in the loss of money or property of the deprivation of honest services'.[226] The Wire Fraud Statute has been described as the 'first line of defence against fraudulent activity'[227] and as providing prosecutors with a broad range of measures.[228] The courts have expanded the application of the Wire Fraud Statute to an ever increasing number of methods of communication and it also applies to a wide range of fraudulent activities.[229]

Another legislative measure designed to prevent fraud is the Bank Fraud Act, which was introduced as part of the Comprehensive Crime Control Act 1984.[230] The Act was a reaction to a large number of fraudulent schemes that targeted financial institutions[231] and the Supreme Court's decision in *Williams v United States*.[232] Here, the court held that people who participated in fraudulent activities such as cheque-kiting

---

222 Pub. L. 100-690, Title VII, §7603(a), 102 Stat, 4181, 4508.

223 Pub. L. 103-322, § 108 Stat. 1796.

224 Greenwood above, n 221, at 719.

225 The Wire Fraud Statute applies to 'scheme or artifice to defraud, or for obtaining money or property by means of false or fraudulent pretenses, representations, or promises, transmits or causes to be transmitted by means of wire, radio, or television communication in interstate or foreign commerce, any writings, signs, signals, pictures, or sounds for the purpose of executing such a scheme or artifice'. 18 U.S.C. § 1343.

226 Stuart, C. 'Mail and wire fraud' (2009) American Criminal Law Review, 46, 813–835, at 816.

227 NuraKami, K. 'Mail and wire fraud' (1987) American Criminal Law Review, 24, 623–637, at 623.

228 Blumel, R. 'Mail and wire fraud' (2005) American Criminal Law Review, 42, 677–698, at 678.

229 *Ibid.*

230 S Rep No. 98-225, 98th Cong, 2d Sess 377. U.S.C. § 1344.

231 Madia, M. 'The bank fraud act: a risk of loss requirement?' (2005) University of Chicago Law Review, 72, 1445–1471, at 1445.

232 458 US 279. See for example Fischer, A. and Sheppard, J. 'Financial institutions fraud' (2008) American Criminal Law Review, 45, 531–578, at 533.

could not be prosecuted for making a misleading statement to the financial institution.[233] As a result of the decision, the Department of Justice was forced to abandon many fraud related prosecutions. Therefore, Congress responded by enacting the Bank Fraud Act, which criminalises schemes that intend to deceive or obtain finances from federally insured financial institutions.[234] The Act criminalises cheque forging, credit card fraud, student loan fraud, mortgage fraud and false financial transactions between offshore shell banks and domestic banks.[235] The scope of the Bank Fraud Act was extended by the Financial Institutions Reform, Recovery and Enforcement Act 1989[236] to include 'financial kingpin crime', which imposes a life sentence for defendants who manage so called financial crime enterprises.[237] The Major Fraud Act 1988 was instituted to tackle procurement fraud,[238] but its scope is limited to frauds that exceed $1m.[239] As a result of the infamous collapse of Enron and WorldCom the Sarbanes–Oxley Act 2002 was introduced.[240] Its objective is to improve the level of regulation for the accountancy profession and to dissuade fraudulent and unethical behaviour.[241] The Act increased the maximum penalty for wire and mail fraud from five years' to 20 years' imprisonment.[242] The Securities Fraud Statute 2003 was introduced following a number of securities frauds that resulted in investors losing over $40bn.[243] There are many other fraud

---

233 Delone and Gwartney stated that the 'Congress passed § 1344 in reaction to this ruling primarily to give the government the means to prosecute check-kiting'. See Delone, C. and Gwartney, S. 'Financial institutions fraud' (2009) American Criminal Law Review, 46, 621–670, at 623.

234 Biskupic, S. 'Fine tuning the bank statute: a prosecutor's perspective' (1999) Marquette Law Review, 82, 381–403, at 382.

235 Delone and Gwartney above, n 233, at 625.

236 Pub.L. No. 101-73, 103 Stat. 187 (1989).

237 Sussman, R. 'Protecting clients from the government's thermonuclear war on bank fraud', (1991) American Law Institute – American Bar Association Continuing Legal Education ALI–ABA Court of Study, C646 213–260, at 215.

238 MacKay, S. 'Major fraud against the United States' (1992) Army Lawyer, September, 7–14, at 8.

239 *Ibid.*

240 Pub. L. No. 107-204, 116 Stat. 745 (2002).

241 Saksena, P. 'The Sarbanes–Oxley Act and occupational fraud: does the law effectively tackle the real problem?' (2009) International Company and Commercial Law Review, 20(2), 37–43, at 37.

242 Sarbanes–Oxley Act 2002, s. 903.

243 Pazicky, L. 'A new arrow in the quiver of federal securities fraud prosecutors: section 807 of the Sarbanes–Oxley Act of 2002' (2003) Washington University Law Quarterly, 81, 801–828, at 801.

statutes, including the Medicaid False Claims Statute 1863,[244] the Medicaid Anti-Kickback Statute 1986[245] and the Health Insurance Portability and Accountability Act 1996.[246] Prosecutors are also able to use the False Claims Act 1863,[247] the False Statements Act 1986,[248] the Social Security Act 1935,[249] the Computer Fraud and Abuse Act 1986,[250] the Identity Theft and Assumption Deterrence Act 1998,[251] the Truth in Lending Act 1968,[252] Credit Card Fraud Act 1984[253] and the Marriage Fraud Act 1986.[254]

Therefore, law enforcement agencies and prosecutors have a vast array of legislative tools at their disposal to tackle white collar criminals associated with the financial crisis. According to Creseney *et al* 'federal regulators and law enforcement agencies, eager to demonstrate they are acting to uncover criminal activity, have responded to the credit crisis by opening a substantial number of investigations'.[255] Podgor added that 'prosecutors understandably feel the necessity to show the public that there will be punishment for criminal conduct'.[256] However, the response of prosecutors in the US must be questioned because there have been no successful prosecutions of high profile contributors to the financial crisis. Pontell *et al* stated that 'the offences that have been prosecuted thus far remain relatively minor compared to the mind-boggling felonies perpetrated by those at the centre or at the top of the largest financial institutions'.[257] Morgenson and Story stated that 'whether prosecutors and regulators have been aggressive enough in pursuing wrongdoing is

---

244 42 U.S.C. § 1320a–7b(a).
245 42 U.S.C. § 1320a–7b(b).
246 Pub. L. No. 104-191, 110 Stat. 1936.
247 18 U.S.C. § 287 (2006).
248 18 U.S.C. § 1001 (2006).
249 42 U.S.C. § 1320a–7b(a).
250 See generally Kleindienst, K., Coughlin, T. and Pasquarella, J. 'Computer crimes' (2009) American Criminal Law Review, 46, 315–392, at 331–333.
251 Pub. L. No. 105-318, 112 Stat. 3007 (1998) (codified as amended 18 U.S.C. § 1028 (1990)).
252 15 U.S.C. § 1643.
253 18 U.S.C. § 1029.
254 I.R.C. § 6663.
255 Creseney, A., Eng, G.E. and Nuttal, S. 'Regulatory investigations and the credit crisis: the search for villains' (2009) American Criminal Law Review, Spring, 46, 225–273, at 235. Hereafter Creseney *et al.*
256 Podgor, E. 'White collar crime and the recession: was the chicken or egg first?' (2010) University of Chicago Legal Forum, 205–222, at 216.
257 Pontell *et al* above, n 132, at 3.

likely to long be a subject of debate. All say they have done the best they could in difficult circumstances.'[258] However, the latter argument can be questioned. For example, the Fraud Enforcement and Recovery Act 2009 provided additional funding for federal prosecutors and law enforcement agencies to tackle crime associated with the financial crisis. Despite the increase in funding the Department of Justice refused to create a specific mortgage task force and the FBI reduced the number of agents investigating allegations of mortgage fraud.[259] Prosecutors have also been criticised because they sometimes 'resort to *shortcut charges* to demonstrate a quick response to the criminal conduct'.[260] Eric Holder has defended the prosecutors and stated that 'our record of success [on fraud] has been nothing less than historic'.[261] The accuracy of this statement must be queried given the robust response of the Department of Justice towards the Savings and Loans Crisis related frauds and the swift reaction of the Corporate Fraud Task Force to the collaspe of Enron and WorldCom. However, Eric Holder did point out that

> we've found that much of the conduct that led to the financial crisis was unethical and irresponsible. But we also have discovered that some of this behavior – while morally reprehensible – may not necessarily have been criminal. Believe me, I understand – and I often hear about – the public desire to, as one pundit put it, see the handcuffs come to Wall Street.[262]

This is a view supported by Abramowitz and Sack, who stated that 'the very depth and breadth of the recent financial crisis makes it difficult to separate criminal behavior from business misjudgment and mistake'.[263]

It is important to emphasise that both the Department of Justice and the FBI did investigate the alleged criminal activities in several banks,

---

258 Morgenson, G. and Story, L. 'In financial crisis, no prosecutions of top figures', 14 April 2011, available from http://www.nytimes.com/2011/04/14/business/14prosecute.html?pagewanted=all&_r=0, accessed 27 September 2013.

259 *Ibid.*

260 See Podgor above, n 256, at 217.

261 Department of Justice 'Attorney General Eric Holder speaks at Columbia University Law School on preventing and combating financial fraud', 23 February 2012, available from http://www.justice.gov/iso/opa/ag/speeches/2012/ag-speech-120223.html, accessed 6 October 2013.

262 *Ibid.*

263 Abramowitz and Sack above, n 175, at 2.

including Merrill Lynch,[264] Lehman Brothers,[265] Countrywide,[266] AIG,[267] Bear Stearns,[268] Goldman Sachs,[269] UBS,[270] Washington Mutual,[271] and Freddie Mac and Fannie Mae.[272] It has been argued that by September

---

264 For a brief commentary see Reuters 'FBI, DoJ investigate BofA's Merril deal', 18 September 2009, available from http://uk.reuters.com/article/2009/09/18/us-bankofamerica-fbi-idUSTRE58H3D220090918, accessed 7 October 2013.

265 See Arena, K. 'FBI probing bailout firms', 24 September 2008, available from http://money.cnn.com/2008/09/23/news/companies/fbi_finance/, accessed 7 October 2013. Huisman stated that 'the FBI started an investigation into Lehman Brothers to see whether the rendering of mortgages involved criminal acts'. See Huisman, Q.W. 'Corporate crime and crisis: causation scenarios' in Deflem, M. (ed.), *Economic crisis and crime* (Emerald: Bingley, 2011) at 112.

266 Simpson, G. and Perez, E. 'FBI investigates Countrywide', 8 March 2008, available from http://online.wsj.com/article/SB120494626642521739.html, accessed 7 October 2013.

267 Johnson, C. and Leonnig, C. 'FBI began investigating AIG in March', 25 September 2008 available from http://articles.washingtonpost.com/2008-09-25/business/36840351_1_mortgage-investments-aig-maurice-r-hank-greenberg, accessed 7 October 2013.

268 Wearden, G. 'FBI investigates sub-prime crisis', 30 January 2008, available from http://www.theguardian.com/business/2008/jan/30/subprimecrisis.creditcrunch, accessed 7 October 2013. Friedrichs stated that 'two hedge fund managers for Bear Stearns, the first high-level Wall Street Executives criminally indicted in the wake of the financial meltdown, were acquitted in the fall of 2009 because their well-funded defence team were able to persuade a jury that their actions took the form of poor investment decisions and not intentional criminal fraud. Such outcomes have the potential to discourage prosecutors from initiating criminal proceedings against financial elites.' See Friedrichs, D. 'Wall Street: crime never sleeps' in Will, S., Handelman, S. and Brotherton, D. (eds), *How they got away with it – white collar criminals and the financial meltdown* (Columbia University Press: New York, 2013) at 8.

269 For a brief but criticial interpretation of the actions of Goldman Sachs see Friedrichs, *ibid.*, at 12–15.

270 See Cantley, B. 'The UBS case: the US attack on Swiss banking sovereignty' (2011) International Law and Management Review, Spring, 7, 1–29.

271 Federal Bureau of Investigation 'Department of Justice closes Washington Mutual investigation with no criminal charges', 5 August 2011, available from http://www.fbi.gov/seattle/press-releases/2011/department-of-justice-closes-washington-mutual-investigation-with-no-criminal-charges, accessed 7 October 2013.

272 Goldfarb, Z. 'Probe into Fannie Mae, Freddie Mac widens', 30 September 2008, available from http://articles.washingtonpost.com/2008-09-30/business/36900204_1_probes-disclosure-and-corporate-governance-fannie-mae, accessed 7 October 2013.

2008 24 banks were under investigation by the FBI.[273] By February 2009 the number of major firms under investigation by the FBI had increased to 38.[274] Creseney *et al* stated that 'as the credit crisis expanded, major financial institutions subsequently collapsed … the focus of federal criminal and regulatory investigations shifted to investigating whether these institutions had misrepresented the value of their assets and whether their disclosures regarding asset writedowns were timely and adequate'.[275] Nonetheless, not one individual in any of these institutions has been held criminally accountable since the start of the financial crisis. The only banker who has been convicted in relation to the financial crisis is Kareem Serageldin.[276] Dooley and Radke took the view that:

> As of yet, however, there have been few criminal prosecutions of financial institutions' executives or Wall Street investment bankers. Instead, the explosion of mortgage loan fraud has been fueled by illegal acts of the little people: the loan brokers; lending agents; management of small and some middle-market mortgage companies; appraisers; a multitude of home-buyers; residential real estate speculators; and property flippers.[277]

However, the SEC has secured the conviction of Rajat Gupta for insider trading,[278] the conviction of several executives of General Electric,[279] the

---

[273] Jordan, L. 'FBI investigating companies at heart of Wall St crisis', 23 September 2008, available from http://www.huffingtonpost.com/2008/09/23/fbi-investigating-compani_n_128759.html, accessed 27 September 2013.

[274] Ryan, J. 'Fraud "directly related" to financial crisis probed', 11 February 2009, available from http://abcnews.go.com/TheLaw/Economy/story?id=6855179&page=1, accessed 27 September 2013.

[275] Creseney *et al* above, n 255, at 243.

[276] United States Attorney's Office 'Former Credit Suisse managing director pleads guilty in connection with scheme to hide losses in mortgage-backed securities trading book', 12 April 2013, available from http://www.justice.gov/usao/nys/pressreleases/April13/SerageldinKareemPleaPR.php, accessed 27 September 2013.

[277] See Dooley and Radke above n 75, at 636.

[278] Department of Justice 'Former chairman of consulting firm and board director, Rajat Gupta, sentenced in Manhattan Federal Court to two years in prison for insider trading', 24 October 2012, available from http://www.justice.gov/usao/nys/pressreleases/October12/GuptaSentencing.php, accessed 2 October 2013.

[279] Department of Justice 'Three former financial services executives sentenced to serve time in prison for roles in conspiracies involving investment contracts for the proceeds of municipal bonds', 18 October 2012, available from http://www.justice.gov/opa/pr/2012/October/12-at-1258.html, accessed 2 October 2013.

mortgage fraud related conviction of Shawn Portmann, the conviction of Joseph Braas for his role in the collapse of the Bank of Lancaster County,[280] the conviction of Peter Madoff[281] and several indictments for other fraud related activities. However, it is important to note that the SEC, unlike the FBI and Department of Justice, has been able to utilise its enforcement powers against some of these financial institutions. For example, Bank of America agreed to pay $150m to settle SEC charges after it 'failed to properly disclose employee bonuses and financial losses at Merrill Lynch before shareholders approved the merger of the companies in December 2008'.[282] Furthermore, Angelo Mozilo, the former CEO of Countrywide, agreed to settle SEC charges and paid a $22.5m penalty for 'misleading investors as the subprime mortgage crisis emerged. The settlement also permanently bars Mozilo from ever again serving as an officer or director of a publicly traded company.'[283] The highest profile enforcement action brought by the SEC was against Goldman Sachs, which agreed to pay a record financial penalty of $550m.[284] The former Goldman Sachs Vice President Fabrice Tourre was held liable for fraud regarding his part in a synthetic CDO that was linked to subprime residential mortgages. The jury concluded that

---

[280] Department of Justice 'Former vice president of Pennsylvania lending institution sentenced to 20 years in prison for fraud scheme', 12 September 2012, available from http://www.stopfraud.gov/iso/opa/stopfraud/PAE-120912.html, accessed 2 October 2013.

[281] Department of Justice 'Peter Madoff, former Chief Compliance Officer and Senior Managing Director at Bernard L. Madoff Investment Securities plc, sentenced in Manhattan Federal Court to 10 years in prison', 20 December 2012, available from http://www.justice.gov/usao/nys/pressreleases/December12/PeterMadoffSentencing.php, accessed 2 October 2013.

[282] Securities and Exchange Commission '*Securities and Exchange Commission v. Bank of America Corporation*, Civil Action No. 09-6829, 10-0215 (S.D.N.Y), Litigation Release No. 21407' 4 February 2010, available from http://www.sec.gov/litigation/litreleases/2010/lr21407.htm, accessed 7 October 2013.

[283] Securities and Exchange Commission 'Former Countrywide CEO Angelo Mozilo to pay SEC's largest-ever financial penalty against a public company's senior executive', 15 October 2010, available from http://www.sec.gov/news/press/2010/2010-197.htm, accessed 7 October 2013. However, the imposition of this financial sanction has been questioned. See Maher above, n 127, at 471–473.

[284] Securities and Exchange Commission 'Goldman Sachs agrees to pay record $550m to settle SEC charges related to subprime mortgage CDO', 15 October 2010, available from http://www.sec.gov/news/press/2010/2010-123.htm, accessed 7 October 2013.

Fabrice Tourre was liable for six of the seven securities law violations and that he had assisted an alleged fraud by Goldman Sachs.[285]

Another reason for the lack of criminal proceedings is the adverse effect that financial crimes have on the stock market. Dooley and Radke stated that 'because of the market's sensitivity to any hint of financial impropriety, the misstatement of financial information by publicly-listed companies, or corporate scandal, any such revelations are likely to trigger a sharp and significant stockprice drop'.[286] This is a view supported by Schuck, who took the view that:

> Notwithstanding their glaring culpability, it is unlikely lending institutions will be prosecuted. High-profile prosecutions of corporations can lead to disastrous consequences, only exacerbating the economic turmoil. The FBI acknowledges that because there are so many mortgage fraud cases to investigate, it can no longer simply pursue individual borrowers. Instead, the government vows to target 'industry insiders,' the mortgage professionals who not only failed to prevent mortgage fraud from occurring, but profited from it.[287]

A graphic illustration of this occurred following the Enron scandal that resulted in Arthur Andersen, which was then regarded as one of the 'Big Five' accountancy firms, first surrendering its licence to practise and then to eventual liquidation.[288]

---

285 Baer, J., Bray, C. and Eaglesham, J. 'Fab trader liable in fraud', 2 August 2013, available from http://online.wsj.com/article/SB10001424127887323681904578641843284450004.html, accessed 7 October 2013. In October 2013 Fabrice Tourre appealed this decision and is seeking a new trial. See Voris, B. and Milford, P. 'Fabrice Tourre asks for reversal, new trial in SEC case', 1 October 2013, available from http://www.bloomberg.com/news/2013-10-01/fabrice-tourre-asks-for-reversal-new-trial-in-sec-case.html, accessed 7 October 2013.

286 Dooley and Radke above, n 75, at 639.

287 Schuck, M. 'A new use for the responsible corporate officer doctrine: prosecuting industry insiders for mortgage fraud' (2010) Lewis and Clark Law Review, 14, 371–395, at 372–373.

288 Markoff above, n 2, at 799. It is important to note that Arthur Andersen was originally convicted of obstruction of justice and fraud relating to the collapse of Enron. However, these convictions were overturned by the United States Supreme Court in *Arthur Andersen LLP v United States*, 544 U.S. 696 (2005). For a more detailed discussion on the lessons from the collapse of Arthur Andersen see Braithwaite, J. 'Restorative justice or banks through negative licensing' (2009) British Journal of Criminology, 49(4), 439–450.

It is necessary to emphasise that investigations and prosecutions in the area of white collar crime are notoriously complex and difficult.[289] The prosecution is further complicated by the sophisticated mechanisms used by white collar criminals to disguise their illegal activities[290] so that the appearance of the proceeds of crime can often appear to be legitimate.[291] It has been argued that prosecutors could utilise the responsible corporate officer doctrine to support the prosecution of instances of mortgage fraud.[292] The responsible corporate officer doctrine provides that 'individuals can be held criminally liable if they fail to prevent fraud from occurring despite having the authority and capacity to do so'.[293] Schuck recommended that 'two possibilities exist to expand the doctrine to mortgage fraud. First, courts can expand the doctrine by applying it to mortgage fraud prosecutions. Alternatively, Congress can amend a statute already used to prosecute mortgage fraud to include "responsible corporate officers".'[294] Another scheme that could be used by prosecutors is to compel companies to cooperate with them by threatening to instigate criminal proceedings against them.[295] Wray and Hur argued that an indictment 'often amounts to a virtual death sentence for business entities, a corporate prosecution provides a government an opportunity for deterrence on a massive scale'.[296] By employing such a tactic the government could be accused of creating an enforcement culture that seeks to rely on deterrence and avoid prosecuting corporations. This is

---

289 Creseney *et al* above, n 255, at 235.

290 Berkeley Journal of Criminal Law 'Developments in White Collar Criminal Law and the Culture of Waiver' (2009) Berkeley Journal of Criminal Law, 14(1), 199–228, at 201. For a more detailed discussion of how the proceeds of crime are disseminated see Unger, B. *The scale and impacts of money laundering* (Edward Elgar: Cheltenham, 2007) at 10–12.

291 Bell, S. 'Criminal procedure within the firm' (2007) Stanford Law Review, 59, 1613–1670, at 1627.

292 Schuck above, n 287, at 373.

293 *Ibid.* The doctrine originated in *United States v Dotterweich* 320 U.S. 277, 284–285 (1943) and has since been extended and upheld in *United States v Park* 421 U.S. 658, 671–673 (1975) and *United States v Brittain* 931 F.2d at 1414.

294 Schuck above, n 287, at 388.

295 Berkeley Journal of Criminal Law above, n 290, at 201.

296 Wray, C. and Hur, R. 'Corporate criminal prosecution in a post-Enron world: the Thompson memo in theory and practice' (2006) American Criminal Law Review, 43, 1095–1188, at 1096.

further supported by the increased use of non-prosecution agreements or deferred prosecution agreements.[297]

4.4.2 Civil Sanctions

As outlined in the previous section of this chapter, it has been extremely difficult for law enforcement agencies to successfully prosecute those who contributed to the financial crisis. Therefore, the most frequently imposed sanction on the culprits of the financial crisis has been the imposition of civil sanctions. These have been imposed by the Department of Justice, the CFTC and by the most prolific agency, the SEC. Montagano took the view that 'in the wake of the Great Recession, the SEC, like countless other federal and state agencies, is using every tool at its disposal to restore confidence in US markets in hopes of restoring the economy'.[298] In 2007, the SEC commenced 776 investigations, and imposed 262 civil actions and approximately 400 administrative proceedings. These enforcement activities were for a broad range of issues including 'financial fraud, abusive backdating of stock options, insider trading, violations by broker-dealers, and fraud related to mutual funds'.[299] Additionally, the enforcement activities of the SEC resulted in $1.6bn of disgorgement and penalties.[300] In 2008, the SEC instigated 671 enforcement activities, which illustrated a 25 per cent increase in the number of insider trading cases and a 45 per cent rise in market manipulation cases.[301] Additionally, the SEC refunded $1bn to damaged investors.[302] In 2009, the SEC was able to redistribute a proportion of $843m to approximately 250,000 failed investors of AIG.[303] It is very

---

297 For a more detailed discussion see Schipanio, C. 'Falling off the corporate ladder: prosecution for financial fraud in the United States' (2011) Company Lawyer, 32(11), 336–342, at 338.

298 Montagano above, n 117, at 577.

299 Securities and Exchange Commission *2007 performance and accountability report* (Securities and Exchange Commission: Washington DC, 2007) at 24.

300 *Ibid.*, at 2.

301 Securities and Exchange Commission *2008 performance and accountability report* (Securities and Exchange Commission: Washington DC, 2008) at 12.

302 *Ibid.*, at 17.

303 Securities and Exchange Commission *2009 performance and accountability report* (Securities and Exchange Commission: Washington DC, 2009) at 29.

interesting to note that in 2009 the SEC spent $980m to enforce the federal securities laws.[304] In 2012, the SEC announced that it had:

> Filed 734 enforcement actions in the fiscal year that ended September 30 2012, one shy of last year's record of 735. Most significantly, that number included an increasing number of cases involving highly complex products, transactions, and practices, including those related to the financial crisis … The SEC also announced that it obtained orders in fiscal year 2012 requiring the payment of more than $3bn in penalties and disgorgement for the benefit of harmed investors. It represents an 11 percent increase over the amount ordered last year. In the past two years, the SEC has obtained orders for $5.9bn in penalties and disgorgement.[305]

The then Chairman of the SEC, Mary Schapiro took the view that 'the record of performance is a testament to the professionalism and perseverance of the staff and the innovative reforms put in place over the past few years … we've now brought more enforcement actions in each of the last two years than ever before including some of the most complex cases we've ever seen'.[306] The Director of the SEC Division of Enforcement, Robert Khuzami stated that 'it's not simply numbers, but the increasing complexity and diversity of the cases we file that shows how successful we've been. The intelligence, dedication, and deep experience of our enforcement staff are, more than any other factors, responsible for the Division's success'.[307] Additionally, the SEC has taken enforcement action against many Ponzi related fraud schemes, including Canopy Financial,[308] Trevor Cook[309] and Mantria Corporation.[310] In 2010, the SEC had acted against more Ponzi

---

304 *Ibid.*, at 28.

305 Securities and Exchange Commission 'SEC's enforcement program continues to show strong results in safeguarding investors and markets', 14 November 2012, available from http://www.sec.gov/News/PressRelease/Detail/PressRelease/1365171485830, accessed 11 August 2013.

306 *Ibid.*

307 Securities and Exchange Commission above, n 303.

308 Securities and Exchange Commission 'SEC obtains asset freeze against co-founder of Canopy Financial in $75 million offering fraud', 2 December 2009, available from http://www.sec.gov/news/press/2009/2009-257.htm, accessed 12 August 2013.

309 Securities and Exchange Commission 'SEC obtains asset freeze in Minnesota-based foreign currency trading scheme', 24 November 2009, available from http://www.sec.gov/news/press/2009/2009-253.htm, accessed 12 August 2013.

310 Securities and Exchange Commission 'SEC charges promoters of "green" investments with operating $30 million Ponzi scheme based in Denver area', 16 November 2009, available from http://www.sec.gov/news/press/2009/2009-247.htm, accessed 12 August 2013.

fraud schemes. Examples include Richard Dalton,[311] Joseph Paul Zada,[312] David Harrold and Bruce Prevost,[313] Robert Anderson,[314] Robert Stinson Jr.,[315] Daniel Spitzer,[316] Trade-LLC,[317] Matthew Jennings,[318] Chimay Capital Management Inc.,[319] Merendon Mining Inc.,[320] Matthew Gagnon,[321]

---

311 Securities and Exchange Commission 'SEC obtained emergency asset freeze in diamond-themed Ponzi scheme', 23 November 2010, available from http://www.sec.gov/news/press/2010/2010-231.htm, accessed 12 August 2013.

312 Securities and Exchange Commission '*SEC v. Joseph Paul Zada and Zada Enterprises*, LLC, Civil Action No. 2:10-cv-14498-DPH-PJK', 10 November 2010, available from http://www.sec.gov/litigation/litreleases/2010/lr21737.htm, accessed 12 August 2013.

313 Securities and Exchange Commission 'SEC charges two Florida-based fund managers with facilitating Petters Ponzi scheme', 14 October 2010, available from http://www.sec.gov/news/press/2010/2010-195.htm, accessed 12 August 2013.

314 Securities and Exchange Commission 'SEC v. Robert R. Anderson and Rosand Enterprises Inc., Civil Action No. 10 CV 6420 (N.D. Illinois)', 7 October 2010, available from http://www.sec.gov/litigation/litreleases/2010/lr21688.htm, accessed 12 August 2013.

315 Securities and Exchange Commission '*SEC v. Robert Stinson, Jr., et al.*, Civil Action No. 10-cv-3130-BMS (E.D. Pa.)', 29 June 2010, available from http://www.sec.gov/litigation/litreleases/2010/lr21584.htm, accessed 12 August 2013.

316 Securities and Exchange Commission 'SEC halts $105 million Ponzi scheme by U.S. Virgin Islands-based money manager', 28 June 2010, available from http://www.sec.gov/news/press/2010/2010-112.htm, accessed 12 August 2013.

317 Securities and Exchange Commission 'SEC charges Palm Beach County investment adviser with running a Ponzi scheme and stealing client funds', 22 June 2010, available from http://www.sec.gov/news/press/2010/2010-107.htm, accessed 12 August 2013.

318 Securities and Exchange Commission '*Securities and Exchange Commission v. Matthew Jennings, Westmoore Management, LLC, Westmoore Investment, L.P., Westmoore Capital Management, Inc., Westmoore Capital, LLC* United States District Court for the Central District of California, Civil Action No. SACV-10-00849-AG (MLGX)', 17 June 2010, available from http://www.sec.gov/litigation/litreleases/2010/lr21561.htm, accessed 12 August 2013.

319 Securities and Exchange Commission 'SEC charges New York-based money manager and firm touting ties to Belgian royal family', 11 June 2010, available from http://www.sec.gov/news/press/2010/2010-100.htm, accessed 12 August 2013.

320 Securities and Exchange Commission 'SEC charges perpetrators of $300 million Ponzi scheme involving purported gold mining investments', 10 June 2010, available from http://www.sec.gov/news/press/2010/2010-99.htm, accessed 12 August 2013.

321 Securities and Exchange Commission '*SEC v. Matthew J. Gagnon*, Case No. 2:10-CV-11891 (E.D. Mich.)', 25 May 2010, available from http://www.sec.gov/litigation/litreleases/2010/lr21532.htm, accessed 12 August 2013.

Nevin Shapiro,[322] McGinn, Smith & Co.[323] and Douglas Vaughan.[324] The SEC continued to tackle an increasing number of Ponzi related frauds in 2011, including Wendell Jacobson and Allen Jacobson,[325] Garfield M. Taylor,[326] Arrowhead Capital Management LLC,[327] Eric Aronson,[328] Doris E. Nelson,[329] James Davis Risher and Daniel Joseph Sebastian,[330] Jeffrey A. Lowrance,[331] David Ronald Allen,[332] AIC Inc.,[333] James

---

[322] Securities and Exchange Commission 'SEC charges prominent Miami Beach businessman in $900 million Ponzi scheme', 21 April 2010, available from http://www.sec.gov/news/press/2010/2010-63.htm, accessed 12 August 2013.

[323] Securities and Exchange Commission 'SEC files emergency action to halt fraudulent scheme at Albany-based firm', 20 April 2010, available from http://www.sec.gov/news/press/2010/2010-62.htm, accessed 12 August 2013.

[324] Securities and Exchange Commission 'SEC charges New Mexico real estate magnate in $80 million Ponzi scheme', available from http://www.sec.gov/news/press/2010/2010-43.htm, 24 March 2010, accessed 12 August 2013.

[325] Securities and Exchange Commission 'SEC halts father–son Ponzi scheme in Utah involving purported real estate investments', 15 December 2011, available from http://www.sec.gov/news/press/2011/2011-266.htm, accessed 12 August 2013.

[326] Securities and Exchange Commission 'SEC charges perpetrator of Washington-area Ponzi scheme', 18 November 2011, available from http://www.sec.gov/news/press/2011/2011-246.htm, accessed 12 August 2013.

[327] Securities and Exchange Commission 'SEC charges feeders to Petters Ponzi scheme', 9 November 2011, available from http://www.sec.gov/news/press/2011/2011-237.htm, accessed 12 August 2013.

[328] Securities and Exchange Commission 'SEC files emergency action to halt green-product themed Ponzi scheme', 6 October 2011, available from http://www.sec.gov/news/press/2011/2011-201.htm, accessed 12 August 2013.

[329] Securities and Exchange Commission '*SEC v. Doris E. Nelson,* Case No. 2:11-cv-00345-RMP (E.D. WA filed September 22, 2011)', 22 September 2011, available from http://www.sec.gov/litigation/litreleases/2011/lr22101.htm, accessed 12 August 2013.

[330] Securities and Exchange Commission 'SEC charges two Florida men in Ponzi scheme defrauding teachers and retirees', 22 August 2011, available from http://www.sec.gov/news/press/2011/2011-171.htm, accessed 12 August 2013.

[331] Securities and Exchange Commission 'SEC charges Forex Ponzi operator who fled after scheme unraveled', 15 July 2011, available from http://www.sec.gov/news/press/2011/2011-147.htm, accessed 12 August 2013.

[332] Securities and Exchange Commission 'SEC halts Ponzi scheme by co-founder of China Voice Holding Corp.', 29 April 2011, available from http://www.sec.gov/news/press/2011/2011-101.htm, accessed 12 August 2013.

[333] Securities and Exchange Commission '*Securities and Exchange Commission v. AIC, Inc., et al.*, Case No. 3:11-CV-00176 (E.D. Tenn.)', 18 April 2011,

Clements and Zeina Smidi,[334] John Scott Clark,[335] Michael Watson and Joshua Escobedo,[336] Fair Finance Company[337] and Francisco Illarramendi.[338] Other notable enforcement actions by the SEC in 2012 and 2013 towards Ponzi fraud schemes included Ricardo Bonilla Rojas and Shadai Yire,[339] Paul Burks and Rex Venture Group,[340] Jim Donnan and Gregory Crabtree,[341] Bridge Premium Finance and Mark Feathers,[342] Wayne

available from http://www.sec.gov/litigation/litreleases/2011/lr21934.htm, accessed 12 August 2013.

334 Securities and Exchange Commission '*SEC v. James Clements and Zeina Smidi*, Civil Action No. 11-cv-60673-LSS, (S.D. Fla.)', 30 March 2011, available from http://www.sec.gov/litigation/litreleases/2011/lr21910.htm, accessed 12 August 2013.

335 Securities and Exchange Commission 'SEC halts $47 million investment fraud at Utah-based payday loan companies', 28 March 2011, available from http://www.sec.gov/news/press/2011/2011-73.htm, accessed 12 August 2013.

336 Securities and Exchange Commission '*Securities and Exchange Commission v. Mike Watson Capital, LLC, Michael P. Watson and Joshua F. Escobedo*, Civil Action No. 2:11-CV-00275 (DB) (D. Utah)', 24 March 2011, available from http://www.sec.gov/litigation/litreleases/2011/lr21898.htm, accessed 12 August 2013.

337 Securities and Exchange Commission 'SEC charges three executives with conducting $230 million investment scheme at Ohio-based company', 16 March 2011, available from http://www.sec.gov/news/press/2011/2011-67.htm, accessed 12 August 2013.

338 Securities and Exchange Commission 'SEC charges Connecticut-based hedge fund manager for fraudulent misuse of investor assets', 28 January 2011, available from http://www.sec.gov/news/press/2011/2011-30.htm, accessed 12 August 2013.

339 Securities and Exchange Commission 'EC brings charges in Puerto Rico-based Ponzi scheme targeting Evangelical Christians and factory workers', 21 August 2012, available from http://www.sec.gov/News/PressRelease/Detail/PressRelease/1365171483948, accessed 12 August 2013.

340 Securities and Exchange Commission 'SEC shuts down $600 million online pyramid and Ponzi scheme', 17 August 2012, available from http://www.sec.gov/News/PressRelease/Detail/PressRelease/1365171483920, accessed 12 August 2013.

341 Securities and Exchange Commission 'SEC charges college football hall of fame coach in $80 million Ponzi scheme', 12 August 2012, available from http://www.sec.gov/News/PressRelease/Detail/PressRelease/1365171483824, accessed 12 August 2013.

342 Securities and Exchange Commission 'SEC shuts down $42 million Ponzi-like scheme', 28 June 2012, available from http://www.sec.gov/News/PressRelease/Detail/PressRelease/1365171482944, accessed 12 August 2013.

Palmer,[343] Gurudeo 'Buddy' Persaud,[344] 14 sales agents,[345] George Levin and Frank Preve,[346] David Connolly,[347] Shervin Neman,[348] Ephren Taylor II,[349] Duncan MacDonald and Gloria Solomon,[350] Mark Morrow and Detroit Memorial Partners,[351] Alvin R. Brown and First Choice Investment,[352]

---

[343] Securities and Exchange Commission 'SEC halts $100 million real-estate based Ponzi scheme', 25 June 2012, available from http://www.sec.gov/News/PressRelease/Detail/PressRelease/1365171482748, accessed 12 August 2013.

[344] Securities and Exchange Commission 'SEC charges Florida broker in astrology-based Ponzi scheme', 21 June 2012, available from http://www.sec.gov/News/PressRelease/Detail/PressRelease/1365171482724, accessed 12 August 2013.

[345] Securities and Exchange Commission 'SEC charges 14 sales agents in $415 million Long Island-based Ponzi scheme', 12 June 2012, available from http://www.sec.gov/News/PressRelease/Detail/PressRelease/1365171482580, accessed 12 August 2013.

[346] Securities and Exchange Commission 'SEC charges two feeders for one of south Florida's largest-ever Ponzi schemes', 22 May 2012, available from http://www.sec.gov/News/PressRelease/Detail/PressRelease/1365171482252, accessed 12 August 2013.

[347] Securities and Exchange Commission 'SEC charges New Jersey man in real estate investment scam', 17 May 2012, available from http://www.sec.gov/News/PressRelease/Detail/PressRelease/1365171489172, accessed 12 August 2013.

[348] Securities and Exchange Commission 'SEC shuts down Ponzi scheme targeting Persian–Jewish community in Los Angeles', 13 April 2012, available from http://www.sec.gov/News/PressRelease/Detail/PressRelease/1365171488330, accessed 12 August 2013.

[349] Securities and Exchange Commission 'SEC charges Ponzi schemer targeting church congregations', 12 April 2012, available from http://www.sec.gov/News/PressRelease/Detail/PressRelease/1365171488284, accessed 12 August 2013.

[350] Securities and Exchange Commission 'SEC charges two executives in Ponzi scheme at Dallas-based medical insurance company', 17 June 2013, available from http://www.sec.gov/News/PressRelease/Detail/PressRelease/1365171574926, accessed 12 August 2013.

[351] Securities and Exchange Commission 'SEC charges Cincinnati resident and Delaware firm with offering fraud', 3 June 2013, available from http://www.sec.gov/litigation/litreleases/2013/lr22712.htm, accessed 12 August 2013.

[352] Securities and Exchange Commission 'SEC shuts down real estate investment scheme in Redondo Beach', 12 March 2013, available from http://www.sec.gov/litigation/litreleases/2013/lr22642.htm, accessed 12 August 2013.

Walter Ng, Kelly Ng, and Bruce Horwitz,[353] and five real estate executives.[354] The SEC took the view that:

> Since fiscal year 2010, the SEC has brought more than 100 enforcement actions against nearly 200 individuals and 250 entities for carrying out Ponzi schemes. In these actions, more than 65 individuals have been barred from working in the securities industry. The SEC also has worked closely with the U.S. Department of Justice and other criminal authorities on parallel criminal and civil proceedings against Ponzi scheme operations.[355]

The CFTC has been heavily involved in the LIBOR scandal and has imposed several financial sanctions on banks. For example, in June 2012 the CFTC fined Barclays $200m for its attempted manipulation and false reporting of LIBOR and EURIBOR.[356] Barclays also agreed to 'implement a series of compliance measures and additional controls with respect to its contributions to the LIBOR'.[357] This has been described as an example of the CFTC 'willing to combat manipulation in commodity staples markets'.[358] The CFTC's Director of Enforcement, David Meister took the view that:

---

353 Securities and Exchange Commission '*Securities and Exchange Commission v. Walter Ng, Kelly Ng, Bruce Horwitz, and The Mortgage Fund, LLC*, Civil Action No. C-13 0895-NC (U.S. District Court for the Northern District of California)', 28 February 2013, available from http://www.sec.gov/litigation/litreleases/2013/lr22628.htm, accessed 12 August 2013.

354 Securities and Exchange Commission 'SEC charges real estate executives in Florida-based $300 million investment scheme', 30 January 2013, available from http://www.sec.gov/News/PressRelease/Detail/PressRelease/1365171513950, accessed 12 August 2013.

355 Securities and Exchange Commission 'SEC enforcement actions against Ponzi schemes', n/d, available from http://www.sec.gov/spotlight/enf-actions-ponzi.shtml, accessed 12 August 2013.

356 Commodities Futures Trading Commission 'FTC orders Barclays to pay $200 million penalty for attempted manipulation of and false reporting concerning LIBOR and Euribor benchmark interest rates', 27 June 2012, available from http://www.cftc.gov/PressRoom/PressReleases/pr6289-12, accessed 12 August 2013. Also see Gensler, G. 'Libor, naked and exposed', 6 August 2012, available from http://www.nytimes.com/2012/08/07/opinion/libor-naked-and-exposed.html?_r=3&ref=opinionpiecesaboutlibor&, accessed 12 August 2013.

357 Feldman, W. 'Staying in compliance: key issues for white collar crime attorneys and their multinational clients' (2013) Aspatore, March, 2–7, at 2.

358 Greenberger, M. 'Striking the right balance: investor and consumer protection in the new financial marketplace' (2013) George Washington Law Review, April, 81, 707–748, at 747.

> The American public and our markets rely upon the integrity of benchmark interest rates like LIBOR and Euribor because they form the basis for hundreds of trillions of dollars of transactions and affect nearly every corner of the global economy … banks that contribute information to those benchmarks must do so honestly. When a bank acts in its own self-interest by attempting to manipulate these rates for profit, or by submitting false reports that result from senior management orders to lower submissions to guard the bank's reputation, the integrity of benchmark interest rates is undermined. The CFTC launched this investigation to protect the markets and the public from such illegal conduct, and today's action demonstrates that we will bring the full force of our authority to bear as we carry out that mission.[359]

Furthermore, CFTC fined UBS $700m for its attempted manipulation and false reporting of LIBOR and EURIBOR.[360] David Meister stated that:

> As our action today makes clear, when a major bank brazenly games some of the world's most important financial benchmarks, the CFTC will respond with the full force of its authority … the American public, as well as people and companies around the globe, rely on interest rate benchmarks every day for mortgages, loans and other transactions, trusting that the underlying benchmark rates are honest. Market integrity is seriously compromised where, as here, a bank spins its rate submissions to boost trading profits, pays off a network of brokers to disseminate false rate information, or makes false submissions to protect its reputation.[361]

In February 2013, the CFTC fined RBS $325m for its manipulation, attempted manipulation and false reporting of the yen and Swiss franc LIBOR.[362] David Meister stated that:

> the integrity of LIBOR depends on truthful information provided by a select group of some of the world's most important banks. The public is deprived of an honest benchmark interest rate when a group of traders sits around a desk

---

[359] Commodities Futures Trading Commission above, n 356.

[360] Commodities Futures Trading Commission 'CFTC orders UBS to pay $700 million penalty to settle charges of manipulation, attempted manipulation and false reporting of LIBOR and other benchmark interest rates', 19 December 2012, available from http://www.cftc.gov/PressRoom/PressReleases/pr6472-12, accessed 12 August 2013.

[361] *Ibid.*

[362] Commodities Futures Trading Commission 'CFTC orders The Royal Bank of Scotland plc and RBS Securities Japan Limited to pay $325 million penalty to settle charges of manipulation, attempted manipulation, and false reporting of yen and Swiss franc LIBOR', 6 February 2013, available from http://www.cftc.gov/PressRoom/PressReleases/pr6510-13, accessed 12 August 2013.

> for years falsely spinning their bank's LIBOR submissions, trying to manufacture winning trades. That's what happened at RBS.[363]

In September 2013, the CFTC fined ICAP Europe Limited $65m civil monetary penalty for 'manipulation, attempted manipulation, false reporting, and aiding and abetting derivatives traders' manipulation and attempted manipulation' of LIBOR.[364] The Chairman of the CFTC, Gary Gensler stated that the

> Order against ICAP once again shows how LIBOR, a critical benchmark interest rate not anchored in sufficient transactions, has been readily rigged. Unfortunately, this is yet another reminder of why we have to coordinate internationally to transition to an alternative to LIBOR to best restore the integrity to markets. Today's Order also highlights the importance of Congress' reforms through the Dodd–Frank Act to bring oversight to swaps trading platforms. Required registration of swap execution facilities becomes a reality next week, finally closing exemptions that had allowed for unregistered, multilateral swaps trading platforms.[365]

Michael Spencer, the ICAP Chief Executive Officer stated:

> We deeply regret and strongly condemn the inexcusable actions of the brokers who sought to assist certain bank traders in their efforts to manipulate YEN Libor. Their conduct contravenes all that ICAP stands for. As soon as their actions came to light, we provided assistance to regulators in the US and UK to understand what had happened. None of the three individuals at the center of the activity remains with the firm. Others are either no longer with the company or are being disciplined. There were no findings that any senior

---

[363] *Ibid.*

[364] Commodities Futures Trading Commission 'CFTC charges ICAP Europe Limited, a subsidiary of ICAP plc, with manipulation and attempted manipulation of yen Libor', 25 September 2013, available from http://www.cftc.gov/PressRoom/PressReleases/pr6708-13, accessed 25 September 2013. Also see Stafford, P., Binham, C. and Scannell, K. 'ICAP agrees to pay £55m to settle Libor claims', 25 September 2013, available from http://www.ft.com/cms/s/0/885dc438-2522-11e3-9b22-00144feab7de.html#axzz2fuu8kZ8W, accessed 25 September 2013 and BBC News 'Libor: ICAP fined $87m by UK and US regulators', 25 September 2013, available from http://www.bbc.co.uk/news/business-24250750, accessed 25 September 2013.

[365] Commodities Futures Trading Commission 'Statement of chairman Gary Gensler on settlement order against ICAP', 25 September 2013, available from http://www.cftc.gov/PressRoom/SpeechesTestimony/genslerstatement092513, accessed 25 September 2013.

management were involved in this matter nor that the firm engaged in deliberate misconduct.[366]

Additionally, the Department of Justice has also attempted to use various civil enforcement mechanisms, including filing a $1bn civil law suit against Bank of America Corporation.[367] It played a key role in obtaining the largest settlement ($25bn) for robo-signing,[368] it also acquired the largest fair lending settlement ($335m) with Countrywide Financial Corporation[369] and the second largest fair lending settlement ($125m) against Wells Fargo Bank.[370] In relation to the manipulation of LIBOR the Department of Justice reached an agreement with Barclays Bank that the latter would pay $160m penalty for its actions. The Department of Justice stated that:

> LIBOR and EURIBOR are critically important benchmark interest rates … because mortgages, student loans, financial derivatives, and other financial products rely on LIBOR and EURIBOR as reference rates, the manipulation of submissions used to calculate those rates can have significant negative effects on consumers and financial markets worldwide. For years, traders at Barclays encouraged the manipulation of LIBOR and EURIBOR submissions in order to benefit their financial positions; and, in the midst of the financial crisis, Barclays management directed that U.S. Dollar LIBOR submissions be artificially lowered. For this illegal conduct, Barclays is paying a significant price. To the bank's credit, Barclays also took a significant step toward

---

[366] ICAP 'ICAP Europe Ltd reaches settlements with FCA and CFTC', 25 September 2013, available from http://www.icap.com/news-events/in-the-news/news/2013/130925-icap-europe-ltd-reaches-settlements-with-fca-and-cftc.aspx, accessed 25 September 2013.

[367] Department of Justice 'Department of Justice sues Bank of America for defrauding investors in connection with sale of over $850 million of residential mortgage-backed securities', 6 August 2013, available from http://www.justice.gov/opa/pr/2013/August/13-ag-886.html, accessed 2 October 2013.

[368] Department of Justice '$25 billion mortgage servicing agreement filed in Federal Court', 12 March 2012, available from http://www.justice.gov/opa/pr/2012/March/12-asg-306.html, accessed 2 October 2013.

[369] Department of Justice 'Justice Department reaches $335 million settlement to resolve allegations of lending discrimination by Countrywide Financial Corporation', 21 December 2012, available from http://www.justice.gov/opa/pr/2011/December/11-ag-1694.html, accessed 2 October 2013.

[370] Department of Justice 'Manhattan U.S. attorney files mortgage fraud lawsuit against Wells Fargo Bank, N.A. seeking hundreds of millions of dollars in damages for fraudulently certified loans', 9 October 2012, available from http://www.justice.gov/usao/nys/pressreleases/October12/WellsFargoLawsuitPR.html, accessed 2 October 2013.

> accepting responsibility for its conduct by being the first institution to provide extensive and meaningful cooperation to the government. Its efforts have substantially assisted the Criminal Division in our ongoing investigation of individuals and other financial institutions in this matter.[371]

In December 2012, the Department of Justice announced that UBS Securities Japan, a subsidiary of UBS, pleaded guilty to wire fraud and its role in manipulating LIBOR.[372] The company has entered into an agreement with the Department of Justice which required it to pay a $100m fine. Additionally, its parent company, UBS AG, entered into a non-prosecution agreement which resulted in the payment of a further $400m fine.[373] The Attorney General stated:

> By causing UBS and other financial institutions to spread false and misleading information about LIBOR, the alleged conspirators we've charged – along with others at UBS – manipulated the benchmark interest rate upon which many transactions and consumer financial products are based. They defrauded the company's counterparties of millions of dollars. And they did so primarily to reap increased profits, and secure bigger bonuses, for themselves … today's announcement – and $1.5 billion global resolution – underscores the Justice Department's firm commitment to investigating and prosecuting such conduct, and to holding the perpetrators of these crimes accountable for their actions.[374]

Additionally, in February 2013 the Department of Justice announced that RBS Securities Japan Limited, a subsidiary of RBS, had pleaded guilty to wire fraud and manipulation as part of the Japense yen LIBOR as part of a deferred prosecution agreement.[375] The Assistant Attorney General stated:

---

[371] Department of Justice 'Barclays Bank PLC admits misconduct related to submissions for the London Interbank Offered Rate and the Euro Interbank Offered Rate and agrees to pay $160 million penalty', 27 June 2012, available from http://www.justice.gov/opa/pr/2012/June/12-crm-815.html, accessed 13 August 2013.

[372] Department of Justice 'UBS Securities Japan Co. Ltd. to plead guilty to felony wire fraud for long-running manipulation of LIBOR benchmark interest rates', 19 December 2012, available from http://www.justice.gov/opa/pr/2012/December/12-ag-1522.html, accessed 13 August 2013.

[373] *Ibid.*

[374] *Ibid.*

[375] Department of Justice 'RBS Securities Japan Limited agrees to plead guilty in connection with long-running manipulation of Libor benchmark interest rates', 6 February 2013, available from http://www.justice.gov/opa/pr/2013/February/13-crm-161.html, accessed 13 August 2013.

> As we have done with Barclays and UBS, we are today holding RBS accountable for a stunning abuse of trust … The bank has admitted to manipulating one of the cornerstone benchmark interest rates in our global financial system, and its Japanese subsidiary has agreed to plead guilty to felony wire fraud. The department's ongoing investigation has now yielded two guilty pleas by significant financial institutions. These are extraordinary results, and our investigation is far from finished. Our message is clear: no financial institution is above the law.[376]

4.5 CONCLUSIONS

> Despite the inevitable criticism, federal law enforcement agencies, including the Justice Department and the SEC, have sought to hold many individuals and institutions accountable for actions contributing to the financial crisis, just not in the manner that the financial industry's harshest critics would want – more criminal cases.[377]

> Although these actions are a step in the right direction, there is no excuse for the lack of prosecutions of any senior executives responsible almost five years after the start of the recession. FERA has been in effect for three years now, and the increased investigations have not rendered any indictments, never mind convictions. Time may be running out for the federal government to show the public that those responsible will face justice. Without such protections, and if Wall Street bankers are permitted to profit from their frauds without a proportionate retributive response, we may be fated to repeat the same economic calamity that has defined our generation.[378]

The initial response to the financial crisis in the US was to introduce and implement a series of legislative measures that attempted to stabilise the US economy. This partly involved providing federal funding for failing institutions whose losses were clearly exposed at the height of the financial crisis. President George Bush introduced several of these legislative measures including the Housing and Economic Recovery Act 2008 and the Emergency Economic Stabilization Act 2008. One of the most controversial aspects of the response from the Bush administration was the creation of the $700bn TARP program, which would later be reduced to $475bn by the Dodd–Frank Wall Street Reform Act 2010. However, as was demonstrated earlier in this monograph, TARP has been targeted and abused by white collar criminals for fraudulent activities. For example, in May 2013 the FBI reported that four people had been

---

376 *Ibid.*

377 Abramowitz and Sack above, n 175, at 2.

378 Maher above, n 127, at 475–476.

convicted of a TARP related fraud that resulted in the collapse of the Bank of the Commonwealth.[379] The response towards the financial crisis and white collar crime in the US has been largely led by the Department of Justice, the FBI, the SEC and the CFTC. Each of these agencies has attempted to adopt a robust stance to the illegal activities within its law enforcement regulatory remit. The origins of the policy or strategy adopted towards white collar crime and the most recent financial crisis were heavily influenced by *misguided* white collar decisions made prior to 2007. For example, following the al-Qaeda terrorist attacks in September 2001 President George Bush instigated the 'War on Terror'. This had a detrimental impact on the efforts of the FBI to tackle the incoming tidal wave of mortgage fraud cases. As a result of the 'War on Terror' and the need to maintain homeland security, President George Bush redirected the resources of the FBI away from white collar crime towards tackling terrorism. Therefore, in the words of former Attorney General Michael Mukasey, 'national security … was an overriding concern'.[380] Three years after the terrorist attacks, the FBI requested additional funding and resources from President George Bush to tackle white collar crime, and in particular mortgage fraud. The then Assistant Director of the FBI, Chris Swecker described the threat posed by mortgage fraud as having 'the potential to be an epidemic' and said that the FBI 'can prevent a problem that could have as much impact as the Savings and Loans Crisis'.[381] This request was rejected, thus limiting the effectiveness of the FBI to deal with mortgage fraud, at a time when reported instances of mortgage fraud had increased 20 fold.[382] The impact of this decision on the FBI was graphically highlighted by Pontell *et al,* who noted that:

> The full extent of law-breaking in the world of subprime lending remains to be seen, although enforcement agencies, concentrating their resources on homeland security, will be hard-pressed to satisfactorily investigate this issue.

---

379 Federal Bureau of Investigation 'Executives, borrower convicted in Virginia of massive fraud scheme that led to collapse of Bank of the Commonwealth', 24 May 2013, available from http://www.fbi.gov/norfolk/press-releases/2013/executives-borrower-convicted-in-virginia-of-massive-fraud-scheme-that-led-to-collapse-of-bank-of-the-commonwealth, accessed 15 October 2013.

380 The Financial Crisis Inquiry Commission *The Financial Crisis Inquiry Commission report* (Financial Crisis Inquiry Commission: Washington DC, 2011) at 15.

381 Frieden, T. 'FBI warns of mortgage fraud "epidemic"', 17 September 2004, available from http://edition.cnn.com/2004/LAW/09/17/mortgage.fraud/, accessed 15 October 2013.

382 Financial Crisis Inquiry Commission above, n 380, at xxii.

> There was a 36% staff reduction beginning in 2001 of FBI agents dealing with white collar crime.[383]

Therefore, when Barack Obama became the 44th President of the US in 2009, he faced a superabundance of economic problems that were fuelled by the largest financial crisis since the Great Depression and Wall Street Crash. Expectedly, this became an area of great importance and resulted in the introduction of several legislative measures, including the American Recovery and Reinvestment Act 2009, the Fraud Enforcement and Recovery Act 2009 and the Dodd–Frank Wall Street Reform Act 2012. These measures aimed to restore confidence in the US banking system and maintain its financial stability. However, the aim of the Fraud Enforcement and Recovery Act 2009 can be contrasted with the other legislative measures because it aimed to tackle white collar crime associated with the financial crisis. The legislation resulted in the *rebalancing* of the amount of federal funding for white collar crime related agencies, including the FBI, SEC and Department of Justice. This has contributed towards a significant increase in the number of investigations, arrests and mortgage fraud related convictions secured by the FBI. However, the results of this additional funding must be questioned when compared with the response to the Savings and Loans Crisis, which resulted in approximately 800 fraud related convictions. The results since the financial crisis have been tainted in the eyes of several commentators because, despite the FBI instigating numerous investigations, there has not been one high profile bank related conviction.[384] Izant took the view that:

> Ultimately, however the prosecution of any criminal case turns on the ability of the government to satisfy its burden of proof. Thus the primary reason why no high-ranking Wall Street executive has faced criminal charges for any wrongdoing that might have contributed to the financial crisis may be the difficulty faced by the government in its obligation to prove mens rea. In order to successfully prosecute a defendant for financial fraud under federal law, the government is required to prove intentional deceit, and prosecutors may not believe that a jury could be persuaded that any potential defendant is guilty beyond a reasonable doubt. Some analysts have therefore concluded

---

383 Pontell *et al* above, n 132, at 2.
384 *Ibid*., at 3.

that the paucity of criminal prosecutions from the financial crisis shows that the real difficulty lies in gathering evidence to prove a crime took place.[385]

Additionally, President Barack Obama authorised the creation of the Financial Fraud Enforcement Task Force to directly tackle white collar crime, including securities and mortgage fraud emanating from the financial crisis. This resulted in immediate action from the Task Force and its members. However, the burst of enthusiasm was short lived, as outlined towards the end of this chapter. Therefore, the response by President Barack Obama to the financial crisis and white collar crime can be categorised as *predictable* as similar responses were made to the threat of corporate bribery in the 1970s, the Savings and Loans Crisis in the 1980s, securities fraud, the so called 'mega frauds', and the collapse of Enron and WorldCom.[386] For example, in response to the collapse of Enron and WorldCom President George Bush introduced the Sarbanes–Oxley Act in 2002. This measure was supported by the creation of the Corporate Fraud Task Force, which in conjunction with the Department of Justice 'obtained nearly 1,300 corporate fraud convictions. These figures include convictions of more than 200 chief executive officers and corporate presidents, more than 120 corporate vice presidents, and more than 50 chief financial officers'.[387]

It is clear that the SEC has been the most active regulatory agency since the start of the financial crisis. The SEC has charged over 160 companies and individuals since the start of the financial crisis and recovered $2.7bn for investors. All of the enforcement activities instigated by the SEC are of a civil nature and either amount to the imposition of a financial sanction or a prohibition order. The SEC has imposed a number of high profile financial sanctions on firms which have breached its rules and regulations. For example, Goldman Sachs agreed to a civil penalty of $550m, JP Morgan paid a penalty of $153.6m and Mizuho Securities USA received a $127.5m penalty. The SEC does not have the ability to instigate criminal proceedings and it is exclusively reliant on the referrals it makes to the Department of Justice. The SEC

---

385 Izant, J. 'Mens rea and the Martin Act: a weapon of choice for securities fraud prosecutions?' (2012) Columbia Business Law Review, 2012, 913–993, at 926.

386 Dooley and Radke above, n 75, at 625–635. It is interesting to note that the United States has a very long history with white collar crime. For example, Huynh took the view that 'due to misconduct of American companies like Wright-Mills in the 1940's and 1960's, public distrust of big business grew'. See Huynh above, n 118, at 108.

387 Corporate Fraud Task Force 2003 above, n 187, at iii.

must be criticised for its weak response to white collar crime associated with the financial crisis. The clearest example of its ineffective approach related to the Ponzi fraud scheme instigated by Bernard Madoff, who the SEC could and should have stopped on numerous occasions. Nonetheless, the SEC has continued to instigate an enforcement strategy that seeks to continuously impose financial sanctions on firms which have breached its regulations. This stance has also been followed by the Department of Justice and the CFTC, which have imposed large financial sanctions on firms since the start of the financial crisis. For example, the CFTC and Department of Justice have imposed record financial penalties on banks which have manipulated LIBOR, an identical stance to regulatory bodies around the world responding to the LIBOR scandal. At the time of writing there have been no criminal convictions of traders allegedly involved in the manipulation of LIBOR. Maher noted that there have been 'zero convictions of executives of the companies responsible for the financial crisis. There are several reasons for the lack of convictions, including the lack of government resources, the difficulty of building a case against a white-collar crime defendant, and a lack of aggression by the Department of Justice.'[388] However, the Department of Justice charged three ICAP traders on several counts of wire fraud in September 2013.

US authorities have a plethora of criminal legislative provisions that could have been used since the financial crisis. A vast majority of the criminal proceedings instigated since 2007 by the Department of Justice and the FBI have generally targeted people involved in mortgage fraud. As outlined earlier in this chapter, the FBI has conducted numerous investigations into banks following the financial crisis. However, the FBI has failed to successfully convict any member of Wall Street associated with the alleged misconduct prior to or during the financial crisis. It is accepted that it is extremely difficult to secure white collar crime related convictions and in many investigations the conduct discovered by law enforcement agencies was irresponsible and unethical, but not necessarily criminal. It appears that US law enforcement agencies have created an enforcement culture that seeks to avoid prosecuting corporations. Therefore, the response towards white collar crime and the financial crisis can be completely contrasted with that adopted for the Savings and Loans Crisis.

388 Maher above, n 127, at 460.

5. United Kingdom – Policy, legislative, regulatory and enforcement responses

Financial crime has attracted considerable attention over the years because of a perception that regulators and law enforcement authorities have taken a relatively lax approach to enforcement and prosecution when compared with other forms of criminality. While this view may be simplistic, in that it ignores the real difficulties in bringing prosecutions in respect of complex financial transactions, it is certainly the case that some individuals found to have engaged in wrongdoing have escaped relatively lightly. A frequently mentioned example is that of Philippe Jabre, an investment manager at a UK hedge fund who was subject to a financial penalty of £750,000 under the FSA's civil market abuse regime. Mr Jabre subsequently relocated to Geneva where he was promptly able to resume fund management activities. The outcome did not present a significant or credible deterrent to others, notwithstanding the relatively high level of the fine imposed on Mr Jabre.[1]

5.1 INTRODUCTION

The aim of this penultimate chapter is to critically consider the response towards the relationship between the financial crisis and white collar crime in the UK. The chapter begins by seeking to identify the UK's policy towards white collar crime since the start of the financial crisis in 2007. This has been achieved by undertaking a detailed and analytical review of the overabundance of policy commissioned reviews published by the former Labour and current Coalition governments. This section of the chapter highlights and critiques the meaningful policy disparities between the governments and is illustrated in two particular instances. First, the contrasting strategies and policies towards banking regulation since the onset of the financial crisis. Secondly, the differing approaches

1 Srivastava, A., Mason, I., Simpson, M. and Litt, M. 'Financial crime' (2011) Compliance Officer Bulletin, May, 86,, 1–23, at 1. Hereafter Srivastava *et al.*

towards white collar crime and the determination of the strategic placement of a dedicated white collar crime enforcement agency. The second part of the chapter outlines and critically considers the impact of the legislative responses towards white collar crime that emanated from the financial crisis. Reference will be made to the central statutory provisions of the Financial Services Act 2012 and the Courts and Crime Act 2013. The penultimate part of the chapter judiciously critiques the regulatory responses to white collar crime associated with the financial crisis. Particular reference is made to the role of the FSA, SFO, NCA and FCA. This final part of the chapter analyses the enforcement response towards white collar crime associated with the financial crisis. Particular attention will be given to the use of financial sanctions at the expense of instigating criminal proceedings.

5.2 POLICY AND LEGISLATIVE RESPONSE

In order to be in a position to critically consider the responses towards white collar crime and the financial crisis, it is essential to identify the initial strategies adopted by the former Labour government towards white collar crime and the regulation of banks. This is important because the Labour government introduced a plethora of white collar crime measures that were initially housed and influenced by its banking regulation policy. Therefore, this section of the chapter outlines the foundations of the former government's policy towards banking regulation following its 1997 general election victory and how it contained several white collar crime initiatives. Furthermore, it also comments on its legislative and regulatory responses to the financial crisis.

5.2.1 The Labour Government

The foundations of the initial policy response by the Labour government towards the financial crisis were heavily influenced by the bold statement made by the then Chancellor of the Exchequer, Gordon Brown MP, in May 1997. He stated that 'the [then] Securities and Investments Board (SIB) will become the *single* [author's emphasis] regulator underpinned by statute. The current system of self-regulation will be replaced by a new and fully statutory system, which will put the public interest first, and increase public confidence in the system.'[2] This statement was followed by the controversial transfer of the banking regulatory powers

---

2 HC Debs. Col. 510, 20 May 1997.

away from the Bank of England to the FSA,[3] the introduction of a single statutory framework via the Financial Services and Markets Act 2000 and the creation of a single financial regulatory agency. The creation of the FSA was a unique and brave attempt by the Labour government to reform a system of banking regulation that had been poorly administered by the Bank of England. The lasting legacy of the Bank of England was overshadowed and tarnished by a series of financial scandals, including the secondary banking crisis, the collapse of Johnson Matthey Bank, Barlow Clowes, the Bank of Credit Commerce International, Barings Bank and Equitable Life. However, the performance of its successor, the FSA, was also hindered by a series of scandals, including Northern Rock and LIBOR. In relation to the well documented collapse of Northern Rock,[4] the FSA published its own review of how it mishandled the regulation of the bank.[5] Additionally, the ineffective regulatory performance of the FSA was condemned by a damning report published by the HM Treasury Select Committee.[6] Following the onset of the financial crisis, the Labour government commissioned Lord Turner to undertake a detailed review of how banks should be regulated. Specifically, he was asked to 'review the causes of the current crisis, and to make recommendations on the changes in regulation and supervisory approach needed to create a more robust banking system'.[7] Lord Turner's final report identified several factors that contributed towards the financial crisis and it also made a set of recommendations aimed at improving the levels of banking regulation.[8] Lord Turner stated that:

---

[3] Bank of England Act 1998, s. 21.

[4] For a detailed discussion of the collapse of Northern Rock see Gray, J. and Akseli, O. *Financial regulation in crisis? The role of law and the failure of Northern Rock* (Edward Elgar: Cheltenham, 2011).

[5] Financial Services Authority *The supervision of Northern Rock: a lessons learned review* (Financial Services Authority: London, 2008).

[6] HM Treasury Select Committee *The run on the Rock* (HM Treasury Select Committee: London, 2008).

[7] Financial Services Authority *The Turner Review: a regulatory response to the global banking crisis* (Financial Services Authority: London, 2009) at 5.

[8] Financial Services Authority 'The FSA publishes the Turner Review: a wide-ranging review of global banking regulation', 18 March 2009, available from http://www.fsa.gov.uk/pages/library/communication/pr/2009/037.shtml, accessed 25 June 2013. For a brief comment on the Turner Review see Anon. 'Turner Review sets out a new approach for banking regulation' (2009) Company Lawyer, 30(7), 211.

> The financial crisis has challenged the intellectual assumptions on which previous regulatory approaches were largely built, and in particular the theory of rational and self-correcting markets. Much financial innovation has proved of little value, and market discipline of individual bank strategies has often proved ineffective. A global market economy remains the best means of delivering global prosperity: it requires a global banking system focused on serving the needs of businesses and households, not in taking risks for quick return. Major changes in regulation and in supervisory approach are required to deliver that. The approach has to build on a system-wide perspective: failure to look at the big picture was far more important to the origins of the crisis than any specific failures in supervising individual firms. And it must reflect the reality of a global financial system without a global government; we need both far more intense international cooperation and greater use of national powers. The changes recommended are profound, and the banking system of the future will be different from that of the last decade. The world's economy will be better served as a result.[9]

The Turner Report made 32 recommendations which applied to a wide range of related areas, including capital adequacy, accounting and liquidity, institutional and geographic coverage of regulation, deposit insurance, bank resolution, CRAs, remuneration, credit default swap market infrastructure, macro-prudential analysis, FSA supervisory approach, firm risk management and governance, utility banking versus investment banking, global cross-border banks and European cross-border banks,[10] the Labour government commissioned the Walker Review, with the following terms of reference:

> to examine corporate governance in the UK banking industry and make recommendations, including in the following areas: the effectiveness of risk management at board level, including the incentives in remuneration policy to manage risk effectively; the balance of skills, experience and independence required on the boards of UK banking institutions; the effectiveness of board practices and the performance of audit, risk, remuneration and nomination committees; the role of institutional shareholders in engaging effectively with companies and monitoring of boards; and whether the UK approach is consistent with international practice and how national and international best practice can be promulgated.[11]

---

[9] Financial Services Authority, *ibid.*

[10] Financial Services Authority above, n 7.

[11] HM Treasury 'Walker Review of corporate governance of UK banking industry', n/d, available from http://webarchive.nationalarchives.gov.uk/+/http:/www.hm-treasury.gov.uk/walker_review_information.htm, accessed 16 September 2013.

The Walker Review made 38 recommendations that dealt with, *inter alia*, bankers' bonuses, the configuration and function of boards, the role of shareholders, risk and remuneration.[12] Both of these reviews were followed by the introduction of the Financial Services Act 2010, which contained numerous amendments to the Financial Services and Markets Act 2000. For example, it included the extension of the statutory objectives of the FSA to include 'financial stability'.[13] The amendments to the Financial Services and Markets Act 2000 were divided into seven parts.[14] First, the FSA was granted innovative powers to establish rules regarding the payment mechanisms of financial services firms.[15] Secondly, the FSA was allowed to create rules relating to recovery and resolution plans.[16] Thirdly, the regulatory agency was permitted to ban short selling.[17] Fourthly, the FSA's powers of intervention against financial services firms were increased.[18] Fifthly, the FSA was granted additional disciplinary powers.[19] Sixthly, the Act introduced a new form of consumer redress scheme.[20] Finally, the FSA was given new powers to force the production of more information by the financial services sector.[21] Therefore, it can be argued that the policy of the Labour government towards banking regulation was initially to create a single financial regulatory agency under a single legislative framework. In

---

12 Anon. 'Final recommendations of Walker review published' (2010) Company Lawyer, 31(3), 81, at 81.

13 Financial Services Act 2010, s. 1.

14 Willmott, N., McGowan, P., Ghusn, M., Brocklehurst, V., Aikens, R., Bailey, S., Scodie, M. and Palme, J. 'Equipping the modern regulator: assessing the new regulatory powers under the Financial Services Act 2010' (2010) Compliance Officer Bulletin, July/August, 78, 1–28, at 3.

15 Financial Services Act 2010, ss. 3–6.

16 Financial Services Act 2010, s. 7.

17 Financial Services Act 2010, s. 8. For a more detailed discussion of the regulation of short selling see Marshall, H., Leonard, C. and Siriwardhane, A. 'The regulation of short selling in the UK' (2009) Compliance Officer Bulletin, February, 63, 1–29. It is also important to note that the European Union has also introduced a series of measures to regulate short selling. See in particular Juurikkala, O. 'Credit default swaps and the EU Short Selling Regulation: a critical analysis' (2012) European Company and Financial Law Review, 9(3), 307–341 and Payne, J. 'The regulation of short selling and its reform in Europe' (2012) European Business Organization Law Review, 13(3), 413–440.

18 Financial Services Act 2010, ss. 9–13.

19 Financial Services Act 2010, ss. 9–13.

20 Financial Services Act 2010, ss. 14–17.

21 Financial Services Act 2010, ss. 18–19.

response to the financial crisis the policy altered to *broaden* the scope of the statutory objectives of the FSA and to grant it *additional* enforcement powers.

It is interesting to note that at this stage there was little or no reference in either the Turner or Walker Review that suggested white collar crime was a contributory factor to the financial crisis. However, this does not mean that the Labour government neglected the area of white collar crime. Indeed, it must be credited with starting to develop and implement a wide range of measures aimed to tackle white collar crime. For example, one of the initial statutory objectives of the FSA was to reduce financial crime.[22] This was one of the most important provisions of the Financial Services and Markets Act 2000 because it provided the FSA with a specific legislative mandate to tackle white collar crime. For example, the FSA was granted extensive investigative powers and was able to prosecute for a wide range of white collar crime related offences.[23] Another important area of the Financial Services and Markets Act 2000 that dealt with white collar crime was the introduction of the market abuse regime.[24] The market abuse regime is used in conjunction with the insider dealing provisions of the Criminal Justice Act 1993.[25] Further evidence of the groundwork of a white collar crime policy was the publication of the UK's anti-money laundering and counter-terrorist financing strategies.[26] Furthermore, the Labour government transformed

---

[22] Financial Services and Markets Act 2000, s. 6.

[23] For a more detailed discussion of this statutory objective of the Financial Services Authority see Ryder, N. 'The Financial Services Authority and money laundering – a game of cat and mouse' (2008) Cambridge Law Journal, 67(3), 635–653.

[24] Financial Services and Markets Act 2000, s. 118. For a more detailed discussion see Harrison, K. and Ryder, N. *The law relating to financial crime in the United Kingdom* (Ashgate: Farnham, 2013) at 111–131.

[25] For an excellent commentary on the legislation relating to insider dealing see Alexander, R. *Insider dealing and money laundering in the EU: law and regulation* (Ashgate: Farnham, 2007) at 113–141. For an interesting discussion of how the insider dealing laws are enforced see Barnes, P. 'Insider dealing and market abuse: the UK's record on enforcement' (2011) International Journal of Law, Crime and Justice, 39, 174–189.

[26] See HM Treasury *Anti-money laundering strategy* (HM Treasury: London, 2004) and HM Treasury *Combating the financing of terrorism* (HM Treasury: London, 2002). For a more detailed commentary on the impact and effectiveness of the policy towards white collar crime as introduced by the Labour government see Ryder, N. 'The fight against illicit finance – a critical review of the Labour government's policy' (2011) Journal of Banking Regulation, 12(3), 252–275.

the failing management of the confiscation of the proceeds of crime and criminalisation of money laundering via the Proceeds of Crime Act 2002.[27] It also commissioned the Fraud Review and introduced the Fraud Act 2006, which have been described as 'a fresh crop of anti-fraud initiatives ... ostensibly demonstrating how fighting fraud [had become] a top priority [for the Labour government] in the UK'.[28] The Fraud Review was commissioned 'to recommend ways of reducing fraud and the harm it does to the economy and society'.[29] In particular, the Fraud Review considered three questions. First, what is the level of fraud? Secondly, what is the appropriate role of the government in dealing with fraud? Thirdly, how could government resources on fraud prevention represent value for money?[30] The Fraud Review was unable to accurately outline the extent of fraud. In relation to the second question, it noted that the government has two functions – to protect public money from fraudsters and to protect consumers and businesses against fraud. The Fraud Review suggested that the government should adopt a holistic approach towards fraud and develop a national fraud strategy which was to be implemented by the NFA.[31] It also suggested that a National Fraud Reporting Centre should be created so that businesses and individuals could report instances of fraud.[32] The National Fraud Intelligence Bureau has become the agency dedicated to analysing and assessing the threat

---

[27] For a more detailed commentary on the management of the confiscation of the proceeds of crime, money laundering and the Proceeds of Crime Act 2002 see Ryder, N. *Money laundering – an endless cycle? A comparative analysis of the anti-money laundering policies in the United States of America, the United Kingdom, Australia and Canada* (Routledge Cavendish: Abingdon, 2012) at 72–102.

[28] Sarker, R. 'Fighting fraud – a missed opportunity?' (2007) Company Lawyer, 28(8), 243–244, at 243. For a more detailed discussion on the counter-fraud strategies adopted by the government in the United Kingdom see Button, M. and Brooks, G. 'Mind the gap, a progress towards developing anti-fraud culture strategies in UK central government bodies' (2009) Journal of Financial Crime, 16(3), 229–244.

[29] Attorney General's Office *Fraud Review – final report* (Attorney General's Office: London, 2006) at 4.

[30] *Ibid.*, at 4–5.

[31] See for example National Fraud Authority *The National Fraud Strategy – a new approach to combating fraud* (National Fraud Authority: London, 2010) at 10.

[32] The National Fraud Reporting Centre is also referred to as 'Action Fraud'. See Action Fraud 'Who is Action Fraud?', n/d, available from http://www.actionfraud.police.uk/about-us/who-we-are, accessed 16 September 2013.

posed by fraud.[33] The Fraud Review also suggested that a national lead police should be established and based in the City of London Police Force.[34]

The introduction of the Fraud Act 2006 represented a significant alteration to statutory deception offences in the Theft Act (1968 and 1978) and the common law offence of conspiracy to defraud. The foundations of the Fraud Act 2006 are to be found in 1998, when the Labour government asked the Law Commission to examine reforming the law relating to fraud.[35] The Law Commission subsequently published a Consultation Paper,[36] and concluded that although the concerns expressed about the existing laws were valid they could be met by extending the existing offences in preference to creating a single offence of fraud.[37] The Law Commission published its final report in 2002, which was followed by the Fraud Act, which came into force on 15 January 2007.[38] The Fraud Act 2006 overhauled and widened the criminal offences available with respect to fraudulent and deceptive behaviour.[39] The new offence, punishable by imprisonment of up to ten

---

[33] See National Fraud Intelligence Bureau 'About us', n/d, available from http://www.cityoflondon.police.uk/CityPolice/About/, accessed 16 September 2013.

[34] For a more detailed discussion of the Fraud Review see Ryder above, n 26, at 257, 261 and 268.

[35] Specifically the Law Commission was asked to 'examine the law on fraud, and in particular to consider whether it: is readily comprehensible to juries; is adequate for effective prosecution; is fair to potential defendants; meets the need of developing technology including electronic means of transfer; and to make recommendations to improve the law in these respects with all due expedition. In making these recommendations to consider whether a general offence of fraud would improve the criminal law.' See HC Debates, 7 April 1998 c.176–177WA.

[36] Law Commission *Legislating the Criminal Code Fraud and Deception – Law Commission Consultation Paper no 155* (Law Commission: London, 1999).

[37] The Law Commission also published an informal discussion paper in 2000. See Law Commission *Fraud and deception – further proposals from the Criminal Law Team* (Law Commission: London, 2000).

[38] The Fraud Act 2006 (Commencement) Order 2006, S.I. 2006/3500.

[39] For a detailed commentary and analysis of the Fraud Act see Ormerod, D. (2007) 'The Fraud Act 2006 – criminalising lying?' Criminal Law Review, March, 193–219. However, it is important to note that not all of the offences under the Theft Act 1968 have been abolished. For example, false accounting (Theft Act 1968, s. 17), the liability of company directors (Theft Act 1968, s. 18), false statements by company directors (Theft Act 1968, s. 19) and dishonest destruction of documents (Theft Act 1968, s. 20(1)).

years and/or an unlimited fine, can be committed in three different ways: fraud by false representation,[40] fraud by failing to disclose information[41] and fraud by abuse of position.[42]

Therefore, the efforts of the Labour government to tackle white collar crime must be commended because they represented the most significant development in this area of law and policy since the recommendations of the Roskill Committee in 1987 and the creation of the SFO. These developments should have laid the foundations for an effective and holistic white collar crime policy that could have been utilised by the Coalition government. However, as the next section of the chapter illustrates, the response to white collar crime by the Coalition government has been lacklustre and generally ineffective.

5.2.2 Coalition Government

The Coalition government has adopted a different approach from its parliamentary predecessor and has focused more on the relationship between the financial crisis and the conduct of banks. For example, the Independent Commission on Banking, or the Vickers Commission, was established in June 2010.[43] George Osborne MP, Chancellor of the Exchequer, stated:

> The worst financial crisis in living memory highlighted the significant detrimental impact that failure in the financial sector can have on the real economy and the public finances. We need a proper debate about the future structure of banks, the relationship between retail and investment banking, and the question of how to ensure greater competition in the banking industry.[44]

The Vickers Commission was asked to consider 'the structure of the UK banking sector, and to look at structural and non-structural measures to

---

[40] Fraud Act 2006, s. 2.

[41] Fraud Act 2006, s. 3.

[42] Fraud Act 2006, s. 4.

[43] HM Treasury 'Speech at The Lord Mayor's Dinner for bankers and merchants of the City of London by The Chancellor of the Exchequer, The Rt Hon George Osborne MP, at Mansion House', 16 June 2010, available from http://webarchive.nationalarchives.gov.uk/20130129110402/http://www.hm-treasury.gov.uk/press_12_10.htm, accessed 25 June 2013.

[44] *Ibid.*

reform the banking system and promote competition'.[45] The Commission published an interim report in April 2011 which concentrated on the idea of ring fencing retail banks, that is, dividing deposit and lending functions from investment banking.[46] The final report, which was published in September 2011,[47] made a broad range of recommendations which were divided into three categories.[48] First, the recommendations are geared towards protecting the delivery of banking services from the fluctuations of the global financial system. Secondly, there are a number of conditions for the 'holding of regulatory capital against risk-weighted assets that exceed the recommendations in the Basel III Accord'.[49] Thirdly, there are a number of proposals to promote and encourage competition within the banking system. The Coalition government published its response in December 2011 and agreed to implement the recommendations.[50] The first sets of proposals were published in June 2012 and have been partially incorporated into the Financial Services Act 2012 and the Financial Services (Banking Reform) Bill 2013.[51] The Financial Services Act 2012 resulted in the abolition of the FSA and the creation of several new financial regulatory agencies, including the FCA,

---

[45] HM Treasury 'Independent Commission on Banking – terms of reference', n/d, available from http://webarchive.nationalarchives.gov.uk/20130129110402/http://www.hm-treasury.gov.uk/d/banking_commission_terms_of_reference.pdf, accessed 25 June 2013.

[46] Independent Commission on Banking *Interim report: consultation on reform options* (Independent Commission on Banking: London, 2011) at 5–6.

[47] Independent Commission on Banking *Final report* (Independent Commission on Banking: London, 2011). For a useful analysis and commentary on the recommendations of the Vickers Commission see Ghosh, S. and Patnaik, S. 'The Independent Banking Commission (Vickers) report: squaring the circle?' (2012) International Journal of Law and Management, 54(2), 141–152.

[48] Baber, G. 'Ring-fenced by the Vickers Report' (2012) Company Lawyer, 33(1), 1–2, at 1.

[49] *Ibid.*

[50] HM Treasury and Department of Business, Innovation and Skills *The Government response to the Independent Commission on Banking* (HM Treasury: London, 2011).

[51] HM Treasury and Department of Business, Innovation and Skills *Banking reform: delivering stability and supporting a sustainable economy* (HM Treasury: London, 2012). For a brief commentary and overview of the White Paper see Andenas, M. and H.-Y. Chiu, I. 'Financial stability and legal integration in financial regulation' (2013) European Law Review, 38(3), 335–359, at 353 and Randell, C. 'The Government's White Paper on the Independent Commission on Banking's recommendations' (2012) Butterworths Journal of International Banking and Financial Law, 27(8), 487–489.

the PRA and FPC. This is in contrast to the regulatory model adopted by Labour in 1997, which was aimed at creating a single regulatory agency that operated within a single legal framework.

The most relevant review commissioned by the Coalition government towards white collar crime and the financial crisis was the Wheatley Review.[52] This was a direct response to the LIBOR scandal,[53] which resulted in the imposition of record financial sanctions on some of the UK's largest banks, including Barclays,[54] UBS[55] and RBS.[56] In July 2012, George Osborne announced that Martin Wheatley, the Chief Executive of the FCA, would undertake a detailed examination of the framework for determining LIBOR. The aim of the review was to devise a set of policy recommendations in three specific areas. First, to reform the legal framework for regulating and determining LIBOR. Secondly, to examine the scope and applicability of the UK's civil and criminal powers towards financial misconduct. Thirdly, to ascertain whether 'similar considerations apply with respect to other price-setting mechanisms in financial markets, and provide provisional policy recommendations in this area'.[57] This announcement was followed by the publication of a discussion paper in August 2012,[58] in which Wheatley took the view that:

---

[52] For a brief commentary and outline of the allegations concerning the rigging of LIBOR see Edwards, C., Hardiman, P., Madden, M. and McClelland, J. 'Implications for commercial organisations of the global investigations into LIBOR' (2012) Banking Law Journal, October, 129, 831.

[53] For an interesting discussion of alternative mechanisms to LIBOR see Tabb, R. and Grundfest, J. 'Alternatives to LIBOR' (2013) Capital Markets Law Journal, 8(3), 229–260.

[54] Financial Services Authority 'Final notice – Barclays Bank', 27 June 2012, available from http://www.fsa.gov.uk/static/pubs/final/barclays-jun12.pdf, accessed 27 June 2013.

[55] Financial Services Authority 'Final notice – UBS', 19 December 2012, available from http://www.fsa.gov.uk/static/pubs/final/ubs.pdf, accessed 27 June 2013.

[56] Financial Services Authority 'Final notice – RBS', 6 February 2013, available from http://www.fsa.gov.uk/static/pubs/final/rbs.pdf, accessed 27 June 2013.

[57] HM Treasury 'The Wheatley Review', 30 June 2012, available from https://www.gov.uk/government/news/the-wheatley-review, accessed 27 June 2013.

[58] HM Treasury *The Wheatley Review of LIBOR: initial discussion paper* (HM Treasury: London, 2012). For a brief yet interesting discussion of the recommendations see Meloni, K. 'New LIBOR new danger?' (2013) Butterworths Journal of International Banking and Financial Law, 28(4), 234–235.

> It is clear that regardless of the outcome of ongoing international investigations, trust in a vital part of the financial system has been badly damaged and timely action is needed to repair it. Today, we are taking the first step in this process by launching the Wheatley Review discussion paper, which seeks responses from a wide range of market experts and international stakeholders. This review aims to ensure that LIBOR is reformed in whichever way fully restores credibility and trust.[59]

The Wheatley Review was published in September 2012 and it made a number of recommendations. For example, this included the creation of a new and stronger regulatory system for LIBOR, the BBA was to be stripped of its accountability for LIBOR, and banks would be required to support their tenders with evidence of the pertinent transactions and alterations to how LIBOR is constructed to prevent further manipulation.[60] Wheatley stated that:

> [the] report sets out my plans for reforming what has become a broken system and to help restore the trust that has been lost. LIBOR needs to get back to doing what it is supposed to do, rather than what unscrupulous traders and individuals in banks wanted it to do. I have concluded that LIBOR can be rehabilitated through a comprehensive and far-reaching programme of reform. Although the current system is broken, it is not beyond repair, and it is up to regulators and market participants to work together towards a lasting and sustainable solution.[61]

The Financial Secretary to the Treasury, Greg Clark MP, described the Wheatley Review as clear and added that 'the self-regulation of LIBOR has failed … LIBOR is a hugely important international benchmark and this report makes a series of comprehensive and practical recommendations designed to restore its credibility'.[62] In response to the recommendations, the Coalition government announced that it would amend the then Financial Services Bill and bring LIBOR within the new regulatory framework, create a new criminal offence of misleading statements and

---

[59] HM Treasury 'Independent review into LIBOR publishes discussion paper', 10 August 2012, available from https://www.gov.uk/government/news/independent-review-into-libor-publishes-discussion-paper, accessed 27 June 2013.

[60] HM Treasury 'Independent review into LIBOR published', 28 September 2012, available from https://www.gov.uk/government/news/independent-review-into-libor-published, accessed 27 June 2013.

[61] *Ibid.*

[62] *Ibid.*

grant the FCA with the ability to make specific rules for LIBOR.[63] Greg Clark added that:

> The Government is determined to restore the credibility of LIBOR. That is why we have accepted Martin Wheatley's recommendations in full and will begin the process of implementing them without delay. The Government's changes to legislation will ensure that those that attempt to manipulate LIBOR face the full force of the law. But this is just one part of the process, the banks and the BBA will have to play their part to ensure that reform is effective and LIBOR's reputation is restored.[64]

In November 2012 the Coalition government published a consultation paper on the regulation of LIBOR.[65] The government invited comments on two proposals: bringing LIBOR within the banking regulation framework and the criminalisation of manipulating LIBOR.[66] In February 2013, the Coalition government created the Hogg Committee that was tasked with recommending a new supervisor for LIBOR.[67] Greg Clark stated that:

> The Government is determined to rebuild the reputation of UK financial services. Establishing confidence that the attempted manipulation of LIBOR can never happen again is crucial. That is why the Committee will follow the principles laid out by the Wheatley Review and recommend an organisation that displays the highest standards of transparency and probity to administer LIBOR.[68]

On 9 July 2013, the Hogg Committee announced that the BBA had accepted its suggestion that NYSE Euronext Rate Administration Limited

---

[63] HM Treasury 'Government accepts recommendations from the Wheatley Review of LIBOR in full', 17 October 2012, available from https://www.gov.uk/government/news/government-accepts-recommendations-from-the-wheatley-review-of-libor-in-full, accessed 27 June 2013.

[64] *Ibid.*

[65] HM Treasury 'The Government launched its public consultation on the regulation of the London Interbank Offered Rate (LIBOR) today', 28 November 2012, available from https://www.gov.uk/government/news/government-publishes-consultation-on-regulation-of-libor, accessed 27 June 2013.

[66] HM Treasury *Implementing the Wheatley Review: draft secondary legislation* (HM Treasury: London, 2012).

[67] HM Treasury 'Government announces LIBOR administrator tendering committee', 25 February 2013, available from https://www.gov.uk/government/news/government-announces-libor-administrator-tendering-committee, accessed 12 July 2013.

[68] *Ibid.*

should be the new LIBOR supervisor.[69] The transfer of the administration of LIBOR from the BBA to NYSE Euronext Rate Administration Limited and its regulation by the FCA will take place in early 2014.

In addition to the Wheatley Review, the Coalition government established the Banking Standards Commission. The Commission was asked to make recommendations on 'professional standards and culture of the UK banking sector, taking account of regulatory and competition investigations into the LIBOR rate-setting process' and to identify what 'lessons could be learned about corporate governance, transparency and conflicts of interest, and their implications for regulation and for government policy'.[70] The Banking Standards Commission published its final report in June 2013,[71] following which Andrew Tyrie MP, the Chairman of the Parliamentary Commission on Banking Standards, stated:

> Recent scandals, not least the fixing of the LIBOR rate that prompted Parliament to establish this Commission, have exposed shocking and widespread malpractice. Taxpayers and customers have lost out. The economy has suffered. The reputation of the financial sector has been gravely damaged. Trust in banking has fallen to a new low. Prudential and conduct failings have many shared causes but there is no single solution that can restore trust in the industry. The Final Report contains a package of recommendations that, together, change banking for good. A lack of personal responsibility has been commonplace throughout the industry. Senior figures have continued to shelter behind an accountability firewall. Risks and rewards in banking have

---

69 Hogg Tendering Advisory Committee for London Interbank Offered Rate 'The Hogg Tendering Advisory Committee announces that NYSE Euronext is to be the new LIBOR administrator', 9 July 2013, available from https://www.gov.uk/government/uploads/system/uploads/attachment_data/file/211330/Hogg_Tendering_Advisory_Committee.pdf, accessed 12 July 2013. Also see BBC 'Libor interest rate to be controlled by NYSE Euronext', 9 July 2013, available from http://www.bbc.co.uk/news/business-23240707, accessed 12 July 2013; Masters, B. and Stafford, P. 'Scandal-plagued Libor moves to NYSE', 9 July 2013, available from http://www.ft.com/cms/s/0/73332222-e87f-11e2-aead-00144feabdc0.html#axzz2YkarYqma, accessed 12 July 2013; and Quinn, J. 'Treasury hands control of Libor to NYSE Euronext', 9 July 2013, available from http://www.telegraph.co.uk/finance/10168894/Treasury-hands-control-of-Libor-to-NYSE-Euronext.html, accessed 12 July 2013. Also see Varriale, G. 'Is NYSE Euronext up to administering Libor?' (2013) International Financial Law Review, 30(27), 12–13.

70 Parliamentary Commission on Banking Standards 'Parliamentary Commission on Banking Standards', n/d, available from http://www.parliament.uk/business/committees/committees-a-z/joint-select/professional-standards-in-the-banking-industry/news/, accessed 25 June 2013.

71 *Ibid.*

> been out of kilter. Given the misalignment of incentives, it should be no surprise that deep lapses in banking standards have been commonplace … where the standards of individuals, especially those in senior roles, have fallen short, clear lines of accountability and enforceable sanctions are needed. They have both been lacking. It is not just bankers that need to change. The actions of regulators and Governments have contributed to the decline in standards. Governments need to get on with the job of implementing these reforms. Regulators and supervisors need rigorously to enforce them.[72]

The Banking Standards Commission recommended replacing the Approved Persons Regime with a new Senior Persons Regime. The aim of this recommendation would be to confirm that the most significant roles in banks are given to identifiable leading individuals who can be held accountable. Furthermore, the Banking Standards Commission suggested the introduction and implementation of a new licensing regime that is supported by the Banking Standards Rules. Additionally, the Commission commended the introduction of a new remuneration code and additional powers for the FCA. What is of particular significance to this monograph is the recommendation for bankers to be imprisoned for a new criminal offence called 'reckless misconduct'.[73] The Banking Standards Commission recommended that:

> there is a strong case in principle for a new criminal offence of reckless misconduct in the management of a bank … the fact that recklessness in carrying out professional responsibilities carries a risk of a criminal conviction and a prison sentence would give pause for thought to the senior officers of UK banks.[74]

---

[72] *Ibid.*

[73] Parliamentary Commission on Banking Standards *Changing banking for good* (Parliamentary Commission on Banking Standards, London, 2013) at 66 para. 243. For a brief comment on the recommendations see Treanor, J. 'Banking commission: bankers should be jailed for "reckless misconduct"', 19 June 2013, available from http://www.guardian.co.uk/business/2013/jun/19/tyrie-report-banking-reform-jail-sentences, accessed 25 June 2013; Wilson, H. 'Banking Commission: bankers should face threat of jail and loss of bonuses', 19 June 2013, available from http://www.telegraph.co.uk/finance/newsbysector/banksand finance/10128750/Banking-Commission-Bankers-should-face-threat-of-jail-and-loss-of-bonuses.html, accessed 25 June 2013; and Pickford, J. 'Banking Commission plans get City staff a little hot under collar', 19 June 2013, available from http://www.ft.com/cms/s/0/b3605ff2-d8fa-11e2-a6cf-00144feab7de.html#axzz2XEtRV9MG, accessed 25 June 2013.

[74] Parliamentary Commission on Banking Standards *ibid.*, at 516, para. 1182. Also see Ed. 'Parliamentary banking commission recommends jailing reckless bankers' (2013) Company Lawyer, 34(9), 283 and Ryder, N. 'The new

The Banking Standards Commission added that the offence would be 'pursued in cases involving only the most serious of failings, such as where a bank failed with substantial costs to the taxpayer, lasting consequences for the financial system, or serious harm to customers'.[75] George Osborne stated that 'we've already supported the recommendations on new criminal sanctions',[76] and in July 2013 the government published its response to the Banking Standards Commission.[77] The government accepted the need to introduce appropriate measures to impose criminal penalties for reckless misconduct for those involved in managing banks.[78] However, this response was severely criticised by the Shadow Chancellor of the Exchequer, Ed Balls MP, who stated 'David Cameron promised to amend the banking reform Bill to implement the Parliamentary Commission's report, including its recommendations on deferring bonuses and criminal penalties for reckless misconduct. But for all the tough talk, he and George Osborne have totally failed to do so.'[79] It is the responsibility of the Coalition government to determine 'which of the recommendations will go forward as amendments to its Banking

criminal offence of reckless misconduct for bankers' (2013) Criminal Lawyer (216), 1–2.

[75] Parliamentary Commission on Banking Standards above, n 73, at 516, para. 1183.

[76] HM Treasury 'Speech by Chancellor of the Exchequer, Rt Hon George Osborne MP, Mansion House 2013', 19 June 2013, available from https://www.gov.uk/government/speeches/speech-by-chancellor-of-the-exchequer-rt-hon-george-osborne-mp-mansion-house-2013, accessed 27 June 2013.

[77] HM Treasury *The Government's response to the Parliamentary Commission on Banking Standards* (HM Treasury: London, 2013).

[78] *Ibid.*, at 11. At the time of writing it is envisaged that these measures will form part of the Banking Reform Bill that will be published in the autumn of 2013. See for example Watt, N. 'Reckless misconduct proposals will be in banking reform bill, says PM', 19 June 2013, available from http://www.guardian.co.uk/business/2013/jun/19/reckless-misconduct-banking-reform-cameron, accessed 11 July 2013; Treanor, J. 'Bankers will face jail for reckless misconduct, says George Osborne', 9 July 2013, available from http://www.guardian.co.uk/business/2013/jul/08/bankers-jail-misconduct-george-osborne, accessed 11 July 2013; and Parker, G. 'George Osborne vows to get tough and raise standards in City', 9 July 2013, available from http://www.ft.com/cms/s/0/1c3a3a66-e71f-11e2-8a57-00144feabdc0.html#axzz2YkarYqma, accessed 11 July 2013.

[79] Labour 'Osborne is continuing to duck the radical banking reform we need – Ed Balls', 8 July 2013, available from http://www.labour.org.uk/osborne-continuing-to-duck-radical-banking-reform-we-need,2013-07-08, accessed 11 July 2013.

Reform Bill'.[80] The Coalition government has adopted a different approach towards white collar crime from that previously adopted by Labour. It has failed to act on the wide ranging measures introduced in the areas of money laundering, confiscation of the proceeds of crime, and fraud.

5.3 LEGISLATIVE RESPONSE

One of the major, but most predictable, related legislative developments was the announcement by the Coalition government to replace the FSA with the FCA. The FSA's tenure as the sole financial regulatory agency was littered with scandals and examples of ineffective regulation. Following the FSA's poor performance during the financial crisis it soon became clear that the Coalition government would instigate an extensive review of the regulation of the UK banking regulatory system. The 2010 Coalition Agreement provided: 'we will reform the regulatory system to avoid a repeat of the financial crisis. We will bring forward proposals to give the Bank of England control of macro-prudential regulation and oversight of micro-prudential regulation.'[81] In June 2010, George Osborne announced that he intended to abolish the FSA and transfer its powers back to the Bank of England,[82] create an FPC within the Bank of England, establish the PRA, establish the Consumer Protection Markets Authority (CPMA), establish ECA, create the Independent Commission on Banking and introduce a specific bank levy.[83] In June 2011 the Coalition government published a White Paper that included a draft

---

[80] Moore, J. and Morris, N. 'Bankers could face jail after report urges the Government to introduce new criminal offence for reckless management', 19 June 2013, available from http://www.independent.co.uk/news/uk/politics/bankers-could-face-jail-after-report-urges-the-government-to-introduce-new-criminal-offence-for-reckless-management-8664137.html, accessed 27 June 2013.

[81] HM Government *The Coalition: our programme for government* (HM Government: London, 2010) at 9. For a more detailed commentary on the abolition of the FSA see Feran, E. 'The break-up of the Financial Services Authority' (2011) Oxford Journal of Legal Studies, 31(3), 455–480.

[82] See HM Treasury *A new approach to financial regulation: consultation on reforming the consumer credit regime* (HM Treasury: London, 2010).

[83] HM Treasury, 'Financial services policy agenda', available from http://www.hm-treasury.gov.uk/fin_policy_agenda_index.htm, accessed 19 July 2011. For a more detailed discussion see Devereux, M. 'Will the bank levy meet its objectives?' (2011) British Tax Review, 1, 33–39.

Financial Services Bill.[84] The Financial Services Act 2012 came into effect on 1 April 2013 and implemented a new structure for banking regulation.

5.3.1 Financial Services Act 2012

The Financial Services Act 2012 brought a fresh approach towards banking regulation[85] that seeks to move away from the tri-partite system to a 'twin peaks' system of regulation.[86] One area of the Financial Services Act 2012 that is relevant here is part 7, which deals with 'offences relating to financial services'. Section 95 of the Financial Services Act 2012 abolished the 'misleading statement and practices' offence created by the Financial Services and Markets Act 2000.[87] The misleading statement and practices offence provided that a person commits an offence if he:

> (a) makes a statement, promise or forecast which he knows to be misleading, false or deceptive in a material particular; (b) dishonestly conceals any material facts whether in connection with a statement, promise or forecast made by him or otherwise; or (c) recklessly makes (dishonestly or otherwise)

---

[84] HM Treasury *A new approach to financial regulation: the blueprint for reform* (HM Treasury: London, 2011).

[85] Harris, J. 'Financial regulation and taking the long-term view' (2012) Company Lawyer, 33(10), 293–294, at 293.

[86] House of Commons Joint Committee on the Draft Financial Services Bill *Draft Financial Services Bill session 2010–12* (House of Commons Joint Committee on the Draft Financial Services Bill: London, 2011) at 9. The 'twin peaks' regulatory model has been successfully used in Australia and Canada. Indeed, it has been argued that this model of financial regulation was extremely effective in countering the problems caused by the 'Credit Crunch'. For example, the Assistant Governor of the Reserve Bank of Australia stated that 'the regulatory culture in Australia may have been different from the one that prevailed in other countries … Some regulatory cultures are more comfortable than others with making use of softer powers. In Australia APRA would describe itself as being towards the end of the spectrum; that is, it would be more comfortable with using its persuasive powers and ability to put pressure on institutions to try to influence the way they behave.' As cited in House of Commons Joint Committee *ibid.*, at 10.

[87] This was originally a criminal offence under the Financial Services Act 1986, s. 47. See Swan, E. 'Market abuse regulation and energy trading' (2004) International Energy Law and Taxation Review, 4, 91–100, at 94. For a detailed commentary on the effectiveness of s. 47 of the Financial Services Act 1986 see Barnett, W. 'Fraud enforcement in the Financial Services Act 1986: an analysis and discussion of s.47' (1996) Company Lawyer, 17(7), 203–210.

a statement, promise or forecast which is misleading, false or deceptive in a material particular.[88]

This misleading statement and practices offence was enforced by the FSA, which only secured one successful prosecution,[89] that of Carl Rigby and Gareth Bailey, who were convicted of 'recklessly making a statement to the market which was misleading, false or deceptive in a material particular'.[90] It has been argued that one of the main reasons why the FSA secured only one criminal conviction is that it was 'not keen' to initiate criminal proceedings.[91] Haynes stated that 'the FSA had a partial success with its one and, so far, only prosecution against directors for recklessly misleading statements'.[92] The 'misleading statement and practices' offence has been replaced by the Financial Services Act 2012 (Misleading Statements and Impressions) Order,[93] which stipulates relevant activities, investments and benchmarks for the purposes of part 7 of the Financial Services Act 2012.[94] Additionally, the 2012 Act reproduces the 'misleading statement and practices' criminal offence. For example s. 89 applies to individuals who:

> '(a) [make] a statement which P knows to be false or misleading in a material respect, (b) [make] a statement which is false or misleading in a material respect, being reckless as to whether it is, or (c) dishonestly [conceal] any material facts whether in connection with a statement made by P or otherwise.[95]

This person will commit an offence if he or she:

---

88 Financial Services and Markets Act 2000, s. 397(1). For a more detailed commentary see Hayes, A. 'Market abuse' (2010) Compliance Officer Bulletin, April, 75, 1–31 and Marsh, J. and McDonnell, B. 'Handling price sensitive information: a guide to the legal and regulatory obligations' (2005) Compliance Officer Bulletin, February, 23, 1–39.

89 Hayes, *ibid.*, at 1.

90 Hayes, *ibid.*, at 1. Also see Financial Services Authority 'FSA secures first conviction in criminal market abuse case', 18 August 2005, available from http://www.fsa.gov.uk/pages/Library/Communication/PR/2005/091.shtml, accessed 26 June 2013.

91 Alcock, A. 'Five years of market abuse' (2007) Company Lawyer, 28(6), 163–171, at 168.

92 *Ibid.*

93 2013/637.

94 The order specifically refers to and identifies LIBOR as the only relevant benchmark.

95 Financial Services Act 2012, s. 89(1).

> makes the statement or conceals the facts with the intention of inducing, or is reckless as to whether making it or concealing them may induce, another person (whether or not the person to whom the statement is made) – (a) to enter into or offer to enter into, or to refrain from entering or offering to enter into, a relevant agreement, or (b) to exercise, or refrain from exercising, any rights conferred by a relevant investment.[96]

Additionally, s. 90 creates the new offence of creating misleading impressions, where a person will be guilty if he or she 'does any act or engages in any course of conduct which creates a false or misleading impression as to the market in or the price or value of any relevant investments and commits an offence if they intend to create the impression'.[97]

5.3.2 Banking Reform Act 2013

The Financial Services (Banking Reform) Bill was introduced in February 2013 and contains a number of provisions aimed at strengthening the regulation of banks. In particular, the Bill seeks to introduce ring fencing to protect the deposits of people and small businesses so that they are kept separate from the dealing floor. Furthermore, the Bill seeks to ensure that banks can be held accountable by the PRA for how they keep their retail and investment activities unattached. Additionally, the Bill grants depositors who are already protected by the FSCS preference if their bank goes into insolvency. Finally, the Bill proposes to grant the government with the power to make banks soak up losses. In October 2013 HM Treasury published a number of amendments to the Banking Reform Bill,[98] one of which was the introduction of criminal sanctions for reckless misconduct by senior managers in the management of a bank. The Banking Reform Act now provides that the new offence of reckless misconduct by senior managers in the management of a bank applies only to people covered by the Senior Managers' Regime. The proposed offence provides that a person commits an offence if:

---

[96] Financial Services Act 2012, s. 89(2).

[97] Financial Services Act 2012, s. 90(1). For a useful commentary on these criminal offences see Callaghan, V. and Ullah, Z. 'The LIBOR scandal – the UK's legislative approach' (2013) Journal of International Banking Law and Regulation, 28(4), 160–165.

[98] HM Treasury *Financial Services (Banking Reform) Bill – Bill overview* (HM Treasury: London, 2013).

> (a) at a time when S is a senior manager in relation to a bank (B), S – (i) takes, or agrees to the taking of, a decision by or on behalf of B as to the way in which the business of a group bank is to be carried on, or (ii) fails to take steps that S could take to prevent such a decision being taken, (b) at the time of the decision, S is aware of a risk that the implementation of the decision may cause the failure of the group bank, (c) in all the circumstances, S's conduct in relation to the taking of the decision falls far below what could reasonably be expected of a person in S's position, and (d) the implementation of the decision causes the failure of the group bank.[99]

HM Treasury took the view that 'these clauses introduce a new criminal offence for reckless misconduct in the management of a bank. The new offence will strengthen individual accountability for senior bankers, and act as a deterrent against misconduct.'[100] HM Treasury added that:

> Senior managers could be liable if they take a decision which leads to the failure of the bank, or fail to take steps available to them to prevent such a decision being taken. The offence will only apply to behaviour which falls far below the standard that could reasonably be expected of a person in that position – this is similar to the test for corporate manslaughter. In addition, at the time the decision was taken, the senior manager must have been aware of a risk that its implementation may cause the failure of the bank.[101]

The Financial Services (Banking Reform) Act 2013 received Royal Assent on 18 December 2013 and criminalises behaviour that amounts to reckless misconduct that leads to a bank failure.[102] The introduction of a new criminal offence of reckless misconduct makes a welcome addition to the armoury of those agencies that have been given the unenviable task of prosecuting white collar crime. The reckless misconduct offence carries a maximum custodial sentence of seven years. It has been argued that the range of prosecutorial tools available for the LIBOR scandal is ineffective in its pursuit of the alleged wrongdoers.[103] For example, it

---

[99] HM Treasury 'Financial Services (Banking Reform) Bill Government annotated amendments: criminal sanctions', 7 October 2013, available from https://www.gov.uk/government/uploads/system/uploads/attachment_data/file/245778/Annotated_Clause_-_Criminal_Sanctions.pdf, accessed 9 October 2013.

[100] HM Treasury *Financial Services (Banking Reform) Bill – Government amendments criminal sanctions* (HM Treasury: London, 2013) at 1.

[101] *Ibid.*, at 1–2.

[102] Financial Services (Banking Reform) Act 2013, s. 36.

[103] Russel, J. 'UK law may struggle to bring prosecutions of Libor traders', 11 December 2012, available from http://www.telegraph.co.uk/finance/libor-scandal/9738417/UK-law-may-struggle-to-bring-prosecutions-of-Libor-traders.html, accessed 27 June 2013. A similar point has been made about the

includes certain provisions of the Theft Act 1968,[104] the Enterprise Act 2002,[105] the Fraud Act 2006[106] and the common law offence of conspiracy to defraud.[107]

5.4 REGULATORY AND ENFORCEMENT RESPONSE

The regulatory response to the financial crisis and white collar crime has seen the abolishment of the FSA, the retention of the SFO, and the creation of two new agencies: the FCA and NCA. This part of the chapter critically reviews the performance of both the FSA and SFO in tackling white collar crime associated with the financial crisis. It then moves on to discuss the likely impact of the FCA and NCA.

5.4.1 Financial Services Authority

One of the most innovative aspects of the Financial Services and Markets Act 2000 was the granting of a statutory duty to reduce financial crime.[108] In order to achieve this statutory objective the FSA was given a plethora of investigative and enforcement powers and a series of preventative measures which *should* have ensured that it was well placed to tackle white collar crime associated with the financial crisis. For

---

prosecutorial powers available in the United States of America. See for example, Elboghdady, D. 'Clock ticking for SEC to pursue fraud charges in financial crisis cases', 19 July 2012, available from http://articles.washingtonpost.com/2012-07-19/business/35487394_1_financial-crisis-fraudulent-activity-federal-securities-regulators, accessed 27 June 2013.

104 For an interesting comment on the Theft Act 1968 and its relationship with the Fraud Act 2006 see Withey, C. 'The Fraud Act 2006 – some early observations and comparisons with the former' (2007) Journal of Criminal Law, 71(3), 220–237.

105 It has been argued that the Serious Fraud Office could use the cartel offence provisions under the Enterprise Act 2002 in relation to the LIBOR scandal. For a more detailed discussion of the cartel offence see Parkinson, S. 'The cartel offence under the Enterprise Act 2002' (2004) Company Lawyer, 25(6), 187–189 and Graham, C. 'The Enterprise Act 2002 and competition law' (2004) Modern Law Review, 67(2), 273–288.

106 For an excellent commentary on the Fraud Act 2006 see Ormerod above, n 39.

107 The use of the common law offence of conspiracy to defraud in relation to the LIBOR scandal has also been questioned. See for example Corker, D. 'Manipulating LIBOR …' (2012) New Law Journal, 162(7524), 980–981.

108 Financial Services and Markets Act 2000, s. 6.

example, the FSA was a prosecuting authority for both money laundering and a limited number of fraud related offences.[109] It also had the power to impose financial sanctions where it had established that there had been a contravention by an authorised person of any of its requirements.[110] Furthermore, the FSA had the power to ban authorised persons and firms from undertaking any regulated activity.[111] However, what transpired after 2007 can be described as a *tepid* approach towards enforcing the white collar crime provisions of the Financial Services and Markets Act 2000. The FSA favoured imposing financial sanctions on firms and individuals as opposed to instigating criminal proceedings, as part of its 'credible deterrence' policy.[112] This was summarised by Peat and Mason, who stated:

> The FSA's policy of credible deterrence in enforcement cases involves bringing action not just against firms, but also against individuals. The normal sanction imposed on a firm is a financial penalty; the firm pays the fine and then carries on with its normal business. In contrast a sanction imposed on an individual may have longer-lasting consequences.[113]

It has been argued that the objective of the credible deterrence policy is to 'deliver a message that breaches of law and/or regulation will result in offenders suffering "meaningful consequences" including imprisonment'.[114] Teasdale stated that the 'credible deterrence agenda has relied upon not only securing meaningful convictions, judgments and regulatory decisions, but also upon clearly advertising them; to the regulated community to dissuade similar behaviour, and to the wider world to

---

109 For example, in 2008 the FSA successfully prosecuted William Radclyffe for offences under the Theft Acts, the Financial Services Act 1986 and the Financial Services and Markets Act 2000. Financial Services Authority, 'Fake stockbroker sentenced to 15 months', available from http://www.fsa.gov.uk/pages/Library/Communication/PR/2008/011.shtml, accessed 28 March 2010.

110 Financial Services and Markets Act 2000, s. 206(1). For a general discussion see Travers Smith Regulatory Investigations Group 'FSA enforcement action: themes and trends' (2011) Compliance Officer Bulletin, June, 87, 1–35.

111 Financial Services and Markets Act 2000, s. 56.

112 Financial Services Authority 'Delivering credible deterrence', speech by Margaret Cole, Director of Enforcement, FSA, Annual Financial Crime Conference, 27 April 2009, available from http://www.fsa.gov.uk/library/communication/speeches/2009/0427_mc.shtml, accessed 8 March 2013.

113 Peat, R. and Mason, I. 'Credible deterrence in action: the FSA brings a series of cases against traders' (2009) Company Lawyer, 30(9), 278–279, at 278.

114 Srivastava *et al* above, n 1, at 8.

engender consumer and market confidence'.[115] Lewis *et al* stated that the FSA 'levied large fines and, at worst, bans, on firms and relevant approved individuals who breached its rules – sometimes regardless of whether the breach has resulted in actual harm to customers'.[116] This point is clearly illustrated by the significant increase in the use of financial sanctions since the start of the financial crisis by the FSA.[117] Srivastava *et al* stated: 'financial sanctions have assumed greater political importance in recent years and as a result there has been increased focus on the part of the FSA in ensuring that firms understand their obligations under the various financial sanctions regimes'.[118] For example, in 2007 the regulatory agency imposed a total of £5.3m in financial sanctions.[119] A year later, the FSA reported that the figure had increased to £22.7m.[120] In 2009 the amount of financial sanctions increased to £35m.[121] The figures for 2010 and 2011 illustrated an increase to £89.1m[122] and a decrease to £66.1m.[123] However, in 2012 the FSA imposed financial sanctions that amounted to £311.5m,[124] a majority of which were associated with the LIBOR scandal. As of April 2013, the FSA had imposed financial sanctions totalling £143.1m.[125] From then, the FCA

---

115 Teasdale, S. 'FSA to FCA: recent trends in UK financial conduct regulation' (2011) Journal of International Banking Law and Regulation, 26(12), 583–586, at 585.

116 Lewis, A., Pretorius, R. and Radmore, E. 'Outsourcing in the financial services sector' (2013) Compliance Officer Bulletin, May, 106, 1–34, at 3.

117 For a more detailed commentary on the approach adopted by the Financial Services Authority towards imposing financial sanctions see Financial Services Authority *Financial services firms' approach to UK financial sanctions* (Financial Services Authority: London, 2009).

118 Srivastava *et al* above, n 1, at 7.

119 Financial Services Authority 'FSA fines table 2007', n/d, available from http://www.fsa.gov.uk/about/press/facts/fines/2007, accessed 8 March 2013.

120 Financial Services Authority 'FSA fines table 2008', n/d, available from http://www.fsa.gov.uk/about/press/facts/fines/2008, accessed 8 March 2013.

121 Financial Services Authority 'FSA fines table 2009', n/d, available from http://www.fsa.gov.uk/about/press/facts/fines/2009, accessed 8 March 2013.

122 Financial Services Authority 'FSA fines table 2010', n/d, available from http://www.fsa.gov.uk/about/press/facts/fines/2010, accessed 8 March 2013.

123 Financial Services Authority 'FSA fines table 2011', n/d, available from http://www.fsa.gov.uk/about/press/facts/fines/2011, accessed 8 March 2013.

124 Financial Services Authority 'FSA fines table 2012', n/d, available from http://www.fsa.gov.uk/about/press/facts/fines/2012, accessed 8 March 2013.

125 Financial Conduct Authority 'Fines table 2013', 1 October 2013, available from http://www.fca.org.uk/firms/being-regulated/enforcement/fines, accessed 7 October 2013.

imposed financial penalties of approximately £202m.[126] Martin Wheatley stated that between 2012 and 2013 regulatory agencies 'handed out a record £312m in fines, more than triple the previous high number of £89m'.[127] Teasdale described these decisions as an example of 'an increase in the FSA's readiness to take decisive action'.[128] Another example of the FSA's credible deterrence policy relates to market abuse cases. For example, the FSA successfully obtained its first conviction for insider dealing in 2009.[129] The then FSA Director of Enforcement and Financial Crime, Margaret Cole stated that:

> the last two years have seen a number of firsts for us and a number of records broken and broken again in close succession ... we've had record totals of fines and prohibitions, records for highest fines ... we're absolutely committed and we will stay committed to achieving our aim of credible deterrence.[130]

However, the record financial penalties imposed by the FSA from the start of the financial crisis were insufficient and represented an insignificant percentage of the annual profits of the guilty firms. Despite producing a series of media friendly headlines, the FSA underperformed given its vast array of other enforcement measures. However, Srivastava *et al* defended the enforcement activities of the FSA and stated:

> The FSA has been criticised for making ineffective use of its enforcement powers and, particularly, for its reluctance to use criminal enforcement powers. In fairness to the FSA, one of the major innovations under FSMA was the FSA's power to impose civil fines for market abuse and thereby overcome the significant evidential difficulties associated with prosecuting insider dealing under the Criminal Justice Act 1993. It is therefore not surprising that the FSA chose to focus on the use of its civil powers during its early years. In response to the criticisms that it has received, the FSA has more recently increased its use of criminal prosecutions. This initiative has

---

[126] *Ibid.* regulated/enforcement/fines

[127] Financial Conduct Authority 'The changing face of financial crime', 1 July 2013, available from http://www.fca.org.uk/news/speeches/the-changing-face-of-financial-crime, accessed 8 July 2013.

[128] Teasdale above, n 115, at 584.

[129] Financial Services Authority 'Solicitor and his father-in-law found guilty in FSA insider dealing case', 27 March 2009, available from http://www.fsa.gov.uk/library/communication/pr/2009/042.shtml, accessed 3 October 2013.

[130] Financial Services Authority 'Introduction to the FSA Enforcement Conference 2010', 22 June 2010, available from http://www.fsa.gov.uk/pages/Library/Communication/Speeches/2010/0622_mc.shtml, accessed 8 July 2013.

> been particularly notable in cases of insider dealing where the FSA has secured a number of convictions.[131]

Additionally, the FSA adopted a series of preventative measures via its Senior Management Arrangements, Systems and Controls, or SYSC, part of the Handbook.[132] Part 3 provides that firms must have in place systems and controls which are appropriate for the firm to conduct its business.[133] In particular, a firm is required to 'take reasonable care to establish and maintain effective systems and controls for compliance with applicable requirements and standards under the regulatory system and for countering the risk that the firm might be used to further financial crime'.[134] Therefore, authorised firms are required to undertake consistent assessments of the adequacy of their systems to prevent themselves from being used to facilitate financial crime,[135] and to allocate a director/senior manager with overall responsibility for establishing the systems.[136] The regime was intended to provide the regulated sector with an even higher degree of flexibility. This means that firms were able to identify the risks and determine how they could best allocate their resources in areas which were most vulnerable.[137] Failure to comply with these measures triggered significant enforcement activity by the FSA.[138] For example, in September 2013 JP Morgan Chase Bank was fined over £137m by the FCA for serious failing relating to the London Whales trades.[139] Tracey McDermott, the FCA's Director of Enforcement and Financial Crime, stated:

---

131 Srivastava *et al* above, n 1, at 8.

132 For a more detailed commentary on the FSA Handbook see Blair, W. and Brent, R. *Banking and financial crime – the international law of tainted money* (Oxford University Press: Oxford, 2008) at 262–266.

133 Financial Services Authority *FSA handbook of senior management arrangements, systems and controls* (Financial Services Authority: London, 2006) at SYSC 3.1.1.

134 *Ibid.*, at SYSC 3.2.6 R.

135 *Ibid.*, at SYSC 3.2.6 C.

136 *Ibid.*, at SYSC 3.2.6 H and I.

137 Bagge, J. 'The future for enforcement under the new Financial Services Authority' (1998) Company Lawyer, 19(7) 194–197, at 194.

138 Examples include fines imposed on Capita Financial Administration Limited, BNP Paribas Private Bank, Nationwide Building Society, Norwich Union Life, Zurich Insurance, Willis Limited and Coutts.

139 Financial Conduct Authority 'JPMorgan Chase Bank N.A. fined £137,610,000 for serious failings relating to its Chief Investment Office's "London Whale" trades', 19 September 2013, available from http://www.fca.org.uk/news/jpmorgan-chase-bank-na-fined, accessed 9 October 2013.

> When the scale of the problems at JPMorgan became apparent, it sent a shock-wave through the markets. Maintaining the integrity of markets is a key part of our wholesale conduct agenda. We consider JPMorgan's failings to be extremely serious such as to undermine the trust and confidence in UK financial markets. This is yet another example of a firm failing to get a proper grip on the risks its business poses to the market. There were basic failings in the operation of fundamental controls over a high risk part of the business. Senior management failed to respond properly to warning signals that there were problems in the Chief Investment Office. As things began to go wrong, the firm didn't wake up quickly enough to the size and the scale of the problems. What is worse, they compounded this by failing to be open and co-operative with us as their regulator.[140]

Other financial sanctions were imposed on ICAP,[141] Barclays,[142] UBS[143] and RBS.[144] It has been argued that the UK has effective preventative white collar crime measures. For example, Huynh argued that the UK has an effective preventative system, when compared with the US.[145] However, the imposition of these financial sanctions can result in only one conclusion: that the measures are ineffective and have failed to prevent breaches of relevant rules by authorised firms. The FSA also had the power to ban authorised persons and firms from undertaking any regulated activity.[146] One area in which the FSA had extensively used these enforcement powers relates to mortgage fraud, which has 'been identified as a contributor to the

---

140 *Ibid.*

141 Financial Conduct Authority 'ICAP Europe Limited fined £14 million for significant failings in relation to LIBOR', 25 September 2013, available from http://www.fca.org.uk/news/icap-europe-limited-fined, accessed 9 October 2013.

142 Financial Services Authority 'Barclays fined £59.5 million for significant failings in relation to LIBOR and EURIBOR', 27 June 2012, available from http://www.fsa.gov.uk/library/communication/pr/2012/070.shtml, accessed 9 October 2013.

143 Financial Services Authority 'UBS fined £160 million for significant failings in relation to LIBOR and EURIBOR', 19 December 2012, available from http://www.fsa.gov.uk/library/communication/pr/2012/116.shtml, accessed 30 June 2013.

144 Financial Services Authority 'RBS fined £87.5m for significant failings in relation to LIBOR', 6 February 2013, available from http://www.fsa.gov.uk/library/communication/pr/2013/011.shtml, accessed 8 February 2013.

145 Huynh, D. 'Preemption v. punishment: a comparative study of white collar crime prosecution in the United States and the United Kingdom' (2010) Journal of International Business and Law, Spring, 9, 105–135, at 134.

146 Financial Services and Markets Act 2000, s. 56. These are commonly referred to as prohibition orders.

financial crisis'.[147] Srivastava *et al* stated that 'the FSA has banned 92 mortgage brokers and imposed fines of around £1.5m'.[148] In 2008/2009, the FSA imposed prohibition orders on 58 individuals,[149] and it is very interesting to note that out of the 58 prohibition orders, 23 were mortgage fraud related.[150] The number of prohibition orders slightly decreased in 2009/2010 to 56,[151] but increased to 71 in 2010/2011.[152] However, the numbers dropped to 47 in 2011[153] and 45 in 2012.[154] The FSA also had the ability to seek criminal prosecutions.[155] In 2008/2009, it successfully obtained two convictions.[156] The number increased in 2009/2010 to three,[157] and also increased to five in 2010/2011.[158] The total number of convictions remained

---

147 Srivastava *et al* above, n 1, at 6.

148 *Ibid.* For a more detailed commentary on the measures introduced by the Financial Services Authority to tackle mortgage fraud see Haines, J. 'Mortgage fraud – FSA report on thematic findings of mortgage lenders systems and controls against mortgage fraud' (2011) Company Lawyer, 32(11), 344–346 and Haines, J. 'Mortgage fraud – have mortgage lenders got their house in order?' (2011) Company Lawyer, 32(3), 86–88.

149 Financial Services Authority *Enforcement annual performance account 2008/2009* (Financial Services Authority: London, 2009) at 7.

150 *Ibid.*, at 4.

151 Financial Services Authority *Enforcement annual performance account 2009/2010* (Financial Services Authority: London, 2010) at 4.

152 Financial Services Authority *Enforcement annual performance account 2010/2011* (Financial Services Authority: London, 2011) at 8.

153 Financial Services Authority *Enforcement annual performance account 2011/2012* (Financial Services Authority: London, 2012) at 8. In 2011, Michael Joseph James Lewis was banned by the FSA from 'advising on mortgages and fined £106,000 for mortgage fraud' and was convicted of 'two counts of making/supplying documentation for use in fraud and ten counts of carrying on a mortgage advisory business despite being prohibited from doing so'. See Financial Services Authority *Final notice – Michael Joseph James Lewis trading as Lewis Partnership* (Financial Services Authority: London, 2011) and Financial Conduct Authority 'Ex-mortgage advisor sentenced to two years after FCA action', 16 July 2013, available from http://www.fca.org.uk/news/exmortgage-advisor-sentenced-to-two-years-after-fca-action, accessed 19 July 2013.

154 Financial Services Authority *Enforcement annual performance account 2012/2013* (Financial Services Authority: London, 2013) at 5.

155 Financial Services and Markets Act 2000, ss. 401 and 402. For an excellent commentary on the prosecutorial powers of the FSA see Wilson, G. and Wilson, S. 'Market misconduct, the Financial Services Authority and creating a system of city grasses' (2010) Company Lawyer, 31(3), 67–80.

156 Financial Services Authority above, n 149, at 7.

157 Financial Services Authority above, n 151, at 8.

158 Financial Services Authority above, n 152, at 8.

unchanged in 2011,[159] but did increase to 13 in 2012.[160] Despite a steady, if unspectacular, increase in the frequency of enforcement activities of the FSA, at the time of writing not one person in the UK who contributed towards the financial crisis has been convicted of any criminal activity.

5.4.2 Serious Fraud Office

The SFO was established following the era of financial deregulation in the 1980s, which resulted in the City of London being perceived as an epicentre for financial criminals.[161] In order to address this problem, the then Conservative government created the SFO, via the Criminal Justice Act 1987.[162] It is important to emphasise that the effectiveness of the SFO *prior* to the financial crisis was questionable.[163] For example, its reputation was tarnished by several notorious prosecutorial failures, including Guinness,[164] Blue Arrow,[165] Maxwell[166] and

---

159 Financial Services Authority above, n 153, at 12.

160 Financial Services Authority above, n 154, at 5.

161 Bosworth-Davies, R. 'Investigating financial crime: the continuing evolution of the public fraud investigation role – a personal perspective' (2009) Company Lawyer, 30(7), 195–199, at 196.

162 See generally Wright, R. 'Fraud after Roskill: a view from the Serious Fraud Office' (2003) Journal of Financial Crime, 11(1), 10–16.

163 See for example Mahendra, B. 'Fighting serious fraud' (2002) New Law Journal, 152(7020), 289; de Grazia, J. *Review of the Serious Fraud Office – final report* (Serious Fraud Office: London, 2008); HM Crown Prosecution Service Inspectorate *Review of the Fraud Prosecution Service* (HM Crown Prosecution Service Inspectorate: London, 2008); and HM Crown Prosecution Service Inspectorate *Report of the Attorney General on the inspection of the Serious Fraud Office* (HM Crown Prosecution Service Inspectorate: London, 2012).

164 For a more detailed discussion see Sarker, R. 'The trials and errors of the Guinness four' (1995) Journal of Financial Crime, 3(1), 86–88 and Page, F. 'Defining fraud: an argument in favour of a general offence of fraud' (1997) Journal of Financial Crime, 4(4), 287–308.

165 For a more detailed discussion of this case see Cohen, H. 'What place does the criminal law have in the regulation of securities markets after the Blue Arrow trials?' (1992) Journal of International Banking Law, 7(10), 420–422 and Kirk, D. 'Blue Arrow: the SFO on trial' (1992) International Company and Commercial Law Review, 3(10), 331–333.

166 For a more detailed discussion see Sarker, R. 'Maxwell: fraud trial of the century (case comment)' (1996) Company Lawyer, 17(4), 116–117 and Honess, T. 'Juror competence in processing complex information: implications from a simulation of the Maxwell trial' (1998) Criminal Law Review, November, 763–773.

Levitt.[167] Furthermore, the SFO has been in the headlines for its handling of the bribery allegations against BAE Systems and its abandonment of the investigation into arms sales in Saudi Arabia.[168] More recently, the SFO has been severely criticised over its poor handling of the Tchenguiz brothers' investigation.[169] However, it is important to emphasise that the SFO *has* increased the frequency of its investigations and prosecutions. For example, between 2001 and 2006 the SFO reported a conviction rate of 61 per cent.[170] This increased to 71 per cent in 2007.[171] By 2008, the conviction rate had fallen slightly

---

[167] For a more detailed discussion see Sarker, R. 'The Serious Fraud Office – quo vadis?' (1995) Company Lawyer, 16(2), 56–61.

[168] For a more detailed discussion see Williams, S. 'The BAE/Saudi Al-Yamamah contracts: implications in law and public procurement' (2008) International and Comparative Law Quarterly, 57(1), 200–209 and Rose, C. 'Legislative comment: the UK Bribery Act 2010 and accompanying guidance: belated implementation of the OECD Anti-Bribery Convention' (2012) International and Comparative Law Quarterly, 61(2), 484–499. The decision by the SFO to terminate its investigation into the sale of arms in Saudi Arabia was subject to a judicial review and the Queen's Bench Divisional Court determined that the decision was unlawful. See *The Queen on the application of (1) Corner House Research (2) Campaign Against Arms Trade v The Director of the Serious Fraud Office (Defendant) and BAE Systems Plc (Interested Party),* Claim No CO/1567/2007, High Court of Justice, Queen's Bench Division, Administrative Court, 18 April 2007. However, this decision was overturned on appeal by the House of Lords. See *R (on the application of Corner House Research and others) v Director of the Serious Fraud Office* [2008] UKHL 60, 30 July 2008, para. 11. For a more detailed discussion of this case and the related legal issues see Yihdego, Z. 'Arms trade and public controls: the right to information perspective' (2008) Northern Ireland Legal Quarterly, 59(4), 379–394; Spencer, J. 'Fiat justicia, ruatque concordia cum Arabe?' (2008) Cambridge Law Journal, 67(3), 456–458; and Roberts, A. 'Prosecution: director of SFO – lawfulness of decision to discontinue prosecution' (2009) Criminal Law Review, 1, 46–49.

[169] See for example Neate, R. 'Tchenguiz brothers seek millions from Serious Fraud Office', 3 December 2012, available from http://m.guardian.co.uk/business/2012/dec/03/tchenguiz-brothers-millions-damages-sfo, accessed 18 March 2013; Russel, J. 'Tchenguiz brothers launch damages case against SFO', 2 December 2012, available from http://www.telegraph.co.uk/finance/financial-crime/9717240/Tchenguiz-brothers-launch-damages-case-against-SFO.html, accessed 18 March 2013.

[170] Serious Fraud Office *Annual Report 2006/2007* (Serious Fraud Office: London, 2007) at 4.

[171] *Ibid.*

to 68 per cent.[172] In 2009, the SFO achieved a conviction rate of 91 per cent.[173] However, this figure fell to 84 per cent in 2010 and 73 per cent in 2011.[174] The regulatory performance of the SFO has been complicated by the introduction of the Bribery Act 2010.[175] This requires the SFO to act as the 'chief prosecutors of offences under the Bribery Act'.[176] Despite being given this additional area of jurisdiction, the SFO has not been granted any additional resources. In July 2012, the SFO announced that it had been liaising with the FSA during its initial investigation into LIBOR and they were 'considering whether it is both appropriate and possible to bring criminal prosecutions'.[177] Four days after this press release, the SFO announced that it had accepted to investigate the alleged manipulation of LIBOR.[178] At the end of July the SFO said that it was satisfied that 'existing criminal offences are capable of covering conduct in relation to the alleged manipulation of LIBOR and related interest rates'.[179] This statement was followed by a further report in December 2012 that the SFO had arrested three people

---

[172] Serious Fraud Office *Annual Report 2007/2008* (Serious Fraud Office: London, 2008) at 5.

[173] Serious Fraud Office *Annual Report 2009/2010* (Serious Fraud Office: London, 2010) at 2.

[174] Serious Fraud Office *Annual Report and accounts 2011/2012* (Serious Fraud Office: London, 2012) at 6.

[175] A full detailed commentary on the Bribery Act 2010 is beyond the scope of this monograph. For a more detailed analysis see Wells, C. 'Who's afraid of the Bribery Act 2010?' (2012) Journal of Business Law, 5, 420–431; Yeoh, P. 'The UK Bribery Act 2010: contents and implications' (2012) Journal of Financial Crime, 19(1), 37–53.

[176] Breslin, B., Ezickson, D. and Kocoras, J. 'The Bribery Act 2010: raising the bar above the US Foreign Corrupt Practices Act' (2010) Company Lawyer, 31(11), 362–369, at 362.

[177] Serious Fraud Office 'LIBOR update', 2 July 2012, available from http://www.sfo.gov.uk/press-room/latest-press-releases/press-releases-2012/libor–update.aspx, accessed 15 July 2013.

[178] Serious Fraud Office 'LIBOR: SFO to investigate', 6 July 2012, available from http://www.sfo.gov.uk/press-room/latest-press-releases/press-releases-2012/libor-sfo-to-investigate.aspx, accessed 15 July 2013.

[179] Serious Fraud Office 'LIBOR: criminal offences are capable of covering conduct', 30 July 2012, available from http://www.sfo.gov.uk/press-room/latest-press-releases/press-releases-2012/libor-criminal-offences-are-capable-of-covering-conduct.aspx, accessed 15 July 2013.

in connection with its investigation into LIBOR.[180] In June 2013, the SFO announced that it had charged Tom Hayes, a former trader at UBS and Citigroup, with conspiracy to defraud in connection with alleged manipulation of LIBOR.[181] In July 2013 it announced that two former brokers of RP Martin Holdings Limited, Terry Farr and James Gilmour, had been charged with conspiracy to defraud in connection with the manipulation of LIBOR.[182] It is interesting to note that the SFO was initially very reluctant to participate in the investigation of LIBOR and it kept referring back to the FSA. Therefore, the investigation into the manipulation of LIBOR rebounded between both agencies. It has been argued that the relationship between the FCA and SFO can be described as 'disconnected', as illustrated over the LIBOR scandal.[183] It has been argued that none of the

> financial institutions implicated in this [LIBOR] scandal might themselves be in jeopardy of prosecution. Indeed, if any such criminal proceedings were a possibility, the FCA would not have sanctioned anyone. The SFO's apparent lack of interest in making a bank accountable is despite the fact that the FCA's investigations concluded that manipulation of LIBOR was endemic and involved senior management at high levels. This therefore goes to demonstrate the continuing reluctance on the part of UK prosecution agencies to prosecute corporate offenders. Prosecutions do not provide the authorities with the same certainty of outcome as that afforded by regulatory investigations leading to an agreed settlement. Whilst the legal difficulties in prosecuting a company should not be under-estimated, criminal prosecutions and convictions serve an important deterrence function and reflect the full range of criminality involved which will lead to increased public confidence in the criminal justice system.[184]

---

180 Serious Fraud Office 'LIBOR: three arrested', 11 December 2012, available from http://www.sfo.gov.uk/press-room/latest-press-releases/press-releases-2012/libor–three-arrested-.aspx, accessed 15 July 2013.

181 Serious Fraud Office 'Trader charged in LIBOR investigation', 18 June 2013, available from http://www.sfo.gov.uk/press-room/latest-press-releases/press-releases-2013/trader-charged-in-libor-investigation.aspx, accessed 15 July 2013.

182 Serious Fraud Office 'Brokers charged in LIBOR investigation', 15 July 2013, available from http://www.sfo.gov.uk/press-room/latest-press-releases/press-releases-2013/brokers-charged-in-libor-investigation.aspx, accessed 15 July 2013.

183 Dyke, C. 'UK prosecution agencies reluctant to prosecute corporate offenders over LIBOR', 7 October 2013, available from http://corkerbinning.com/blog/uk-prosecution-agencies-reluctant-to-prosecute-corporate-offenders-over-libor/#page=1, accessed 9 October 2013.

184 *Ibid.*

Therefore, one possible way forward to resolve the regulatory infighting would have been the creation of a single Economic Crime Agency as promised by the Coalition government in 2010. However, this proposal was abandoned in favour of a broader NCA.

5.4.3 National Crime Authority

As outlined in the previous section of this chapter, there was a clear overlap between the regulatory remit of the FSA and SFO, a position that could have been resolved by the creation of the ECA. In the 'Coalition Agreement' it was proclaimed that the government would merge the SFO, the OFT and the FSA into a single ECA.[185] Srivastava *et al* stated 'the coalition government has made clear its intention to reform the United Kingdom's financial crime regime and sweep away much of what it considers being an ineffectual bureaucracy, described by George Osborne while in Opposition as a "confused alphabet soup of law enforcement agencies"'.[186] This proposal resulted in the Coalition government's initial response to white collar crime being referred to as 'energetic' and that there would be 'significant changes in the approach to financial crime'.[187] Initially, it was thought that the ECA would be 'responsible for investigating and bringing criminal prosecutions for economic crimes in the UK including insider dealing, market manipulation, fraud, bribery and corruption'.[188] Rawlings stated that this agency would 'acquire responsibility for serious economic crime from the various departments and agencies, such as the SFO and the OFT'.[189] However, it was initially proposed that the FSA's Enforcement and Financial Crime Division would not be transferred to the ECA, but to the CPMA.[190] The Coalition government stated that 'we take white collar crime as seriously as other crime and we are determined to simplify the confusing and overlapping responsibilities in this area in order to

---

185 Perry, J., Moulton, R., Barwick, G., Small, R., Green, J. and Kay, N. 'The new UK regulatory landscape' (2001) Compliance Officer Bulletin, March, 84, 1–33, at 3. Also see Teasdale above, n 115, at 583.

186 Srivastava *et al* above, n 1, at 1.

187 *Ibid.*

188 See Willmott *et al* above, n 14, at 22.

189 Rawlings, P. 'Reform of bank regulation in the United Kingdom: the opening salvo' (2010) Journal of International Banking Law and Regulation, 25(10), 522–528, at 523.

190 McDonnell, J., Bell, O., Butler, J., De Marco, L., Heaton, E., Purewal, J. and Maxwell, B. 'Annual review 2010' (2010/2011) Compliance Bulletin Officer, December/January, 8, 1–39, at 36.

improve detection and enforcement'.[191] The government acknowledged that the then existing white collar crime structure was unworkable due to conflicting priorities, overlapping roles and ineffective outcomes.[192] This point was supported by Kirk, who noted that 'the main argument originally advanced in support of the creation of an ECA was that it would gather under one roof all the "alphabet soup" of authorities which currently operate in the area of corporate fraud and economic crime'.[193] The creation of ECA has been questioned and described as amounting to no less than simply 'rearranging the deckchairs'.[194] Sadly, the formation of the ECA has been obstructed by differences of opinion within the Coalition government over its proposed remit and the unparalleled enforcement reaction from the SFO and FSA since the financial crisis.[195] The most significant factor that prevented its creation is the uncertainty over its ownership. The ECA was to be managed by the Home Office, which hoped to end the UK's 'piecemeal' approach towards tackling financial crime.[196] The Home Office decided against creating the ECA, and turned its attention to establishing the broader NCA, which was to tackle several issues, not just white collar crime.[197] On announcing the formation of the NCA, the Home Secretary, Teresa May stated:

> The impact of serious and organised crime is felt across the UK in the everyday lives of people and neighbourhoods. For too long we have lacked a strong, collaborative national response in the fight for criminal justice, with a fragmented approach to policy, prevention and investigation. It is time for a fresh start. By creating a powerful new body of operational crime fighters – the National Crime Agency – we will confront the serious and organised criminality that threatens the safety and security of the UK. The NCA will work in partnership with the police, law enforcement agencies, businesses and the public to ensure those who commit serious and organised crime are

---

[191] HM Treasury above, n 43.

[192] See generally Ryder above, n 26.

[193] Kirk, D. 'Serious about fraud?' (2011) Journal of Criminal Law, 75(4), 249–252, at 249.

[194] Rider, B. 'A serious fraud?' (2010) Company Lawyer, 31(12), 381–382, at 381.

[195] See for example Palmer, A. and Ryder, N. 'The Economic Crime Agency' (2011) Financial Regulation International, April, 1–3.

[196] Home Office, Press Release, 'Home Office to take lead on economic crime', 17 January 2011, available from http://www.homeoffice.gov.uk/media-centre/news/economic-crime, accessed 23 October 2011.

[197] Bazley, S. 'FSA enforcement activity, reflections on 2010 and the challenges of regulatory change' (2011) Company Lawyer, 32(1), 1–2, at 2.

> tracked down, pursued, brought to justice and their ill-gotten gains are stripped away.[198]

This included tackling organised crime, fraud, cybercrime, maintaining border protection and protecting children and young people. The NCA is to be divided into four Command areas: Organised Crime Command, Border Policing Command, Economic Crime Command, and the Child Exploitation and Online Protection Centre.[199] The Home Office envisages the role of the Economic Crime Command to:

> Ensure an innovative and improved capability to deal with economic crimes, including those carried out by organised criminals. It will co-ordinate effective action to tackle complex economic crime and will ensure the coherent use of resources across all national economic crime fighting agencies including the Serious Fraud Office and City of London Police.[200]

It was also envisaged that the Economic Crime Command 'is intended to co-ordinate and improve communication between the SFO, the FCA and other prosecutors of economic crime, which has gained in prominence in the wake of the financial crisis'.[201] However, Kirk was sceptical if the NCA would work and stated:

> There is a risk that economic crime, far from being given a higher profile by the arrangements set out in the National Crime Agency plan, will slide down the scale of priorities because the SFO has been so damaged by recent events that its capacity to fight fraud has been diminished, and no credible alternative, with the required skills and budget, will be available to take over the important work that it undertakes.[202]

---

198 Home Office 'New National Crime Agency (NCA) to fight serious and organised crime', 8 June 2011, available from https://www.gov.uk/government/news/new-national-crime-agency-nca-to-fight-serious-and-organised-crime, accessed 16 September 2013.

199 The Home Office *The National Crime Agency – a plan for the creation of a national crime-fighting capability* (London: Home Office, 2011).

200 Home Office above, n 198.

201 Binham, C. and Warell, H. 'Top fraud investigator quits UK crime agency role', 18 August 2013, available from http://www.ft.com/cms/s/0/dae8e0f2-0691-11e3-9bd9-00144feab7de.html#axzz2f4C0WdBO, accessed 16 September 2013.

202 Kirk above, n 193, at 252.

The NCA was established by virtue of the Crime and Courts Act 2013,[203] which received Royal Assent on 25 April 2013.[204] The Act provides the NCA with two specific functions – crime reduction[205] and crime intelligence.[206] It is important to note that the NCA does not have any prosecutorial functions, which clearly contradicts the initial proposal to grant the ECA such powers. Therefore, the creation of the NCA must be questioned, and it merely amounts to the creation of yet another law enforcement agency with little bite.

5.4.4 Financial Conduct Authority

By virtue of the Financial Services Act 2012, the FCA replaced the FSA for dealing with white collar crime in relation to its financial regulatory remit.[207] The 'financial crime' statutory objective of the FSA under the Financial Services and Markets Act 2000 has been removed and it is now associated with the FCA's consumer protection and market integrity objectives.[208] Hill stated that 'in accordance with its consumer protection objective, the FCA must also have regard to taking action in relation to financial crime. This will be a freestanding duty to take action in relation to any fraud, dishonesty, misconduct and handling the proceeds of crime.'[209] Tackling white collar crime is an integral part of the FCA's regulatory remit.[210] Tracey McDermott stated that 'one of our objectives is to ensure the integrity of the markets … a key part of that is ensuring that our markets operate honestly and that the firms we regulate understand, and manage, the financial crime risks that they face'.[211] The

---

[203] The Crime and Courts Act 2013, s. 1. For a brief overview of the Crime and Courts Act 2013 see Anon. 'Administration of justice' (2013) Public Law, July, 637–640, at 637.

[204] McGowan, L. 'Criminal law legislation update' (2013) Journal of Criminal Law, 77(4), 279–280, at 279.

[205] The Crime and Courts Act 2013, s. 1(4).

[206] The Crime and Courts Act 2013, s. 1(5).

[207] Srivastava *et al* above, n 1, at 4.

[208] Financial Conduct Authority 'Fighting financial crime', 31 March 2013, available from http://www.fca.org.uk/about/what/protecting/financial-crime, accessed 8 July 2013.

[209] Hill, C. 'Fund management update' (2013) Compliance Officer Bulletin, March, 104, 1–36, at 30.

[210] Financial Conduct Authority 'Keynote address: financial crime in the FCA world, Tracey McDermott', 1 July 2013, available from http://www.fca.org.uk/news/speeches/financial-crime-in-the-fca-world, accessed 8 July 2013.

[211] *Ibid.*

FCA will concentrate its resources towards maintaining 'standards of conduct in the financial services industry'.[212] This means that the FCA will adopt a very similar approach towards the reduction of white collar crime to that adopted by the FSA, namely that regulated firms must have appropriate systems and controls. Another legacy left by the FSA which the FCA will be able to use is the 'tools that are currently available to the FSA. It will be able to impose penalties for market abuse, instigate criminal proceedings for insider dealing and market manipulation and it will act as a "competent authority" in relation to money laundering.'[213] Furthermore, the FCA will be expected to follow and further develop the FSA's credible deterrence strategy.[214] This will involve the FCA continuing to 'tak[e] tough, targeted, effective and public action against misconduct perpetrated by firms and individuals'.[215] However, it is important to note that there is an expectation that the FCA will be more proactive than the FSA was in using its enforcement powers and that it will seek to initiate more cases that levy stronger penalties.[216] Thus the policy adopted by the FCA towards white collar crime is identical to that of the FSA. We are likely to see for the foreseeable future nothing more than the imposition of more financial penalties. The Coalition government has missed a significant opportunity to create the ECA, an agency that would have had sufficient prosecutorial and investigative powers towards white collar crime.

5.5 ENFORCEMENT RESPONSE

The response of regulatory and law enforcement agencies towards instances of white collar crime during the financial crisis in the UK is very similar to that adopted in the US. It is largely based on the production of damning reports, the imposition of 'media friendly', tokenistic financial sanctions, several LIBOR related arrests, meaningless statements from politicians and, therefore, more broken promises. This

---

[212] Srivastava *et al* above, n 1, at 9. For a more detailed discussion of this approach see Financial Conduct Authority *Financial crime: a guide for firms part 1: a firm's guide to preventing financial crime* (Financial Conduct Authority: London, 2013) and Financial Conduct Authority *Financial crime: a guide for firms part 2: financial crime thematic reviews* (Financial Conduct Authority: London, 2013).

[213] Hill above, n 209, at 30.

[214] Srivastava *et al* above, n 1, at 10.

[215] Hill above, n 209, at 30.

[216] Marshall *et al* above, n 17, at 18.

section of the chapter analyses the array of enforcement mechanisms, both civil and criminal, that have been used since the start of the financial crisis.

5.5.1 Criminal Sanctions

> Serious bank failure results in severe economic disruption and considerable losses for taxpayers. In the wake of the financial crisis, £65 billion of taxpayers' money was used to bail out banks on the brink of failure, and the annual cost of financial crises to the UK economy as a whole has been estimated by the Independent Commission on Banking at approximately 3 per cent of GDP, or around £40 billion in 2010 terms.[217]

One of the problems associated with those who were allegedly engaged in misconduct during the financial crisis is determining what laws they have broken. Law enforcement agencies have a multitude of statutory provisions that should have covered the alleged misconduct. For example, the Fraud Act 2006 provides that the offence can be committed in three different ways: by a false representation,[218] by a failure to disclose information when there is a legal duty to do so[219] and by abuse of position.[220] There are also a number of secondary offences including the possession or control of articles for use either in the course of or in connection with frauds,[221] making, adapting, supplying or offering to supply articles for use in frauds,[222] participating in fraudulent trading as a sole trader[223] and obtaining services dishonestly where the defendant either intends not to pay or not to pay in full.[224] Yet, the SFO decided *against* charging the alleged perpetrators of the LIBOR scandal under the Fraud Act 2006, favouring the conspiracy to defraud charges. Another legislative possibility is false accounting under the Theft Act 1968, which provides that a person is guilty if he:

> dishonestly (a) destroys, defaces, conceals or falsifies any account or any record or document made or required for any accounting purpose; or (b) in

---

217 HM Treasury above, n 100, at 1.
218 Fraud Act 2006, s. 2.
219 Fraud Act 2006, s. 3.
220 Fraud Act 2006, s. 4. For a more detailed discussion see Collins, J. 'Fraud by abuse position: theorizing section 4 of the Fraud Act 2006' (2011) Criminal Law Review, 7, 513–523.
221 Fraud Act 2006, s. 6.
222 Fraud Act 2006, s. 7.
223 Fraud Act 2006, s. 9.
224 Fraud Act 2006, s. 11.

> furnishing information for any purpose produces or makes use of any account, or any such record or document as aforesaid, which to his knowledge is or may be misleading, false or deceptive in a material particular; he shall, on conviction on indictment, be liable to imprisonment for a term not exceeding seven years.[225]

However, the usefulness and appropriateness of this in relation to LIBOR have been questioned by Corker, who noted that:

> LIBOR submissions are a mass of financial data all on one sheet which would be alleged to be false or misleading … the problem … is that this information is not created for an accounting purpose which the offence requires a prosecutor to prove … [which is] beyond the scope of this offence.[226]

It has also been suggested that the SFO could use its powers relating to price fixing under what is referred to as the 'Cartel Offence'.[227] A person is guilty of an offence if they 'agree with one or more other persons to make or implement, or to cause to be made or implemented, arrangements of the following kind relating to at least two undertakings'.[228] The Cartel Offence also provides that the arrangements:

> must be ones which, if operating as the parties to the agreement intend, would – (a) directly or indirectly fix a price for the supply by A in the United Kingdom (otherwise than to B) of a product or service, (b) limit or prevent supply by A in the United Kingdom of a product or service, (c) limit or prevent production by A in the United Kingdom of a product, (d) divide between A and B the supply in the United Kingdom of a product or service to a customer or customers, (e) divide between A and B customers for the supply in the United Kingdom of a product or service, or (f) be bid-rigging arrangements.[229]

It is important to note that the enforcement of the Cartel Offence is limited due to the overlapping prosecutorial roles of the SFO and OFT.[230]

---

225 Theft Act 1969, s. 17(1).
226 Corker above, n 107, at 980.
227 Enterprise Act 2002, s. 188.
228 Enterprise Act 2002, s. 188(1).
229 Enterprise Act 2002, s. 188(2).
230 Furse, M. 'The cartel offence – "great for a headline but not much else"?' (2011) European Competition Law Review, 32(5), 223–230, at 223. For a more detailed discussion of the cartel offence see Lever, J. and Pike, J. 'Cartel agreements, criminal conspiracy and the statutory "cartel offence": part 2' (2005) European Competition Law Review, 26(3), 164–172 and Stephan, A. 'How dishonesty killed the cartel offence' (2011) Criminal Law Review, 6, 446–455.

Furthermore, it must also be taken into account that in its previous attempts to initiate criminal proceedings for price fixing, the SFO was accused of 'misunderstand[ing] the law so badly that the case collapse[d] at the first hurdle'.[231] The failure of the SFO to gain a successful prosecution in *R. v GG Plc* has been described as an 'embarrassment for choosing the wrong charges'.[232]

Additionally, the FSA has the ability to prosecute for a wide range of criminal activities.[233] For example, the FSA can prosecute carrying on or purporting to carry on a regulated activity without authorisation or exemption,[234] making false claims to be authorised or exempt,[235] communicating an invitation or inducement to engage in investment activity in breach of the restrictions on financial promotion,[236] misleading the FSA and other contraventions in relation to the exercise of Treaty rights,[237] performing or agreeing to perform functions in breach of a prohibition order[238] and failing to register a copy of listing particulars on or before publication.[239] Furthermore, the FSA is able to pursue criminal proceedings where someone offers securities to the public before publishing a prospectus required by listing rules,[240] issuing an advertisement, or other information specified in the listing rules, without prior approval or authorisation from the competent authority,[241] failing to cooperate with, or giving false information to, FSA appointed investigators,[242] failing to

---

[231] See Corker above, n 107, at 980 and *R. v GG Plc* [2009] 2 All E.R. 738. For a brief discussion of this case see Ormerod, D. 'Conspiracy: conspiracy to defraud – whether scope of offence extends to price fixing' (2009) Criminal Law Review, 6, 433–437. For a wider discussion of the legal issues in this case see Whelan, P. 'Legal certainty and cartel criminalisation within the EU Member States' (2012) Cambridge Law Journal, 71(3), 677–702 and Danagher, L. 'The criminalisation of cartels: a European and trans-Atlantic perspective' (2012) European Competition Law Review, 33(11), 522–525.

[232] Trafford, M. 'Losing on LIBOR' (2013) Butterworths Journal of International Banking and Financial Law, 28(4), 238–239, at 238.

[233] Financial Services and Markets Act 2000, ss. 401 and 402.

[234] Financial Services and Markets Act 2000, s. 23.

[235] Financial Services and Markets Act 2000, s. 24.

[236] Financial Services and Markets Act 2000, s. 25.

[237] Financial Services and Markets Act 2000, schedule 4, para. 6.

[238] Financial Services and Markets Act 2000, s. 56(4).

[239] Financial Services and Markets Act 2000, s. 83(3).

[240] Financial Services and Markets Act 2000, s. 85(2).

[241] Financial Services and Markets Act 2000, s. 98(2).

[242] Financial Services and Markets Act 2000, s. 177.

comply with provisions about control over authorised persons,[243] carrying on, or purporting to carry on, business in contravention of a consumer credit prohibition,[244] making false claims to be a person to whom the general prohibition does not apply,[245] providing false or misleading information to an auditor,[246] disclosing confidential information,[247] failure by a director of an insurer carrying on long-term insurance business to notify the FSA of a general meeting to propose a resolution for voluntary winding up,[248] misleading statements and practices offences[249] and misleading the FSA.[250] Additionally, the FSA is able to commence prosecutions for insider dealing,[251] money laundering[252] and terrorist financing.[253] However, there is some *uncertainty* if the FSA is able to enforce its *own* fraud policy and instigate criminal proceedings.[254] For example, the FSA has stated that 'we cannot prosecute most types of fraud and dishonesty … in contrast with money laundering; we have no direct powers to prosecute fraud or dishonesty offences. Prosecution is

---

243 Financial Services and Markets Act 2000, s. 191.
244 Financial Services and Markets Act 2000, s. 203(9).
245 Financial Services and Markets Act 2000, s. 333.
246 Financial Services and Markets Act 2000, s. 346.
247 Financial Services and Markets Act 2000, s. 352.
248 Financial Services and Markets Act 2000, s. 366(3).
249 Financial Services and Markets Act 2000, s. 397.
250 Financial Services and Markets Act 2000, s. 398.
251 Financial Services and Markets Act 2000, s. 402 (1)(a). For a more detailed discussion of this section see Ormerod, D. 'Prosecution: insider dealing – Criminal Justice Act 1993 s.61' (2009) Criminal Law Review, 6, 445–449.
252 Financial Services and Markets Act 2000, s. 402 (1)(b). For a general discussion of the ability of the FSA to initiate prosecutions for money laundering see Taylor, N. 'FSA prosecutions: offences of money laundering – power to prosecute' (2010) Criminal Law Review, 10, 772–775.
253 Financial Services and Markets Act 2000, s. 402 (1)(c). For a detailed discussion of this see Goldby, M. 'The impact of Schedule 7 of the Counter-Terrorism Act 2008 on banks and their customers' (2010) Journal of Money Laundering Control, 13(4), 351–371.
254 The fraud policy of the Financial Services Authority can be divided into four parts and includes a direct approach, increased supervisory activity, promoting a more joined up approach and Handbook modifications. See Ryder, N. *Financial crime in the 21st century: law and policy* (Edward Elgar: Cheltenham, 2011) at 130.

the responsibility of other law enforcement agencies.'[255] This explanation was reiterated by Lord Turner, the former Chairman of the FSA, who said:

> My understanding is that the FSA is *not* [author's emphasis] able to bring a criminal case in the UK. If it falls within the category of fraud, which is a general category of malfeasance quite separate from financial regulation, the Serious Fraud Office has a right to look at it, and we have been in contact with the SFO throughout this. I think that it announced a week or so ago that it would increase its focus on this issue. In the UK, this issue – as I understand it, but I would defer to my legal expert here – is *not* one where we, the FSA, have an ability to bring a criminal case.[256]

Further uncertainty was also expressed by Tracey McDermott of the FSA, who added: 'we are *not* a general fraud prosecutor … we have spent quite a lot of time and energy on prosecuting both section 397 offences and indeed insider dealing offences … we do *not* have a remit to prosecute false accounting, conspiracy'.[257] However, it is strongly suggested that the FSA *does* have the regulatory remit to prosecute certain fraudulent activity based on the following cases. For example, in March 2000 the FSA *successfully* prosecuted Paul Haslam for breaches of the Banking Act 1987.[258] Furthermore, in February 2008 the FSA successfully prosecuted William Anthony 'Robin' Radclyffe, who was convicted after pleading guilty to a series of offences under the Theft Acts, the Financial Services Act 1986 and Financial Services and Markets Act 2000. The defendant, who was not authorised by the FSA, made a series

---

[255] Financial Services Authority *Developing our policy on fraud and dishonesty – discussion paper 26* (Financial Services Authority: London, 2003) at 18.

[256] HM Treasury Select Committee *Fixing LIBOR: some preliminary findings* (HM Treasury: London, 2012) at 102.

[257] *Ibid.*

[258] Section 35 of the Banking Act 1987 provides that a person commits the offence of fraudulent inducement to make a deposit if a person '(a) makes a statement, promise or forecast which he knows to be misleading, false or deceptive, or dishonestly conceals any material facts; or (b) recklessly makes (dishonestly or otherwise) a statement, promise or forecast which is misleading, false or deceptive, is guilty of an offence if he makes the statement, promise or forecast or conceals the facts for the purpose of inducing, or is reckless as to whether it may induce, another person (whether or not the person to whom the statement, promise or forecast is made or from whom the facts are concealed) – (i) to make, or refrain from making, a deposit with him or any other person; or (ii) to enter, or refrain from entering, into an agreement for the purpose of making such a deposit'.

of false and misleading statements to his clients.[259] Margaret Cole, the then Director of the FSA, said 'our prosecution of this case is indicative of the FSA's determination to deter wrongdoing of this sort'.[260] Therefore, it is unsurprising that HM Treasury Select Committee criticised the decision of the FSA not to initiate criminal proceedings in relation to LIBOR:

> The FSA's decision whether to initiate a criminal prosecution should not be influenced by the fact that its income is derived from firms which it regulates. The FSA has an obligation under section 2(1)(b) of FSMA to discharge its functions in the way in which it considers most appropriate for the purpose of meeting its regulatory objectives. Under section 2(2)(d) the reduction of financial crime is one of these objectives. Financial crime is defined in section 6(3) as including not only misconduct in relation to a financial market but also any criminal offence of fraud or dishonesty. The FSA took a narrow view of its power to initiate criminal proceedings for fraudulent conduct in this case.[261]

This was also supported by George Osborne, who stated that the then legislation contained 'gaping holes' and that amendments would be made to the Financial Services Act 2012.[262] Therefore, the inability of the FSA to prosecute those involved in white collar crime during the financial crisis must be criticised. The Coalition government could have addressed this weakness by granting the FCA a specific mandate to tackle white collar crime. However, this was not forthcoming and the Financial Services Act 2012 only merged the financial crime statutory objective with the other FCA objectives. The FCA has determined to follow the 'credible deterrence' approach that was adopted by its regulatory predecessor the FSA, which, as outlined above, resulted in the imposition of more financial sanctions.

---

[259] Financial Services Authority 'Fake stockbroker sentenced to 15 months', 13 February 2008, available from http://www.fsa.gov.uk/library/communication/pr/2008/011.shtml, accessed 12 November 2012.

[260] *Ibid.* Also see Griffiths, K. 'Fraudulent broker gets 15 months', 14 February 2008, available from http://www.telegraph.co.uk/finance/markets/2784369/Fraudulent-broker-gets-15-months.html, accessed 12 November 2012.

[261] HM Treasury Select Committee above, n 256, at 103.

[262] HM Treasury 'Statement by the Chancellor of the Exchequer, Rt Hon George Osborne MP, on LIBOR', 2 July 2012, available from https://www.gov.uk/government/speeches/statement-by-the-chancellor-of-the-exchequer-rt-hon-george-osborne-mp-on-libor, accessed 15 July 2013. Also see Anon. 'Banks in big bother' (2012) New Law Journal, 6 July, at 885.

5.5.2 Civil Sanctions

The Financial Services and Markets Act 2000 provides the FSA with the power to ensure that authorised people are both fit and proper to perform the functions for which they were employed. Enforcement within the context of the Financial Services and Markets Act incorporates two broad concepts. First, preventing those who are not authorised to conduct banking or investment business from doing so; and secondly, to ensure that those who are authorised to conduct such businesses do so properly.[263] The Financial Services and Markets Act 2000 states that the FSA has the power to require information or documents that may reasonably be required in connection with the discharge of its functions under the FSMA.[264] The information or documents can be required from any person. This would include an authorised person, a formerly authorised person, a person connected with an authorised person, an operator, a recognised investment exchange and a recognised clearing house. Furthermore, the Financial Services and Markets Act 2000 grants the FSA the power to require an authorised person or a formerly authorised person to commission and provide to the FSA in any manner in which the FSA might specify.[265] The FSA is provided with such powers to issue public statements or impose financial penalties where the rules under the FSMA have been contravened. For example, the FSA has the power to issue a public statement concerning a breach by an authorised person of any requirement that is imposed by the 2000 Act.[266]

The FSA also has the power to impose financial sanctions where it establishes that there has been a contravention by an authorised person of any requirement under the Financial Services and Markets Act.[267] The highest profile financial sanctions imposed have been over the manipulation or rigging of LIBOR. The FSA alleged that Barclays Bank attempted to manipulate the dollar LIBOR and the EURIBOR rates of interest after being asked by derivative traders and other banking institutions. The misconduct took place in both London and New York. The FSA also concluded that Barclays acted inappropriately between September 2007 and May 2009 by 'making LIBOR submissions which took into account concerns over the negative media perception of

263 Bagge above, n 137, at 196.
264 Financial Services and Markets Act 2000, s. 165.
265 Financial Services and Markets Act 2000, s. 166.
266 Financial Services and Markets Act 2000, s. 205.
267 Financial Services and Markets Act 2000, s. 206 (1).

Barclays' LIBOR submissions'.[268] This is of particular relevance to the link between the financial crisis and the illegal activities of Barclays. This was a point raised by the FSA, which reported:

> Liquidity issues were a particular focus for Barclays and other banks during the financial crisis and banks' LIBOR submissions were seen by some commentators as a measure of their ability to raise funds. Barclays was identified in the media as having higher LIBOR submissions than other contributing banks at the outset of the financial crisis. Barclays believed that other banks were making LIBOR submissions that were too low and did not reflect market conditions. The media questioned whether Barclays' submissions indicated that it had a liquidity problem. Senior management at high levels within Barclays expressed concerns over this negative publicity.[269]

The FSA added that the concerns raised by members of senior management at Barclays resulted in 'instructions being given by less senior managers at Barclays to reduce LIBOR submissions in order to avoid negative media comment'.[270] The FSA concluded that this conduct breached several of its Principles of Business.[271] The FSA noted that Barclays breached Principle 3 by 'failing to have adequate risk management systems or effective controls in place in relation to its LIBOR and EURIBOR submissions processes'.[272] Barclays had no specific systems and controls in place relating to its LIBOR and EURIBOR submissions processes until December 2009.[273] The FSA fined Barclays £59.5m and concluded:

> Barclays' misconduct was serious, widespread and extended over a number of years. The integrity of benchmark reference rates such as LIBOR and EURIBOR is of fundamental importance to both UK and international financial markets. Firms making submissions must not use those submissions as tools to promote their own interests. Making submissions to try to benefit trading positions is wholly unacceptable. This was possible because Barclays failed to ensure it had proper controls in place. Barclays' behaviour threatened the integrity of the rates with the risk of serious harm to other market participants. The FSA continues to pursue a number of other significant cross-border investigations in this area and the action we have taken against

---

268 Financial Services Authority *Final notice to Barclays Bank Plc* (Financial Services Authority: London, 2012) at 3.

269 *Ibid.*

270 Financial Services Authority above, n 268, at 3.

271 *Ibid.*, at 2.

272 Financial Services Authority above, n 268, at 3.

273 *Ibid.*, at 3.

> Barclays should leave firms in no doubt about the serious consequences of this type of failure.[274]

The HM Treasury Select Committee concluded that these findings have 'been a reputational disaster for Barclays. They have led directly to the loss of its Chief Executive and its Chief Operating Officer.'[275] Furthermore, the conduct of Barclays resulted in condemnation from HM Treasury Select Committee:

> The attempted manipulation of Barclays' LIBOR submissions with the intention of personal gain continued for four years. It is shocking that it flourished for so long. Any system may fail for a short period, but compliance at Barclays was persistently ineffective. Even when Barclays' compliance had indications that something was awry, it failed to take the opportunity to strengthen the bank's controls. Nor was there any pressure from senior executives within Barclays to ensure that effective LIBOR controls were in place, as it was considered low-risk, in particular where LIBOR setters sat, with no presence of the compliance function. These are serious failures of governance within Barclays, for which the board is responsible.[276]

It is very important to note that Barclays received a significant discount on the financial penalty imposed.

The second bank to be fined by the FSA due to its manipulation of LIBOR was UBS, which was fined £160m in December 2012.[277] The FSA determined that between January 2005 and December 2010, UBS breached Regulations 3 and 5 of the FSA's Principles of Business when the bank engaged in illegal behaviour regarding the calculation of LIBOR and EURIBOR. The FSA stated that:

> The findings we have set out in our notice today do not make for pretty reading. The integrity of benchmarks such as LIBOR and EURIBOR is of fundamental importance to both UK and international financial markets. UBS traders and managers ignored this. They manipulated UBS's submissions in order to benefit their own positions and to protect UBS's reputation, showing a total disregard for the millions of market participants around the world who were also affected by LIBOR and EURIBOR. UBS's misconduct was all the more serious because of the orchestrated attempts to manipulate the JPY LIBOR submissions of other banks as well as its own and the collusion with

---

274 Financial Services Authority above, n 142.

275 HM Treasury Select Committee above, n 256, at 10.

276 *Ibid.*, 21.

277 Financial Services Authority 'Final notice RBS', 19 December 2012, available from http://www.fsa.gov.uk/static/pubs/final/ubs.pdf, accessed 30 June 2013.

> interdealer brokers and other panel banks in coordinated efforts to manipulate the fix. Over an extended period UBS allowed this to happen through its failure to control its business appropriately to ensure that LIBOR and EURIBOR submissions properly reflected the relevant requirements. There should be no doubt about how seriously the FSA views these failings. This is our largest penalty to date and demonstrates our commitment to ensuring that those in the wholesale markets do not put their own interests above those of the markets as a whole.[278]

> In February 2013 the Royal Bank of Scotland became the third bank to be fined by the FSA following the revelations of LIBOR rigging. The FSA fined RBS £87.5m for its conduct between January 2006 and November 2010.[279]

It has already been established that the SEC has used its power on numerous occasions to ban those individuals who it believes contributed towards the financial crisis. Therefore, it will be useful at this stage to determine if any comparisons can be made with the ability of the FSA to issue prohibition orders to authorised persons and firms from undertaking any regulated activity.[280] An illustration of the FSA issuing a prohibition order was Peter Cummings, a former CEO of HBOS.[281] Additionally, he was fined £500,000 for his 'breaching Statement of Principle 6 of the FSA's Code of Practice for Approved Persons, by failing to exercise due

---

[278] Financial Services Authority above, n 143.

[279] Financial Services Authority 'RBS fined £87.5m for significant failings in relation to LIBOR', 6 February 2013, available from http://www.fsa.gov.uk/library/communication/pr/2013/011.shtml, accessed 8 February 2013.

[280] Financial Services and Markets Act 2000, s. 56. For example, in April 2008 the FSA banned John Paul Keay, who operated as Jack Keay Mortgage Services, 'for not being competent or capable to perform any functions related to regulated activities, including giving advice'. See Financial Services Authority 'Final notice to Mr John Paul Keay trading as Jack Keay Mortgage Services', 21 April 2008, available from http://www.fsa.gov.uk/pubs/final/JKMS.pdf, accessed 30 June 2013. For further examples see Financial Services Authority 'FSA bans four more brokers for mortgage fraud as the Tribunal dismisses broker's appeal', 19 April 2011, available from http://www.fsa.gov.uk/pages/Library/Communication/PR/2011/038.shtml, accessed 30 June 2013.

[281] Financial Services Authority 'FSA issues ban and fine of £500,000 against former HBOS executive, Peter Cummings', 12 September 2012, available from http://www.fsa.gov.uk/library/communication/pr/2012/087.shtml, accessed 30 June 2013. Also see Treanor, J. 'Ex-HBOS banker Cummings banned for life and fined £500,000', 12 September 2012, available from http://www.guardian.co.uk/business/2012/sep/12/hbos-banker-peter-cummings-banned-fined-fsa, accessed 30 June 2013.

skill, care and diligence in managing HBOS's Corporate Division'.[282] The FSA stated that:

> Despite being aware of the weaknesses in his division and growing problems in the economy, Cummings presided over a culture of aggressive growth without the controls in place to manage the risks associated with that strategy. Instead of reacting to the worsening environment, he raised his targets as other banks pulled out of the same markets. It is essential that senior executives understand that incentivising revenue over risk is a dangerous folly. Growth is a sound ambition for any business but risk must be properly managed and robust controls are imperative to ensure growth is achieved in a way that is both stable and sustainable.[283]

The financial predicament that HBOS faced just after the start of the financial crisis was succinctly summarised by Tomasic and Akinbami, who stated 'the deterioration in the financial position of HBOS was largely attributable to heavy lending to its corporate customers involved in property development; while its retail arm was scheduled to make a profit of £1.2bn … its corporate lending arm was scheduled to make a loss of almost £6.8bn'.[284] Willmott and James described this issue of a prohibition order against Peter Cummings as

> the first case that the FSA has pursued in which disciplinary action is taken in relation to the core business risks taken by the firm … in this case, the bank's decision as to whether or not to lend its own money to customers … This is unprecedented in the 11 years of the FSA's existence and marks a very important shift in the FSA's own view of its regulatory remit.[285]

Another instance of the FSA utilising prohibition orders was illustrated in July 2010, when it banned and fined the former Finance Director of Northern Rock, David Jones, for misrepresenting mortgage arrears figures.[286] Further, the FSA also fined and banned the former Deputy Chief Executive and Credit Director of Northern Rock also for misreporting

---

282 *Ibid.*

283 Financial Services Authority above, n 281.

284 Tomasic, R. and Akinbami, F. 'Towards a new corporate governance after the global financial crisis' (2011) International Company and Commercial Law Review, 22(8), 237–249, at 243.

285 Willmott, N. and James, P. 'Reading between the lines: understanding the FSA's unwritten expectations of significant influence function holders on appointment and beyond' (2012) Compliance Officer Bulletin, November, 101, 1–28, at 13.

286 Financial Services Authority 'FSA bans and fines former Northern Rock finance director £320,000 for misreporting mortgage arrears figures', 27 July

mortgage arrears figures.[287] However, the implementation of a prohibition order against Peter Cummings can be contrasted with the lack of enforcement action against two other bankers, Fred Goodwin and Johnny Cameron. Johnny Cameron, the former Executive Director of RBS, was under investigation by the FSA. However, unlike Peter Cummings, the FSA reached a settlement with Johnny Cameron, who agreed that he will not 'perform any significant influence function in relation to any regulated activity carried on by any authorised person, exempt person or exempt professional firm' or 'undertake any further full time employment in the financial services industry'.[288] It is important to stress that Johnny Cameron made no admission of guilt, and in response to the decision by the FSA he stated: 'given the losses sustained by RBS in 2008, as a director of the RBS, I recognise that it is appropriate that I take my share of responsibility, and I will not be seeking another managerial role in the financial services industry'.[289] The highest profile former banker who the FSA decided not to take action against was Fred Goodwin, who was the CEO of RBS between 2001 and 2009. During his tenure, Fred Goodwin oversaw what can be classified as a boom time for RBS. By 2008, the bank had demonstrated rapid growth; its assets totalled £1.9tn and it was the fifth largest bank on the stock exchange. Fred Goodwin was 'deemed by the banking world and by the government to have a Midas touch. He advised the government on banking matters and was knighted for his services. He could do no wrong.'[290] However, this persona changed after RBS's ill-advised purchase in 2007 of ABN Amro for £48bn,[291] which was unsurprising given Goodwin's eagerness to

---

2010, available from http://www.fsa.gov.uk/pages/Library/Communication/PR/2010/126.shtml, accessed 1 July 2013.

287 Financial Services Authority 'FSA fines and bans former Northern Rock deputy chief executive and credit director for misreporting mortgage arrears figures', 13 April 2010, available from http://www.fsa.gov.uk/pages/Library/Communication/PR/2010/066.shtml, accessed 1 July 2013.

288 Financial Services Authority 'FSA statement on Johnny Cameron', 18 May 2010, available from http://www.fsa.gov.uk/pages/Library/Communication/PR/2010/081.shtml, accessed 1 July 2013.

289 Anon. 'Former RBS investment bank chief Johnny Cameron banned from City', 18 May 2010, available from http://www.telegraph.co.uk/finance/financialcrisis/7736540/Former-RBS-investment-bank-chief-Johnny-Cameron-banned-from-City.html, accessed 7 July 2013.

290 Kirk, D. 'Criminalising bad bankers' (2012) Journal of Criminal Law, 76(6), 439–441, at 440.

291 BBC News 'RBS secures takeover of ABN Amro', 8 October 2007, available from http://news.bbc.co.uk/1/hi/business/7033176.stm, accessed 2 July

expand the size of RBS via acquiring other banks.[292] Huisman stated that 'Fred Goodwin … is the embodiment of all that is apparently wrong in the financial sectors and which caused the financial crisis. He is seen as responsible for the disastrous acquisition of … ABN Amro Bank and the resulting rescue operation of the government.'[293] Tomasic and Akinbami noted that Goodwin's approach was flawed and extremely risky and he was 'known for the way in which he aggressively cut costs within the bank'.[294] This created the perfect cocktail of events that contributed to the bank suffering the largest annual corporate loss in UK history,[295] and the part nationalisation of RBS. The FSA decided against pursuing any action against Fred Goodwin.[296] Despite no action being taken against him, Fred Goodwin has offered a 'profound and unqualified apology for all of the distress that has been caused'.[297] Despite no action being taken by the FSA against Fred Goodwin, the Department of Business, Innovation and Skills (DBIS) stated in June 2012 that there is 'prosecutable evidence' to pursue disqualification proceedings under the Company Directors Disqualification Act 1986.[298] In May 2013, the Telegraph

---

2013. It is interesting to note that during its purchase of ABN Amro, RBS did not undertake any due diligence. See House of Commons Treasury Committee *Banking crisis: reforming corporate governance and pay in the City, HC 519* (House of Commons Treasury Committee: London, 2009) at 22, as cited in Tomasic and Akinbami above, n 284, at 243.

292 *Ibid.*

293 Huisman, Q.W. 'Corporate crime and crisis: causation scenarios' in Deflem, M. (ed.), *Economic crisis and crime* (Emerald: Bingley, 2011) at 119.

294 Tomasic and Akinbami above, n 284, at 243.

295 See for example BBC News 'RBS reports record corporate loss', 26 February 2009, available from http://news.bbc.co.uk/1/hi/business/7911722.stm, accessed 2 July 2013; Treanor, J. 'RBS record losses raise prospect of 95% state ownership', 26 February 2009, available from http://www.guardian.co.uk/business/2009/feb/26/rbs-record-loss, accessed 2 July 2013; and CNN 'RBS posts record $34 billion loss', 27 February 2009, available from http://edition.cnn.com/2009/BUSINESS/02/26/uk.rbs.recordloss/, accessed 2 July 2013.

296 For an explanation of the reasons for not pursuing action against Fred Goodwin see Financial Services Authority *The failure of the Royal Bank of Scotland – FSA board report* (Financial Services Authority: London, 2009) at 405–406.

297 House of Commons Treasury Committee above, n 291, at 58, as cited in Tomasic, R. 'The financial crisis and the haphazard pursuit of financial crime' (2011) Journal of Financial Crime, 18(1), 7–31, at 13.

298 Quinn, J. 'Vince Cable: RBS report recommends prosecution', 17 June 2012, available from http://www.telegraph.co.uk/finance/newsbysector/banksand

reported that the DBIS had contacted Lord Wallace, the government's principal legal adviser in Scotland, 'demanding to know when a decision will be made on whether to ban the former bankers from sitting on company boards'.[299] However, at the time of writing no action has been taken by the DBIS against *any* director in relation to the financial crisis. At the Liberal Democrat annual conference in September 2013, Vince Cable MP announced that he was 'preparing to legislate to make it easier to prosecute and ban rogue directors who repeatedly walk away from their debts and their customers'.[300] Despite the continued political rhetoric from politicians and the DBIS, the stark reality remains, that not one company director has been disqualified for conduct relating to the financial crisis.[301]

5.6 CONCLUSION

The regulatory response to the financial crisis in the UK is very similar to that outlined in the previous chapter for the US. We have seen the publication of numerous reports, consultation papers, the creation of several new regulatory agencies, the introduction of new legislation and criminal offences to criminalise the reckless misconduct of bankers. The former Labour government must be credited with actually attempting to tackle white collar crime by introducing and implementing the money laundering, counter-terrorist financing, confiscation of the proceeds of crime and anti-fraud strategies between 1997 and 2010. Furthermore, several white collar crime mechanisms were contained in the Financial Services and Markets Act 2000 and the FSA was given the statutory

---

finance/9336327/Vince-Cable-RBS-report-recommends-prosecution.html, accessed 2 July 2013.

[299] Hurley, J. 'Speed up action against Fred Goodwin, Vince Cable tells Scottish prosecutors', 1 May 2013, available from http://www.telegraph.co.uk/finance/newsbysector/banksandfinance/10029013/Speed-up-action-against-Fred-Goodwin-Vince-Cable-tells-Scottish-prosecutors.html, accessed 2 July 2013.

[300] Liberal Democrats 'Vince Cable F21 speech to the Liberal Democrat Autumn Conference', 16 September 2013, available from http://www.libdems.org.uk/speeches_detail.aspx?title=Vince_Cable_F21_speech_to_the_Liberal_Democrat_Autumn_Conference&pPK=e4e269ed-a26f-4177-bd2f-6a9dd18131a9, accessed 20 September 2013.

[301] For a more detailed analysis of the liability of bank directors see Arsalidou, D. 'The banking crisis: rethinking and refining the accountability of bank directors' (2010) Journal of Business Law, 4, 284–310 and HM Treasury *Sanctions for the directors of failed banks* (HM Treasury: London, 2012).

objective of reducing financial crime. These measures laid the foundations for an effective white collar crime strategy that the Coalition government could have utilised. The FSA and now the FCA has continued to adopt its credible deterrence strategy which has resulted in the continued imposition of financial sanctions on both firms and individuals who have breached its regulations. Both the FCA and its regulatory predecessor the FSA imposed increasing and record levels of financial penalties on those firms which manipulated LIBOR, yet it decided against instigating criminal proceedings and left that with the SFO. The decision over whether or not the FSA was able to bring criminal proceedings in relation to LIBOR remains unclear as the evidence provided above suggests that it did have the ability to initiate criminal proceedings for fraud, despite contradictory statements from the FSA. Nonetheless, the FSA must be credited for increasing the number of insider dealing convictions and vigorously enforcing the market abuse regime. However, the FSA and FCA must be criticised for its initial response to LIBOR, which amounted to nothing more than playing regulatory tennis with the most serious financial scandal in the UK since the collapse of Barings Bank. The Coalition government has not continued the white collar crime strategies introduced by the former Labour government. For example, it had the ideal opportunity to create a single agency that would have exclusively tackled white collar crime – the ECA. However, the Coalition government decided to create the NCA that contains an Economic Crime Command. One can only feel that an ideal opportunity has been missed to create a single white collar crime agency that would merge the existing, overlapping and competing agencies into the ECA.

One of the major criticisms of the response to white collar crime emanating from the financial crisis has been the lack of criminal prosecutions. During the height of the financial crisis, and while leader of the Conservative party, David Cameron boldly proclaimed that the City of London faced a 'Day of Reckoning' and that severe penalties would be imposed for those bankers whose reckless activities caused the financial crisis.[302] During his 'Day of Reckoning' speech, David Cameron stressed the importance of punishment and deterrence and stated:

---

[302] Prince, R. 'Cameron calls for criminal charges against bankers responsible for credit crunch', 15 December 2008, available from http://www.telegraph.co.uk/finance/financetopics/bernard-madoff/3775925/Cameron-calls-for-criminal-charges-against-bankers-responsible-for-credit-crunch.html, accessed 7 May 2013.

> [the] most important step we must take in enforcing responsibility in the City is to make sure that when rules are broken, and culprits are found, they are properly punished. That's only fair – because those responsible must be held to account … around the world, bankers sat up and took notice not when global finance ministers issued some new communiqué on unauthorized speculative trading – it was when Nick Leeson was caught and put behind bars. And corporate America really understood the consequences of dodgy accounting not just when Enron collapsed – but when Jeffrey Skilling was given a twenty-four year jail sentence. The problem in Britain … is that there just doesn't seem to be the will to see appropriate justice done at the highest level. Not from the Government. Despite the fact that the FSA itself admits: 'that the prospect of criminal proceedings acts as a significantly greater deterrent to those contemplating misconduct than does a fine of almost any size' it still prefers fines and mediation to the full application of the law. I welcome the recent comments by Jamie Symington of the FSA that they would 'bring more criminal prosecutions in the future'. But the truth remains that in the last twelve months, they have only brought four cases to trial. And only one of these has any connection to the current crisis – a mortgage advisor who lied and submitted forged documents in his application to become an FSA approved person. The other three all involved incidences of insider dealing that occurred before the debt crisis. This is not, at root, about more legislation. The laws are already there. Rather, it's about implementation and law enforcement.[303]

A number of interesting points can be raised from this section of the speech. For example, David Cameron stated that when 'rules are broken, and culprits are found, they are properly punished'. This raises a very important question: how many of those who are responsible for the financial crisis or contributed to it have been held accountable since the Coalition government was formed in 2010? The answer at the time of writing is zero. For example, not one director of a bank has been disqualified by the DBIS under the Company Director Disqualification Act 1986.[304] David Cameron also claimed that 'corporate America really understood the consequences of dodgy accounting not just when Enron collapsed – but when Jeffrey Skilling was given a twenty-four year jail sentence'. This part of the speech must be questioned: as previously

---

303 Conservatives 'David Cameron: a day of reckoning', 15 December 2008, available from http://www.conservatives.com/News/Speeches/2008/12/David_Cameron_A_day_of_reckoning.aspx, accessed 29 June 2013.

304 For a more detailed commentary on the Directors Disqualification Act 1986 see Griffin, S. 'The disqualification of unit directors and the protection of the public interest' (2002) Northern Ireland Legal Quarterly, 53(3), 207–231, and Wheeler, S. 'Directors disqualification: insolvency practitioners and the decision making process' (1995) Legal Studies, 15, 283–305.

argued in Chapter 4, there have been no high profile prosecutions, let alone convictions, for those who contributed towards the financial crisis. US law enforcement and regulatory agencies have concentrated on imposing what were initially perceived as impressive financial penalties on the culprits and also pursuing deferred or non-prosecution agreements. Sadly, authorities in the UK have adopted a similar, rather limp approach. David Cameron added that:

> the Serious Fraud Office has an important part to play too. But its effectiveness was called into question earlier this year in a review conducted by American prosecutor Jessica de Grazia. This has to change. The FSA and the SFO should be following up every lead, investigating every suspect transaction. And the government should be urging them on, because we need to make it one hundred per cent clear: those who break the law should face prosecution.[305]

In order for the SFO to 'follow up' every lead it is essential that it is granted the appropriate levels of funding by the UK government. However, since the creation of the Coalition government in 2010, the SFO, like many other government departments and agencies, has had its budget cut as part of a glut of extensive austerity measures.[306] For example, the annual budget of the SFO in 2008/2009 was £53.2m, £32.1m in 2013/2014 and £30.8m in 2014/2015.[307] The decision to reduce the budget of the SFO, at a time when white collar crime has increased and the duties of the SFO have been expanded to incorporate the enforcement of the Bribery Act 2010, has been questioned and criticised.[308] However, it is important to note that fraud is an extremely

---

[305] Conservatives above, n 303.

[306] For the most recent government funding cutbacks in the United Kingdom see HM Treasury *Spending review* (HM Treasury: London, 2013); HM Treasury *Spending round 2013: distributional analysis* (HM Treasury: London, 2013); HM Treasury *Spending round 2013: policy costings* (HM Treasury: London, 2013); and HM Treasury 'Spending round 2013: speech', 26 June 2013, available from https://www.gov.uk/government/speeches/spending-round-2013-speech, accessed 30 June 2013.

[307] Serious Fraud Office *Serious Fraud Office annual report and accounts 2011–2012* (Serious Fraud Office: London, 2012) at 7. Also see for example Purkiss, A. 'U.K. Fraud Office hit by budget cuts, staff losses', 28 March 2011, available from http://www.bloomberg.com/news/2011-03-28/u-k-fraud-office-hit-by-budget-cuts-staff-losses-ft-reports.html, accessed 30 June 2013.

[308] See for example Masters, B. 'Fraud watchdog weakened by budget cuts', 27 March 2011, available from http://www.ft.com/cms/s/0/8221aba2-58b5-11e0-9b8a-00144feab49a.html#axzz2XgX4w3hV, accessed 30 June 2013; Russel, J.

difficult criminal offence to detect and prosecute, and is expensive to enforce.[309] This was clearly illustrated by the 1994 SFO prosecution of Virani, in which 50 per cent of the trial costs were associated with accountants who assisted with the prosecution.[310] The imposition of budgetary cuts on the SFO since 2010 adversely affected its investigation into the alleged manipulation of LIBOR.[311] The Wall Street Journal reported that the SFO was unable to accept the offer to investigate LIBOR in 2011, due to significant budget cuts.[312] However, it has also been argued that the former Director of the SFO, Richard Alderman, refused to investigate LIBOR and handed over to the FSA.[313] It is important to note that the Coalition government responded by increasing

---

'The case to answer for the Serious Fraud Office', 26 May 2012, available from http://www.telegraph.co.uk/finance/financial-crime/9292046/The-case-to-answer-for-the-Serious-Fraud-Office.html, accessed 30 June 2013; Armitage, J. 'Cuts hamper fight against crime, warns SFO director', 5 April 2012, available from http://www.independent.co.uk/news/business/news/cuts-hamper-fight-against-crime-warns-sfo-director-7619339.html, accessed 30 June 2013.

[309] For an excellent discussion of the practical difficulties in prosecuting fraud cases see Lloyd-Bostock, S. 'The Jubilee Line jurors: does their experience strengthen the argument for judge-only trial in long and complex fraud cases?' (2007) Criminal Law Review, April, 255–273; Julian, R. 'Judicial perspectives in serious fraud cases – the present status of and problems posed by case management practices, jury selection rules, juror expertise, plea bargaining and choice of mode of trial' (2008) Criminal Law Review, 10, 764–783; and Julian, R. 'Judicial perspectives on the conduct of serious fraud trials' (2007) Criminal Law Review, October, 751–768.

[310] Savla, S. 'Serious Fraud Office powers under section 2 of the Criminal Justice Act 1987 and Police and Criminal Evidence Act 1984' (1997) Journal of Financial Crime, 4(3), 223–231, at 225.

[311] See for example Brady, B. and Owen, J. 'Budget cuts killed off LIBOR inquiry', 1 July 2012, available from http://www.independent.co.uk/news/uk/politics/budget-cuts-killed-off-libor-inquiry-7901940.html, accessed 18 March 2013; Russell, J. 'SFO given just £2m to enforce Bribery Act', 30 January 2011, available from http://www.telegraph.co.uk/finance/newsbysector/banksandfinance/8290808/SFO-given-just-2m-to-enforce-Bribery-Act.html, accessed 18 March 2013; Reyes, E. 'News focus: who will bring a Libor claim?', 5 July 2012, available from http://www.lawgazette.co.uk/news/news-focus-who-will-bring-a-libor-claim, accessed 30 June 2013.

[312] Colchester, M. 'U.K. Fraud Office opens Libor investigation', 6 July 2012, available from http://online.wsj.com/article/SB10001424052702303962304577510534226515306.html, accessed 30 June 2013.

[313] Adamson, R. 'SFO's priorities' (2013) Tolley's Practical Audit and Accounting, 24(7), 81–82, at 81.

the SFO budget for the investigation of LIBOR.[314] Indeed, the Financial Times reported that the SFO had been given £10.5m to fund its investigation into LIBOR.[315] In March 2013, the Director of the SFO, Sir David Green QC, announced that:'We have an agreement with HM Treasury that where any case costs over a certain percentage of our budget in any one year, we can have access to the reserve for a sum covering that cost, ring fenced for that case. Libor is the first example'.[316] However, it is important to note that the amount of funding provided to support the SFO and combat fraud is likely to be limited by drastic cuts to the legal aid budget.[317] Michael Turner QC, the Chairman of the Criminal Bar Association, advised the Justice Committee that one way to reduce the amount of taxpayers' money committed to fraud prosecutions was to introduce an insurance system that would involve banks contributing towards the cost of such prosecutions.[318] He added:

> At present, when a bank loses any money, the only person who suffers is the taxpayer. The bank is allowed to write the money off against tax; the taxpayer pays for the investigation; the taxpayer pays for the prosecution. If the

---

314 See for example Anon. 'SFO to launch criminal investigation into Libor scandal', 6 July 2012, available from http://www.telegraph.co.uk/finance/newsbysector/banksandfinance/9381683/SFO-to-launch-criminal-investigation-into-Libor-scandal.html, accessed 30 June 2013, and Binham, C. and Parker, G. 'SFO secures cash for Libor investigation', 6 July 2012, available from http://www.ft.com/cms/s/0/3b590260-c6cd-11e1-943a-00144feabdc0.html#axzz2XgX4w3hV, accessed 30 June 2013.

315 Shoffman, M. 'SFO given £10.5m for Libor probe', 20 February 2013, available from http://www.ftadviser.com/2013/02/20/regulation/regulators/sfo-given-m-for-libor-probe-uza6iEIER2ai2LZejszgLJ/article.html, accessed 30 June 2013. It has also been argued that the SFO was initially granted an additional £3.5m of funding to investigate LIBOR. See Adamson above, n 313, at 81.

316 Serious Fraud Office 'Inaugural fraud lawyers association, Inner Temple, speech by David Green CB QC Director, Serious Fraud Office', 26 March 2013, available from http://www.sfo.gov.uk/about-us/our-views/director's-speeches/speeches-2012/inaugural-fraud-lawyers'-association.aspx, accessed 30 June 2013.

317 Judd, T. 'Hundreds of millions from legal aid budget helps banks defend fraud cases', 11 June 2013, available from http://www.independent.co.uk/news/uk/home-news/hundreds-of-millions-from-legal-aid-budget-helps-banks-defend-fraud-cases-8654539.html, accessed 30 June 2013.

318 House of Commons 'Oral evidence by Michael Turner QC, taken before the Judicial Committee Price Competitive Tendering Proposals in the Government's Transforming Legal Aid Consultation', 11 June 2013, available from http://www.publications.parliament.uk/pa/cm201314/cmselect/cmjust/uc91-i/uc9101.htm, accessed 30 June 2013.

> prosecution is successful, lo and behold, the bank is delivered free of charge all it needs to get its civil recovery.[319]

One way in which the SFO has attempted to loosen the imposed budgetary constraints is to rely on 'investigations conducted and paid for by the target companies themselves'.[320] In January 2009, David Cameron stated that:

> I think that we need to look at the behaviour of banks and bankers and, where people have behaved inappropriately, that needs to be identified and if anyone has behaved criminally, in my view, there is a role for the criminal law and I don't understand why in this country the regulatory authorities seem to be doing so little to investigate it, whereas in America they're doing quite a lot.[321]

There is evidence to suggest that law enforcement agencies have been very proactive since the start of the financial crisis. For example, President Barack Obama granted the Department of Justice and FBI additional funding to tackle the threat posed by mortgage fraud during the financial crisis. However, it is essential to note that concerns have been raised by several commentators who have sought an answer to a simple question: why have there been no prosecutions of the high profile contributors of the financial crisis?[322]

---

319 *Ibid.*

320 Masters above, n 308.

321 Porter, A. 'David Cameron calls for criminal actions against bankers', 27 January 2009, available from http://www.telegraph.co.uk/finance/newsbysector/banksandfinance/4348801/David-Cameron-calls-for-criminal-actions-against-bankers.html, accessed 7 May 2013.

322 See for example Morgenson, G. and Story, L. 'In financial crisis, no prosecutions of top figures', 14 April 2011, available from http://www.nytimes.com/2011/04/14/business/14prosecute.html?pagewanted=all&_r=0, accessed 30 June 2013.

6. Conclusions and recommendations

In 2002, after a series of corporate scandals and financial frauds shocked the securities market, caused huge losses to investors, and outraged the public, Congress passed into law the Sarbanes–Oxley Act. Parts of Sarbanes–Oxley added new criminal penalties for various white-collar criminal offenses and increased the severity of penalties for, among others, securities fraud, mail and wire fraud, and conspiracy to commit securities fraud. At that time, the thinking of legislators, securities regulators, and law enforcement authorities was that 'enhanced' prison sentences, penalties, and fines would deter others from following in the footsteps of the likes of Bernie Ebbers (WorldCom's CEO), Jeff Skilling (Enron's COO), John Rigas (Adelphia's CEO), and Walter Forbes (Cendant's CEO). Yet, only seven years later, instead of the corporate securities frauds of Messrs. Ebbers, Skilling, Rigas, and Forbes, we now have Messrs. Bernie Madoff, Scott Rothstein, and Allen Stanford and their multi-billion dollar 'Ponzi' schemes; instead of the corporate financial scandals of the early 2000s, now at the end of the decade we have mortgage-lending fraud and related financial crimes. It is déjà vu all over again.[1]

Although we will never be able to stop white collar crime entirely, it is possible for us to alter the systemic and environmental factors that lead 'opportunists' and members of the 'go along' crowd to engage in deleterious behavior. Increased resources should be dedicated to investigating and prosecuting white collar crime in good economic times as well as bad. Excessive practices with negative consequences for society should be criminalized, and penalties should be raised on other crimes to increase their deterrent value. Better regulatory systems should be developed. Perhaps most importantly, we should foster a spirit of transparency in the business world through the use of mandatory disclosure.[2]

---

[1] Dooley, D. and Radke, M. 'Does severe punishment deter financial crimes?' (2010) Charleston Law Review, Spring, 4, 619–658, at 619.

[2] Valukas, A. 'White-collar crime and economic recession' (2010) University of Chicago Legal Forum, 1–21, at 12.

6.1 INTRODUCTION

This monograph has attempted to add to the existing literature on the factors that have contributed towards the most recent financial crisis. It is the author's contention that one of the previously unattributed and under-researched variables that contributed to, exploited and benefited from the worst economic conditions since the Great Depression and Wall Street Crash is white collar crime. It is important to note and accept that white collar crime was *not* the sole and *only* cause of the financial crisis. For example, as outlined in the second chapter of this monograph, it has been correctly asserted by many leading economists, the IMF, the World Bank, nation states, governments and other commentators that the foundations of the financial crisis were laid as a result of the collapse of the US subprime mortgage market in 2007. Others have argued that the groundwork of the financial crisis was placed by the continued imposition of low interest rates by the Federal Reserve. This economic policy was used by successive US governments in the 1980s and 1990s as a preventative measure to avoid economic turmoil. The policy of adopting low interest rates was continued by President George Bush and the Federal Reserve following the terrorist attacks in September 2001. Other well documented factors, which are beyond the scope of the monograph, include the deregulation of banking laws in the US and UK, and the development and promotion by lenders of access to convenient credit. This, when combined with the irresponsible lending practices, or what many US commentators refer to as predatory lending, of financial institutions contributed towards record levels of personal debt, individual and corporate insolvencies, and extreme levels of overindebtedness. Lenders must take some responsibility for adopting aggressive and at times illegal or even fraudulent lending practices by deliberately offering and granting loans to borrowers who did not have the financial capability to meet their repayment obligations. Such lending practices are at the heart of the subprime mortgage crisis, which has further worsened the levels of personal debt. However, it is important to emphasise that in many circumstances the borrower must accept some of the responsibility for engaging in irresponsible borrowing practices.

Another well documented factor that contributed towards the financial crisis was ineffective banking regulation. This is abundantly clear in the UK following the publication of several damning reports into the regulatory performance of the FSA in the run-up to the collapse and part nationalisation of Northern Rock in 2008. Likewise, banking regulatory agencies in the US have been severely criticised. For example, the SEC was largely condemned for its sluggish response to the Ponzi fraud scheme of Bernard Madoff. Therefore, both President Barack Obama and the Prime Minister David Cameron have managed and overseen radical changes towards the regulation of banks since the start of the financial crisis. As previously outlined in this monograph, there are a wide range of variables that contributed towards the financial crisis which have resulted in a great deal of literature from economists, academics, think tanks and commissioned government reports. It is the author's contention that white collar crime is an equally important factor that contributed towards the financial crisis.

6.2 THE FINANCIAL CRISIS AND WHITE COLLAR CRIME

Initially, the link between the financial crisis and white collar crime was difficult to quantify and establish. Sadly, there is no individual or super-villain that has become the face of white collar crime during the financial crisis, despite the illegal activities of notorious white collar criminals including Bernard Madoff and Allen Stanford. It has recently been suggested by several commentators that the face of white collar crime during the financial crisis is not any one individual but the banking profession. Such commentators have criticised the weak response by law enforcement agencies towards the activities, conduct and actions of banks that contributed towards the financial crisis.[3] Nonetheless, this monograph has attempted to identify several perceived instances of white collar crime that has interacted with the traditional variables that contributed towards the financial crisis. For example, this includes:

1. the relationship between subprime mortgages and mortgage fraud;
2. the alleged illegal activities of CRAs;
3. increased instances of predatory lending;
4. Ponzi fraud schemes;
5. the instigation of the 'War on Terror' and the 'Financial War on Terrorism';
6. market misconduct; and
7. the manipulation or rigging of LIBOR.

---

[3] For a more detailed illustration of this see Chapters 1, 2 and 3.

The relationship between subprime mortgages and mortgage fraud is clearly illustrated by reference to the enforcement activities of the FBI and the number of related SARs filed by deposit taking institutions with FinCEN. As a result of the financial crisis and the implementation of mortgage fraud related legislation by President Barack Obama in 2009, mortgage fraud was identified as one of the most widespread and uncontrolled white collar crimes associated with the financial crisis. This monograph has presented evidence that the FBI has pushed mortgage fraud to the top of its white collar crime agenda. For example, the FBI has secured over 1,200 mortgage fraud related convictions since 2009, launched numerous investigations, created a plethora of mortgage fraud task forces, and attempted to recompense lenders and borrowers who have been victims of this white collar crime. The explosion of instances of mortgage fraud was clearly illustrated by the dramatic increase in the number of mortgage fraud related SARs filed with FinCEN. Finally, the link between the financial crisis and mortgage fraud was illustrated in October 2013 when the Bank of America was found liable for mortgage fraud.[4] Predatory lending is inherently associated with the subprime mortgage sector and subprime lending. There is evidence to suggest that subprime lenders have either engaged in immoral, unethical or fraudulent lending prior to and during the financial crisis. There have been several legislative attempts to regulate predatory lending, a majority of which relates to the regulation of consumer credit agreements and their terms and conditions. These laws are enforced by a number of regulatory agencies, including the Federal Trade Commission and Department of Justice. However, they provide very little protection to borrowers and it is to the surprise of the author that no criminal proceedings have been instigated against subprime lenders under the plethora of US anti-fraud legislation. The contribution of CRAs towards the financial crisis is extremely well documented and some commentators have suggested that these institutions have become too powerful and that the current systems of regulation and accountability are ineffective.[5] The latter point is evident from the lacklustre legislative measures introduced by President George Bush to regulate CRAs in 2006, when the SEC was not granted the authorisation to regulate CRAs. This decision must be criticised given the contribution of CRAs towards the collapse of Enron at the start of the new millennium. The relationship between CRAs, the financial crisis and

---

[4] BBC News 'Bank of America found liable in US mortgage fraud trial', 24 October 2013, available from http://www.bbc.co.uk/news/business-24649063, accessed 25 October 2013.

[5] For a more detailed illustration see Chapter 4.

white collar crime is extremely difficult to determine as, at the time of writing, the civil fraud suit pursued by the Department of Justice has not been settled. If, as some commentators have suggested, the court decides in favour of the Department of Justice, Standard and Poor's could be forced to agree to a financial sanction in the region of $5bn. As previously outlined, there is no face, no 'super-villain' or 'evil mastermind' who has cleverly orchestrated the financial crisis. However, as a result of a dramatic increase in Ponzi fraud schemes during the financial crisis it could be argued that white collar criminals such as Bernard Madoff or Allen Stanford have become the face or faces of the financial crisis. The link between this type of white collar crime and the financial crisis is illustrated by research that suggests there was a 400 per cent increase in Ponzi fraud schemes between 2007 and 2009. This is further supported by evidence presented by the FBI, SEC and CFTC, which have all concluded that due to the financial crisis there has been a significant increase in this type of white collar crime.

Perhaps the most controversial conclusion of this monograph is the argument that the 'War on Terror' and instigation of the 'Financial War on Terrorism' indirectly contributed towards the financial crisis. A vast majority of the literature on the causes of the financial crisis has argued that the only link with the terrorist attacks in September 2001 relates to the continued policy by the Federal Reserve to maintain very low interest rates. However, it is my contention that realigning the priorities of the FBI towards tackling terrorism and maintaining homeland security contributed towards the financial crisis. This decision by President George Bush resulted in the FBI being under-prepared to tackle the incoming surge of mortgage fraud related activities. The decision by President George Bush to ignore the *numerous* warnings from the FBI must be questioned and criticised. The FBI and related law enforcement agencies were ill-equipped to deal with the rampant spread of mortgage fraud prior to the financial crisis. The final instance of white collar crime and the financial crisis discussed in this monograph is the global manipulation of LIBOR. The activities of traders in the US, UK, Japan and Switzerland before and during the financial crisis could potentially affect millions of borrowers around the globe. The manipulation of LIBOR has resulted in the imposition of a plethora of record breaking financial sanctions in the US and UK. The Department of Justice and the SFO have arrested and charged three traders in relation to the alleged manipulation of LIBOR and it is likely that the trials will commence in 2014.

6.3 THE UNITED STATES OF AMERICA

The first legislative measure that was introduced to counter the threat of the financial crisis was the Emergency Economic Stabilization Act in 2008. This legislative measure, which was signed by President George Bush, was designed to permit the US government to pursue bad or troubled assets and to protect the financial system and taxpayers and prevent further economic disturbances. As outlined in Chapter 4, the most important part of this Act was the creation of TARP, which resulted in the government providing $700bn of financial support. Another legislative measure was the Housing and Economic Recovery Act 2008, which aimed to improve the regulation of Fannie Mae and Freddie Mac, after they were heavily exposed to record financial losses in the subprime mortgage sector. In response to the problems associated with the financial crisis, President Barack Obama introduced an embarrassment of policy documents and legislative measures aimed at the answering and solving the questions and problems associated with the financial crisis. For example, the initial proposals were contained in the publication of a White Paper entitled *Financial regulatory reform – a new foundation: rebuilding financial supervision and regulation*. The White Paper proposed to introduce a series of regulatory reforms aimed at creating a more rigorous system of regulation for financial firms that would ultimately aim to protect consumers and firms from financial abuse.[6] Subsequently, President Barack Obama signed the American Recovery and Reinvestment Act 2009. This law has also been referred to as the 'Recovery' or 'Stimulus Act'. In contrast to the legislation introduced by President Bush, the aim of this legislation was to reduce the financial benefits of those firms which had utilised and received TARP funding. Furthermore, these measures were aimed at improving the US system of banking regulation and they also attempted to regalvanise the economy. However, for the purpose of this monograph the most important legislation was the Fraud Enforcement and Recovery Act 2009. Importantly, the enactment of this legislation was a direct response to 'chronic misconduct which may have helped foster economic instability'.[7] Specifically,

---

[6] Department of Treasury *Financial regulatory reform – a new foundation: rebuilding financial supervision and regulation* (Department of Treasury: Washington, DC, 2009) at 2–4. For a more detailed discussion of these objectives see Walker, G. 'US regulatory reform' (2009) Journal of Banking Regulation, 11(1), 1–5.

[7] Reidy, J. 'The problem of proceeds in the era of FERA' (2010) American Journal of Criminal Law, Summer, 5, 295–323, at 318. The other legislation

the Act granted additional necessary funding for the FBI and Department of Justice, it increased the custodial sentences for those convicted of mortgage fraud, it amended fraud and money laundering legislation and it increased the regulation of TARP. The final piece of legislation introduced in the US was the highly anticipated Dodd–Frank Wall Street Reform Act 2010. The Act was signed by President Barack Obama in July 2010 with the aim of promoting and maintaining financial stability. Importantly, the Act altered the US system of banking regulation and created the Council of Federal Regulators, Financial Stability Oversight Council and the Consumer Financial Protection Bureau and abolished the Office of Thrift Supervision.[8] The legislative response to the financial crisis under President George Bush was initially aimed at attempting to stabilise the economy by providing access to emergency liquidity for failing financial institutions. This approach was partly followed by President Barack Obama, yet the legislation aimed to contradict some of the anomalies created by the distribution of the TARP funds, as discussed in Chapter 4.

The US has presented an aggressive legislative, policy and enforcement stance towards white collar crime emanating from the financial crisis. As outlined previously in Chapter 4, President Barack Obama boldly declared on numerous occasions that his administration would take an aggressive stance against the perpetrators of the financial crisis. A wide range of legislative measures, namely the Fraud Enforcement and Recovery Act 2009, have been introduced that have provided essential funding for law enforcement agencies and regulatory bodies. These measures provided a welcome addition to the already extensive legislative armoury of the Department of Justice, SEC and the FBI. Nonetheless, these measures are a stark contrast to the ill-advised white collar crime policies adopted by President George Bush following the terrorist attacks in September 2001. The FBI has made significant steps towards targeting those involved in mortgage fraud. Therefore, it is peculiar that both the Department of Justice and FBI declined to create a designated mortgage fraud task force and reduced the number of field agents investigating mortgage fraud.[9] It is important to stress that in the early

introduced was the Housing and Economic Recovery Act, the Emergency Economic Stabilization Act and the American Recovery and Reinvestment Act.

[8] Krawiec, K. 'Don't screw Joe the plumber: the sausage-making of financial reform' (2013) Arizona Law Review, Spring, 55, 53–103, at 54.

[9] Morgenson, G. and Story, L. 'Financial crisis, no prosecutions of top figures', 14 April 2011, available from http://www.nytimes.com/2011/04/14/business/14prosecute.html?pagewanted=all&_r=0, accessed 12 September 2013.

stages of the financial crisis the FBI did instigate over 25 investigations into the conduct of the largest banks. However, it was unable to obtain any criminal convictions and at the time of writing the FBI has failed to successfully obtain a conviction of any senior employee of the US banks whose actions directly contributed towards the financial crisis.

As a result of the Fraud Enforcement and Recovery Act 2009, President Barack Obama created the Financial Fraud Enforcement Task Force via a Presidential Executive Order. The aim of this Task Force was to tackle white collar crime that originated during the financial crisis. However, when the performance of this Task Force is compared with the performance of its predecessor, the Corporate Fraud Task Force, the FFETF has failed to meet the expectations of President Barack Obama. Therefore, the merits of creating *another* task force and replacing an already existing and successful one must also be questioned. Therefore, a very important question that must be considered is why no high profile contributors to a financial crisis that has seen numerous corporations collapse, record global corporate losses, countries receiving bailouts by the international community and economic hardship have been prosecuted. The ability of prosecutorial agencies to prosecute chief executive officers or chief financial officers of those corporations which were involved in either risky, unethical, immoral or illegal business practices that contributed to the financial crisis has been limited by several factors. This includes for instance the myriad and complex nature of the financial markets and the thousands of transactions in which such firms are involved. Thus the collection of evidence is problematic and extremely difficult. Nonetheless, there is evidence to suggest that a concerted and aggressive effort to investigate those involved in the financial crisis could have resulted in prosecutions and convictions. For example, as a result of the Savings and Loans Crisis prosecutors successfully instigated criminal proceedings against approximately 800 bank officials. It is also interesting to compare the contrasting policies of the Department of Justice after the Savings and Loans Crisis and the financial crisis. In relation to the Savings and Loans Crisis it was claimed that the 'Department of Justice is now giving special attention to the investigation and prosecution of banking crimes, particularly crimes connected with failed savings and loans institutions'.[10] Therefore, it is strongly recommended that a mortgage fraud statute should be introduced in the US to assist in the

[10] Green, M. 'After the fall: the criminal law enforcement response to the S&L crisis' (1991) Fordham Law Review, May, 59, 155–192, at 155.

prosecution of this criminal offence. In response to this criticism, in his 2012 State of the Union Address President Barack Obama announced that he would:

> establish a Financial Crimes Unit of highly trained investigators to crack down on large-scale fraud and protect people's investments. Some financial firms violate major anti-fraud laws because there's no real penalty for being a repeat offender. That's bad for consumers, and it's bad for the vast majority of bankers and financial service professionals who do the right thing. So pass legislation that makes the penalties for fraud count.[11]

He added that:

> I'm asking my Attorney General to create a special unit of federal prosecutors and leading state attorney generals to expand our investigations into the abusive lending and packaging of risky mortgages that led to the housing crisis. This new unit will hold accountable those who broke the law, speed assistance to homeowners, and help turn the page on an era of recklessness that hurt so many Americans.[12]

The Department of Justice has recently scored a number of important victories in its pursuit of conduct that contributed towards the financial crisis. For example, in October 2013 Bank of America's Countrywide Financial unit was found answerable for defrauding Fannie Mae and Freddie Mac.[13] Furthermore, it has been reported that JP Morgan has tentatively reached an agreement with the Department of Justice in relation to mortgage backed securities. At the time of writing the settlement has not been ratified, but it has been reported that the settlement will exceed $13bn.[14]

---

[11] The White House 'Remarks by the President in State of the Union Address', 26 January 2012, available from http://www.whitehouse.gov/photos-and-video/video/2012/01/25/2012-state-union-address-enhanced-version#transcript, accessed 12 September 2013.

[12] *Ibid.*

[13] United States Attorney's Office of Southern District of New York 'Statement of Manhattan U.S. Attorney Preet Bharara on the Countrywide, Bank of America, and Rebecca Mairone verdicts', 23 October 2013, available from http://www.justice.gov/usao/nys/pressreleases/October13/BoAVerdictStatement.php, accessed 25 October 2013.

[14] See Aldrick, P. 'JPMorgan agrees $13bn settlement with US Justice Department', 20 October 2013, available from http://www.telegraph.co.uk/finance/newsbysector/banksandfinance/10391383/JPMorgan-agrees-13bn-settlement-with-US-Justice-Department.html, accessed 29 October 2013.

6.4 COMPARING THE US AND UK

What becomes clear after reviewing the policy, legislative and enforcement responses from within both the US and UK is that there are a number of similarities. For example, both the US and UK governments have attempted to introduce new legislation aimed at improving the level of banking regulation via the Dodd–Frank Act 2012 and the Financial Services Act 2012. Likewise, the Coalition government expressed its desire to reform the then banking regulation system under the Financial Services and Markets Act 2000 that was administered by the FSA in 2010. After the publication of numerous consultation papers and reports commissioned by the government, the FSA was replaced by the FCA, the PRA and the FPC, which are housed and managed by the Bank of England. One important distinction between the approaches adopted in the US and UK has been their legislative approach towards white collar crime and the financial crisis. For example, as outlined above and in Chapter 4, one of the first legislative measures introduced by President Barack Obama was the Fraud Enforcement and Recovery Act 2009. The objective of this Act was to improve the enforcement of white collar crimes associated with the financial crisis, including mortgage fraud, securities and commodities fraud, financial institution fraud and fraud related to financial support provided by the US government. This position can be contrasted with the stance adopted in the UK. The US legislation increased the allocation of funding for the Department of Justice and the FBI, which had previously been diverted by President George Bush towards the War on Terror following the terrorist attacks in September 2001. The benefits of providing the additional funding are evidenced by the significant increase in mortgage fraud related investigations, arrests and convictions obtained by the FBI since the enactment of this legislation. It is interesting to note that during his two terms of office President George Bush refused to redirect any funding towards the FBI, which predicted the threat posed by mortgage fraud in 2004. This decision must be questioned and its adverse effects are abundantly clear as the true extent of the interaction between mortgage fraud and financial crisis becomes clearer. Furthermore, the results achieved by the 'War on Terror' and the 'Financial War on Terror' are derisory at best. The Fraud Enforcement and Recovery Act 2009 also established a designated Financial Fraud Task Force to investigate the association between white collar crime and the financial crisis. This in itself is an important factor illustrating the principal objective of this monograph, but it must be noted that other task forces have been created following such financial scandals as Enron and WorldCom. However, it must be pointed out that the Task Force has had little effect on the wrongdoers who operate in Wall Street. This stance can be completely contrasted with the policy adopted in the UK, where there has been no specific white collar crime legislation to combat the illegal activities during the financial crisis. The Coalition government has decided to rely on already existing common law offences such as conspiracy to defraud, and to create new minor offences within the parameters of the Financial Services Act 2012 and Financial Services (Banking Reform) Bill 2013. Furthermore, the UK stance towards white collar crime emanating from the financial crisis has been adversely affected because there has not been a coordinated policy from the Coalition government. What we have witnessed from the government amounts to nothing more than customary political rhetoric, as illustrated by the Prime Minister's 'Day of Reckoning' speech and the 'We take white collar crime seriously' speech by George Osborne. In fact, it can be concluded that the Coalition government has not added to the foundations of a white collar crime strategy that were laid down by the Labour government following the publication of its money laundering strategy in 2004, the Fraud Review in 2006 and its 2007 counter-terrorist financing strategy. The Coalition government boldly asserted that it would tackle white collar crime and briefly considered the idea of creating a single Economic Crime Agency to tackle white collar crime, as previously outlined by Fisher. Sadly, the excellent vision of the ECA as outlined by Fisher was never achieved, largely due to political infighting and the desire of the government to cut costs and reduce the budgetary deficit. This clearly illustrates that the 'Day of Reckoning' and 'We take white collar crime seriously' speeches are nothing more than examples of empty political promises. It is to the bemusement of the author that the Coalition government has steadfastly refused to provide any additional funding to such agencies as the SFO. In fact, the government has reduced the funding of the SFO by 25 per cent since coming into office. This resulted in the SFO going 'cap in hand' to HM Treasury to provide additional funding so that it could complete its investigation into the manipulation of LIBOR. This is hardly the ideal picture that needs to be presented of the SFO. The Coalition government decided to create the NCA, a multifaceted organisation that would seek to tackle white collar crime as part of its wider agenda when compared with the previously narrow focused ECA. However, as opposed to merging the then existing white collar crime agencies into the NCA, we are left with an elaborate regulatory and law enforcement spider's web that has given different agencies overlapping roles leading to confusion and delay.

Another similarity between the US and UK relates to their enforcement stances towards those involved in white collar crime during the financial crisis. President Barack Obama and Prime Minister David Cameron have pledged to bring the perpetrators to justice. However, these bold statements have amounted to little more than sporadic attempts to prosecute those who allegedly contributed towards the financial crisis. For example, despite the advances made by the FBI towards tackling mortgage fraud, not one member of Wall Street has been convicted of a criminal offence in relation to the financial crisis. This can be contrasted with the tougher and comprehensive response of law enforcement agencies after the Savings and Loans Crisis in the 1980s and the response to the collapse of Enron and WorldCom. It is the conclusion of this monograph that US law enforcement and regulatory agencies have deliberately steered away from pursuing criminal proceedings and have sought to impose inadequate media friendly financial sanctions, which represent a very small percentage of a firm's annual profits. The SEC and the Department of Justice are both culpable of adopting ill-considered approaches towards the enforcement of white collar crime legislation. For example, this was clearly illustrated by the meagre fines imposed by US authorities against several banks which manipulated or rigged LIBOR. None of the parties to the deferred prosecution agreements has been found criminally responsible for one of the largest global frauds that concerned banks. This is also evident from the imposition of a 'record' fine by the SEC on Goldman Sachs. Sadly, the position is comparable with the enforcement activities in the UK by the FSA and FCA, which have also imposed a set of media friendly headline grabbing financial penalties on banks which manipulated LIBOR. The position has not been assisted by an inadequate legislative and regulatory framework that resulted in LIBOR not amounting to a regulated activity, thus exempting it from regulation by the FSA. We were left in a very unsatisfactory position where LIBOR was managed and administered by the BBA, thus representing the continuation of a 'relic' or the 'dark side' of banking regulation, namely self-regulation.

Therefore, it is my contention that white collar crime is a key variable that contributed towards the financial crisis in 2007. The response of both governments in Washington and London has been to introduce new means of banking regulation, a series of economic measures aimed at maintaining the financial stability of both countries and some attempt to punish those who contributed towards the financial crisis. However, the enforcement response in both countries has been unsatisfactory. This is due to the paucity of the financial sanctions imposed by related law enforcement and regulatory agencies, the continued use of deferred prosecution agreements and the lack of any related successful prosecutions. The response to this financial crisis can be contrasted with that towards the Savings and Loans Crisis and the collapse of Enron and WorldCom. It is extremely likely that the efforts of law enforcement agencies and regulators will continue to utilise financial penalties and there will be a small number of criminal prosecutions for low level traders.

Bibliography

Abdurakhmanova, S. 'Using unsolicited credit ratings to regulate the credit rating agencies' (2013) Fordham Journal of Corporate and Financial Law, 18, 451–488.

Abramovich, A. 'Comparative analysis of stress testing in the United States and Europe' (2011) North Carolina Banking Institute, March, 15, 333–353.

Abramowitz, E. and Sack, J. 'Why so few prosecutions connected to the financial crisis?' (2013) New York Law Journal, 250(46), 1–3.

Action Fraud 'Who is Action Fraud?' n/d, available from http://www.actionfraud.police.uk/about-us/who-we-are, accessed 16 September 2013.

Adamson, R. 'SFO's priorities' (2013) Tolley's Practical Audit and Accounting, 24(7), 81–82.

Akseli, O. 'Securitisation, the financial crisis and the need for effective risk retention' (2013) European Business Organization Law Review, 14(1), 1–27.

Alcock, A. 'Five years of market abuse' (2007) Company Lawyer, 28(6), 163–171.

Aldrick, P. 'JPMorgan agrees $13bn settlement with US Justice Department', 20 October 2013, available from http://www.telegraph.co.uk/finance/newsbysector/banksandfinance/10391383/JPMorgan-agrees-13bn-settlement-with-US-Justice-Department.html, accessed 29 October 2013.

Alexander, K. 'The nature of modern credit markets' in Alexander, K. and Dhumale, R. (eds) *Research handbook on international financial regulation* (Edward Elgar: Cheltenham, 2012).

Alexander, K. and Dhumale, R. *Research handbook on international financial regulation* (Edward Elgar: Cheltenham, 2012).

Alexander, R. *Insider dealing and money laundering in the EU: law and regulation* (Ashgate: Farnham, 2007).

Allen, K. 'Quantitative easing boosted by £75bn by Bank of England', 6 October 2011, available from http://www.guardian.co.uk/business/2011/oct/06/quantitative-easing-75bn-bank-of-england, accessed 26 February 2013.

Allen, K. 'Recession pushes white-collar crime to new highs', 31 December 2009, available from http://www.guardian.co.uk/business/2009/dec/31/fraud-recession-kpmg-report, accessed 18 March 2013.

Altman, J. 'A test case in international bankruptcy protocols: the Lehman Brothers insolvency' (2011) San Diego International Law Journal, 12, 463–495.
Ament, H. 'Predatory lending: what will stop it?' (2009) Journal of Business and Technology Law, 4, 371–394.
Andenas, M. and H.-Y. Chiu, I. 'Financial stability and legal integration in financial regulation' (2013) European Law Review, 38(3), 335–359.
Anderberg, K. and Epstein, J. 'Transatlantic developments' (2008) Compliance Officer Bulletin, October, 60, 1–40.
Anderson, C. 'Ponzi schemes' collapses nearly quadrupled in '09', 29 December 2009, available from http://www.law.com/jsp/article.jsp?id=1202437299784, accessed 20 October 2013.
Anderson, T., David, L. and Fox, M. 'The US financial sector status update: road to recovery or highway to hell?' (2009) Journal of International Banking Law and Regulation, 24(10), 491–500.
Anderson, T., Lane, H. and Fox, M. 'Consequences and responses to the Madoff fraud' (2009) Journal of International Banking Law and Regulation, 24(11), 548–555.
Angelides, P. 'FICF and the crisis: preventing the next financial meltdown' (2012) UMKC Law Review, Summer, 80, 949–964.
Anon. 'Administration of justice' (2013) Public Law, July, 637–640.
Anon. 'Banking and financial services policy report' (2010) The Monitor, 29(4), 19–23.
Anon. 'Banks in big bother' (2012) New Law Journal, 6 July, 885.
Anon. 'Bernard Madoff: the Ponzi scam', 16 June 2009, available from http://www.telegraph.co.uk/finance/financetopics/bernard-madoff/5547213/Bernard-Madoff-the-Ponzi-scam.html, accessed 3 June 2013.
Anon. 'Final recommendations of Walker review published' (2010) Company Lawyer, 31(3), 81.
Anon. 'Former RBS investment bank chief Johnny Cameron banned from City', 18 May 2010, available from http://www.telegraph.co.uk/finance/financialcrisis/7736540/Former-RBS-investment-bank-chief-Johnny-Cameron-banned-from-City.html, accessed 7 July 2013.
Anon. 'Reform of financial regulation gathers pace with son of FSA' (2011) Company Law Newsletter, 297, 103.
Anon. 'SFO to launch criminal investigation into Libor scandal', 6 July 2012, available from http://www.telegraph.co.uk/finance/newsbysector/banksandfinance/9381683/SFO-to-launch-criminal-investigation-into-Libor-scandal.html, accessed 30 June 2013.
Anon. 'Turner Review sets out a new approach for banking regulation' (2009) Company Lawyer, 30(7), 211.

Arena, K. 'FBI probing bailout firms', 24 September 2008, available from http://money.cnn.com/2008/09/23/news/companies/fbi_finance/, accessed 7 October 2013.

Armitage, J. 'Cuts hamper fight against crime, warns SFO director', 5 April 2012, available from http://www.independent.co.uk/news/business/news/cuts-hamper-fight-against-crime-warns-sfo-director-7619339.html, accessed 30 June 2013.

Arnold, T. '"It's déjà vu all over again": using bounty hunters to leverage gatekeepers duties' (2010) Tulsa Law Review, 45, 419–469.

Arogeti, J. 'How much cooperation between government agencies is too much? Reconciling United States v Scrushy, the corporate fraud task force, and the nature of parallel proceedings' (2006) Georgia State University Law Review, Winter, 23, 427–453.

Arora, A. 'The corporate governance failings in financial institutions and directors' legal liability' (2011) Company Lawyer, 32(1), 3–18.

Arsalidou, D. 'The banking crisis: rethinking and refining the accountability of bank directors' (2010) Journal of Business Law, 4, 284–310.

Ashcroft, J. 'Reflections on events and changes at the Department of Justice' (2009) Harvard Journal of Law & Public Policy, Summer, 32, 813–830.

Association of Chief Police Officers 'Police committed to tackling mortgage fraud' Press Release, 5 March 2008, available from www.acpo.police.uk, accessed 15 May 2013.

Atkinson, T., Luttrell, D. and Rosenblum, H. 'How bad was it? The costs and consequences of the 2007–09 financial crisis' (2013) Dallas Fed, Staff Papers, 1–22.

Attorney General's Office *Fraud Review – final report* (Attorney General's Office: London, 2006).

Attorney General's Office and Sandra Quinn 'The National Fraud Strategy', speech to Council of Mortgage Lenders, 13 February 2008, available from www.attorneygeneral.gov.uk, accessed 15 May 2013.

Baber, G. 'Ring-fenced by the Vickers Report' (2012) Company Lawyer, 33(1), 1–2.

Baer, J., Bray, C. and Eaglesham, J. 'Fab trader liable in fraud', 2 August 2013, available from http://online.wsj.com/article/SB10001424127887323681904578641843284450004.html, accessed 7 October 2013.

Baer, M. 'Choosing punishment' (2012) Boston University Law Review, March, 92, 577–640.

Bagehot, W. *Lombard Street – a description of the money market* (John Murray: London, 1922).

Bagge, J. 'The future for enforcement under the new Financial Services Authority' (1998) Company Lawyer, 19(7) 194–197.

Bai, L. 'The performance disclosures of credit rating agencies: are they effective reputational sanctions?' (2010) NYU Journal of Law and Business, 7, 47–104.

Bailey, S. 'Chopping at the roots: a proposal to change the focus of criminal laws dealing with savings and loans fraud' (1997) American Journal of Criminal Law, Spring, 24, 401–439.

Bainbridge, S. 'A critique of the Insider Trading Sanctions Act 1984' (1985) Virginia Law Review, April, 71, 455–498.

Baker, J. 'Reforming corporations through threats of federal prosecution' (2004) Cornell Law Review, January, 89, 310–353.

Bale, R. and Volpe, T. 'Ponzi schemes and financial fraud regulation' (2011) Brief, Summer, 40, 8.

Barak, G. 'The flickering desires for white collar crime studies in the post-financial crisis: will they ever shine brightly?' (2013) Western Criminology Review, 13(3), 61–71.

Barfield, R., Du Plessis, S. and Fell, P. 'Basel III – implications for risk management and supervision' (2011) Compliance Officer Bulletin, September, 89, 1–26.

Bar-Gill, O. 'Seduction by plastic' (2004) Northwestern University Law Review, 98, 1373–1434.

Bar-Gill, O. 'The law, economics and psychology of subprime mortgage contracts' (2009) Cornell Law Review, 93, Rev., 1073–1151.

Barnes, P. 'Insider dealing and market abuse: the UK's record on enforcement' (2011) International Journal of Law, Crime and Justice, 39, 174–189.

Barnett, H. 'The securitization of mortgage fraud' in Deflem, M. (ed.), *Economic crisis and crime* (Emerald: Bingley, 2011).

Barnett, W. 'Fraud enforcement in the Financial Services Act 1986: an analysis and discussion of s.47' (1996) Company Lawyer, 17(7), 203–210.

Barr, C. 'SEC charges Goldman Sachs with fraud', 16 April 2010, available from http://money.cnn.com/2010/04/16/news/companies/sec.goldman.fortune/, accessed 18 June 2013.

Bates, C., Gibbons, K., Gray, R., Machin, J., Motani, H. and Plews, T. 'Bradford and Bingley plc: break-up under the Banking (Special Provisions) Act 2008' (2008) Financial Regulation International, November, 1–4.

Bavoso, V. 'Financial innovation and structured finance: the case of securitisation' (2012) Company Lawyer, 34(1), 3–12.

Bazley, S. 'FSA enforcement activity, reflections on 2010 and the challenges of regulatory change' (2011) Company Lawyer, 32(1), 1–2.

BBC 'Libor interest rate to be controlled by NYSE Euronext', 9 July 2013, available from http://www.bbc.co.uk/news/business-23240707, accessed 12 July 2013.

BBC 'Sub-prime crisis to cost IKB $1bn', 3 September 2007, available from http://news.bbc.co.uk/1/hi/business/6976517.stm, accessed 21 November 2012.

BBC News 'Bank of America found liable in US mortgage fraud trial', 24 October 2013, available from http://www.bbc.co.uk/news/business-24649063, accessed 25 October 2013.

BBC News 'Credit crunch fuels fraud cases', 30 April 2008, available from http://news.bbc.co.uk/1/hi/business/7375091.stm, accessed 28 March 2013.

BBC News 'Credit crunch enters the lexicon', 3 July 2008, available from http://news.bbc.co.uk/1/hi/business/7487608.stm, accessed 21 November 2012.

BBC News 'Europe markets follow Asia's down after Cyprus bailout deal', 18 March 2013, available from http://www.bbc.co.uk/news/business-21823432, accessed 18 March 2013.

BBC News 'Europe's PIGS: country by country', 11 February 2011, available from http://news.bbc.co.uk/1/hi/business/8510603.stm, accessed 26 February 2013.

BBC News 'Fitch downgrades UK credit rating to AA+', 19 April 2013, available from http://www.bbc.co.uk/news/business-22219382, accessed 7 October 2013.

BBC News 'Greece's debt reaches 300bn euros', 10 December 2009, available from http://news.bbc.co.uk/1/hi/business/8406665.stm, accessed 26 February 2013.

BBC News 'Irish Republic 85bn euro bail-out agreed', 20 November 2010, available from http://www.bbc.co.uk/news/world-europe-11855990, accessed 26 February 2013.

BBC News 'Libor: ICAP fined $87m by UK and US regulators', 25 September 2013, available from http://www.bbc.co.uk/news/business-24250750, accessed 25 September 2013.

BBC News 'Northern Rock gets bank bailout', 13 September 2007, available from http://news.bbc.co.uk/1/hi/business/6994099.stm, accessed 21 November 2012.

BBC News 'Portugal's 78bn euro bail-out is formally approved', 17 May 2011, available from http://www.bbc.co.uk/news/business-13408497, accessed 26 February 2013.

BBC News 'RBS reports record corporate loss', 26 February 2009, available from http://news.bbc.co.uk/1/hi/business/7911722.stm, accessed 2 July 2013.

BBC News 'RBS secures takeover of ABN Amro', 8 October 2007, available from http://news.bbc.co.uk/1/hi/business/7033176.stm, accessed 2 July 2013.

BBC News 'Timeline: Libor-fixing scandal', 26 September 2012, available from http://www.bbc.co.uk/news/business-18671255, accessed 1 October 2012.

BBC News 'Timeline: sub-prime losses', 19 May 2008, available from http://news.bbc.co.uk/1/hi/business/7096845.stm, accessed 21 November 2012.

BBC News 'Timeline: The unfolding eurozone crisis', 13 June 2012, available from http://www.bbc.co.uk/news/business-13856580, accessed 11 March 2013.

BBC News 'UK loses top AAA credit rating for first time since 1978', 23 February 2013, available from http://www.bbc.co.uk/news/business-21554311, accessed 26 February 2013.

BBC News 'Why Cyprus's rescue matters to us', 16 March 2013, available from http://www.bbc.co.uk/news/business-21812853, accessed 18 March 2013.

Bell, S. 'Clarity and predictability at the SEC: Abacus, Citigroup, and the political economy of securities fraud settlements' (2012) Columbia Business Law Review, 865–912.

Bell, S. 'Criminal procedure within the firm' (2007) Stanford Law Review, 59, 1613–1670.

Ben-Ishai, S. and Lubben, S. 'A comparative study of bankruptcy as bailout' (2011) Brooklyn Journal of Corporate, Financial and Commercial Law, 6, 79–101.

Benson, M.L. and Simpson, S.S. *White-collar crime: an opportunity perspective*, Criminology and Justice Series (Routledge: New York, 2009).

Berenson, A. 'S.E.C. opens investigation into Enron', 1 November 2001, available from http://www.nytimes.com/2001/11/01/business/sec-opens-investigation-into-enron.html, accessed 18 October 2013.

Berenson, A. 'Watching the firms that watch the books', 5 December 2001, available from http://www.nytimes.com/2001/12/05/business/05INVE.html?pagewanted=1, accessed 4 June 2013.

Berger, J. 'DOJ, FBI admit they inflated claims about mortgage fraud crackdown last year', 14 August 2013, available from http://www.foxnews.com/politics/2013/08/14/doj-fbi-admit-inflated-claims-about-mortgage-fraud-crackdown-last-year/, accessed 14 October 2013.

Berkeley Journal of Criminal Law 'Developments in white collar criminal law and the culture of waiver' (2009), Berkeley Journal of Criminal Law, 14(1), 199–228.

Bernanke, B. and Lown, C.S. 'The Credit Crunch', Brookings Papers on Economic Activity, 2, 205–247.

Berthelsen, C., Eaglesham, J. and Jones, K. 'SEC, two banks settle over loans', 16 November 2012, available from http://online.wsj.com/article/SB10001424127887324735104578123242727307524.html, accessed 18 June 2013.

Binham, C. and Parker, G. 'SFO secures cash for Libor investigation', 6 July 2012, available from http://www.ft.com/cms/s/0/3b590260-c6cd-11e1-943a-00144feabdc0.html#axzz2XgX4w3hV, accessed 30 June 2013.

Binham, C. and Warell, H. 'Top fraud investigator quits UK crime agency role', 18 August 2013, available from http://www.ft.com/cms/s/0/dae8e0f2-0691-11e3-9bd9-00144feab7de.html#axzz2f4C0WdBO, accessed 16 September 2013.

Biskupic, S. 'Fine tuning the bank statute: a prosecutor's perspective' (1999), Marquette Law Review, 82, 381–403.

Black, B. 'Should the SEC be a collection agency for defrauded investors?' (2008) Business Lawyer, February, 63, 317–346.

Black, K. 'Neo-classical economic theories, methodology, and praxis optimize criminogenic environments and produce recurrent intensifying crisis' (2011) Creighton Law Review, 44, 597–644.

Black, W. 'The Department of Justice "chases mice while lions roam the campsite": why the department has failed to prosecute elite frauds that drove the financial crisis' (2012) UMKC Law Review, Summer, 80, 987–1019.

Blackden, R. 'SEC investigates role of ratings agencies Moody's and Standard & Poor's ahead of the financial crisis', 18 June 2011, available from http://www.telegraph.co.uk/finance/financialcrisis/8583387/SEC-investigates-role-of-ratings-agencies-Moodys-and-Standard-and-Poors-ahead-of-the-financial-crisis.html, accessed 29 May 2013.

Blair, W. and Brent, R. *Banking and financial crime – the international law of tainted money* (Oxford University Press: Oxford, 2008).

Block, C. 'A continuum approach to systemic risk and too-big-to-fail' (2012) Brooklyn Journal of Corporate, Financial and Commercial Law, Spring, 6, 289.

Blumel, R. 'Mail and wire fraud' (2005) American Criminal Law Review, 42, 677–698.

Bonewitz, P. 'Implications of reputation economics on regulatory reform of the credit rating industry' (2010) William and Mary Business Law Review, April, 1, 391–430.

Bookman, Z. 'Convergences and omissions in reporting corporate and white collar crime', (2008) DePaul Business and Commercial Law Journal, 6, 347–392.

Bosworth-Davies, R. 'Investigating financial crime: the continuing evolution of the public fraud investigation role – a personal perspective' (2009) Company Lawyer, 30(7), 195–199.

Boylan, S. 'Will credit rating agency reforms be effective?' (2012) Journal of Financial Regulation and Compliance, 20(4), 356–366.

Brady, B. and Owen, J. 'Budget cuts killed off LIBOR inquiry', 1 July 2012, available from http://www.independent.co.uk/news/uk/politics/budget-cuts-killed-off-libor-inquiry-7901940.html, accessed 18 March 2013.

Braithwaite, J. 'Restorative justice or banks through negative licensing' (2009) British Journal of Criminology, 49(4), 439–450.

Brescia, R. 'Tainted loans: the value of mass torts approach in subprime mortgage litigation' (2009) University of Cincinnati Law Review, 78, 1–79.

Breslin, B., Ezickson, D. and Kocoras, J. 'The Bribery Act 2010: raising the bar above the US Foreign Corrupt Practices Act' (2010) Company Lawyer, 31(11), 362–369.

Brewer, E. and Klingenhagen, A. 'Be careful what you wish for: the stock market reactions to bailing out large financial institutions: evidence from the USA' (2010) Journal of Financial Regulation and Compliance, 16(1), 56–69.

Brickey, K. 'Enron's legacy' (2004) Buffalo Criminal Law Review, 8, 221–276.

British Bankers' Association 'About us', n/d, available from http://www.bba.org.uk/about-us, accessed 1 October 2012.

British Bankers' Association 'LIBOR definitions', n/d, available from http://www.bbalibor.com/bbalibor-explained/definitions, accessed 1 October 2012.

Brody, R. and Kiehl, K. 'From white-collar crime to red-collar crime' (2010) Journal of Financial Crime, 17(3), 351–364.

Brooks, B. 'Law enforcement's role in US counterterrorism strategy' (2010) Police Journal, 83(2), 113–125.

Brotman, E. and Dougherty, E. 'Blue collar tactics in white collar crime' (2011) Champion, September, 35, 16–20.

Broughman, A. 'The collapse of Bear Stearns, or: skinny dipping on the street' (2010) Ohio Northern University Law Review, 36, 191–213.

Brown, A. and Rice, B. 'Financial Services Act 2012' (2013) Company Secretary's Review, 36(21), 166–167.

Brown, E. 'A comparison of the handling of the financial crisis in the United States, the United Kingdom and Australia' (2010) Villanova Law Review, 55, 509–574.

Brown, M. 'First credit crunch traced back to Roman republic', 28 November 2008, available from http://www.guardian.co.uk/business/2008/nov/28/credit-crunch-roman-republic-lecture, accessed 1 February 2013.

Browning, L. 'Ex-officer faults mortgage giants for "orgy" of nonprime loans', 9 December 2008, available from http://www.nytimes.com/2008/12/10/business/10fannie.html, accessed 25 March 2013.

Brownlow, B. 'Rating agency reform: preserving the registered market for asset backed securities' (2011) North Carolina Banking Institute, March, 15, 111–138.

Bruce, H., Gruenstein, D., Herbert, C. and Scheessele, R. 'Subprime foreclosures: the smoking gun of predatory lending?', n/d, available from http://www.huduser.org/publications/polleg/hpcproceedings.html, accessed 21 October 2013.

Buchheit, L. and Mitu Gulati, G. 'The Eurozone debt crisis: the options now' (2013) Capital Markets Law Journal, 8(1), 54–61.

Buell, S. 'Is the white collar offender privileged?' (2014) Duke Law, 63(4), 823–889.

Buell, S. 'What is securities fraud?' (2011) Duke Law Journal, December, 61, 511–581.

Bunting, W. 'The trouble with investment banks: cluelessness, not greed' (2011) San Diego Law Review, Summer, 48, 993–1073.

Burton, T. 'Petters gets 50-year term for running Ponzi scheme', 9 April 2010, available from http://online.wsj.com/article/SB10001424052702304198004575171881879666308.html, accessed 3 June 2013.

Button, M. 'Editorial: fraud, corruption and the financial crisis' (2011) International Journal of Law, Crime and Justice, 29, 137–139.

Button, M. and Brooks, G. 'Mind the gap, a progress towards developing anti-fraud culture strategies in UK central government bodies' (2009) Journal of Financial Crime, 16(3), 229–244.

Callaghan, V. and Ullah, Z. 'The LIBOR scandal – the UK's legislative approach' (2013) Journal of International Banking Law and Regulation, 28(4), 160–165.

Cane, M., Shamir, A. and Jodar, T. 'Below investment grade and above the law: a past, present and future look at the accountability of credit rating agencies' (2012) Fordham Journal of Corporate and Financial Law, 17, 1063–1126.

Cantley, B. 'The UBS case: the US attack on Swiss banking sovereignty' (2011) International Law and Management Review, Spring, 7, 1–29.

Carnell, R. 'Handling the failure of a government-sponsored enterprise' (2005) Washington Law Review, 80, 565–642.
Carrillo, J. 'Dangerous loans: consumer challenges to adjustable rate mortgages' (2008) Berkeley Business Law Journal, 5, 1–43.
Cava, B. 'Quid pro quo corruption is "so yesterday": restoring honest services fraud after Skilling and Black' (2011) University of California, Fall, 12, 1–29.
Cerulus, S. 'Central clearing for credit default swaps: a legal analysis of the new central clearing regulations in Europe and the US' (2012) Journal of Financial Regulation and Compliance, 20(2), 212–244.
Charles, K. 'Regulatory imperialism: the worldwide export of European regulatory principles on credit rating agencies' (2010) Minnesota Journal of International Law, Summer, 19, 399–451.
Chason, E. 'The uneasy case for deferring banker pay' (2013) Louisiana Law Review, Summer, 73, 923–977.
Choi, J. and Papaioannou, M. 'Financial crisis and risk management: reassessing the Asian financial crisis in light of the American financial crisis' (2010) East Asia Law Review, Summer, 5, 442–466.
CIFAS '2007 fraud trends', January 2008, available from http://www.cifas.org.uk/secure/contentPORT/uploads/documents/Press%20Release/2008/A%20-%202007%20Fraud%20Trends.pdf, accessed 28 March 2013.
CIFAS 'Fraud trends and recession go hand in hand', n/d, available from www.cifas.org.uk/default.asp?edit_id=899-5, accessed 19 October 2013.
CIFAS *Fraudscape – depicting the UK's fraud landscape* (CIFAS: London, 2013).
Clair, R. and Tucker, P. 'Six causes of the credit crunch (or, why is it so hard to get a loan?)' (1993) Federal Reserve Bank of Dallas Economic Review, 1–19.
Clayton, N. 'Many hands make light work: the tripartite arrangement as part of the legislative reforms to banking legislation in the UK – a spectrum of views from a spectrum of institutions' (2010) Law and Financial Markets Review, 4(4), 366–393.
CNN 'Italian Cabinet OKs 47 billion-euro austerity package', 30 June 2011, available from http://articles.cnn.com/2011-06-30/world/italy.austerity.measures_1_austerity-package-finance-minister-giulio-tremonti-pierluigi-bersani?_s=PM:WORLD, accessed 26 February 2013.
CNN 'RBS posts record $34 billion loss', 27 February 2009, available from http://edition.cnn.com/2009/BUSINESS/02/26/uk.rbs.recordloss/, accessed 2 July 2013.

Cohen, H. 'What place does the criminal law have in the regulation of securities markets after the Blue Arrow trials?' (1992) Journal of International Banking Law, 7(10), 420–422.

Colchester, M. 'U.K. Fraud Office opens Libor investigation', 6 July 2012, available from http://online.wsj.com/article/SB10001424052702303962304577510534226515306.html, accessed 30 June 2013.

Colesanti, J. 'Another Madoff masquerade? Questioning "securities fraud" in the crime and its cleanup' (2012) Saint Louis University Law Journal, 56, 521–565.

Collins, J. 'Fraud by abuse position: theorizing section 4 of the Fraud Act 2006' (2011) Criminal Law Review, 7, 513–523.

Committee of European Securities Regulators *CESR's report to the European Commission on the compliance of credit rating agencies with the IOSCO Code* (Committee of European Securities Regulators: Paris, 2006).

Committee on Banking and Currency *Stock exchange practices* (United States Government: Washington DC, 1934).

Committee on Governmental Affairs, United States Senate *Financial oversight of Enron: the SEC and private-sector watchdogs* (Committee on Governmental Affairs, United States Senate: Washington DC, 2002).

Commodities Futures Trading Commission 'CFTC charges ICAP Europe Limited, a subsidiary of ICAP plc, with manipulation and attempted manipulation of yen Libor', 25 September 2013, available from http://www.cftc.gov/PressRoom/PressReleases/pr6708-13, accessed 8 October 2013.

Commodity Futures Trading Commission 'CFTC orders Barclays to pay $200 million penalty for attempted manipulation of and false reporting concerning LIBOR and Euribor benchmark interest rates', 27 June 2012, available from http://www.cftc.gov/PressRoom/PressReleases/pr6289-12, accessed 1 October 2012.

Commodities Futures Trading Commission 'CFTC orders The Royal Bank of Scotland plc and RBS Securities Japan Limited to pay $325 million penalty to settle charges of manipulation, attempted manipulation, and false reporting of yen and Swiss franc LIBOR', 6 February 2013, available from http://www.cftc.gov/PressRoom/PressReleases/pr6510-13, accessed 12 August 2013.

Commodities Futures Trading Commission 'CFTC orders UBS to pay $700 million penalty to settle charges of manipulation, attempted manipulation and false reporting of LIBOR and other benchmark interest rates', 19 December 2012, available from http://www.cftc.gov/PressRoom/PressReleases/pr6472-12, accessed 12 August 2013. http://www.cftc.gov/PressRoom/PressReleases/pr6289

Commodity Futures Trading Commission *Order instituting proceedings pursuant to sections 6(c) and 6(d) of the Commodity Exchange Act, as amended, making findings and imposing remedial sanctions* (Commodity Futures Trading Commission: Washington DC, 2012).

Commodities Futures Trading Commission 'Statement of chairman Gary Gensler on settlement order against ICAP', 25 September 2013, available from http://www.cftc.gov/PressRoom/SpeechesTestimony/genslerstatement092513, accessed 25 September 2013.

Connecticut Department of Banking 'Ameriquest to pay $325 million for predatory lending practices that bilked consumers', 23 January 2006, available from http://www.ct.gov/dob/cwp/view.asp?a=2245&q=309018, accessed 21 October 2013.

Conservatives 'David Cameron: a day of reckoning', 15 December 2008, available from http://www. conservatives.com/News/Speeches/2008/12/David_Cameron_A_day_of_reckoning.aspx, accessed 29 June 2013.

Cooper, H. 'Obama signs overhaul of financial system', 21 July 2010, available from http://www.nytimes.com/2010/07/22/business/22regulate.html?_r=0, accessed 3 August 2013.

Coors, C. 'Credit rating agencies – too big to fail?' (2012) Journal of International Banking Law and Regulation, 27(1), 27–32.

CoreLogic *2011 Mortgage fraud trends report* (CoreLogic: Irvine, 2011).

Corker, D. 'Manipulating LIBOR …' (2012) New Law Journal, 162(7524), 980–981.

Coskun, D. 'Credit rating agencies in a post-Enron world: Congress revisits the NRSRO concept' (2008) Journal of Banking Regulation, 9(4), 264–283.

Coskun, D. 'Supervision of credit rating agencies: the role of credit rating agencies in finance decisions' (2009) Journal of International Banking Law and Regulation, 24(5), 252–261.

Coskun, D. 'Credit-rating agencies in the Basel II framework: why the standardised approach is inadequate for regulatory capital purposes' (2010) Journal of International Banking Law and Regulation, 25(4), 157–169.

Costello, M. and Spence, A. 'Lenders face huge hit on mortgages fraudulently obtained by crime gangs', 30 August 2008, available from http://www.thetimes.co.uk/tto/business/industries/banking/article2158313.ece, accessed 23 May 2013.

Council of Economic Advisers *Economic report of the President* (Government Printing Office: Brussels, 1992).

Council of Mortgage Lenders '£700 million fraud claim not substantiated' (2008) Council of Mortgage Lenders News and Views, 5(18), 5.

Creseney, A., Eng, G.E. and Nuttal, S. 'Regulatory investigations and the credit crisis: the search for villains' (2009) American Criminal Law Review, Spring, 46, 225–273.

Cresswell, J. 'Mortgage lender New Century Financial files for bankruptcy', 2 April 2007, available from http://www.nytimes.com/2007/04/02/business/worldbusiness/02iht-loans.5.5118838.html, accessed 21 November 2012.

Crutsinger, M. 'IMF trims loss estimate from financial crisis', 20 April 2010, available from http://www.nbcnews.com/id/36662585/, accessed 21 October 2013.

Curzon, E., Kaswell, S. and Rosenblat, A. 'SEC proposed for registration of credit rating agencies' (2007) Banking Law Journal, May, 124, 438.

Danagher, L. 'The criminalisation of cartels: a European and trans-Atlantic perspective' (2012) European Competition Law Review, 33(11), 522–525.

Davenport, T. 'An American nightmare: predatory lending in the sub-prime home mortgage industry' (2003) Suffolk University Law Review, 36, 531–557.

Davidoff, S. and Hill, C. 'Limits of disclosure' (2013) Seattle University Law Review, 36, 599–637.

Davidoff, S. and Zaring, D. 'Regulation by deal: the government's response to the financial crisis' (2009) Administrative Law Review, Summer, 61, 463–541.

Davidoff, S., Morrison, A. and Wilhelm Jr, W. 'The SEC v Goldman Sachs: reputation, trust, and fiduciary duties in investment banking' (2012) Journal of Corporation Law, 37, 529–553.

de Grazia, J. *Review of the Serious Fraud Office – final report* (Serious Fraud Office: London, 2008).

Deckant, N. 'Criticisms of collateralised debt obligations in the wake of the Goldman Sachs scandal' (2010) Review of Banking and Financial Law, Fall, 30, 407–442.

Deeds, J. 'The flawed logic of congress in the Economic Stimulus Act of 2008' (2010) Journal of Law and Family Studies, 12, 299–313.

Delone, C. and Gwartney, S. 'Financial institutions fraud' (2009) American Criminal Law Review, 46, 621–670.

Department of Justice '$25 billion mortgage servicing agreement filed in Federal Court', 12 March 2012, available from http://www.justice.gov/opa/pr/2012/March/12-asg-306.html, accessed 2 October 2013.

Department of Justice 'Accomplishments under the leadership of Attorney General Eric Holder', n/d, available from http://www.justice.gov/accomplishments/accomplishments.pdf, accessed 2 October 2013.

Department of Justice 'Attorney General Eric Holder speaks at Columbia University Law School on preventing and combating financial fraud',

23 February 2012, available from http://www.justice.gov/iso/opa/ag/speeches/2012/ag-speech-120223.html, accessed 6 October 2013.

Department of Justice 'Attorney General Eric Holder speaks at the Distressed Homeowner Initiative press conference', 9 October 2012, available from http://www.justice.gov/iso/opa/ag/speeches/2012/ag-speech-1210091.html, accessed 1 August 2013.

Department of Justice 'Attorney General Eric Holder speaks at the press conference announcing lawsuit against S&P', 5 February 2013, available from http://www.justice.gov/iso/opa/ag/speeches/2013/ag-speech-130205.html, accessed 28 May 2013.

Department of Justice 'Attorney General Eric Holder testifies before the Financial Crisis Inquiry Commission', 14 January 2010, available from http://www.justice.gov/ag/testimony/2010/ag-testimony-100114.html, accessed 2 October 2013.

Department of Justice 'Barclays Bank PLC admits misconduct related to submissions for the London Interbank Offered Rate and the Euro Interbank Offered Rate and agrees to pay $160 million penalty', 27 June 2012, available from http://www.justice.gov/opa/pr/2012/June/12-crm-815.html, accessed 1 October 2012.

Department of Justice 'Coinciding with one-year anniversary of "Operation Stolen Dreams," three loan officers and a title agent charged in $2.5 million reverse mortgage and loan modification scheme', 6 July 2011, available from http://www.justice.gov/opa/pr/2011/July/11-civ-884.html, accessed 1 August 2013.

Department of Justice 'Department of Justice sues Bank of America for defrauding investors in connection with sale of over $850 million of residential mortgage-backed securities', 6 August 2013, available from http://www.justice.gov/opa/pr/2013/August/13-ag-886.html, accessed 2 October 2013.

Department of Justice 'Department of Justice sues Standard & Poor's for fraud in rating mortgage-backed securities in the years leading up to the financial crisis', 5 February 2013, available from http://www.justice.gov/opa/pr/2013/February/13-ag-156.html, accessed 28 May 2013.

Department of Justice 'Financial Fraud Enforcement Task Force announces results of broadest mortgage fraud sweep in history', 17 June 2010, available from http://www.justice.gov/opa/pr/2010/June/10-opa-708.html, accessed 1 August 2013.

Department of Justice *First year report to the President – the Corporate Fraud Task Force* (Department of Justice: Washington DC, 2003).

Department of Justice 'Former chairman of consulting firm and board director, Rajat Gupta, sentenced in Manhattan Federal Court to two years in prison for insider trading', 24 October 2012, available from

http://www.justice.gov/usao/nys/pressreleases/October12/GuptaSentencing.php, accessed 2 October 2013.
Department of Justice 'Former vice president of Pennsylvania lending institution sentenced to 20 years in prison for fraud scheme', 12 September 2012, available from http://www.stopfraud.gov/iso/opa/stopfraud/PAE-120912.html, accessed 2 October 2013.
Department of Justice 'Ft. Lauderdale man convicted of money laundering and obstruction of justice in connection with MBC fraud', 8 February 2013, available from http://www.justice.gov/usao/fls/PressReleases/130228-01.html, accessed 3 June 2013.
Department of Justice 'Justice Department reaches $335 million settlement to resolve allegations of lending discrimination by Countrywide Financial Corporation', 21 December 2012, available from http://www.justice.gov/opa/pr/2011/December/11-ag-1694.html, accessed 2 October 2013.
Department of Justice 'Justice Department reaches settlement with Wells Fargo resulting in more than $175 million in relief for homeowners to resolve fair lending claims', 12 July 2012, available from http://www.justice.gov/opa/pr/2012/July/12-dag-869.html, accessed 21 October 2013.
Department of Justice 'Manhattan U.S. attorney files mortgage fraud lawsuit against Wells Fargo Bank, N.A. seeking hundreds of millions of dollars in damages for fraudulently certified loans', 9 October 2012, available from http://www.justice.gov/usao/nys/pressreleases/October12/WellsFargoLawsuitPR.html, accessed 2 October 2013.
Department of Justice 'Peter Madoff, former Chief Compliance Officer and Senior Managing Director at Bernard L. Madoff Investment Securities plc, sentenced in Manhattan Federal Court to 10 years in prison', 20 December 2012, available from http://www.justice.gov/usao/nys/pressreleases/December12/PeterMadoffSentencing.php, accessed 2 October 2013.
Department of Justice 'RBS Securities Japan Limited agrees to plead guilty in connection with long-running manipulation of Libor benchmark interest rates', 6 February 2013, available from http://www.justice.gov/opa/pr/2013/February/13-crm-161.html, accessed 13 August 2013.
Department of Justice *Second year report to the President – the Corporate Fraud Task Force* (Department of Justice: Washington DC, 2004).
Department of Justice *The Corporate Fraud Task Force report* (Department of Justice: Washington DC, 2008).
Department of Justice 'Three former financial services executives sentenced to serve time in prison for roles in conspiracies involving

investment contracts for the proceeds of municipal bonds', 18 October 2012, available from http://www.justice.gov/opa/pr/2012/October/12-at-1258.html, accessed 2 October 2013.

Department of Justice 'UBS Securities Japan Co. Ltd. to plead guilty to felony wire fraud for long-running manipulation of LIBOR benchmark interest rates', 19 December 2012, available from http://www.justice.gov/opa/pr/2012/December/12-ag-1522.html, accessed 13 August 2013.

Department of Treasury '31 CFR Part 30 RIN 1505–AC09 TARP standards for compensation and corporate governance' 28394 Federal Register, Vol. 74, No. 113, 15 June 2009/Rules and Regulations, available from http://www.gpo.gov/fdsys/pkg/FR-2009-06-15/pdf/E9-13868.pdf, accessed 6 August 2013.

Department of Treasury 'Bank investment programs', n/d, available from http://www.treasury.gov/initiatives/financial-stability/TARP-Programs/bank-investment-programs/Pages/default.aspx, accessed 5 August 2013.

Department of Treasury 'Credit market programs', n/d, available from http://www.treasury.gov/initiatives/financial-stability/TARP-Programs/credit-market-programs/Pages/default.aspx, accessed 5 August 2013.

Department of Treasury 'Executive compensation', n/d, available from http://www.treasury.gov/initiatives/financial-stability/TARP-Programs/executive-comp/Pages/default.aspx, accessed 5 August 2013.

Department of Treasury *Financial regulatory reform – a new foundation: rebuilding financial supervision and regulation* (Department of Treasury: Washington DC, 2009).

Department of Treasury 'Financial Stability Oversight Council – about FSOC', n/d, available from http://www.treasury.gov/initiatives/fsoc/about/Pages/default.aspx, accessed 23 September 2013.

Department of Treasury 'Investment in American International Group (AIG)', n/d, available from http://www.treasury.gov/initiatives/financial-stability/TARP-Programs/aig/Pages/default.aspx, accessed 5 August 2013.

Department of Treasury 'President's Working Group on Financial Markets, policy statement on financial markets developments', 13 March 2008, available from http://www.treasury.gov/resource-center/fin-mkts/Documents/pwgpolicystatemktturmoil_03122008.pdf, accessed 14 August 2012.

Department of Treasury 'Secretary Geithner introduces financial stability plan', 2 October 2009, available from http://www.treasury.gov/press-center/press-releases/Pages/tg18.aspx, accessed 7 August 2013.

Department of Treasury 'TARP programs', n/d, available from http://www.treasury.gov/initiatives/financial-stability/TARP-Programs/Pages/default.aspx, accessed 5 August 2013.

Department of Treasury 'Testimony by Secretary Henry M. Paulson, Jr. before the Senate Banking Committee on turmoil in US credit markets: recent actions regarding government sponsored entities, investment banks and other financial institutions', 23 September 2008, available from http://www.treasury.gov/press-center/press-releases/Pages/hp1153.aspx, accessed 7 August 2013.

Department of Treasury, Office of Comptroller, Federal Reserve System, Federal Deposit Insurance Corporation, Office of Thrift Supervision and National Credit Union Association 'Statement on subprime mortgage lending', 29 June 2007, available from http://www.occ.gov/news-issuances/news-releases/2007/nr-ia-2007-64a.pdf, accessed 5 March 2013.

Department of Treasury Task Force on Predatory Lending *Curbing predatory home mortgage lending* 1 (Treasury Task Force on Predatory Lending: Washington DC, 2000).

Detrixhe, J. 'Libor reported as rigged in '08 proving 2012's revelation', 19 July 2012, available from http://www.bloomberg.com/news/2012-07-18/libor-reported-as-rigged-in-08-crisis-proving-revelation-in-12.html, accessed 3 October 2012.

Devereux, M. 'Will the bank levy meet its objectives?' (2011) British Tax Review, 1, 33–39.

Diamant, S. 'Neil Barofsjy's sig tarp: "difficult, rigorous, and independent" oversight of the TARP' (2011) North Carolina Banking Institute, 15, 313–332.

Dickerson, M. 'Over-indebtedness, the subprime mortgage crisis, and the effect on US cities' (2009) Fordham Urban Law Journal, 36, 395–425.

Dilley, B. and Weller, F. 'Mortgage fraud and the credit crunch' (2008) Fighting Fraud, Summer, 35, 1–31.

Doise, D. 'Subprime: price of infringements' (2008) International Business Law Journal, 4, 558–568.

Donnini, G. 'White collar fraud investigations leading lawyers on analyzing recent trends, building a defense strategy, and developing compliance programs analyzing recent fraud trends' (2009) Aspatore, November, 1–12.

Dooley, D. and Radke, M. 'Does severe punishment deter financial crimes?' (2010) Charleston Law Review, Spring, 4, 619–659.

Dorn, N. 'Regulatory sloth and activism in the effervescence of financial crisis' (2011) University of Denver Law and Policy, 33(3), 428–448.

Dose, D. 'Subprime: price of infringements' (2008) International Business Law Journal, 4, 558–568.

Drew, J. and Drew, M. 'Ponzimonium: Madoff and the red flags of fraud' (2012) Griffith Business School Discussion Papers Finance, 2010-07.

Drew, J. and Drew, M. 'The identification of Ponzi schemes – can a picture tell a thousand frauds?' (2010) Griffiths Law Review, 19, 51–70.

Dunbar, K. 'Forecasting and stress testing the risk-based capital requirements for revolving retail exposures' (2012) Journal of Banking Regulation, 13(3), 249–263.

Duran, C. 'The economic crisis and the role of law in monetary policy: a study of the political and social accountability of the Brazilian Central Bank (Bacen), the European Central Bank (ECB) and the Federal Reserve (Fed)' (2012) Journal of International Banking Law and Regulation, 27(8), 306–317.

Dyke, C. 'UK prosecution agencies reluctant to prosecute corporate offenders over LIBOR', 7 October 2013, available from http://corkerbinning.com/blog/uk-prosecution-agencies-reluctant-to-prosecute-corporate-offenders-over-libor/#page=1, accessed 9 October 2013.

Eckard, E. 'FBI shift crimps white-collar crime probes – with more agents moved to anti-terrorism duty, corporate fraud cases are routinely put on hold, prosecutors say', 30 August 2004, available from http://articles.latimes.com/2004/aug/30/business/fi-fbi30, accessed 3 May 2013.

Ed. 'Credit rating agencies to be regulated' EU Focus, 2008, 244, 2–4.

Ed. 'Parliamentary banking commission recommends jailing reckless bankers' (2013) Company Lawyer, 34(9), 283.

Ed. 'RBS measure and restructuring plan approved' EU Focus, 2010, 33–34.

Edmonds, T., Jarrett, T. and Woodhouse, J. *Credit crunch time line* (House of Commons Library: London, 2010).

Edwards, C., Hardiman, P., Madden, M. and McClelland, J. 'Implications for commercial organisations of the global investigations into LIBOR' (2012) Banking Law Journal, October, 129, 831.

Effinger, S. and Masciandaro, D. *Handbook of central banking, financial regulation and supervision* (Edward Elgar: Cheltenham, 2011).

Elboghdady, D. 'Clock ticking for SEC to pursue fraud charges in financial crisis cases', 19 July 2012, available from http://articles.washingtonpost.com/2012-07-19/business/35487394_1_financial-crisis-fraudulent-activity-federal-securities-regulators, accessed 27 June 2013.

Elliot, L. 'Credit crisis – how it all began', 5 August 2008, available from http://www.guardian.co.uk/business/2008/aug/05/northernrock.banking, accessed 8 February 2013.

Ellis, N., Fairchild, L. and D'Souza, F. 'Is imposing liability of credit rating agencies a good idea? Credit rating agency reform in the aftermath of the global financial crisis' (2012) Stanford Journal of Law, Business and Finance, Spring, 17, 175–222.

Emerson, C. 'A troubled house of cards: examining how the Housing and Economic Recovery Act of 2008 fails to resolve the foreclosure crisis' (2008) Oklahoma Law Review, 61, 561–584.

Engel, K. and McCoy, P. 'A tale of three markets: the law and economics of predatory lending' (2002) Texas Law Review, 80(6), 1255–1281.

Engert, A. 'Transnational hedge fund regulation' (2010) European Business Organization Law Review, 11(3), 329–378.

Estrada, E. 'The immediate and lasting impacts of the 2008 economic collapse – Lehman Brothers, General Motors and the secured credit markets' (2011) University of Richmond Law Review, 45, 1111–1142.

EURIBOR 'About EURIBOR', n/d, available from http://www.euribor-ebf.eu/euribor-org/about-euribor.html, accessed 1 October 2012.

European Commission *Report of the High-Level Group on Financial Supervision in the EU* (European Commission: Brussels, 2009).

Evans, A. 'The investor compensation fund' (2007), Journal of Corporation Law, Fall, 33, 233–290.

Evans, C. 'What makes you so special? Ending the credit rating agencies' special status and access to confidential information' (2012) Valparaiso University Law Review, Summer, 46, 1091–1137.

Fairfax, L. 'The legal origins of theory in crisis' (2009) Brigham Young University Law Review, 1571–1617.

Federal Bureau of Investigation '2008 mortgage fraud report', n/d, available from http://www.fbi.gov/stats-services/publications/mortgage-fraud-2008/2008-mortgage-fraud-report, accessed 8 August 2013.

Federal Bureau of Investigation '2009 mortgage fraud report', n/d, available from http://www.fbi.gov/stats-services/publications/mortgage-fraud-2009, accessed 8 August 2013.

Federal Bureau of Investigation 'Allen Stanford convicted in Houston for orchestrating $7 billion investment fraud scheme', 6 March 2012, available from http://www.fbi.gov/houston/press-releases/2012/allen-stanford-convicted-in-houston-for-orchestrating-7-billion-investment-fraud-scheme, accessed 4 June 2012.

Federal Bureau of Investigation 'Allen Stanford gets 110 years for orchestrating $7 billion investment fraud scheme', 14 June 2012, available from http://www.fbi.gov/houston/press-releases/2012/allen-stanford-gets-110-years-for-orchestrating-7-billion-investment-fraud-scheme, accessed 4 June 2013.

Federal Bureau of Investigation 'Chris Swecker, Assistant Director, Criminal Investigative Division, Federal Bureau of Investigation, before the House Financial Services Subcommittee on Housing and Community Opportunity', 7 October 2004, available from http://www.fbi.

gov/news/testimony/fbis-efforts-in-combating-mortgage-fraud, accessed 8 August 2013.

Federal Bureau of Investigation 'Department of Justice closes Washington Mutual investigation with no criminal charges', 5 August 2011, available from http://www.fbi.gov/seattle/press-releases/2011/department-of-justice-closes-washington-mutual-investigation-with-no-criminal-charges, accessed 7 October 2013.

Federal Bureau of Investigation 'Executives, borrower convicted in Virginia of massive fraud scheme that led to collapse of Bank of the Commonwealth', 24 May 2013, available from http://www.fbi.gov/norfolk/press-releases/2013/executives-borrower-convicted-in-virginia-of-massive-fraud-scheme-that-led-to-collapse-of-bank-of-the-common wealth, accessed 15 October 2013.

Federal Bureau of Investigation 'Financial crimes report to the public', available from http://www.fbi.gov/stats-services/publications/financial-crimes-report-2010-2011/financial-crimes-report-2010-2011#Financial, accessed 21 March 2012.

Federal Bureau of Investigation 'Financial crimes report to the public – fiscal years 2010–2011', n/d, available from http://www.fbi.gov/stats-services/publications/financial-crimes-report-2010-2011/financial-crimes-report-2010-2011#Mortgage, accessed 8 August 2013.

Federal Bureau of Investigation 'Inside the FBI – podcast', 11 October 2012, available from http://www.fbi.gov/news/podcasts/inside/distressed-homeowner-mortgage-fraud.mp3/view, accessed 14 October 2013.

Federal Bureau of Investigation 'John S. Pistole, Deputy Director Federal Bureau of Investigation, statement before the House Committee on the Judiciary', 1 April 2009, available from http://www.fbi.gov/news/testimony/fbi-efforts-to-combat-mortgage-fraud-and-other-financial-frauds, accessed 17 June 2013.

Federal Bureau of Investigation 'Looking ahead resolve not to be scammed', 29 December 2006, available from http://www.fbi.gov/news/stories/2006/december/scams_122906, accessed 23 May 2013.

Federal Bureau of Investigation 'Mortgage fraud report 2006', May 2007, available from http://www.fbi.gov/stats-services/publications/mortgage-fraud-2006/2006-mortgage-fraud-report#mf06_key, accessed 8 August 2013.

Federal Bureau of Investigation 'Mortgage fraud report 2007', April 2008, available from http://www.fbi.gov/stats-services/publications/mortgage-fraud-2007, accessed 18 October 2013.

Federal Bureau of Investigation 'Mortgage fraud report 2008', 2009, available from http://www.fbi.gov/stats-services/publications/mortgage-fraud-2008/2008-mortgage-fraud-report, accessed 17 June 2013.

Federal Bureau of Investigation 'Mortgage fraud', n/d, available from http://www.fbi.gov/about-us/investigate/white_collar/mortgage-fraud/mortgage_fraud, accessed 23 May 2013.

Federal Bureau of Investigation 'Operation Stolen Dreams: hundreds arrested in mortgage fraud sweep', 17 June 2010, available from http://www.fbi.gov/news/stories/2010/june/mortgage-fraud-sweep, accessed 1 August 2013.

Federal Bureau of Investigation 'Swecker, C. former FBI Assistant Director, Criminal Investigative Division, introductory statement: House Financial Services Subcommittee on Housing and Community Opportunity' 7 October 2004, available from http://www.fbi.gov/news/testimony/fbis-efforts-in-combating-mortgage-fraud, accessed 22 October 2013.

Federal Reserve 'Press Release', 21 December 2007, available from http://www.federalreserve.gov/newsevents/press/monetary/20071212a.htm, accessed 8 August 2012.

Federal Reserve 'Press Release', 14 March 2008, available from http://www.federalreserve.gov/newsevents/press/monetary/20080314a.htm, accessed 8 August 2012.

Federal Reserve 'Term Auction Facility', n/d, available from http://www.federalreserve.gov/newsevents/reform_taf.htm, accessed 23 September 2013.

Federal Reserve 'Term Securities Lending Facility', n/d, available from http://www.federalreserve.gov/monetarypolicy/tslf.htm, accessed 8 August 2012.

Federal Reserve 'Why are interest rates being kept at a low level?', n/d, available from http://www.federalreserve.gov/faqs/money_12849.htm, accessed 23 September 2013.

Federal Reserve Board *Flow of funds accounts of the United States: flows and outstandings third quarter 2008* (Board of Governors of the Federal Reserve System: Washington DC, 2008).

Federal Trade Commission 'Bear Stearns and EMC Mortgage to pay $28 million to settle FTC charges of unlawful mortgage servicing and debt collection practices', 9 September 2008, available from http://www.ftc.gov/opa/2008/09/emc.shtm, accessed 21 October 2013.

Federal Trade Commission 'Predatory lending practices in the subprime industry', 24 May 2000, available from http://www.ftc.gov/os/2000/05/predatorytestimony.htm, accessed 21 October 2013.

Feldman, W. 'Staying in compliance: key issues for white collar crime attorneys and their multinational clients' (2013) Aspatore, March, 2–7.

Felsenfeld, C. 'The savings and loan crisis' (1991) Fordham Law Review, May, 59, 7–56.

Feran, E. 'The break-up of the Financial Services Authority' (2011) Oxford Journal of Legal Studies, 31(3), 455–480.

Ferran, E. and Alexander, K. 'Can soft law bodies be effective? The special case of the European Systemic Risk Board' (2010) European Law Review, 35(6), 751–776.

Ferren, E., Moloney, N., Hill, J. and Coffee, J. *The regulatory aftermath of the global financial crisis* (Cambridge University Press: Cambridge, 2012).

Financial Conduct Authority 'Ex-mortgage advisor sentenced to two years after FCA action', 16 July 2013, available from http://www.fca.org.uk/news/exmortgage-advisor-sentenced-to-two-years-after-fca-action, accessed 19 July 2013.

Financial Conduct Authority 'Fighting financial crime', 31 March 2013, available from http://www.fca.org.uk/about/what/protecting/financial-crime, accessed 8 July 2013.

Financial Conduct Authority *Financial crime: a guide for firms part 1: a firm's guide to preventing financial crime* (Financial Conduct Authority: London, 2013).

Financial Conduct Authority *Financial crime: a guide for firms part 2: financial crime thematic reviews* (Financial Conduct Authority: London, 2013).

Financial Conduct Authority 'Fines table 2013', 1 October 2013, available from http://www.fca.org.uk/firms/being-regulated/enforcement/fines, accessed 7 October 2013.

Financial Conduct Authority 'ICAP Europe Limited fined £14 million for significant failings in relation to LIBOR', 25 September 2013, available from http://www.fca.org.uk/news/icap-europe-limited-fined, accessed 9 October 2013.

Financial Conduct Authority 'JPMorgan Chase Bank N.A. fined £137,610,000 for serious failings relating to its Chief Investment Office's "London Whale" trades', 19 September 2013, available from http://www.fca.org.uk/news/jpmorgan-chase-bank-na-fined, accessed 9 October 2013.

Financial Conduct Authority 'Keynote address: financial crime in the FCA world, Tracey McDermott', 1 July 2013, available from http://www.fca.org.uk/news/speeches/financial-crime-in-the-fca-world, accessed 8 July 2013.

Financial Conduct Authority 'The changing face of financial crime', 1 July 2013, available from http://www.fca.org.uk/news/speeches/the-changing-face-of-financial-crime, accessed 8 July 2013.

Financial Crimes Enforcement Network 'Financial Fraud Enforcement Task Force', n/d, available from http://www.fincen.gov/fraudenftaskforce.html, accessed 18 March 2013.

Financial Crimes Enforcement Network *Mortgage loan fraud* (Financial Crime Enforcement Network: Washington DC, 2012).

Financial Crimes Enforcement Network *Mortgage loan fraud: an industry assessment based upon suspicious activity: report analysis* (Financial Crimes Enforcement Network: Washington DC, 2006).

Financial Crimes Enforcement Network *Mortgage loan fraud: an update on trends based on analysis of suspicious activity reports April 2008* (Financial Crimes Enforcement Network: Washington DC, 2008).

Financial Crimes Enforcement Network *Mortgage loan fraud update – suspicious activity report filings from January 1–December 31 2010* (Financial Crime Enforcement Network: Washington DC, 2011).

Financial Crimes Enforcement Network 'Remarks of Jennifer Shashly Calvery, Director of FinCEN Enforcement Network, Mortgage Bankers Association, Fraud Issues Conference', 15 April 2013, available from http://www.fincen.gov/news_room/speech/pdf/20130415.pdf, accessed 1 August 2013.

Financial Crisis Inquiry Commission *Final report of the National Commission on the causes of the financial and economic crisis in the United States* (Financial Crisis Inquiry Commission: Washington DC, 2011).

Financial Crisis Inquiry Commission *Financial Crisis Inquiry Commission report* (Financial Fraud Enforcement Task Force: Washington DC, 2010).

Financial Industry Regulatory Authority *Report of the 2009 special review committee on FINRA's examination program in light of the Stanford and Madoff schemes* (Financial Industry Regulatory Authority: Washington DC, 2010).

Financial Services Authority 'Barclays fined £59.5 million for significant failings in relation to LIBOR and EURIBOR', 27 June 2012, available from http://www.fsa.gov.uk/library/communication/pr/2012/070.shtml, accessed 9 October 2013.

Financial Services Authority 'Delivering credible deterrence', speech by Margaret Cole, Director of Enforcement, FSA, Annual Financial Crime Conference, 27 April 2009, available from http://www.fsa.gov.uk/library/communication/speeches/2009/0427_mc.shtml, accessed 8 March 2013.

Financial Services Authority *Developing our policy on fraud and dishonesty – discussion paper 26* (Financial Services Authority: London, 2003).

Financial Services Authority *Enforcement annual performance account 2008/2009* (Financial Services Authority: London, 2009).

Financial Services Authority *Enforcement annual performance account 2009/2010* (Financial Services Authority: London, 2010).

Financial Services Authority *Enforcement annual performance account 2010/2011* (Financial Services Authority: London, 2011).
Financial Services Authority *Enforcement annual performance account 2011/2012* (Financial Services Authority: London, 2012).
Financial Services Authority *Enforcement annual performance account 2012/2013* (Financial Services Authority: London, 2013).
Financial Services Authority 'Fake stockbroker sentenced to 15 months', 13 February 2008, available from http://www.fsa.gov.uk/library/communication/pr/2008/011.shtml, accessed 12 November 2012.
Financial Services Authority 'Final notice – Barclays Bank', 27 June 2012, available from http://www.fsa.gov.uk/static/pubs/final/barclays-jun12.pdf, accessed 27 June 2013.
Financial Services Authority *Final notice – Michael Joseph James Lewis trading as Lewis Partnership* (Financial Services Authority: London, 2011).
Financial Services Authority 'Final notice – RBS', 6 February 2013, available from http://www.fsa.gov.uk/static/pubs/final/rbs.pdf accessed 27 June 2013.
Financial Services Authority 'Final notice – UBS', 19 December 2012, available from http://www.fsa.gov.uk/static/pubs/final/ubs.pdf, accessed 27 June 2013.
Financial Services Authority *Final notice to Barclays Bank Plc* (Financial Services Authority: London, 2012).
Financial Services Authority 'Final notice to Mr John Paul Keay trading as Jack Keay Mortgage Services', 21 April 2008, available from http://www.fsa.gov.uk/pubs/final/JKMS.pdf, accessed 30 June 2013.
Financial Services Authority *Financial risk outlook 2009* (Financial Services Authority: London, 2009).
Financial Services Authority *Financial services firms' approach to UK financial sanctions* (Financial Services Authority: London, 2009).
Financial Services Authority 'FSA bans and fines former Northern Rock finance director £320,000 for misreporting mortgage arrears figures', 27 July 2010, available from http://www.fsa.gov.uk/pages/Library/Communication/PR/2010/126.shtml, accessed 1 July 2013.
Financial Services Authority 'FSA bans four more brokers for mortgage fraud as the Tribunal dismisses broker's appeal', 19 April 2011, available from http://www.fsa.gov.uk/pages/Library/Communication/PR/2011/038.shtml, accessed 30 June 2013.
Financial Services Authority 'FSA fines and bans former Northern Rock deputy chief executive and credit director for misreporting mortgage arrears figures', 13 April 2010, available from http://www.fsa.gov.uk/pages/Library/Communication/PR/2010/066.shtml, accessed 1 July 2013.

Financial Services Authority 'FSA fines table 2007', n/d, available from http://www.fsa.gov.uk/about/press/facts/fines/2007, accessed 8 March 2013.

Financial Services Authority 'FSA fines table 2008', n/d, available from http://www.fsa.gov.uk/about/press/facts/fines/2008, accessed 8 March 2013.

Financial Services Authority 'FSA fines table 2009', n/d, available from http://www.fsa.gov.uk/about/press/facts/fines/2009, accessed 8 March 2013.

Financial Services Authority 'FSA fines table 2010', n/d, available from http://www.fsa.gov.uk/about/press/facts/fines/2010, accessed 8 March 2013.

Financial Services Authority 'FSA fines table 2011', n/d, available from http://www.fsa.gov.uk/about/press/facts/fines/2011, accessed 8 March 2013.

Financial Services Authority 'FSA fines table 2012', n/d, available from http://www.fsa.gov.uk/about/press/facts/fines/2012, accessed 8 March 2013.

Financial Services Authority 'FSA fines table 2013', n/d, available from http://www.fsa.gov.uk/about/press/facts/fines/2013, accessed 8 March 2013.

Financial Services Authority *FSA handbook of senior management arrangements, systems and controls* (Financial Services Authority: London, 2006).

Financial Services Authority 'FSA issues ban and fine of £500,000 against former HBOS executive, Peter Cummings', 12 September 2012, available from http://www.fsa.gov.uk/library/communication/pr/2012/087.shtml, accessed 30 June 2013.

Financial Services Authority 'FSA secures first conviction in criminal market abuse case', 18 August 2005, available from http://www.fsa.gov.uk/pages/Library/Communication/PR/2005/091.shtml, accessed 26 June 2013.

Financial Services Authority 'FSA statement on Johnny Cameron', 18 May 2010, available from http://www.fsa.gov.uk/pages/Library/Communication/PR/2010/081.shtml, accessed 1 July 2013.

Financial Services Authority 'Introduction to the FSA Enforcement Conference 2010', 22 June 2010, available from http://www.fsa.gov.uk/pages/Library/Communication/Speeches/2010/0622_mc.shtml, accessed 8 July 2013.

Financial Services Authority *Mortgage fraud against lenders – a thematic review of lenders' systems and controls to detect and prevent mortgage fraud* (Financial Services Authority: London, 2011).

Financial Services Authority 'RBS fined £87.5m for significant failings in relation to LIBOR' 6 February 2013, available from http://www.fsa.gov.uk/library/communication/pr/2013/011.shtml, accessed 8 February 2013.

Financial Services Authority 'Solicitor and his father-in-law found guilty in FSA insider dealing case', 27 March 2009, available from http://www.fsa.gov.uk/library/communication/pr/2009/042.shtml, accessed 3 October 2013.

Financial Services Authority 'Speech by Thomas F. Huertas, Director, Banking Sector, FSA and Vice Chairman, CEBS, Wharton School of Management, University of Pennsylvania Philadelphia', 16 February 2010, available from http://www.fsa.gov.uk/pages/Library/Communication/Speeches/2010/0212_th.shtml, accessed 7 October 2013.

Financial Services Authority *Stress and scenario testing – feedback on CP08/24 and final rules* (Financial Services Authority: London, 2009).

Financial Services Authority 'Stress testing', n/d, available from http://www.fsa.gov.uk/about/what/international/stress_testing, accessed 4 February 2012.

Financial Services Authority *The failure of the Royal Bank of Scotland – FSA Board report* (Financial Services Authority: London, 2009).

Financial Services Authority 'The FSA publishes the Turner Review: a wide-ranging review of global banking regulation', 18 March 2009, available from http://www.fsa.gov.uk/pages/library/communication/pr/2009/037.shtml, accessed 25 June 2013.

Financial Services Authority *The supervision of Northern Rock: a lessons learned review* (Financial Services Authority: London, 2008).

Financial Services Authority *The Turner Review: a regulatory response to the global banking crisis* (Financial Services Authority: London, 2009).

Financial Services Authority 'UBS fined £160 million for significant failings in relation to LIBOR and EURIBOR', 19 December 2012, available from http://www.fsa.gov.uk/library/communication/pr/2012/116.shtml, accessed 30 June 2013.

Financial Services Bill *Draft Financial Services Bill session 2010–12* (House of Commons Joint Committee on the draft Financial Services Bill: London, 2011).

Financial Times Lexicon, n/d, available from http://lexicon.ft.com/Term?term=credit-crunch, accessed 21 November 2012.

Fischer, A. and Sheppard, J. 'Financial institutions fraud' (2008) American Criminal Law Review, 45, 531–578.

Fisher, J. *Fighting fraud and financial crime – a new architecture for the investigation and prosecution of serious fraud, corruption and financial market crimes* (Policy Exchange: London, 2010).

Fisher, L. 'Target marketing of subprime loans: racialised consumer fraud and reverse redlining' (2009) Journal of Law and Policy, 18, 121–155.
Fitzpatrick, T. and Sagers, C. 'Faith-based financial regulation: a primer on oversight of credit rating organizations' (2009) Administrative Law Review, Summer, 61, 557–610.
Fleming, M. *FSA's Scale & Impact of Financial Crime project (phase one): Critical Analysis Occasional Paper Series 37* (Financial Services Authority: London, 2009).
Foley, S. 'McGraw-Hill reveals $77m S&P settlement', 30 April 2013, available from http://www.ft.com/cms/s/0/97d716bc-b187-11e2-9315-00144feabdc0.html#axzz2UgVAYfge, accessed 29 May 2013.
Forrester, J. 'Still mortgaging the American dream: predatory lending, pre-emption, and federally supported lenders' (2006) University of Cincinnati Law Review, Summer, 74, 1303–1371.
Fox, M. and David, H. 'Lessons from the US subprime mortgage crisis' (2008) Journal of International Banking Law & Regulation, 23(9), 449–457.
Fraud Advisory Panel *11th annual review 2008/2009* (Fraud Advisory Panel: London, 2009).
Frieden, T. 'FBI warns of mortgage fraud "epidemic"', 17 September 2004, available from http://edition.cnn.com/2004/LAW/09/17/mortgage.fraud/, accessed 15 October 2013.
Friedrichs, D. *Trusted criminals: white collar crime in contemporary society* (Wadsworth Cengage Learning: Bellmont, 2010).
Friedrichs, D. 'Wall Street: crime never sleeps' in Will, S., Handelman, S. and Brotherton, D. (eds), *How they got away with it – white collar criminals and the financial meltdown* (Columbia University Press: New York, 2013).
Furse, M. 'The cartel offence – "great for a headline but not much else"?' (2011) European Competition Law Review, 32(5), 223–230.
Gabel, J. 'Midnight in the garden of good faith: using clawback actions to harvest the equitable roots of bankrupt ponzi schemes' (2011) Case Western Reserve Law Review, 62, 19–78.
Gabilondo, J. 'Dodd–Frank, liability structure, and financial instability cycles: neither a (ponzi) borrower nor a lender be' (2011) Wake Forest Law Review, Fall, 46, 469–489.
Galbraith, J. *The great crash 1929* (Houghton: Boston, 1988).
Gallagher, J., Lauchlan, J. and Steven, M. 'Polly Peck: the breaking of an entrepreneur?' (1996) Journal of Small Business and Enterprise Development, 3(1), 3–12.
Gans, K. 'Anatomy of a mortgage meltdown: the story of the subprime crisis, the role of fraud, and the efficacy of the Idaho Safe Act' (2011) Idaho Law Review, 48, 123–174.

Gee, J. 'Fraud 2009 bad, 2010 better?' (2010) Computer Fraud and Security, 2010, February, 2, 13–15.
Gensler, G. 'Libor, naked and exposed', 6 August 2012, available from http://www.nytimes.com/2012/08/07/opinion/libor-naked-and-exposed.html?_r=3&ref=opinionpiecesaboutlibor&, accessed 12 August 2013.
Gevurtz, G. 'The role of corporate law in preventing a financial crisis: reflections on in re Citigroup Inc shareholder derivative litigation' (2010) Pacific McGeorge Global Business and Development Law Journal, 23, 113.
Ghosh, S. and Mohamed, S. 'The troubled asset relief program (TARP) and its limitations: an analysis' (2010) International Journal of Law and Management, 52(2), 124–143.
Ghosh, S. and Patnaik, S. 'The Independent Banking Commission (Vickers) report: squaring the circle?' (2012) International Journal of Law and Management, 54(2), 141–152.
Gilbert, M. 'Barclays takes a money-market beating', 3 September 2012, available from http://www.bloomberg.com/apps/news?pid=newsarchive&sid=a8uEKKBYY7As, accessed 1 October 2012.
Gill, M. 'Fraud and recessions: views from fraudsters and fraud managers' (2011) International Journal of Law, Crime and Justice, 39, 204–214.
Gilligan, G. 'The problem of, and with, financial crime' (2012) Northern Ireland Legal Quarterly, 63(4), 495–508.
Goddard, J., Molyneux, P. and Wilson, J. 'The financial crisis in Europe: evolution, policy responses and lessons for the future' (2009) Journal of Financial Regulation and Compliance, 17(4), 362–380.
Goldby, M. 'The impact of Schedule 7 of the Counter-Terrorism Act 2008 on banks and their customers' (2010) Journal of Money Laundering Control, 13(4), 351–371.
Goldfarb, Z. 'Probe into Fannie Mae, Freddie Mac widens', 30 September 2008, available from http://articles.washingtonpost.com/2008-09-30/business/36900204_1_probes-disclosure-and-corporate-governance-fannie-mae, accessed 7 October 2013.
Gonon, F. 'Greece and Armageddon' (2011) European Lawyer, 109, 5.
Gottschalk, P. 'Categories of financial crime' (2010) Journal of Financial Crime 17(4), 441–458.
Gottschalk, P. 'Executive positions involved in white-collar crime' (2011) Journal of Money Laundering Control, 14(4), 300–312.
Gottschalk, P. 'Gender and white-collar crime: only four per cent female criminals' (2012) Journal of Money Laundering Control, 15(3), 362–373.
Gradwohl, D. and Corbett, K. 'Equity receiverships for ponzi schemes' (2010) Seton Hall Legislative Journal, 34, 181–225.

Graham, C. 'The Enterprise Act 2002 and competition law' (2004) Modern Law Review, 67(2), 273–288.

Graham, T. 'Financial Services and Markets Bill: investigations and enforcement in the context of the financial crime objective' (2000) Journal of International Financial Markets, 2(3), 88–93.

Gray, E. 'Warnings ignored: the politics of the crisis' (1990) Stanford Law and Policy Review, Spring, 2, 138–145.

Gray, J. and Akseli, O. *Financial regulation in crisis? The role of law and the failure of Northern Rock* (Edward Elgar: Cheltenham, 2011).

Green, M. 'After the fall: the criminal law enforcement response to the S&L crisis' (1991) Fordham Law Review, May, 59, 155–192.

Green, S. 'The concept of white collar crime in law and legal theory' (2004) Buffalo Criminal Law Review, 8, 1–34.

Greenberger, M. 'Striking the right balance: investor and consumer protection in the new financial marketplace' (2013) George Washington Law Review, April, 81, 707–748.

Greenwood, L. 'Mail and wire fraud' (2008) American Criminal Law Review, 45, 717–740.

Griffin, S. 'The disqualification of unit directors and the protection of the public interest' (2002) Northern Ireland Legal Quarterly, 53(3), 207–231.

Griffiths, K. 'Fraudulent broker gets 15 months', 14 February 2008, available from http://www.telegraph.co.uk/finance/markets/2784369/Fraudulent-broker-gets-15-months.html, accessed 12 November 2012.

Grinshteyn, A. 'Horseshoes and hand grenades: the Dodd–Frank Act's (almost) attack on credit rating agencies' (2011) Hofstra Law Review, Summer, 39, 937–978.

Guentes, N. 'Defrauding the American dream: predatory lending in Latin communities and reform of California's lending law' (2009) California Law Review, August, 97, 1279–1335.

Haines, J. 'Mortgage fraud – FSA report on thematic findings of mortgage lenders' systems and controls against mortgage fraud' (2011) Company Lawyer, 32(11), 344–346.

Haines, J. 'Mortgage fraud – have mortgage lenders got their house in order?' (2011) Company Lawyer, 32(3), 86–88.

Halligan, L. 'Obama signs a bill that lets banks have US over a barrel once more', 26 July 2010, available from http://www.telegraph.co.uk/finance/comment/liamhalligan/7908516/Obama-signs-a-bill-that-lets-banks-have-US-over-a-barrel-once-more.html, accessed 3 August 2013.

Handwerker, J., Solomon, M., Davar, M. and Harne, K. 'Congress declares checkmate: how the Fraud Enforcement and Recovery Act of 2009 strengthens the Civil False Claims Act and counters the courts' (2010) Journal of Business and Technology Law, 5, 295–323.

Hardouin, P. 'The aftermath of the financial crisis' (2011) Journal of Financial Crime, 18(2), 148–161.

Harper, S. 'Credit rating agencies deserve credit for the 2007–2008 financial crisis: an analysis of CRA liability following the enactment of the Dodd–Frank Act' (2011) Washington and Lee Law Review, 68, 1925–1972.

Harrell, A. 'The great credit contraction: who, what, when, where and why?' (2010) Georgia State University Law Review, Summer, 26, 1209–1258.

Harris, J. 'Financial regulation and taking the long-term view' (2012) Company Lawyer, 33(10), 293–294.

Harris, J. 'Getting over Madoff: how the SEC must restore its credibility' (2010) Company Lawyer, 31(2), 33–34.

Harrison, K. and Ryder, N. *The law relating to financial crime in the United Kingdom* (Ashgate: Farnham, 2013).

Hatchett, D. 'Sox it to 'em: using Sarbanes–Oxley as a model for regulating conflicts of interest in the credit rating industry' (2012) Alabama Law Review, 63, 407–428.

Hausemann, Y. and Bechtold-Orth, E. 'Changing remuneration systems in Europe and the United States: a legal analysis of recent developments in the wake of the financial crisis' (2010) European Business Organization Law Review, 11(2), 195–229.

Hawles, A. 'Italy downgrade adds to eurozone contagion fears', 20 September 2011, available from http://www.guardian.co.uk/business/2011/sep/20/italy-downgrade-eurozone-contagion-fear, accessed 26 February 2013.

Hayes, A. 'Market abuse' (2010) Compliance Officer Bulletin, April, 75, 1–31.

Hays, K. and Driver, A. 'Former Enron CEO Skilling's sentence cut to 14 years', 22 June 2013, available from http://uk.reuters.com/article/2013/06/21/us-enron-skilling-idUSBRE95K12520130621, accessed 18 October 2013.

Henning, J. 'Making sure the buck stops here: barring executives for corporate violations' (2012) University of Chicago Legal Forum, 91–128.

Henry, J. and Kotlikoff, L. 'Financial reform, R.I.P.', 15 July 2010, available from http://www.forbes.com/2010/07/15/dodd-frank-failure-regulation-opinions-contributors-james-henry-laurence-kotlikoff-wall-street.html, accessed 3 August 2013.

Heroy, J. 'Other people's money: how a time-gap in credit reporting may lead to fraud' (2008) North Carolina Banking Institute, 12, 321–351.

Hill, C. 'Fund management update' (2013) Compliance Officer Bulletin, March, 104, 1–36.

Hill, C. 'Limits on Dodd–Frank's rating agency reform' (2011) Chapman Law Review, Spring, 15, 133–148.

Hiznay, H. 'How the Bernard Madoff scandal exposed weaknesses in asset management regulation' (2009) Review of Banking and Financial Law, Spring, 28, 413–425.

HM Crown Prosecution Service Inspectorate *Report of the Attorney General on the inspection of the Serious Fraud Office* (HM Crown Prosecution Service Inspectorate: London, 2012).

HM Crown Prosecution Service Inspectorate *Review of the Fraud Prosecution Service* (HM Crown Prosecution Service Inspectorate: London, 2008).

HM Government *The Coalition: our programme for government* (HM Government: London, 2010).

HM Treasury *A new approach to financial regulation: consultation on reforming the consumer credit regime* (HM Treasury: London, 2010).

HM Treasury *A new approach to financial regulation: the blueprint for reform* (HM Treasury: London, 2011).

HM Treasury *Anti-money laundering strategy* (HM Treasury: London, 2004).

HM Treasury 'Bradford & Bingley plc', 29 September 2007, available from http://webarchive.nationalarchives.gov.uk/+/http://www.hm-treasury.gov.uk/press_97_08.htm, accessed 8 December 2012.

HM Treasury *Combating the financing of terrorism* (HM Treasury: London, 2002).

HM Treasury *Financial Services (Banking Reform) Bill – Bill overview* (HM Treasury: London, 2013).

HM Treasury 'Financial Services (Banking Reform) Bill Government annotated amendments: criminal sanctions', 7 October 2013, available from https://www.gov.uk/government/uploads/system/uploads/attachment_data/file/245778/Annotated_Clause_-_Criminal_Sanctions.pdf, accessed 9 October 2013.

HM Treasury *Financial Services (Banking Reform) Bill – Government amendments, criminal sanctions* (HM Treasury: London, 2013).

HM Treasury, 'Financial services policy agenda', n/d, available from http://www.hm-treasury.gov.uk/fin_policy_agenda_index.htm, accessed 19 July 2011.

HM Treasury 'Government accepts recommendations from the Wheatley Review of LIBOR in full', 17 October 2012, available from https://www.gov.uk/government/news/government-accepts-recommendations-from-the-wheatley-review-of-libor-in-full, accessed 27 June 2013.

HM Treasury 'Government announces LIBOR administrator tendering committee', 25 February 2013, available from https://www.gov.uk/

government/news/government-announces-libor-administrator-tendering-committee, accessed 12 July 2013.

HM Treasury 'Government guarantee arrangements: Bradford & Bingley plc', 29 September 2008, available from http://webarchive.nationalarchives.gov.uk/+/http://www.hm-treasury.gov.uk/press_98_08.htm, accessed 13 August 2012.

HM Treasury *Implementing the Wheatley Review: draft secondary legislation* (HM Treasury: London, 2012).

HM Treasury 'Independent Commission on Banking – terms of reference', n/d, available from http://webarchive.nationalarchives.gov.uk/20130129110402/http://www.hm-treasury.gov.uk/d/banking_commission_terms_of_reference.pdf, accessed 25 June 2013.

HM Treasury 'Independent review into LIBOR published', 28 September 2012, available from https://www.gov.uk/government/news/independent-review-into-libor-published, accessed 27 June 2013.

HM Treasury 'Independent review into LIBOR publishes discussion paper', 10 August 2012, available from https://www.gov.uk/government/news/independent-review-into-libor-publishes-discussion-paper, accessed 27 June 2013.

HM Treasury 'LIBOR tendering process launched', 26 February 2013, available from https://www.gov.uk/government/news/libor-tendering-process-launched, accessed 12 July 2013.

HM Treasury 'Northern Rock plc deposits', 9 October 2007, available from http://webarchive.nationalarchives.gov.uk/20100407010852/http://www.hm-treasury.gov.uk/press_104_07.htm, accessed 28 February 2013.

HM Treasury *Sanctions for the directors of failed banks* (HM Treasury: London, 2012).

HM Treasury 'Speech at The Lord Mayor's Dinner for bankers and merchants of the City of London by The Chancellor of the Exchequer, The Rt Hon George Osborne MP, at Mansion House', 16 June 2010, available from http://webarchive.nationalarchives.gov.uk/20130129110402/http://www.hm-treasury.gov.uk/press_12_10.htm, accessed 25 June 2013.

HM Treasury 'Speech by Chancellor of the Exchequer, Rt Hon George Osborne MP, Mansion House 2013', 19 June 2013, available from https://www.gov.uk/government/speeches/speech-by-chancellor-of-the-exchequer-rt-hon-george-osborne-mp-mansion-house-2013, accessed 27 June 2013.

HM Treasury 'Speech by Financial Secretary to the Treasury, Rt Hon Greg Clark MP; Wheatley Review final report', 28 September 2012, available from https://www.gov.uk/government/speeches/speech-by-financial-secretary-to-the-treasury-rt-hon-greg-clark-mp-wheatley-review-final-report, accessed 27 June 2013.

HM Treasury *Spending review* (HM Treasury: London, 2013).
HM Treasury *Spending round 2013: distributional analysis* (HM Treasury: London, 2013).
HM Treasury *Spending round 2013: policy costings* (HM Treasury: London, 2013).
HM Treasury 'Spending round 2013: speech', 26 June 2013, available from https://www.gov.uk/government/speeches/spending-round-2013-speech, accessed 30 June 2013.
HM Treasury 'Statement by the Chancellor of the Exchequer, Rt Hon George Osborne MP, on LIBOR', 2 July 2012, available from https://www.gov.uk/government/speeches/statement-by-the-chancellor-of-the-exchequer-rt-hon-george-osborne-mp-on-libor, accessed 15 July 2013.
HM Treasury 'The Asset Protection Scheme', n/d, available from http://www.hm-treasury.gov.uk/apa_aps.htm, accessed 2 December 2012.
HM Treasury 'The Government launched its public consultation on the regulation of the London Interbank Offered Rate (LIBOR) today', 28 November 2012, available from https://www.gov.uk/government/news/government-publishes-consultation-on-regulation-of-libor, accessed 27 June 2013.
HM Treasury *The Government's response to the Parliamentary Commission on Banking Standards* (HM Treasury: London, 2013).
HM Treasury 'The Hogg Tendering Advisory Committee for LIBOR: pre-tender questionnaire', 26 February 2013, available from https://www.gov.uk/government/publications/the-hogg-tendering-advisory-committee-for-libor-pre-tender-questionnaire, accessed 12 July 2013.
HM Treasury 'The Wheatley Review', 30 June 2012, available from https://www.gov.uk/government/news/the-wheatley-review, accessed 27 June 2013.
HM Treasury *The Wheatley Review of LIBOR: initial discussion paper* (HM Treasury: London, 2012).
HM Treasury 'Walker Review of corporate governance of UK banking industry', n/d, available from http://webarchive.nationalarchives.gov.uk/+/http:/www.hm-treasury.gov.uk/walker_review_information.htm, accessed 16 September 2013.
HM Treasury and Department of Business, Innovation and Skills *Banking reform: delivering stability and supporting a sustainable economy* (HM Treasury: London, 2012).
HM Treasury and Department of Business, Innovation and Skills *The Government response to the Independent Commission on Banking* (HM Treasury: London, 2011).
HM Treasury Select Committee *Fixing LIBOR: some preliminary findings* (HM Treasury: London, 2012).
HM Treasury Select Committee *The run on the Rock* (HM Treasury Select Committee: London, 2008).

Hogg Tendering Advisory Committee for London Interbank Offered Rate 'The Hogg Tendering Advisory Committee announces that NYSE Euronext is to be the new LIBOR administrator', 9 July 2013, available from https://www.gov.uk/government/uploads/system/uploads/attachment_data/file/211330/Hogg_Tendering_Advisory_Committee.pdf, accessed 12 July 2013.

Home Office 'New National Crime Agency (NCA) to fight serious and organised crime', 8 June 2011, available from https://www.gov.uk/government/news/new-national-crime-agency-nca-to-fight-serious-and-organised-crime, accessed 16 September 2013.

Home Office, Press Release, 'Home Office to take lead on economic crime', 17 January 2011, available from http://www.homeoffice.gov.uk/media-centre/news/economic-crime, accessed 23 October 2011.

Home Office *The National Crime Agency – a plan for the creation of a national crime-fighting capability* (London: Home Office, 2011).

Honess, T. 'Juror competence in processing complex information: implications from a simulation of the Maxwell trial' (1998) Criminal Law Review, November, 763–773.

House Lawyer 'Con artists fleece desperate homeowners', 14 December 2012, available from http://articles.washingtonpost.com/2012-12-14/news/35846475_1_lender-distressed-homeowner-initiative-loan-data, accessed 1 August 2013.

House of Commons 'Oral evidence by Michael Turner QC, taken before the Judicial Committee Price Competitive Tendering Proposals in the Government's Transforming Legal Aid Consultation', 11 June 2013, available from http://www.publications.parliament.uk/pa/cm201314/cmselect/cmjust/uc91-i/uc9101.htm, accessed 30 June 2013.

House of Commons Joint Committee on the Draft Financial Services Bill *Draft Financial Services Bill session 2010–12* (House of Commons Joint Committee on the Draft Financial Services Bill: London, 2011).

House of Commons Treasury Committee *Banking crisis: reforming corporate governance and pay in the City, HC 519* (House of Commons Treasury Committee: London, 2009).

Huisman, Q.W. 'Corporate crime and crisis: causation scenarios' in Deflem, M. (ed.), *Economic crisis and crime* (Emerald: Bingley, 2011).

Huisman, W. 'White-collar crime and the economic crisis' (2012/2013) Newsletter of the European Society of Criminology, 11.

Hunt, C. 'In the racial crosshairs: reconsidering racially targeted predatory lending under a new theory of economic hate crime' (2003) University of Toledo Law Review, Winter, 3, 211–315.

Hurley, C. 'Paying the price for too big to fail' (2010) Entrepreneurial Business Law Journal, 4, 349–387.

Hurley, J. 'Speed up action against Fred Goodwin, Vince Cable tells Scottish prosecutors', 1 May 2013, available from http://www.telegraph.co.uk/finance/newsbysector/banksandfinance/10029013/Speed-up-action-against-Fred-Goodwin-Vince-Cable-tells-Scottish-prosecutors.html, accessed 2 July 2013.

Hurst, T. 'The role of credit rating agencies in the current worldwide financial crisis' (2009) Company Lawyer, 30(2), 61–66.

Hurt, C. 'Evil has a new name (and a new narrative): Bernard Madoff' (2009) Michigan State Law Review, Winter, 947–987.

Hurt, C. 'Of breaches of the peace, home invasions, and securities fraud' (2007) American Criminal Law Review, 44, 1365–1380.

Hurtado, P. 'Paul Greenwood, WG Trading hedge fund manager, pleads guilty to fraud', 28 July 2010, available from http://www.bloomberg.com/news/2010-07-28/paul-greenwood-wg-trading-hedge-fund-manager-to-plead-guilty-to-fraud.html, accessed 28 October 2013.

Hutchins, A. 'Flip that prosecution strategy: an argument for using RICO to prosecute large-scale mortgage fraud' (2011) Buffalo Law Review, 59(1), 293.

Huynh, D. 'Preemption v. punishment: a comparative study of white collar crime prosecution in the United States and the United Kingdom' (2010) Journal of International Business and Law, Spring, 9, 105–135.

ICAP 'ICAP Europe Ltd reaches settlements with FCA and CFTC', 25 September 2013, available from http://www.icap.com/news-events/in-the-news/news/2013/130925-icap-europe-ltd-reaches-settlements-with-fca-and-cftc.aspx, accessed 25 September 2013.

Independent Commission on Banking *Final report* (Independent Commission on Banking: London, 2011).

Independent Commission on Banking *Interim report on consultation on reform options* (Independent Commission on Banking: London, 2011).

International Monetary Fund *Global financial stability report: containing systemic risks and restoring financial soundness* (International Monetary Fund: Washington DC, 2008).

International Organization of Securities Commission 'IOSCO update on credit rating agencies oversight' 3 March 2009, available from http://www.iosco.org/news/pdf/IOSCONEWS138.pdf, accessed 24 April 2013.

International Organization of Securities Commission *Report on the activities of credit rating agencies* (International Organization of Securities Commission: Madrid, 2003).

International Organization of Securities Commission *Report on the activities of credit rating agencies* (International Organization of Securities Commission: Madrid, 2008).

Isidore, C. 'Bailout plan under fire', 23 September 2008, available from http://money.cnn.com/2008/09/23/news/economy/bailout_hearing/, accessed 7 August 2013.

Isidore, C. 'BofA settles unfair lending claims for $335 million', 21 December 2011, available from http://money.cnn.com/2011/12/21/news/companies/bank_america_settlement/, accessed 21 October 2013.

Izant, J. 'Mens rea and the Martin Act: a weapon of choice for securities fraud prosecutions?' (2012) Columbia Business Law Review, 2012, 913–993.

Jackson, K. 'The scandal beneath the financial crisis: getting a view from a moral–cultural mental model' (2010) Harvard Journal of Law and Public Policy, 33, 735–778.

Jackson, W. *Glass–Steagall Act: commercial vs. investment banking* (Congressional Research Services: Washington DC, 1987).

Jacobsen, B. and Barnhill, M. 'Drawing the short straw – mortgage fraud and straw buyers' (2008) Utah Bar Journal, July/August, 21, 9–13.

Jacobus, C. 'Mortgage fraud: recognition and prevention' (2008) Texas Bar Journal, March, 71, 188–192.

Johannson, T. 'Regulating credit rating agencies: the issue of conflicts of interest in the rating of structured finance products' (2010) Journal of Banking Regulation, 12, 1–23.

Johnson, A. 'Bush signs $700 billion financial bailout bill', 3 October 2013, available from http://www.nbcnews.com/id/26987291/ns/business-stocks_and_economy/t/bush-signs-billion-financial-bailout-bill/, accessed 5 August 2013.

Johnson, C. 'U.S. promotes its record on corporate crime', 18 July 2007, available from http://www.washingtonpost.com/wp-dyn/content/article/2007/07/17/AR2007071701767.html, accessed 31 July 2013.

Johnson, C. and Leonnig, C. 'FBI began investigating AIG in March', 25 September 2008, available from http://articles.washingtonpost.com/2008-09-25/business/36840351_1_mortgage-investments-aig-maurice-r-hank-greenberg, accessed 7 October 2013.

Johnston, K., Greer, J., Biermacher, J. and Hummel, J. 'The subprime morass: past, present and future' (2008) North Carolina Banking Institute, March, 12, 125–139.

Johnston, K., Johnson, K. and Hummel, J. 'Ponzi schemes litigation risks: what every financial services company should know' (2010) North Carolina Banking Institute, 14, 29–57.

Jones, R. 'The need for a negligence standard of care for credit rating agencies' (2010) William and Mary Business Law Review, 1, 201–231.

Jordan, L. 'FBI investigating companies at heart of Wall St crisis', 23 September 2008, available from http://www.huffingtonpost.com/2008/09/23/fbi-investigating-compani_n_128759.html, accessed 27 September 2013.

Jordan, S. 'Victimisation on main street: Occupy Wall Street and the mortgage fraud crisis' (2011) Fordham Urban Law Journal, December, 39, 485–510.

Judd, T. 'Hundreds of millions from legal aid budget helps banks defend fraud cases', 11 June 2013, available from http://www. independent.co.uk/news/uk/home-news/hundreds-of-millions-from-legal-aid-budget-helps-banks-defend-fraud-cases-8654539.html, accessed 30 June 2013.

Julian, R. 'Judicial perspectives in serious fraud cases – the present status of and problems posed by case management practices, jury selection rules, juror expertise, plea bargaining and choice of mode of trial', (2008) Criminal Law Review, 10, 764–783.

Julian, R. 'Judicial perspectives on the conduct of serious fraud trials' (2007) Criminal Law Review, October, 751–768.

Juurikkala, O. 'Credit default swaps and the EU Short Selling Regulation: a critical analysis' (2012) European Company and Financial Law Review, 9(3), 307–341.

K&L Gates 'Financial services reform alert: Dodd Frank next steps', 16 August 2010, available from http://www.klgates.com/dodd-frank-next-steps-08-16-2010/, accessed 3 August 2013.

Kaal, W. and Painter, R. 'Initial reflections on evolving standards: constraints on risk taking by directors and officers in Germany and the United States' (2010) Seton Hall Law Review, 40, 1433–1485.

Kamin, S.B. and DeMarco, L.P. *How did a domestic housing slump turn into a global financial crisis?*, Board of Governors of the Federal Reserve System International Finance Discussion Papers No. 994, January 2010.

Karnitschnig, M., Solomon, D., Pleven, L. and Hilsenrath, J. 'U.S. to take over AIG in $85 billion bailout; central banks inject cash as credit dries up', 16 September 2008, available from http://online.wsj.com/article/SB122156561931242905.html, accessed 25 March 2013.

Kathuria, S. 'Best practices for compliance with new government contractor compliance and ethics rules under the federal acquisition regulation' (2009) Public Contract Law Journal, Summer, 38, 803–856.

Kelly, J. 'Transparency and bank supervision' (2010) Albany Law Review, 73, 421–446.

Kempa, M. 'Combating white-collar crime in Canada: serving victim needs and market integrity' (2010) Journal of Financial Crime, 17(2), 251–264.

Kenagy, R., Anderson, T. and Fox, M. 'Regulation and the impact of political lobbying on the investment banking industry' (2013) Journal of International Banking Law and Regulation, 28(5), 171–180.

Kennedy, K. 'Excessive executive compensation: prior federal attempts to curb perceived abuses' (2010) Houston Business and Tax Law Journal, 10, 196–261.

Kirk, D. 'Blue Arrow: the SFO on trial' (1992) International Company and Commercial Law Review, 3(10), 331–333.

Kirk, D. 'Criminalising bad bankers' (2012) Journal of Criminal Law, 76(6), 439–441.

Kirk, D. 'Serious about fraud?' (2011) Journal of Criminal Law, 75(4), 249–252.

Kirkland Alert, 'The Fraud Enforcement and Recovery Act 2009', Kirkland and Ellis LLP.

Kleindienst, K., Coughlin, T. and Pasquarella, J. 'Computer crimes', (2009) American Criminal Law Review, 46, 315–392.

Kliesen, K. and Tatom, J. 'The recent credit crunch: the neglected dimensions' (1992) Federal Reserve Bank of St. Louis Review, 74(5), 18–36.

Klock, M. 'Lessons learned from Bernard Madoff: why we should partially privatise the Barney Fifes at the SEC' (2010) Arizona State Law Journal, 42, 783–835.

Koller, C. *Diffusion of innovation and fraud in the subprime mortgage market*. OhioLink ETD, 2010, available from http://etd.ohiolink.edu/send-pdf.cgi/Koller%20Cynthia.pdf?ucin1282050951, accessed 23 May 2013.

KPMG 'Boom time for fraudsters as austerity bites', 30 January 2012, available from http://www.kpmg.com/uk/en/issuesandinsights/articles publications/newsreleases/pages/fraud-barometer-boom-time-for-fraudsters-as-austerity-bites.aspx, accessed 18 March 2013.

Krawiec, K. 'Financial reform during the Great Recession: Dodd–Frank, executive compensation, and the Card Act – don't screw Joe the plumber: the sausage-making of financial reform' (2013) Arizona Law Review, Spring, 55, 53–103.

Krebs, J. 'The rating agencies: where we have been and where do we go from here?' (2009) Journal of Business, Entrepreneurship and the Law, Fall, 3, 133–164.

Krehely, K. 'Government sponsored enterprises: a discussion of the federal subsidy of Fannie Mae and Freddie Mac' (2002) North Carolina Banking Institute, 6, 519–544.

Kuttner, R. 'A real Pecora Commission', 31 May 2009, available from http://www.huffingtonpost.com/robert-kuttner/a-real-pecora-commission_b_209572.html, accessed 11 June 2013.

Labour 'Osborne is continuing to duck the radical banking reform we need – Ed Balls', 8 July 2013, available from http://www.labour.org.uk/osborne-continuing-to-duck-radical-banking-reform-we-need,2013-07-08, accessed 11 July 2013.

Lander, M. and Myers, S. 'Buyout plan for Wall Street is a hard sell on Capitol Hill', 23 September 2008, available from http://www. nytimes.com/2008/09/24/business/economy/24fannie.html?_r=1&, accessed 7 August 2013.

Lastra, R. 'Lender of last resort, an international perspective' (1999) International and Comparative Law Quarterly, 48(2), 340–361.

Lathrop, D. 'FBI lacks resources to fight boom in mortgage fraud: 2,500 agents reassigned to terrorism weren't replaced', 5 July 2007 available from http://www.highbeam.com/doc/1G1-125637095.html, accessed 3 May 2013.

Laughlin, R. 'Causes of the savings and loan crisis' (1991) Fordham Law Review, 59, 6(11), 301–322.

Lavargna, C. 'Government-sponsored enterprises are "too big to fail" balancing public and private interests' (1993) Hastings Law Journal, 44, 991–1083.

Law Commission *Fraud and deception – further proposals from the Criminal Law Team*, Informal Discussion Paper (Law Commission: London, 2000).

Law Commission *Legislating the criminal code: fraud and deception – Law Commission Consultation Paper no 155* (Law Commission: London, 1999).

Lee, J. 'Regulatory regimes and norms for directors' remuneration: EU, UK and Belgian law compared' (2012) European Business Organization Law Review, 13(4), 599–637.

Lehman Brothers Holdings Inc. *Quarterly report* (Form 10-Q), 89,31 May 2008, available from http://www.rns-pdf.londonstockexchange.com/rns/8436Z_1-2008-7-24.pdf, accessed 25 March 2013.

Leong, A. 'Definitional analysis: the war on terror and organised crime' (2004) Journal of Money Laundering Control, 8(1), 19–36.

Lever, J. and Pike, J. 'Cartel agreements, criminal conspiracy and the statutory "cartel offence": part 2' (2005) European Competition Law Review, 26(3), 164–172.

Levitin, A. 'The crisis without a face: emerging narratives of the financial crisis' (2009) University of Miami Law Review, 63, 999–1010.

Lewis, A., Pretorius, R. and Radmore, E. 'Outsourcing in the financial services sector' (2013) Compliance Officer Bulletin, May, 106, 1–34.

Lewis, K. 'Rebuilding a house of cards: envisioning sustainable housing policy housing' (2009) Washington University Journal of Law and Policy, 35, 473–517.

Lewis, M. and Einhorn, D. 'The end of the financial world as we know it', 3 January 2009, available from http://www.nytimes.com/2009/01/04/opinion/04lewiseinhorn.html?pagewanted=all&_r=0, accessed 2 October 2013.

Lexis Nexis *The Lexis Nexis 14th annual mortgage fraud report* (Lexis Nexis: London, 2012).

Liberal Democrats 'Vince Cable F21 speech to the Liberal Democrat Autumn Conference', 16 September 2013, available from http://www.libdems.org.uk/speeches_detail.aspx?title=Vince_Cable_F21_speech_to_the_Liberal_Democrat_Autumn_Conference&pPK=e4e269ed-a26f-4177-bd2f-6a9dd18131a9, accessed 20 September 2013.

Lichtblau, E., Johnston, D. and Nixon, E. 'F.B.I. struggles to handle financial fraud cases', 19 October 2008, available from http://www.nytimes.com/2008/10/19/washington/19fbi.html?pagewanted=all&_r=0, accessed 8 August 2013.

Ligere, E. 'Legislative comment EU Regulation 3642/09 on credit rating agencies' (2010) Journal of International Banking Law and Regulation, 25(1), 1–4.

Lim, C. 'Libor, strategy, and the international cartel investigations' (2013) Journal of European Competition Law and Practice, first published online 8 January 2013, doi:10.1093/jeclap/lps077.

Lin, D. 'Bank recapitalizations: a comparative perspective' (2013) Harvard Journal on Legislation, Summer, 50, 513–544.

Linn, C. 'The way we live now: the case for mandating fraud reporting by persons involved in real estate closings and settlements' (2009) Journal of Financial Crime, 16(1), 7–27.

Lloyd-Bostock, S. 'The Jubilee Line jurors: does their experience strengthen the argument for judge-only trial in long and complex fraud cases?' (2007) Criminal Law Review, April, 255–273.

Lopez, L. and Viswanatha, A. 'S&P asks federal judge to dismiss U.S. civil fraud lawsuit', 22 April 2013, available from http://www.reuters.com/article/2013/04/22/sandp-fraud-lawsuit-idUSN9E8KE00P20130422, accessed 29 May 2013.

Lover, C. 'The Fraud Enforcement and Recovery Act of 2009 and the expansion of the liability under the False Claims Act' (2012) Utah Law Review, 1129–1154.

Lowell, A. and Arnold, K. 'Corporate crime after 2000: a new law enforcement challenge or déjà vu?' (2003) American Criminal Law Review, Spring, 40, 219–240.

Luhrs, J. 'Encouraging litigation: why Dodd–Frank goes too far in eliminating the procedural difficulties in Sarbanes–Oxley' (2012) Hastings Business Law Journal, Winter, 8, 175–189.

Lupica, L. 'Credit rating agencies, structured securities, and the way out of the abyss' (2009) Review of Banking and Financial Law, Spring, 28, 639–673.

Lynch, T. 'Deeply and persistently conflicted: credit rating agencies in the current regulatory environment' (2009) Case Western Reserve Law Review, Winter, 59, 227–304.

Macchiavello, E. 'Securitisation in microfinance and global financial crisis: innovation or Trojan horse?' (2013) Journal of International Banking Law and Regulation, 28(3), 109–122.

MacDonald, R. 'Setting examples, not settling: towards a new SEC enforcement paradigm' (2012) Texas Law Review, 91, 419–447.

MacKay, S. 'Major fraud against the United States' (1992) Army Lawyer, September, 7–14.

Madia, M. 'The bank fraud act: a risk of loss requirement?' (2005) University of Chicago Law Review, 72, 1445–1471.

Mahallati, N. 'Chapter 174: California's dedicated mortgage fraud statute' (2010) McGeorge Law Review, 41, 712–724.

Mahendra, B. 'Fighting serious fraud' (2002) New Law Journal, 152(7020), 289.

Maher, C. 'Crisis not averted: lack of criminal prosecutions leaves limited consequences for those responsible for the financial crisis' (2013) New England Journal on Criminal and Civil Confinement, 39, 459–476.

Malkawi, B. 'Financial derivatives between Western legal tradition and Islamic finance: a comparative approach' (2011) Journal of International Banking Law and Regulation, 26(6), 276–284.

Markoff, G. 'Arthur Andersen and the myth of the corporate death penalty: corporate criminal convictions in the twenty-first century' (2013) University of Pennsylvania Journal of Business Law, 15, 797–836.

Markopolos, H. *No one would listen* (Wiley: New Jersey, 2010).

Markopolos, H. 'Testimony before the US Senate Banking, Housing and Urban Affairs Committee', 4 February 2009, available from http://www.banking.senate.gov/public/index.cfm?FuseAction=Files.View&FileStore_id=a157968b-2c5f-4477-a9d6-7042fec46593, accessed 14 October 2013.

Marsh, J. and McDonnell, B. 'Handling price sensitive information: a guide to the legal and regulatory obligations' (2005) Compliance Officer Bulletin, February, 23, 1–39.

Marshall, H., Leonard, C., Bibby, R.P., Paul, R. and Zahabi, E. 'Annual review 2012' (2013) Compliance Officer Bulletin, January, 102, 1–30.

Marshall, H., Leonard, C. and Siriwardhane, A. 'The regulation of short selling in the UK' (2009) Compliance Officer Bulletin, February, 63, 1–29.

Marshall, J. *The financial crisis in the US: key events, causes and responses – House of Commons Research Paper 09/034* (House of Commons Library: London, 2009).

Marshall, J. *US Congressional debates on the financial crisis: key players, policy and future regulation – House of Commons Research Paper 09/58* (House of Commons Library: London, 2009).

Mason, H. 'No one saw it coming – again systemic risk and state foreclosure proceedings: why a national uniform foreclosure law is necessary' (2012) University of Miami Law Review, Fall, 67, 41–93.

Masters, B. 'Corporate fraud rises to £1.2bn', 19 January 2009, available from http://www.ft.com/cms/s/0/344179e6-e5c9-11dd-afe4-0000779fd2ac.html#axzz2OpRGItRM, accessed 28 March 2013.

Masters, B. 'Fraud watchdog weakened by budget cuts', 27 March 2011, available from http://www.ft.com/cms/s/0/8221aba2-58b5-11e0-9b8a-00144feab49a.html#axzz2XgX4w3hV, accessed 30 June 2013.

Masters, B. and Stafford, P. 'Scandal-plagued Libor moves to NYSE', 9 July 2013, available from http://www.ft.com/cms/s/0/73332222-e87f-11e2-aead-00144feabdc0.html#axzz2YkarYqma, accessed 12 July 2013.

Mattingly, P. and Schoenberg, T. 'U.S. mortgage fraud initiative included Bush-era case', 11 October 2012, available from http://www.bloomberg.com/news/2012-10-10/u-s-mortgage-fraud-initiative-data-included-older-cases.html, accessed 1 August 2013.

Mattingly, P. and Schoenberg, T. 'U.S. mortgage group forced to correct initiative stats', 9 August 2013, available from http://www.bloomberg.com/news/2013-08-09/u-s-mortgage-group-forced-to-correct-initiative-stats.html, accessed 14 October 2013.

Maximilian, J. 'The sub-prime crisis, the credit squeeze and Northern Rock: the lessons to be learned' (2008) Journal of Financial Regulation and Compliance, 16(1), 19–34.

McCann, N. 'Federal law enforcement in the home mortgage lending market enhanced by the Fraud Enforcement and Recovery Act of 2009' (2010) Loyola Consumer Law Review, 22, 354–390.

McDonald, J. 'Similarities between the savings & loans crisis and today's current financial crisis: what the past can tell us about the future' (2009) Defence Counsel Journal, October, 76, 470–480.

McDonald, O. 'The American mortgage market' (2012) Company Lawyer, 33(6), 183–184.

McDonnel, B. 'Don't panic! Defending cowardly interventions during and after the financial crisis' (2011) Penn State Law Review, Summer, 116, 1–75.
McDonnell, J., Bell, O., Butler, J., De Marco, L., Heaton, E., Purewal, J. and Maxwell, B. 'Annual review 2010' (2010/2011) Compliance Bulletin Officer, December/January, 82, 1–39.
McGowan, L. 'Criminal law legislation update' (2013) Journal of Criminal Law, 77(4), 279–280.
McNonagle, D. 'In pursuit of safety and soundness: an analysis of the OCC's anti-predatory lending standard' (2004) Fordham Urban Law Journal, November, 31, 1533–1554.
McVea, H. 'Credit rating agencies, the subprime mortgage debacle and global governance: the EU strikes back' (2010) International and Comparative Law Quarterly, 59(3), 701–730.
McVea, H. 'Hedge fund asset valuations and the work of the International Organization of Securities Commissions (IOSCO)' (2008) International and Comparative Law Quarterly, 57(1), 1–24.
Meloni, K. 'New LIBOR new danger?' (2013) Butterworths Journal of International Banking and Financial Law, 28(4), 234–235.
Messerschmitt, D. 'Overview of the subprime mortgage market' (2007) Review of Banking and Financial Law, Fall, 27, 3–11.
Michaud, C. 'FBI resources limited for economic probes: report', 18 October 2008, available from http://www.reuters.com/article/2008/10/18/us-fbi-resources-idUSTRE49H23S20081018?feedType=RSS&feedName=domesticNews, accessed 3 May 2013.
Minder, R. 'Portugal agrees to a $116 billion bailout', 3 May 2011, available from http://www.nytimes.com/2011/05/04/business/global/04portugal.html?_r=0, accessed 26 February 2013.
Mitchell, T. 'Growing inequality and racial economic gaps' (2013) Howard Law Journal, Spring, 56, 849–890.
Mizen, P. 'The credit crunch of 2007–2008: a discussion of the background, market reactions, and policy responses' (2008) Federal Reserve Bank of St. Louis Review, 90(5), 531–567.
Mollenkamp, C. 'Bankers cast doubt on key rate amid crisis', 16 April 2008, available from http://online.wsj.com/article/SB120831164167818299.html, accessed 1 October 2012.
Moloney, N. 'Reform or revolution? The financial crisis, EU financial markets law, and the European Securities and Markets Authority' (2011) International and Comparative Legal Quarterly, 60(2), 521–533.
Monteith, C. 'The Bribery Act 2010: part 3: enforcement' (2011) Criminal Law Review, 2, 111–121.

Moohr, G. 'The balance among corporate criminal liability, private civil suits, and regulatory enforcement' (2009) American Criminal Law Review, Fall, 46, 1459–1479.

Moore, J. and Morris, N. 'Bankers could face jail after report urges the Government to introduce new criminal offence for reckless management', 19 June 2013, available from http://www.independent.co.uk/news/uk/politics/bankers-could-face-jail-after-report-urges-the-government-to-introduce-new-criminal-offence-for-reckless-management-8664137.html, accessed 27 June 2013.

Moosa, I. 'The regulation of short selling: a pragmatic view' (2012) Journal of Banking Regulation, 13(3), 211–227.

Morgan, G. 'Reforming OTC markets: the politics and economics of technical fixes' (2012) European Business Organization Law Review, 13(3), 391–412.

Morgan, H. 'Credit rating agencies and regulatory reform: the case of Moody's Investors Services' (2012) Journal of International Banking Law and Regulation, 26(8), 389–397.

Morgenson, G. and Story, L. 'In financial crisis, no prosecutions of top figures', 14 April 2011, available from http://www.nytimes.com/2011/04/14/business/14prosecute.html?pagewanted=all&_r=0, accessed 27 September 2013.

Mortgage Bankers' Association 'MBA Signs memorandum of agreement with FBI to promote use of FBI's Mortgage Fraud Warning Notice', 8 March 2007, available from http://www.mortgagebankers.org/NewsandMedia/PressCenter/50728.htm, accessed 8 August 2013.

Moye, J. 'Are we bulletproof? A defensive business strategy to protect health care companies from False Claims Act litigation and corporate integrity agreements' (2010) University of Baltimore Law Forum, Fall, 41, 24–42.

Moye, J. 'Let's put the fear in the FERA! Suggestions to make the Fraud Enforcement and Recovery Act of 2009 a strong fraud deterrent' (2011) Southern Illinois University Law Journal, Spring, 35, 421–432.

Mulligan, C. 'From AAA to F: the credit rating agencies failed America and what can be done to protect investors' (2009) Boston College Law Review, September, 50, 1275–1305.

Murdock, C. 'The Dodd–Frank Wall Street Reform and Consumer Protection Act: what caused the financial crisis and will Dodd–Frank prevent future crises?' (2011) SMU Law Review, Fall, 64, 1243–1327.

Murdock, C. 'Why not tell the truth? Deceptive practices and the economic meltdown' (2010) Loyola University Chicago Law Journal, Summer, 41, 801–884.

Murphy, B. 'Credit rating immunity? How the hands-off approach towards credit rating agencies led to the subprime credit crisis and the

need for greater accountability' (2010) Oklahoma Law Review, Summer, 62, 735–792.
National Fraud Authority *Annual fraud indicator 2010* (National Fraud Authority: London, 2010).
National Fraud Authority *Annual fraud indicator 2011* (National Fraud Authority: London, 2011).
National Fraud Authority *Annual fraud indicator 2012* (National Fraud Authority: London, 2012).
National Fraud Authority *Annual fraud indicator 2013* (National Fraud Authority: London, 2013).
National Fraud Authority *The National Fraud Strategy – a new approach to combating fraud* (National Fraud Authority: London, 2010).
National Fraud Authority *Working together to stop mortgage fraud: progress report* (National Fraud Authority: London, 2011).
National Fraud Intelligence Bureau 'About us', n/d, available from http://www.cityoflondon.police.uk/CityPolice/About/, accessed 16 September 2013.
Nationwide White Collar Crime Centre *National public survey on white collar crime* (Nationwide White Collar Crime Centre: Fairmont, 2011).
Neate, R. 'Tchenguiz brothers seek millions from Serious Fraud Office', 3 December 2012, available from http://m.guardian.co.uk/business/2012/dec/03/tchenguiz-brothers-millions-damages-sfo, accessed 18 March 2013.
Nemeroff, M. 'Dodd–Frank: frankly an inefficient form of corporate governance' (2012) University of Florida Journal of Law and Public Policy, December, 23, 431–445.
Nesvetailova, A. 'The crisis of invented money: liquidity illusion and the global credit meltdown' (2010) Theoretical Inquiries in Law, January, 11, 125–147.
Neuman, N. 'A Sarbanes–Oxley for credit rating agencies? A comparison of the roles of auditors' and credit rating agencies' conflicts of interest played in recent financial crises' (2010) University of Pennsylvania Journal of Business Law, Spring, 12, 921–946.
New York Federal Reserve 'USD Libor', 28 August 2008, available from http://www.newyorkfed.org/newsevents/news/markets/2012/libor/August_28_2007_mass_distribution_emails.pdf, accessed 1 October 2012.
New York Times 'Bernanke: subprime hit could top $100bn', 19 July 2007, available from http://money.cnn.com/2007/07/19/news/economy/bernanke/, accessed 21 November 2012.
New York Times 'Text of draft proposal for Bailout Plan', 20 September 2008, available from http://www.nytimes.com/2008/09/21/business/21draftcnd.html, accessed 7 August 2013.

Nguyen, T. and Pontell, H. 'Fraud and inequality in the subprime mortgage crisis' in Deflem, M. (ed.), *Economic crisis and crime* (Emerald: Bingley, 2011).

Nguyen, T. and Pontell, H. 'Mortgage origination fraud and the global economic crisis' (2010) Criminology and Public Policy, 9(3), 591–612.

Nichols, C. 'Addressing inept SEC enforcement efforts: lessons from Madoff, the hedge fund industry, and title IV of the Dodd–Frank Act for the US and global financial systems' (2011) Northwestern Journal of International Law and Business, 31, 637–698.

Nikolić, B. 'Rise and fall of regulatory state in financial markets' (2013) Journal of International Banking Law and Regulation, 28(1), 1–8.

Novogradac, M. and Graff, G. 'Impact of the Housing and Economic Recovery Act of 2008 on current and future low-income housing tax credit properties' (2008) Journal of Affordable Housing, 18(1), 47–70.

Nunziato, M. 'Aiding and abetting, a Madoff family affair: why secondary actors should be held accountable for securities fraud through the restoration of the private right of action for aiding and abetting liability under the federal security laws' (2010) Albany Law Review, 73, 603–643.

NuraKami, K. 'Mail and wire fraud' (1987) American Criminal Law Review, 24, 623–637.

Nwogugu, M. 'Corporate governance and high-risk finance: alternative methods for financing domestic/foreign emerging growth companies with inadequate collateral' (2005) Journal of International Banking Law and Regulation, 20(10), 541–558.

Nwogugu, M. 'Illegality of securitisation: bankruptcy issues and theories of securitisation' (2008) Journal of International Banking Law and Regulation, 23(7), 363–377.

Nwogugu, M. 'Securitisation is illegal: racketeer influenced and corrupt organisations, usury, antitrust and tax issues' (2008) Journal of International Banking Law and Regulation, 23(6), 316–332.

O'Donnell, M. and Planer, K. 'If it sounds too good to be true: identifying and avoiding common mortgage fraud scams' (2008) New Jersey Lawyer, October, 254, 54–57.

Omarova, S. 'The Dodd–Frank Act: a new deal for a new age?' (2011) North Carolina Banking Institute, March, 15, 83–98.

Ormerod, D. 'Conspiracy: conspiracy to defraud – whether scope of offence extends to price fixing' (2009) Criminal Law Review, 6, 433–437.

Ormerod, D. 'Prosecution: insider dealing – Criminal Justice Act 1993 s.61' (2009) Criminal Law Review, 6, 445–449.

Ormerod, D. 'The Fraud Act 2006 – criminalising lying?' (2007) Criminal Law Review, March, 193–219.

Owens, R. and Schreft, S. 'Identifying credit crunches' (1995) Contemporary Economic Policy, 13(2), 63–76.

Paez, G. 'LTCM and other major hedge fund failures: part 2' (2009) Journal of International Banking Law and Regulation, 24(6), 304–312.

Page, F. 'Defining fraud: an argument in favour of a general offence of fraud' (1997) Journal of Financial Crime, 4(4), 287–308.

Palmer, A. and Ryder, N. 'The Economic Crime Agency' (2011) Financial Regulation International, April, 1–3.

Parker, G. 'George Osborne vows to get tough and raise standards in City', 9 July 2013, available from http://www.ft.com/cms/s/0/1c3a3a66-e71f-11e2-8a57-00144feabdc0.html#axzz2YkarYqma, accessed 11 July 2013.

Parkinson, S. 'The cartel offence under the Enterprise Act 2002' (2004) Company Lawyer, 25(6), 187–189

Parliamentary Commission on Banking Standards *Changing banking for good* (Parliamentary Commission on Banking Standards: London, 2013).

Parliamentary Commission on Banking Standards 'Parliamentary Commission on Banking Standards', n/d, available from http://www.parliament.uk/business/committees/committees-a-z/joint-select/professional-standards-in-the-banking-industry/news/, accessed 25 June 2013.

Partnoy, F. 'Rethinking regulation of credit-rating agencies: an institutional investor perspective' (2010) Journal of International Banking Law and Regulation, 25(4), 188–199.

Patel, A. 'The bailout of Fannie Mae and Freddie Mac' (2008) Review of Banking and Financial Law, 28, 21–30.

Patterson, L. and Koller, C. 'Diffusion of fraud through subprime lending' in Deflem, M. (ed.), *Economic crisis and crime* (Emerald: Bingley, 2011).

Payne, J. 'The regulation of short selling and its reform in Europe' (2012) European Business Organization Law Review, 13(3), 413–440.

Pazicky, L. 'A new arrow in the quiver of federal securities fraud prosecutors: section 807 of the Sarbanes–Oxley Act of 2002' (2003) Washington University Law Quarterly, 81, 801–828.

Peat, R. and Mason, I. 'Credible deterrence in action: the FSA brings a series of cases against traders' (2009) Company Lawyer, 30(9), 278–279.

Peek, J. and Rosengren, E. Crunching the recovery: bank capital and the role of bank credit. *Conference Series[Proceedings]* (1992). Federal Reserve Bank of Boston, 151–186.

Perri, F. and Brody, R. 'The optics of fraud: affiliations that enhance offender credibility' (2012) Journal of Financial Crime, 19(4), 355–370.

Perry, J., Moulton, R., Barwick, G., Small, R., Green, J. and Kay, N. 'The new UK regulatory landscape' (2001) Compliance Officer Bulletin, March, 84, 1–33.

Peters, J. and Romeo, S. 'Enron founder dies before sentencing', 5 July 2006, available from http://www.nytimes.com/2006/07/05/business/05cnd-lay.html?_r=0, accessed 18 October 2013.

Peterson, C. 'Federalism and predatory lending: unmasking the deregulatory agenda' (2005) Temple Law Review, Spring, 1–98.

Peterson, C. 'Predatory structured finance' (2007) Cardozo Law Review, April, 28, 2185–2282.

Pickford, J. 'Banking Commission plans get City staff a little hot under collar', 19 June 2013, available from http://www.ft.com/cms/s/0/b3605ff2-d8fa-11e2-a6cf-00144feab7de.html#axzz2XEtRV9MG, accessed 25 June 2013.

Piekarski, M. 'Ratings agency accountability' (2008) Review of Banking and Financial Law, Spring, 27, 272–284.

Pizzo, S., Fricker, M. and Muolo, P. *Inside job: the looting of America's savings and loans* (McGraw-Hill: New York, 1989).

Podgor, E. 'Criminal fraud' (1999) American University Law Review, 48, 729–768.

Podgor, E. 'Introduction: examining white collar crime with trifocals' (2011) Fordham Urban Law Journal, December, 39, 299–308.

Podgor, E. 'White collar crime: a letter from the future' (2007) Ohio State Journal of Criminal Law, 5, 247–255.

Podgor, E. 'White-collar-crime and the recession: was the chicken or egg first?' (2010) University of Chicago Legal Forum, 205–222.

Pontell, H. and Calavita, K. 'The savings and loans industry' (1993) Crime and Justice, 18, 203–242.

Pontell, H., Black, W. and Geis, G. 'Too big to fail, too powerful to prosecute? On the absence of criminal prosecutions after the 2009 financial meltdown' (2014) Crime, Law and Society, 61(1), 1–13.

Porter, A. 'David Cameron calls for criminal actions against bankers', 27 January 2009, available from http://www.telegraph.co.uk/finance/newsbysector/banksandfinance/4348801/David-Cameron-calls-for-criminal-actions-against-bankers.html, accessed 7 May 2013.

Poser, N. 'Why the SEC failed: regulators against regulation' (2009) Brooklyn Journal of Corporate, Financial and Commercial Law, Spring, 3, 289.

Posner, E. and Vermeule, A. 'Crisis governance in the administrative state: 9/11 and the financial meltdown of 2008' (2009) University of Chicago Law Review, Fall, 76, 1613–1681.

President Barack Obama 'Protecting homeowners, protecting the economy', 24 August 2009, available from http://www.whitehouse.gov/blog/Protecting-Homeowners-Protecting-the-Economy, accessed 20 June 2013.

President Barack Obama 'Remarks upon signing the American Recovery & Reinvestment Act', 17 February 2009, available from http://www.presidentialrhetoric.com/speeches/02.17.09.html, accessed 27 March 2013.

Price Waterhouse Cooper *Fraud in a downturn* (Price Waterhouse Cooper: London, 2008).

Prime Minister's Office 'Prime Minister's speech', 2 May 2010, available from http://www.primeminister.gov.gr/english/2010/05/02/meeting-of-cabinet-prime-ministers-speech/, accessed 26 February 2013.

Prince, R. 'Cameron calls for criminal charges against bankers responsible for credit crunch', 15 December 2008, available from http://www.telegraph.co.uk/finance/financetopics/bernard-madoff/3775925/Cameron-calls-for-criminal-charges-against-bankers-responsible-for-credit-crunch.html, accessed 7 May 2013.

Prior, I. and Skehill, L. 'Beware the federal government bearing gifts: how the American Recovery and Reinvestment Act of 2009 could become a whistleblowing trojan horse' (2010) Suffolk University Law Review, 43, 565–586.

Protess, B. 'Post-Madoff, a greater awareness of ponzi schemes', 14 November 2011, available from http://dealbook.nytimes.com/2011/11/14/post-madoff-a-greater-awareness-of-ponzi-schemes/, accessed 3 June 2013.

Purkiss, A. 'U.K. Fraud Office hit by budget cuts, staff losses', 28 March 2011, available from http://www.bloomberg.com/news/2011-03-28/u-k-fraud-office-hit-by-budget-cuts-staff-losses-ft-reports.html, accessed 30 June 2013.

Putney, A. 'Rules, standards, and suitability: finding the correct approach to predatory lending' (2003) Fordham Law Review, April, 71, 2101–2139.

Quinn, J. 'Treasury hands control of Libor to NYSE Euronext', 9 July 2013, available from http://www.telegraph.co.uk/finance/10168894/Treasury-hands-control-of-Libor-to-NYSE-Euronext.html, accessed 12 July 2013.

Quinn, J. 'Vince Cable: RBS report recommends prosecution', 17 June 2012, available from http://www.telegraph.co.uk/finance/newsby

sector/banksandfinance/9336327/Vince-Cable-RBS-report-recommends-prosecution.html, accessed 2 July 2013.

Quintin, Y. 'Alis … da in wonderland or Greek tragedy? The dynamics of credit default swaps and the "voluntary" Greek restructuring of 2011/2012' (2012) International Business Law Journal, 2, 277–291.

Raaijmakers, G., Silverentand, L., Rank, P. and Noome, M. 'Living wills for banks' (2011) Financial Regulation International, May, 16–19.

Ramirez, K. 'Prioritizing justice: combating corporate crime from task force to top priority' (2011) Marquette Law Review, Spring, 93, 971–1019.

Ramirez, M. 'Criminal affirmance: going beyond the deterrence paradigm to examine the social meaning of declining prosecution of elite crime' (2013) Connecticut Law Review, February, 45, 865–931.

Ramirez, S. 'Dodd–Frank as maginot line' (2011) Chapman Law Review, Spring, 15, 109–132.

Randell, C. 'The Government's White Paper on the Independent Commission on Banking's recommendations' (2012) Butterworths Journal of International Banking and Financial Law, 27(8), 487–489.

Rappis, J. 'Tax aspects of the American Recovery and Reinvestment Act of 2009: on the road to recovery?' (2009) Wisconsin Lawyer, 82, 10–14.

Rasnak, S. 'USTP's civil enforcement activity targets mortgage fraud and mortgage rescue schemes' (2010) American Bankruptcy Institute Journal, March, 29, 18.

Rawlings, P. 'Reform of bank regulation in the United Kingdom: the opening salvo' (2010) Journal of International Banking Law and Regulation, 25(10), 522–528.

Rayner, G. 'Families turning to insurance fraud to beat credit crunch', 25 December 2008, available from http://www.telegraph.co.uk/finance/financialcrisis/3949048/Families-turning-to-insurance-fraud-to-beat-credit-crunch.html, accessed 28 March 2013.

Recovery.gov 'The Recovery Act', n/d, available from http://www.recovery.gov/about/pages/the_act.aspx, accessed 8 August 2012.

Reidy, J. 'The problem of proceeds in the era of FERA' (2010) American Journal of Criminal Law, Summer, 5, 295–323.

Reinhart, C. and Rogoff, K. *This time is different – eight centuries of financial folly* (Princeton University Press: Princeton, 2009).

Reinhart, V. 'A year of living dangerously: the management of the financial crisis' (2011) Journal of Economic Perspectives, 25(1), 71–90.

Reiss, D. 'Fannie Mae and Freddie Mac and the future of federal housing finance policy: a study of regulatory privilege' (2011) Alabama Law Review, 62, 907–955.

Reiss, D. 'The role of the Fannie Mae/Freddie Mac duopoly in the American housing market' (2009) Journal of Financial Regulation and Compliance, 17(3), 336–348.

Reuters 'FBI, DoJ investigate BofA's Merril deal', 18 September 2009, available from http://uk.reuters.com/article/2009/09/18/us-bankof america-fbi-idUSTRE58H3D220090918, accessed 7 October 2013.

Reuters 'Timeline: the credit crunch of 2007/2008', 5 August 2008, available from http://www.reuters.com/article/gc06/idUSL1555645 20080805, accessed 10 August 2012.

Reuters, 'Timeline: UBS investment bank mishaps and upheavals', 15 September 2007, available from http://mobile.reuters.com/article/ topNews/idUSTRE78E2FM20110915, accessed 21 November 2012.

Reuters 'UBS writes off $10 billion in subprime losses', 12 October 2007, available from http://www.msnbc.msn.com/id/22180574/ns/ business-real_estate/t/ubs-writes-billion-subprime-losses/, accessed 13 June 2013.

Reyes, E. 'News focus: who will bring a Libor claim?', 5 July 2012, available from http://www.lawgazette.co.uk/news/news-focus-who-will-bring-a-libor-claim, accessed 30 June 2013.

Richards-Carpenter, P., Sautter, E., Hayes, A., Kynoch, N., Stark, P., Baker, M., Dehra, S., Rosser, S., Plange, V. and Ali, M. 'Annual review for 2008' (2008/2009) Compliance Officer Bulletin December/January 62, 1–38.

Richman, D. and Stuntz, W. 'Al Capone's revenge: an essay on the political economy of pretextual prosecution' (2005) Columbia Law Review, March, 105, 583–639.

Rider, B. 'A serious fraud?' (2010) Company Lawyer, 31(12), 381–382.

Riley, C. and Johnston, J. 'Fraud Enforcement and Recovery Act of 2009: expanding fraud and False Claims Act liability and increasing enforcement in the wake of the economic crisis' (2009) Banking and Financial Services Policy Report, July, 28(7), 1–7.

Roberts, A. 'Prosecution: director of SFO – lawfulness of decision to discontinue prosecution' (2009) Criminal Law Review, 1, 46–49.

Romano, R. 'The Sarbanes–Oxley Act and the making of quack corporate governance' (2005) Yale Law Journal, May, 114, 1521–1603.

Rosato, J. 'Down the road to perdition: how the flaws of Basel II led to the collapse of Bear Stearns and Lehman Brothers' (2011) Connecticut Insurance Law Journal, 17, 475–500.

Rose, C. 'Legislative comment: the UK Bribery Act 2010 and accompanying guidance: belated implementation of the OECD Anti-Bribery Convention' (2012) International and Comparative Law Quarterly, 61(2), 484–499.

Rosemeyer, M. 'Is the government's takeover of AIG constitutionally permissible?' (2009) Entrepreneurial Business Law Journal, 4, 243–266.

Rowlett, J. 'The chilling effect of the Financial Institutions Reform, Recovery and Enforcement Act of 1989 and the Bank Fraud Prosecution Act of 1990: has Congress gone too far?' (1993) American Journal of Criminal Law, Winter, 20, 239–262.

Rowley, E. 'Serious Fraud Office needs proper funding, warns Tchenguiz judge', 24 May 2012, available from http://www.telegraph.co.uk/finance/financial-crime/9288330/Serious-Fraud-Office-needs-proper-funding-warns-Tchenguiz-judge.htmlm, accessed 18 March 2013.

Ruben, M. 'Forgive us our trespasses? The rise of consumer debt in modern America', February 2009, available from http://www.csa.com/discoveryguides/debt/review.pdf, accessed 14 August 2012.

Ruby, J. 'Sound and fury, confused alarms and oversight: congress, delegation, and effective responses to financial crises' (2010) Harvard Journal on Legislation, 47, 209–252.

Russel, J. 'Tchenguiz brothers launch damages case against SFO', 2 December 2012, available from http://www.telegraph.co.uk/finance/financial-crime/9717240/Tchenguiz-brothers-launch-damages-case-against-SFO.html, accessed 18 March 2013.

Russel, J. 'The case to answer for the Serious Fraud Office', 26 May 2012, available from http://www.telegraph.co.uk/finance/financial-crime/9292046/The-case-to-answer-for-the-Serious-Fraud-Office.html, accessed 30 June 2013.

Russel, J. 'UK law may struggle to bring prosecutions of Libor traders', 11 December 2012, available from http://www.telegraph.co.uk/finance/libor-scandal/9738417/UK-law-may-struggle-to-bring-prosecutions-of-Libor-traders.html, accessed 27 June 2013.

Russell, J. 'SFO given just £2m to enforce Bribery Act', 30 January 2011, available from http://www.telegraph.co.uk/finance/newsbysector/banksandfinance/8290808/SFO-given-just-2m-to-enforce-Bribery-Act.html, accessed 18 March 2013.

Ryan, J. 'Fraud "directly related" to financial crisis probed', 11 February 2009, available from http://abcnews.go.com/TheLaw/Economy/story?id=6855179&page=1, accessed 27 September 2013.

Ryder, N. 'A false sense of security? An analysis of legislative approaches towards the prevention of terrorist finance in the United States and the United Kingdom' (2007) Journal of Business Law, November, 821–850.

Ryder, N. 'An unhappy coupling' (2008) New Law Journal, 158(7319), 609.

Ryder, N. *Financial crime in the 21st century: law and policy* (Edward Elgar: Cheltenham, 2011).

Ryder, N. *Money laundering – an endless cycle? A comparative analysis of the anti-money laundering policies in the United States of America, the United Kingdom, Australia and Canada* (Routledge Cavendish: Abingdon, 2012).

Ryder, N. 'The fight against illicit finance – a critical review of the Labour government's policy' (2011) Journal of Banking Regulation, 12(3), 252–275.

Ryder, N. 'The Financial Services Authority and money laundering – a game of cat and mouse' (2008) Cambridge Law Journal, 67(3), 635–653.

Ryder, N. 'The new criminal offence of reckless misconduct for bankers' (2013) Criminal Lawyer, (216), 1–2.

Saksena, P. 'The Sarbanes–Oxley Act and occupational fraud: does the law effectively tackle the real problem?' (2009) International Company and Commercial Law Review, 20(2), 37–43.

Saladrigas, C. 'Corporate criminal liability: lessons from the Rothstein debacle' (2012) University of Miami Law Review, Winter, 66, 435–469.

Santanu, R. and Chakrabarti, B. 'Operational risk and the banking sector' (2005) Journal of International Banking Law and Regulation, 20(10), 535–540.

Sarker, R. 'Fighting fraud – a missed opportunity?' (2007) Company Lawyer, 28(8), 243–244.

Sarker, R. 'Maxwell: fraud trial of the century (case comment)' (1996) Company Lawyer, 17(4), 116–117.

Sarker, R. 'The Serious Fraud Office – quo vadis?' (1995) Company Lawyer, 16(2), 56–61.

Sarker, R. 'The trials and errors of the Guinness four' (1995) Journal of Financial Crime, 3(1), 86–88.

Savla, S. 'Serious Fraud Office powers under section 2 of the Criminal Justice Act 1987 and Police and Criminal Evidence Act 1984' (1997) Journal of Financial Crime, 4(3), 223–231.

Scannel, K. 'US cracks down on mortgage fraud', 9 October 2012, available from http://www.ft.com/cms/s/0/bcf3465c-122a-11e2-868d-00144feabdc0.html#axzz2aheJherM, accessed 1 August 2013.

Schaefer, E. 'The Credit Card Act of 2009 was not enough: a national usury rate would provide consumers with the protection they need' (2012) University of Baltimore Law Review, Summer, 41, 741–767.

Schammo, P. 'The European Securities and Markets Authority: lifting the veil on the allocation of powers' (2011) Common Market Law Review, 48(6), 1879–1913.

Schapiro, M. 'SEC Chair Mary L. Schapiro, testimony concerning the state of the financial crisis before the Financial Crisis Inquiry Commission', 14 January 2013, available from http://www.sec.gov/news/testimony/2010/ts011410mls.htm, accessed 4 June 2013.

Schipanio, C. 'Falling off the corporate ladder: prosecution for financial fraud in the United States' (2011) Company Lawyer, 32(11), 336–342.

Schuck, C. 'A new use of the responsible corporate officer doctrine: prosecuting industry insiders for mortgage fraud' (2010) Lewis and Clark Law Review, 14, 371–395.

Schwarcz, S. 'The future of securitisation' (2008) *Duke Public Law and Legal Theory Research Paper Series No. 223*.

Scott, H. 'A general evaluation of the Dodd–Frank US financial reform legislation' (2010) Journal of International Banking Law and Regulation, 25(10), 477–480.

Scott, H. 'The competitive impact of financial regulatory reform' (2011) Journal of International Banking Law and Regulation, 26(11), 527–530.

Securities and Exchange Commission *2007 performance and accountability report* (Securities and Exchange Commission: Washington DC, 2007).

Securities and Exchange Commission *2008 performance and accountability report* (Securities and Exchange Commission: Washington DC, 2008).

Securities and Exchange Commission *2009 performance and accountability report* (Securities and Exchange Commission: Washington DC, 2009).

Securities and Exchange Commission 'About the division of enforcement', n/d, available from http://www.sec.gov/divisions/enforce/about.htm, accessed 8 August 2013.

Securities and Exchange Commission 'Citigroup to pay $285 million to settle SEC charges for misleading investors about CDO tied to housing market', 19 October 2011, available from http://www.sec.gov/news/press/2011/2011-214.htm, accessed 17 June 2013.

Securities and Exchange Commission 'Court approves SEC settlements with two former Bear Stearns hedge fund portfolio managers; SEC bars managers from regulated industries', 25 June 2012, available from http://www.sec.gov/litigation/litreleases/2012/lr22398.htm, accessed 18 June 2013.

Securities and Exchange Commission 'CR Intrinsic agrees to pay more than $600 million in largest-ever settlement for insider trading case', 15 March 2013, available from http://www.sec.gov/news/press/2013/2013-41.htm, accessed 18 March 2013.

Securities and Exchange Commission 'Credit agreement between American International Group and Federal Reserve Bank of New York', 22

September 2008, available from http://www.sec.gov/Archives/edgar/data/5272/000095012308011496/y71452exv99w1.htm, accessed 25 March 2013.

Securities and Exchange Commission 'EC brings charges in Puerto Rico-based Ponzi scheme targeting Evangelical Christians and factory workers', 21 August 2012, available from http://www.sec.gov/News/PressRelease/Detail/PressRelease/1365171483948, accessed 12 August 2013.

Securities and Exchange Commission 'Former Countrywide CEO Angelo Mozilo to pay SEC's largest-ever financial penalty against a public company's senior executive', 15 October 2010, available from http://www.sec.gov/news/press/2010/2010-197.htm, accessed 7 October 2013.

Securities and Exchange Commission 'Goldman Sachs agrees to pay record $550m to settle SEC charges related to subprime mortgage CDO', 15 October 2010, available from http://www.sec.gov/news/press/2010/2010-123.htm, accessed 7 October 2013.

Securities and Exchange Commission 'J.P. Morgan to pay $153.6 million to settle SEC charges of misleading investors in CDO tied to U.S. housing market', 21 June 2011, available from http://www.sec.gov/news/press/2011/2011-131.htm, accessed 17 June 2013.

Securities and Exchange Commission 'N.Y.-based investment advisory firm and founder settle SEC charges for fraudulent management of CDOS', 7 September 2012, available from http://www.sec.gov/news/press/2012/2012-184.htm, accessed 17 June 2013.

Securities and Exchange Commission *Office of Investigation's investigation of failure of the SEC to uncover Bernard Madoff's Ponzi scheme* (Securities and Exchange Commission: Washington DC, 2009).

Securities and Exchange Commission 'Remarks during news conference call about enforcement actions against J.P. Morgan and Credit Suisse', 16 November 2012, available from http://www.sec.gov/news/speech/2012/spch111612rk.htm, accessed 18 June 2013.

Securities and Exchange Commission *Report on the role and function of credit rating agencies in the operation of the securities markets* (Securities and Exchange Commission: Washington DC, 2002).

Securities and Exchange Commission 'SEC charges 14 sales agents in $415 million Long Island-based Ponzi scheme', 12 June 2012, available from http://www.sec.gov/News/PressRelease/Detail/PressRelease/1365171482580, accessed 12 August 2013.

Securities and Exchange Commission 'SEC charges Cincinnati resident and Delaware firm with offering fraud', 3 June 2013, available from http://www.sec.gov/litigation/litreleases/2013/lr22712.htm, accessed 12 August 2013.

Securities and Exchange Commission 'SEC charges Citigroup and two executives for misleading investors about exposure to subprime mortgage assets', 29 July 2010, available from http://www.sec.gov/news/press/2010/2010-136.htm, accessed 17 June 2013.

Securities and Exchange Commission 'SEC charges college football hall of fame coach in $80 million Ponzi scheme', 12 August 2012, available from http://www.sec.gov/News/PressRelease/Detail/PressRelease/1365171483824, accessed 12 August 2013.

Securities and Exchange Commission 'SEC charges Connecticut-based hedge fund manager for fraudulent misuse of investor assets', 28 January 2011, available from http://www.sec.gov/news/press/2011/2011-30.htm, accessed 12 August 2013.

Securities and Exchange Commission 'SEC charges feeders to Petters Ponzi scheme', 9 November 2011, available from http://www.sec.gov/news/press/2011/2011-237.htm, accessed 12 August 2013.

Securities and Exchange Commission 'SEC charges Florida broker in astrology-based Ponzi scheme', 21 June 2012, available from http://www.sec.gov/News/PressRelease/Detail/PressRelease/1365171482724, accessed 12 August 2013.

Securities and Exchange Commission 'SEC charges Forex Ponzi operator who fled after scheme unraveled', 15 July 2011, available from http://www.sec.gov/news/press/2011/2011-147.htm, accessed 12 August 2013.

Securities and Exchange Commission 'SEC charges former American Home Mortgage executives for misleading investors about company's financial condition', 28 April 2009, available from http://www.sec.gov/news/press/2009/2009-92.htm, accessed 17 June 2013.

Securities and Exchange Commission 'SEC charges former officers of subprime lender New Century with fraud', 7 December 2009, available from http://www.sec.gov/news/press/2009/2009-258.htm, accessed 18 June 2013.

Securities and Exchange Commission 'SEC charges Goldman Sachs with fraud in structuring and marketing of CDO tied to subprime mortgages', 16 April 2010, available from http://www.sec.gov/news/press/2010/2010-59.htm, accessed 17 June 2013.

Securities and Exchange Commission 'SEC charges J.P. Morgan and Credit Suisse with misleading investors in RMBS offerings', 16 November 2012, available from http://www.sec.gov/news/press/2012/2012-233.htm, accessed 17 June 2013.

Securities and Exchange Commission 'SEC charges Mizuho Securities USA with misleading investors by obtaining false credit ratings for CDO', 18 July 2012, available from http://www.sec.gov/news/press/2012/2012-139.htm, accessed 18 June 2013.

Securities and Exchange Commission 'SEC charges New Jersey man in real estate investment scam', 17 May 2012, available from http://www.sec.gov/News/PressRelease/Detail/PressRelease/1365171489172, accessed 12 August 2013.
Securities and Exchange Commission 'SEC charges New Mexico real estate magnate in $80 million Ponzi scheme', 24 March 2010, available from http://www.sec.gov/news/press/2010/2010-43.htm, accessed 12 August 2013.
Securities and Exchange Commission 'SEC charges New York-based money manager and firm touting ties to Belgian royal family', 11 June 2010, available from http://www.sec.gov/news/press/2010/2010-100.htm, accessed 12 August 2013.
Securities and Exchange Commission 'SEC charges Palm Beach County investment adviser with running a Ponzi scheme and stealing client funds', 22 June 2010, available from http://www.sec.gov/news/press/2010/2010-107.htm, accessed 12 August 2013.
Securities and Exchange Commission 'SEC charges perpetrator of Washington-area Ponzi scheme', 18 November 2011, available from http://www.sec.gov/news/press/2011/2011-246.htm, accessed 12 August 2013.
Securities and Exchange Commission 'SEC charges perpetrators of $300 million Ponzi scheme involving purported gold mining investments', 10 June 2010, available from http://www.sec.gov/news/press/2010/2010-99.htm, accessed 12 August 2013.
Securities and Exchange Commission 'SEC charges Ponzi schemer targeting church congregations', 12 April 2012, available from http://www.sec.gov/News/PressRelease/Detail/PressRelease/1365171488284, accessed 12 August 2013.
Securities and Exchange Commission 'SEC charges prominent Miami Beach businessman in $900 million Ponzi scheme', 21 April 2010, available from http://www.sec.gov/news/press/2010/2010-63.htm, accessed 12 August 2013.
Securities and Exchange Commission 'SEC charges promoters of "green" investments with operating $30 million Ponzi scheme based in Denver area', 16 November 2009, available from http://www.sec.gov/news/press/2009/2009-247.htm, accessed 12 August 2013.
Securities and Exchange Commission 'SEC charges real estate executives in Florida-based $300 million investment scheme', 30 January 2013, available from http://www.sec.gov/News/PressRelease/Detail/PressRelease/1365171513950, accessed 12 August 2013.
Securities and Exchange Commission 'SEC charges Schwab entities and two executives with making misleading statements', 11 January 2011,

available from http://www.sec.gov/news/press/2011/2011-7.htm, accessed 28 October 2013.
Securities and Exchange Commission 'SEC charges three executives with conducting $230 million investment scheme at Ohio-based company', 16 March 2011, available from http://www.sec.gov/news/press/2011/2011-67.htm, accessed 12 August 2013.
Securities and Exchange Commission 'SEC charges two executives in Ponzi scheme at Dallas-based medical insurance company', 17 June 2013, available from http://www.sec.gov/News/PressRelease/Detail/PressRelease/1365171574926, accessed 12 August 2013.
Securities and Exchange Commission 'SEC charges two feeders for one of south Florida's largest-ever Ponzi schemes', 22 May 2012, available from http://www.sec.gov/News/PressRelease/Detail/PressRelease/1365171482252, accessed 12 August 2013.
Securities and Exchange Commission 'SEC charges two Florida men in Ponzi scheme defrauding teachers and retirees', 22 August 2011, available from http://www.sec.gov/news/press/2011/2011-171.htm, accessed 12 August 2013.
Securities and Exchange Commission 'SEC charges two Florida-based fund managers with facilitating Petters Ponzi scheme', 14 October 2010, available from http://www.sec.gov/news/press/2010/2010-195.htm, accessed 12 August 2013.
Securities and Exchange Commission 'SEC charges two former Bear Stearns hedge fund managers with fraud', 19 June 2008, available from http://www.sec.gov/news/press/2008/2008-115.htm, accessed 18 June 2013.
Securities and Exchange Commission 'SEC enforcement actions addressing misconduct that led to or arose from the financial crisis', 1 September 2013, available from http://www.sec.gov/spotlight/enf-actions-fc.shtml, accessed 7 October 2013.
Securities and Exchange Commission 'SEC enforcement actions against Ponzi schemes', n/d, available from http://www.sec.gov/spotlight/enf-actions-ponzi.shtml, accessed 28 October 2013.
Securities and Exchange Commission 'SEC files emergency action to halt fraudulent scheme at Albany-based firm', 20 April 2010, available from http://www.sec.gov/news/press/2010/2010-62.htm, accessed 12 August 2013.
Securities and Exchange Commission 'SEC files emergency action to halt green-product themed Ponzi scheme', 6 October 2011, available from http://www.sec.gov/news/press/2011/2011-201.htm, accessed 12 August 2013.
Securities and Exchange Commission 'SEC halts $47 million investment fraud at Utah-based payday loan companies', 28 March 2011, available

from http://www.sec.gov/news/press/2011/2011-73.htm, accessed 12 August 2013.

Securities and Exchange Commission 'SEC halts $100 million real-estate based Ponzi scheme', 25 June 2012, available from http://www.sec.gov/News/PressRelease/Detail/PressRelease/1365171482748, accessed 12 August 2013.

Securities and Exchange Commission 'SEC halts $105 million Ponzi scheme by U.S. Virgin Islands-based money manager', 28 June 2010, available from http://www.sec.gov/news/press/2010/2010-112.htm, accessed 12 August 2013.

Securities and Exchange Commission 'SEC halts father–son Ponzi scheme in Utah involving purported real estate investments', 15 December 2011, available from http://www.sec.gov/news/press/2011/2011-266.htm, accessed 12 August 2013.

Securities and Exchange Commission 'SEC halts Ponzi scheme by co-founder of China Voice Holding Corp.', 29 April 2011, available from http://www.sec.gov/news/press/2011/2011-101.htm, accessed 12 August 2013.

Securities and Exchange Commission 'SEC obtained emergency asset freeze in diamond-themed Ponzi scheme', 23 November 2010, available from http://www.sec.gov/news/press/2010/2010-231.htm, accessed 12 August 2013.

Securities and Exchange Commission 'SEC obtains asset freeze against co-founder of Canopy Financial in $75 million offering fraud', 2 December 2009, available from http://www.sec.gov/news/press/2009/2009-257.htm, accessed 12 August 2013.

Securities and Exchange Commission 'SEC obtains asset freeze in Minnesota-based foreign currency trading scheme', 24 November 2009, available from http://www.sec.gov/news/press/2009/2009-253.htm, accessed 12 August 2013.

Securities and Exchange Commission 'SEC shuts down $42 million Ponzi-like scheme', 28 June 2012, available from http://www.sec.gov/News/PressRelease/Detail/PressRelease/1365171482944, accessed 12 August 2013.

Securities and Exchange Commission 'SEC shuts down $600 million online pyramid and Ponzi scheme', 17 August 2012, available from http://www.sec.gov/News/PressRelease/Detail/PressRelease/1365171483920, accessed 12 August 2013.

Securities and Exchange Commission 'SEC shuts down Ponzi scheme targeting Persian-Jewish community in Los Angeles', 13 April 2012, available from http://www.sec.gov/News/PressRelease/Detail/PressRelease/1365171488330, accessed 12 August 2013.

Securities and Exchange Commission 'SEC shuts down real estate investment scheme in Redondo Beach', 12 March 2013, available from http://www.sec.gov/litigation/litreleases/2013/lr22642.htm, accessed 12 August 2013.
Securities and Exchange Commission '*SEC v. Doris E. Nelson*, Case No. 2:11-cv-00345-RMP (E.D. WA filed September 22, 2011)', 22 September 2011, available from http://www.sec.gov/litigation/litreleases/2011/lr22101.htm, accessed 12 August 2013.
Securities and Exchange Commission '*SEC v. James Clements and Zeina Smidi*, Civil Action No. 11-cv-60673-LSS (S.D. Fla.)', 30 March 2011, available from http://www.sec.gov/litigation/litreleases/2011/lr21910.htm, accessed 12 August 2013.
Securities and Exchange Commission '*SEC v. Joseph Paul Zada and Zada Enterprises*, LLC, Civil Action No. 2:10-cv-14498-DPH-PJK', 10 November 2010, available from http://www.sec.gov/litigation/litreleases/2010/lr21737.htm, accessed 12 August 2013.
Securities and Exchange Commission '*SEC v. Matthew J. Gagnon*, Case No. 2:10-CV-11891 (E.D. Mich.)', 25 May 2010, available from http://www.sec.gov/litigation/litreleases/2010/lr21532.htm, accessed 12 August 2013.
Securities and Exchange Commission '*SEC v. Robert R. Anderson and Rosand Enterprises Inc.*, Civil Action No. 10 CV 6420 (N.D. Illinois.)', 7 October 2010, available from http://www.sec.gov/litigation/litreleases/2010/lr21688.htm, accessed 12 August 2013.
Securities and Exchange Commission '*SEC v. Robert Stinson, Jr., et al.*, Civil Action No. 10-cv-3130-BMS (E.D. Pa.)', 29 June 2010, available from http://www.sec.gov/litigation/litreleases/2010/lr21584.htm, accessed 12 August 2013.
Securities and Exchange Commission 'SEC's enforcement program continues to show strong results in safeguarding investors and markets', 14 November 2012, available from http://www.sec.gov/News/PressRelease/Detail/PressRelease/1365171485830, accessed 11 August 2013.
Securities and Exchange Commission '*Securities and Exchange Commission v. AIC, Inc., et al.*, Case No. 3:11-CV-00176 (E.D. Tenn.)', 18 April 2011, available from http://www.sec.gov/litigation/litreleases/2011/lr21934.htm, accessed 12 August 2013.
Securities and Exchange Commission '*Securities and Exchange Commission v. Bank of America Corporation*, Civil Action No. 09-6829, 10-0215 (S.D.N.Y), Litigation Release No. 21407', 4 February 2010, available from http://www.sec.gov/litigation/litreleases/2010/lr21407.htm, accessed 7 October 2013.

Securities and Exchange Commission '*Securities and Exchange Commission v. Matthew Jennings, Westmoore Management, LLC, Westmoore Investment, L.P., Westmoore Capital Management, Inc., Westmoore Capital, LLC* United States District Court for the Central District of California, Civil Action No. SACV-10-00849-AG (MLGX)', 17 June 2010, available from http://www.sec.gov/litigation/litreleases/2010/lr21561.htm, accessed 12 August 2013.

Securities and Exchange Commission '*Securities and Exchange Commission v. Mike Watson Capital, LLC, Michael P. Watson and Joshua F. Escobedo*, Civil Action No. 2:11-CV-00275 (DB) (D. Utah)', 24 March 2011, available from http://www.sec.gov/litigation/litreleases/2011/lr21898.htm, accessed 12 August 2013.

Securities and Exchange Commission '*Securities and Exchange Commission v. Walter Ng, Kelly Ng, Bruce Horwitz, and The Mortgage Fund, LLC*, Civil Action No. C-13 0895-NC (U.S. District Court for the Northern District of California)', 28 February 2013, available from http://www.sec.gov/litigation/litreleases/2013/lr22628.htm, accessed 12 August 2013.

Securities and Exchange Commission *Summary report of issues identified in the Commission staff's examinations of select credit rating agencies* (Securities and Exchange Commission: Washington DC, 2008).

Securities and Exchange Commission 'The investor's advocate: how the SEC protects investors, maintains market integrity, and facilitates capital formation', n/d, available from http://www.sec.gov/about/whatwedo.shtml, accessed 9 August 2013.

Securities Exchange Commission 'The world's largest hedge fund is a fraud', 7 November 2005, available from http://www.sec.gov/news/studies/2009/oig-509/exhibit-0293.pdf, accessed 13 October 2013.

Seitz, N., Gilsinan, J., Fisher, J., Harshman, E., Islam, M., Yeager, F. and Millar, J. 'The U.S. subprime mortgage crisis: what have we learned?' (2010) Company Lawyer, 31(11), 355–361.

Seitz, N., Gilsinan, J., Millar, J., Fisher, J., Harshman, E., Islam, M. and Yeager, F. 'Bank integrity: the case of subprime lending' (2009) Company Lawyer, 30(9), 271–276.

Sekhon, V. 'Enforcement of material non-disclosure under federal securities laws' (2011) Stanford Journal of Law, Business and Finance, Spring, 16, 273–287.

Selvarajah, P. 'The AIG bailout and AIG's prospects for repaying government loans' (2010) Review of Banking and Financial Law, 29, 363–371.

Serious Fraud Office *Annual report 2006/2007* (Serious Fraud Office: London, 2007).

Serious Fraud Office *Annual report 2007/2008* (Serious Fraud Office: London, 2008).

Serious Fraud Office *Annual report 2009/2010* (Serious Fraud Office: London, 2010).

Serious Fraud Office *Annual report and accounts 2011/2012* (Serious Fraud Office: London, 2012).

Serious Fraud Office 'Brokers charged in LIBOR investigation', 15 July 2013, available from http://www.sfo.gov.uk/press-room/latest-press-releases/press-releases-2013/brokers-charged-in-libor-investigation.aspx, accessed 15 July 2013.

Serious Fraud Office 'Inaugural fraud lawyers' association, Inner Temple, speech by David Green CB QC Director, Serious Fraud Office', 26 March 2013, available from http://www.sfo.gov.uk/about-us/our-views/director's-speeches/speeches-2012/inaugural-fraud-lawyers'-association.aspx, accessed 30 June 2013.

Serious Fraud Office 'LIBOR: criminal offences are capable of covering conduct', 30 July 2012, available from http://www.sfo.gov.uk/press-room/latest-press-releases/press-releases-2012/libor-criminal-offences-are-capable-of-covering-conduct.aspx, accessed 15 July 2013.

Serious Fraud Office 'LIBOR: SFO to investigate', 6 July 2012, available from http://www.sfo.gov.uk/press-room/latest-press-releases/press-releases-2012/libor-sfo-to-investigate.aspx, accessed 15 July 2013.

Serious Fraud Office 'LIBOR: three arrested', 11 December 2012, available from http://www.sfo.gov.uk/press-room/latest-press-releases/press-releases-2012/libor–three-arrested-.aspx, accessed 15 July 2013.

Serious Fraud Office 'LIBOR update', 2 July 2012, available from http://www.sfo.gov.uk/press-room/latest-press-releases/press-releases-2012/libor–update.aspx, accessed 15 July 2013.

Serious Fraud Office 'Trader charged in LIBOR investigation', 18 June 2013, available from http://www.sfo.gov.uk/press-room/latest-press-releases/press-releases-2013/trader-charged-in-libor-investigation.aspx, accessed 15 July 2013.

Serious Fraud Office 'Who we are', n/d, available from http://www.sfo.gov.uk/about-us/who-we-are.aspx, accessed 11 March 2013.

Seyad, S. 'The impact of the proposed banking union on the unity and integrity of the European Union's single market' (2013) Journal of International Banking Law and Regulation, 28(3), 99–108.

Shah, A. 'Emergency Economic Stabilization Act of 2008' (2009) Harvard Journal on Legislation, Summer, 46, 569–589.

Shelley, M. and Jackson, M. 'Sub-prime lending, its deficiencies and the government responses' (2008) Journal of International Banking Law and Regulation, 23(10), 523–537.

Sheppard, M. and Dougherty, E. 'Tapping into Wall Street – the government employs tougher tactics against money crimes', Criminal Justice, Winter, 26, 20–29.

Shoffman, M. 'SFO given £10.5m for Libor probe', 20 February 2013, available from http://www.ftadviser.com/2013/02/20/regulation/regulators/sfo-given-m-for-libor-probe-uza6iEIER2ai2LZejszgLJ/article.html, accessed 30 June 2013.

Silva, Y. 'The "too big to fail" doctrine and the credit crisis' (2008) Review of Banking and Financial Law, 28, 115–131.

Simpson, G. and Perez, E. 'FBI investigates Countrywide', 8 March 2008, available from http://online.wsj.com/article/SB120494626642521739.html, accessed 7 October 2013.

Simpson, S. 'Making sense of white-collar crime: theory and research' (2011) Ohio State Journal of Criminal Law, Spring, 8, 481–502.

Simpson, S. 'White collar crime: a review of recent developments and promising directions for future research' (2013) Annual Review of Sociology, 39, 309–331.

Singh, D. 'The UK Banking Act 2009, pre-insolvency and early intervention: policy and practice' (2011) Journal of Business Law, 1, 20–42.

Singh, D. 'UK approach to financial crisis management' (2011) Transnational Law and Contemporary Problems, 19, 868–922.

Singh, D. and LaBrosse, J. 'Northern Rock, depositors and deposit insurance coverage: some critical reflections' (2010) Journal of Business Law, 2, 55–84.

Slevin, P. 'Bad vibrations: subprime-sparked legal action' (2007) European Lawyer, 72, 18–19.

Smith, A. 'Madoff sentenced to 150 years, CNN', 30 June 2009, available from http://money.cnn.com/2009/06/29/news/economy/madoff_prison_sentence/index.htm, accessed 17 August 2012.

Smith, A. 'Stocks slump on AIG, housing', 17 September 2008, available from http://money.cnn.com/2008/09/17/markets/stockswatch/index.htm, accessed 25 March 2013.

Smith, F. 'Madoff ponzi scheme exposes "the myth of the sophisticated investor"' (2010) University of Baltimore Law Review, 40, 215–283.

Smith, J. 'The structural causes of mortgage fraud' (2010) Syracuse Law Review, 60, 473–500.

Smith, M. 'The legal nature of credit default swaps' (2010) Lloyd's Maritime and Commercial Law Quarterly, August, 3, 386–410.

Smith, R. and Emshwiller, J. 'Enron faces collapse as Dynegy bolts and stock price, credit standing dive', 29 November 2001, available from

http://online.wsj.com/article/SB1006963515929275680.html, accessed 13 October 2013.
Smith, S. 'Reforming the law of adhesion contracts: a judicial response to the subprime mortgage crisis' (2010) Lewis and Clark Law, Fall, 1035–1121.
Soothill, K. 'Blacklists and black sheep' (2010) Police Journal, 83(1), 5–10.
Sorkin, A. 'Bailout above the law', 22 September 2009, available from http://www.nytimes.com/2008/09/23/business/23sorkin.html?_r=0, accessed 7 August 2013.
Sorkin, A. 'JP Morgan pays $2 a share for Bear Stearns', 17 March 2008, available from http://www.nytimes.com/2008/03/17/business/17bear.html?_r=0, accessed 7 October 2013.
Sorkin, A. and Thomas Jnr, L. 'JP Morgan acts to buy ailing Bear Sterns at huge discount', 16 March 2008, available from http://www.nytimes.com/2008/03/16/business/16cnd-bear.html?_r=0, accessed 25 March 2013.
Spencer, J. 'Fiat justicia, ruatque concordia cum Arabe?' (2008) Cambridge Law Journal, 67(3), 456–458.
Squire, R. 'Shareholder opportunism in a world of risky debt' (2010) Harvard Law Review, 123, 1151–1213.
Srivastava, A., Mason, I., Simpson, M. and Litt, M. 'Financial crime' (2011) Compliance Officer Bulletin, May, 86, 1–23.
Stafford, P., Binham, C. and Scannell, K. 'ICAP agrees to pay £55m to settle Libor claims', 25 September 2013, available from http://www.ft.com/cms/s/0/885dc438-2522-11e3-9b22-00144feab7de.html#axzz2fuu8kZ8W, accessed 25 September 2013.
Standard&Poor's Rating Service 'S&P brief in support of motion to dismiss', 22 April 2013, available from http://www.standardandpoors.com/spf/upload/Ratings_US/USvMcGraw-HillMemorandumin SupportofDefendantsnMotion.pdf, accessed 29 May 2013.
Standard&Poor's Rating Service 'Standard & Poor's says DOJ civil lawsuit is unjustified and without legal merit', 5 February 2013, available from http://img.en25.com/Web/StandardPoorsRatings/DOJ Lawsuit.pdf, accessed 29 May 2013.
Stephan, A. 'How dishonesty killed the cartel offence' (2011) Criminal Law Review, 6, 446–455.
Strickland, J. 'The proposed regulatory changes to Fannie Mae and Freddie Mac: an analysis' (2004) Northern Carolina Banking Institute, 8, 267–287.
Stuart, C. 'Mail and wire fraud' (2009) American Criminal Law Review, 46, 813–835.

Stutts, W. and Watts, W. 'Of herring and sausage: nordic responses to banking crises as examples for the United States' (2009) Texas International Law Journal, Summer, 44, 577–627.

Succurro, M. 'Bankruptcy systems and economic performance across countries: some empirical evidence' (2012) European Journal of Law and Economics, 33(1), 101–126.

Sussman, R. 'Protecting clients from the government's thermonuclear war on bank fraud', (1991) American Law Institute–American Bar Association Continuing Legal Education ALI–ABA Court of Study, C646 213-260.

Sutherland, E. 'The white collar criminal', (1940) American Sociological Review, 5(1), 1–12.

Sutherland, E. *White collar crime* (Dryden: New York, 1949).

Swan, E. 'Market abuse regulation and energy trading' (2004) International Energy Law and Taxation Review, 4, 91–100.

Tabb, R. and Grundfest, J. 'Alternatives to LIBOR' (2013) Capital Markets Law Journal, 8(3), 229–260.

Taylor, N. 'FSA prosecutions: offences of money laundering – power to prosecute' (2010) Criminal Law Review, 10, 772–775.

Taylor III, P., Pinguelo, D. and Cedrone, T. 'The reverse-morals clause: the unique way to save talent's reputation and money in a new era of corporate crimes and scandals' (2010) Cardozo Arts and Entertainment Law Journal, 28, 65–113.

Teasdale, S. 'FSA to FCA: recent trends in UK financial conduct regulation' (2011) Journal of International Banking Law and Regulation, 26(12), 583–586.

The Chancellor of the Exchequer (Mr. Alistair Darling), HC Deb, 13 October 2008, c539-42, available from http://www.publications.parliament.uk/pa/cm200708/cmhansrd/cm081013/debtext/81013-0003.htm#0810132000002 , accessed 8 December 2012.

The Economist 'America's Justice Department charges Standard & Poor's with fraud', 13 February 2013, available from http://www.economist.com/news/finance-and-economics/21571448-americas-justice-department-charges-standard-poors-fraud-victim-support, accessed 28 May 2013.

The White House *Annual report to the President on progress implementing the American Recovery and Reinvestment Act of 2009* (White House: Washington DC, 2010).

The White House 'Barack Obama, President of the United States, state of the union', 24 January 2012, available from www.whitehouse.gov/the-press-office/2012/01/24/remarks-president-state-union-address, accessed 21 October 2013.

The White House 'Memorandum for the heads of executive departments and agencies', 20 March 2009, available from http://www.whitehouse.gov/the_press_office/Memorandum-for-the-Heads-of-Executive-Departments-and-Agencies-3-20-09/, accessed 7 August 2013.

The White House 'President Bush discusses Emergency Economic Stabilization Act of 2008', 3 October 2008, available from http://georgewbush-whitehouse.archives.gov/news/releases/2008/10/20081003-11.html, accessed 5 August 2013.

The White House 'President Bush signs H.R. 5140, the Economic Stimulus Act of 2008', 13 February 2008, available from http://georgewbush-whitehouse.archives.gov/news/releases/2008/02/20080213-3.html, accessed 23 September 2013.

The White House 'President Obama announces financial regulation reform', 18 June 2009, available from http://www.whitehouse.gov/video/President-Obama-Announces-Financial-Regulation-Reform/#transcript, accessed 6 August 2013.

The White House 'Reforms for American homeowners and consumers – President Obama signs the Helping Families Save their Homes Act and the Fraud Enforcement and Recovery Act', 20 May 2009, available from http://www.whitehouse.gov/the_press_office/Reforms-for-American-Homeowners-and-Consumers-President-Obama-Signs-the-Helping-Families-Save-their-Homes-Act-and-the-Fraud-Enforcement-and-Recovery-Act, accessed 28 October 2013.

The White House 'Remarks by the President at signing of Dodd–Frank Wall Street Reform and Consumer Protection Act', 21 July 2010, available from http://www.whitehouse.gov/the-press-office/remarks-president-signing-dodd-frank-wall-street-reform-and-consumer-protection-act, accessed 3 August 2012.

The White House 'Remarks by the President at the signing of the Helping Families Save Their Homes Act and the Fraud Enforcement and Recovery Act', 20 May 2009, available from http://www.whitehouse.gov/the_press_office/Remarks-by-the-President-at-Signing-of-the-Helping-Families-Save-Their-Homes-Act-and-the-Fraud-Enforcement-and-Recovery-Act/, accessed 17 June 2013.

The White House 'Wall Street reform: the Dodd–Frank Act', n/d, available from http://www.whitehouse.gov/economy/middle-class/dodd-frank-wall-street-reform, accessed 3 August 2013.

Thelwell, E. 'Northern Rock customers queue for cash as crisis hits high street', 14 September 2007, available from http://www.telegraph.co.uk/finance/markets/2815686/Northern-Rock-customers-queue-for-cash-as-crisis-hits-high-street.html, accessed 8 December 2012.

Titolo, M. 'Retroactivity and the Fraud Enforcement and Recovery Act of 2009' (2011) Indiana Law Journal, Winter, 86, 257–302.

Tomasic, R. 'The financial crisis and the haphazard pursuit of financial crime' (2011) Journal of Financial Crime, 18(1), 7–31.

Tomasic, R. and Akinbami, F. 'Towards a new corporate governance after the global financial crisis' (2011) International Company and Commercial Law Review, 22(8), 237–249.

Touryalai, H. 'Fraud charges against ratings agencies won't help investors', 17 June 2011, available from http://www.forbes.com/sites/halahtouryalai/2011/06/17/fraud-charges-against-ratings-agencies-wont-help-investors/, accessed 29 May 2013.

TRAC Reports 'Slump in FBI white collar crime prosecutions', 24 September 2013, available from http://trac.syr.edu/whatsnew/email.130924.html, accessed 17 October 2013.

Tracer, Z. 'AIG stock sale repays bailout as U.S. Government profits', 11 September 2012, available from http://www.bloomberg.com/news/2012-09-11/aig-stock-prices-at-32-50-share-as-treasury-cuts-stake.html, accessed 28 March 2012.

Trafford, M. 'Losing on LIBOR' (2013) Butterworths Journal of International Banking and Financial Law, 28(4), 238–239.

Travers Smith Regulatory Investigations Group 'FSA enforcement action: themes and trends' (2011) Compliance Officer Bulletin, June, 87, 2–35.

Travers Smith Regulatory Investigations Group 'FSA enforcement action: themes and trends' (2012) Compliance Officer Bulletin, May, 96, 1–30.

Treanor, J. 'Bankers will face jail for reckless misconduct, says George Osborne', 9 July 2013, available from http://www.guardian.co.uk/business/2013/jul/08/bankers-jail-misconduct-george-osborne, accessed 11 July 2013.

Treanor, J. 'Banking commission: bankers should be jailed for "reckless misconduct"', 19 June 2013, available from http://www.guardian.co.uk/business/2013/jun/19/tyrie-report-banking-reform-jail-sentences, accessed 25 June 2013.

Treanor, J. 'Ex-HBOS banker Cummings banned for life and fined £500,000', 12 September 2012, available from http://www.guardian.co.uk/business/2012/sep/12/hbos-banker-peter-cummings-banned-fined-fsa, accessed 30 June 2013.

Treanor, J. 'RBS record losses raise prospect of 95% state ownership', 26 February 2009, available from http://www.guardian.co.uk/business/2009/feb/26/rbs-record-loss, accessed 2 July 2013.

Tschoepe, J. 'A fraud against one is apparently a fraud against all: the Fraud Enforcement and Recovery Act's unprecedented expansion of liability under the False Claims Act' (2010) Houston Law Review, Fall, 47, 741–778.

Tuch, A. 'Conflicted gatekeepers: the Volcker Rule and Goldman Sachs' (2012) Virginia Law and Business Review, Fall, 7, 365–420.

Unger, B. *The scale and impacts of money laundering* (Edward Elgar: Cheltenham, 2007).

United States Attorney's Office 'Former Credit Suisse managing director pleads guilty in connection with scheme to hide losses in mortgage-backed securities trading book', 12 April 2013, available from http://www.justice.gov/usao/nys/pressreleases/April13/SerageldinKareemPleaPR.php, accessed 27 September 2013.

United States Attorney's Office of Southern District of New York 'Statement of Manhattan U.S. Attorney Preet Bharara on the Countrywide, Bank of America, and Rebecca Mairone verdicts', 23 October 2013, available from http://www.justice.gov/usao/nys/pressreleases/October13/BoAVerdictState ment.php, accessed 25 October 2013.

United States Department of Justice 'Financial Fraud Enforcement Task Force members reveal results of Distressed Homeowner Initiative', 9 October 2012, available from http://www.justice.gov/opa/pr/2012/October/12-ag-1216.html, accessed 1 August 2013.

United States Department of Justice 'Letter to The Honorable Patrick J. Leahy Chairman, Committee on the Judiciary', 1 April 2009, available from http://www.justice.gov/ola/views-letters/111-1/040109-s386-fraud-enforcement-recovery-act.pdf, accessed 20 June 2013.

United States Department of Justice Statement of Assistant Attorney General for the Criminal Division Lanny A. Breuer before the Senate Committee on the Judiciary', 26 January 2011, available from http://www.justice.gov/criminal/pr/testimony/2011/crm-testimony-110126.html, accessed June 2013.

United States Department of Justice 'Statement of Lanny A. Breuer, Assistant Attorney General before the United States Senate Committee on the Judiciary', 22 September 2010, available from http://www.justice.gov/ola/testimony/111-2/09-22-10-breuer-financial-fraud.pdf, accessed 20 June 2013.

United States General Accounting Office *Savings and loan crisis – federal response to fraud in financial institutions* (United States General Accounting Office: Washington DC, 1990).

United States Senate Permanent Subcommittee on Investigations – Committee on Homeland Security and Governmental Affairs *Wall Street and the financial collapse* (United States Senate Permanent Subcommittee on Investigations – Committee on Homeland Security and Governmental Affairs: Washington DC, 2011).

University of Oxford 'World's first credit crunch?', 27 November 2008, available from http://www.ox.ac.uk/media/news_releases_for_journalists/081127.html, accessed 1 February 2013.

Vacco, P. 'RESPA and avoiding mortgage fraud: what goes on the HUD settlement statement?' (2008) Illinois Bar Journal, May, 96, 248–249.

Valukas, A. 'White-collar crime and economic recession' (2010) University of Chicago Legal Forum, 1–21.

Valukas, A.R., Examiner In re Lehman Brothers Holding Inc., Report, Chapter 11 Case No. 08-13555, United States Bankruptcy Court for the Southern District of New York, available from http://www.distressedvolatility.com/2010/03/full-examiner-report-of-lehman-brothers.html, accessed 25 March 2013.

Varriale, G. 'Is NYSE Euronext up to administering Libor?' (2013) International Financial Law Review, 30(27), 12–13.

Velikonja, U. 'Leverage, sanctions, and deterrence of accounting fraud' (2011) UC Davis Law Review, 44, 1281–1345.

Veronesi, P. and Zingales, L. 'Paulson's gift', 2008, unpublished working paper, University of Chicago Booth School of Business, available from http://faculty.chicagobooth.edu/brian.barry/igm/P_gift.pdf, accessed 6 August 2013.

Verret, J. 'The bailout through a public choice lens: government controlled corporations as a mechanism for rent transfer' (2010) Seton Hall Law Review, 40, 1521–1579.

Viswanatha, A. and LaCapra, L. 'U.S. government slams S&P with $5 billion fraud lawsuit', 5 February 2013, available from http://mobile.reuters.com/article/idUSBRE9130U120130205?irpc=932, accessed 29 May 2013.

Voreacos, D. 'Wholesale grocery owner gets 20-year sentence in $930 million Ponzi scam', n/d, available from http://www.bloomberg.com/news/2011-06-07/nevin-shapiro-gets-20-years-in-880-million-ponzi-scheme.html, accessed 4 June 2013.

Voris, B. and Milford, P. 'Fabrice Tourre asks for reversal, new trial in SEC case', 1 October 2013, available from http://www.bloomberg.com/news/2013-10-01/fabrice-tourre-asks-for-reversal-new-trial-in-sec-case.html, accessed 7 October 2013.

Wagner, D. and Rexrode, C. 'S&P lawsuit: U.S. accuses ratings agency of fraud in lead up to financial crisis', 5 February 2013, available from http://www.huffingtonpost.com/2013/02/05/sp-lawsuit_n_2621561.html, accessed 28 May 2013.

Walker, G. 'Prudential regulation authority' (2011) Financial Regulation International, October, 7–11.

Walker, G. 'US regulatory reform' (2009) Journal of Banking Regulation, 11(1), 1–5.

Watt, N. 'Reckless misconduct proposals will be in banking reform bill, says PM', 19 June 2013, available from http://www.guardian.co.uk/

business/2013/jun/19/reckless-misconduct-banking-reform-cameron, accessed 11 July 2013.

Wearden, G. 'FBI investigates sub-prime crisis', 30 January 2008, available from http://www.theguardian.com/business/2008/jan/30/subprimecrisis.creditcrunch, accessed 7 October 2013.

Wearden, G., Teather, D. and Treanor, J. 'Banking crisis: Lehman Brothers files for bankruptcy protection', 15 September 2008, available from http://www.guardian.co.uk/business/2008/sep/15/lehmanbrothers.creditcrunch, accessed 21 November 2012.

Weintraub, L. 'Crime of the century: use of the mail fraud statute against authors' (1987) Boston University Law Review, 67, 507–549.

Wells, C. 'Who's afraid of the Bribery Act 2010?' (2012) Journal of Business Law, 5, 420–431.

Wen, S. 'The magnitude of shareholder value as the overriding objective in the UK: the post-crisis perspective' (2011) Journal of International Banking Law and Regulation, 26(7), 325–337.

Westercamp, K. 'A crack in the façade and the whole building came tumbling down: a critical examination of the central banks' response to the sub-prime mortgage loan crisis and global financial economic turmoil' (2009) Transnational Law and Contemporary Problems, Winter, 11, 197–244.

Wheeler, S. 'Directors' disqualification: insolvency practitioners and the decision making process' (1995) Legal Studies, 15, 283–305.

Whelan, P. 'Legal certainty and cartel criminalisation within the EU Member States' (2012) Cambridge Law Journal, 71(3), 677–702.

White, A. 'The case for banning subprime mortgages' (2008) University of Cincinnati Law Review, Winter, 77, 617–644.

White, L. 'Credit-rating agencies and the financial crisis: less regulation of CRAs is a better response' (2010) Journal of International Banking Law and Regulation, 25(4), 170–179.

Williams, S. 'The BAE/Saudi Al-Yamamah contracts: implications in law and public procurement' (2008) International and Comparative Law Quarterly, 57(1), 200–209.

Willmott, N. and James, P. 'Reading between the lines: understanding the FSA's unwritten expectations of significant influence function holders on appointment and beyond' (2012) Compliance Officer Bulletin, November, 101, 1–28.

Willmott, N., McGowan, P., Ghusn, M., Brocklehurst, V., Aikens, R., Bailey, S., Scodie, M. and Palme, J. 'Equipping the modern regulator: assessing the new regulatory powers under the Financial Services Act 2010' (2010) Compliance Officer Bulletin July/August, 78, 1–28.

Wilmarth Jr, A. 'The Dodd–Frank Act: a flawed and inadequate response to the too-big-to-fail problem' (2011) Oregon Law Review, 89, 951–1057.

Wilson, G. and Wilson, S. 'Can the general fraud offence "get the law right"? Some perspectives on the "problem" of financial crime' (2007) Journal of Criminal Law, 71(1), 36–53.

Wilson, G. and Wilson, S. 'Market misconduct, the Financial Services Authority and creating a system of city grasses' (2010) Company Lawyer, 31(3), 67–80.

Wilson, H. 'Banking Commission: bankers should face threat of jail and loss of bonuses', 19 June 2013, available from http://www.telegraph.co.uk/finance/newsbysector/banksandfinance/10128750/Banking-Commission-Bankers-should-face-threat-of-jail-and-loss-of-bonuses.html, accessed 25 June 2013.

Wilson, S. 'Collaring the crime and the criminal? Jury psychology and some criminological perspectives on fraud and the criminal law' (2006) Journal of Criminal Law, 70(1), 75–92.

Wilson, S. 'Former Enron boss Jeffrey Skilling has jail sentence cut to 14 years', 21 June 2013, available from http://www.telegraph.co.uk/news/worldnews/northamerica/usa/10136104/Former-Enron-boss-Jeffrey-Skilling-has-jail-sentence-cut-to-14-years.html, accessed 18 October 2013.

Withey, C. 'The Fraud Act 2006 – some early observations and comparisons with the former' (2007) Journal of Criminal Law, 71(3), 220–237.

Wojnilower, A.M. 'The central role of credit crunches in recent financial history' (1980) Brookings Papers on Economic Activity, 2, 277–339.

Wray, C. and Hur, R. 'Corporate criminal prosecution in a post-Enron world: the Thompson memo in theory and practice' (2006) American Criminal Law Review, 43, 1095–1188.

Wright, R. 'Fraud after Roskill: a view from the Serious Fraud Office' (2003) Journal of Financial Crime, 11(1), 10–16.

Yeager, F., Seitz, N., Islam, M., Harshman, E., Gilsinan, J., Fisher, J. and Millar, J. 'US legislation designed to improve corporate governance: an exploration' (2012) Company Lawyer, 33(1), 25–32.

Yeoh, P. 'Hedge funds: from privileged child to locust and now bogeyman?' (2012) Company Lawyer, 33(2), 42–49.

Yeoh, P. 'Self-regulation, regulation, co-regulation: the credit rating industry case' (2013) Journal of Business Law, 2, 186–211.

Yeoh, P. 'The UK Bribery Act 2010: contents and implications' (2012) Journal of Financial Crime, 19(1), 37–53.

Yihdego, Z. 'Arms trade and public controls: the right to information perspective' (2008) Northern Ireland Legal Quarterly, 59(4), 379–394.

Yoon, A. 'Total global losses from financial crisis: $15 trillion' 1 October 2012, available from http://blogs.wsj.com/economics/2012/10/01/total-global-losses-from-financial-crisis-15-trillion/, accessed 21 October 2013.

Zimring, F. and Hawkins, G. 'Crime, justice and the savings and loans crisis' (1993) Crime and Justice, 18, 247–288.

Zywicki, T. 'The Consumer Financial Protection Bureau: savior or menace?' (2013) George Washington Law Review April, 81, 856–928.

Index